AF772449

Knowledge Discovery and Data Mining: Challenges and Realities

Xingquan Zhu
Florida Atlantic University, USA

Ian Davidson
University of Albany, State University of New York, USA

Information Science REFERENCE

INFORMATION SCIENCE REFERENCE

Hershey · New York

Acquisitions Editor:	Kristin Klinger
Development Editor:	Kristin Roth
Senior Managing Editor:	Jennifer Neidig
Managing Editor:	Sara Reed
Assistant Managing Editor:	Sharon Berger
Copy Editor:	April Schmidt and Erin Meyer
Typesetter:	Jamie Snavely
Cover Design:	Lisa Tosheff
Printed at:	Yurchak Printing Inc.

Published in the United States of America by
Information Science Reference (an imprint of IGI Global)
701 E. Chocolate Avenue, Suite 200
Hershey PA 17033
Tel: 717-533-8845
Fax: 717-533-8661
E-mail: cust@idea-group.com
Web site: http://www.info-sci-ref.com

and in the United Kingdom by
Information Science Reference (an imprint of IGI Global)
3 Henrietta Street
Covent Garden
London WC2E 8LU
Tel: 44 20 7240 0856
Fax: 44 20 7379 0609
Web site: http://www.eurospanonline.com

Copyright © 2007 by IGI Global. All rights reserved. No part of this publication may be reproduced, stored or distributed in any form or by any means, electronic or mechanical, including photocopying, without written permission from the publisher.

Product or company names used in this set are for identification purposes only. Inclusion of the names of the products or companies does not indicate a claim of ownership by IGI Global of the trademark or registered trademark.

Library of Congress Cataloging-in-Publication Data

Knowledge discovery and data mining : challenges and realities / Xingquan Zhu and Ian Davidson, editors.

p. cm.

Summary: "This book provides a focal point for research and real-world data mining practitioners that advance knowledge discovery from low-quality data; it presents in-depth experiences and methodologies, providing theoretical and empirical guidance to users who have suffered from underlying low-quality data. Contributions also focus on interdisciplinary collaborations among data quality, data processing, data mining, data privacy, and data sharing"--Provided by publisher.

Includes bibliographical references and index.

ISBN 978-1-59904-252-7 (hardcover) -- ISBN 978-1-59904-254-1 (ebook)

1. Data mining. 2. Expert systems (Computer science) I. Zhu, Xingquan, 1973- II. Davidson, Ian, 1971-

QA76.9.D343K55 2007

005.74--dc22

2006033770

British Cataloguing in Publication Data
A Cataloguing in Publication record for this book is available from the British Library.

All work contributed to this book set is new, previously-unpublished material. The views expressed in this book are those of the authors, but not necessarily of the publisher.

Table of Contents

Section IV
Mining Image Data Repository

Section V
Data Mining and Business Intelligence

Section VI
Data Mining and Ontology Engineering

Section VII
Traditional Data Mining Algoritms

Detailed Table of Contents

This chapter explores applications of data-mining for pharmaceutical clinical trials particularly for the purpose of improving clinical trial design. The authors provide a detailed case study for analysis of the clinical trials of a drug to treat schizophrenia. More specifically, they design a decision tree algorithm that is particularly useful for the purpose of identifying the characteristics of individuals who respond considerably different than expected.

This chapter explores mining from various modalities (aspects) of video clips: image, audio and transcribed text. The authors represent the multi-media data as a graph and use a random walk algorithm to find correlations. In particular, their approach requires few parameters to estimate and scales well to large datasets. The results on image captioning indicate an improvement of over 50% when compared to traditional mining techniques.

This chapter proposes an image mining framework to discover implicit, previously unknown and potentially useful information from digital image and video repositories for automatic image diagnosis. A detailed case study for cell classification and in particular the identification of antinuclear autoantibodies (ANA) is described

This chapter studies the applications of decision trees for remotely sensed image data so as to generate human interpretable rules that are useful for classification. The authors propose a new iterative algorithm that creates a series of linked decision trees, which is superior in interpretability and accuracy than existing techniques for Land cover data obtained from satellite images and Urban change data from southern China.

Section V
Data Mining and Business Intelligence

This chapter studies the problem of measuring the fiscal impact of a predictive model by using simple metrics such as confusion tables. Several counter-intuitive insights are provided such as accuracy can be a misleading measure due to typical skewness in financial applications

This chapter addresses the problem of credit scoring via modeling credit risk. Details and modeling solutions for predicting expected dollar loss (rather than accuracy) and overcoming sample bias are presented.

Section VI
Data Mining and Ontology Engineering

This chapter provides a survey of the effect of ontologies on data mining and also the effects of mining on ontologies to create a close-loop style mining process. More specifically, the author attempts to answer two explicit questions: How can domain specific ontologies help in knowledge discovery and how can web and text mining help to build ontologies.

This chapter examines the problem of using protein ontologies for mining. They begin by describing a well known protein ontology and then describe how to incorporate this information into clustering. In particular they show how to use ontology to create an appropriate distance matrix and subsequently name the clusters. A case study shows the benefits of their approach.

Foreword

Recent development in computer technology has significantly advanced the generation and consumption of data in our daily life. As a consequence, challenges, such as the growing data warehouses, the needs of intelligent data analysis and the scalability for large or continuous data volumes, are now moving to the desktop of business managers, data experts or even end users. Knowledge discovery and data mining (KDD), grounded on established disciplines such as machine learning, artificial intelligence and statistics, is dedicated to solving the challenges by exploring useful information from a massive amount of data.

Although the objective of data mining is simple—discovering buried knowledge, it is the reality of the underlying real-world data which frequently imposes severe challenges to the mining tasks, where complications such as data modality, data quality, data accessibility, and data privacy often make existing tools invalid or difficult to apply. For example, when mining large data sets, we require mining algorithms to scale well; for applications where getting instances is expensive, the mining algorithms must manipulate precious small data sets; when data suffering from corruptions such as erroneous or missing values, it is desirable to enhance the underlying data before being mined; in situations, such as privacy preserving data mining and trustworthy data sharing, it is desirable to explicitly and intentionally add perturbations to the original data such that sensitive data values and data privacy can be preserved. For multimedia data such as images, audio and videos, data mining algorithms are severely challenged by the reality: finding knowledge from a huge and continuous volume of data items where the internal relationships among data items are yet to be found. When data are characterized by all/some of the above real-world complexities, traditional data mining techniques often work ineffectively, because the input to these algorithms is often assumed to confirm to strict assumptions, such as having a reasonable data volume, specific data distributions, no missing and few inconsistent or incorrect values. This creates the challenges between the real-world data and the available data mining solutions.

Motivated by these challenges, this book addresses data mining techniques and their implementations on the real-world data, such as human genetic and medical data, software engineering data, financial data and remote sensing data. One unique features of the book is that many contributors are the experts of their own areas, such as genetics, biostatistics, clinical research development, credit risk management, computer vision and applied computer science, and of course, traditional computer science and engineering. The diverse background of the authors renders this book a useful tool of overseeing real-world data mining challenges from different domains, not necessarily from the computer scientists and engineers' perspectives. The introduction of the data mining methods in all these areas will allow interested readers to start building their own models from the scratch, as well as resolve their own challenges in an effective way. In addition, the book will help data mining researchers to better understand the requirements of the real-world applications and motivate them to develop practical solutions.

I expect that this book will be a useful reference to academic scholars, data mining novices and experts, data analysts and business professionals, who may find the book interesting and profitable. I am confident that the book will be a resource for students, scientists and engineers interested in exploring the broader uses of data mining.

Philip S. Yu
IBM Thomas J. Watson Research Center

Philip S. Yu *received a BS in electrical engineering from National Taiwan University, MS and PhD in electrical engineering from Stanford University, and an MBA from New York University. He is currently the manager of the software tools and techniques group at the IBM Thomas J. Watson Research Center in Yorktown Heights, New York. His research interests include data mining, data stream processing, database systems, Internet applications and technologies, multimedia systems, parallel and distributed processing, and performance modeling. Dr. Yu has published more than 450 papers in refereed journals and conferences. He holds or has applied for more than 250 U.S. patents. Dr. Yu is a fellow of the ACM and the IEEE. He is associate editor of* ACM Transactions on the Internet Technology *and* ACM Transactions on Knowledge Discovery in Data. *He is a member of the IEEE Data Engineering steering committee and is also on the steering committee of IEEE Conference on Data Mining. He was the editor-in-chief of* IEEE Transactions on Knowledge and Data Engineering *(2001-2004), an editor, advisory board member and also a guest co-editor of the special issue on mining of databases. He had also served as an associate editor of* Knowledge and Information Systems. *In addition to serving as program committee member on various conferences, he will be serving as the general chair of 2006 ACM Conference on Information and Knowledge Management and the program chair of the 2006 joint conferences of the 8th IEEE Conference on E-Commerce Technology (CE '06) and the 3rd IEEE Conference on Enterprise Computing, E-Commerce and E-Services (EEE '06). He was the program chair or co-chairs of the 11th IEEE International Conference on Data Engineering, the 6th Pacific Area Conference on Knowledge Discovery and Data Mining, the 9th ACM SIGMOD Workshop on Research Issues in Data Mining and Knowledge Discovery, the 2nd IEEE Intl. Workshop on Research Issues on Data Engineering: Transaction and Query Processing, the PAKDD Workshop on Knowledge Discovery from Advanced Databases and the 2nd IEEE International Workshop on Advanced Issues of E-Commerce and Web-based Information Systems. He served as the general chair of the 14th IEEE International Conference on Data Engineering and the general co-chair of the 2nd IEEE International. Conference on Data Mining. He has received several IBM honors including two IBM Outstanding Innovation Awards, an Outstanding Technical Achievement Award, two Research Division Awards and the 85th plateau of Invention Achievement Awards. He received an Research Contributions Award from IEEE International Conference on Data Mining (2003) and also an IEEE Region 1 Award for "promoting and perpetuating numerous new electrical engineering concepts" (1999). Dr. Yu is an IBM master inventor.*

Preface

As data mining evolves into an exciting research area spanning multiple disciplines such as machine learning, artificial intelligence, bioinformatics, medicine and business intelligence, the need to apply data mining techniques to more demanding real-world problem arises. The application of data mining techniques to domains with considerable complexity has become a major hurdle for practitioners and researchers alike. The academic study of data mining typically makes assumptions such as plentiful, correctly labeled, well organized, and error free data which often do not hold. The reality is that in real-world situations, complications occur such as the data availability data quality, data volume, data privacy and data accessibility. This presents challenges of how to apply existing data mining techniques to these new data environments from both design and implementation perspectives.

A major source of challenges is how to expand data mining algorithms into data mining systems. There is little doubt that the importance and usefulness of data mining have been well recognized by many practitioners from the outside of the data mining community, such as business administrators and medical experts. However, when referring to data mining techniques for solutions, the way people review data mining will crucially determine the success of their projects. For example, if data mining were treated just as a tool or a algorithm rather than a systematic solution, practitioners may often find their initial results unsatisfactory, partially because of the realities such as the unmanageable poor quality data, inadequate training examples or lack of integration with the domain knowledge. All these issues require that each data mining project should be customized to meet the needs of different real-world applications, hence, require a data mining practitioner to have a comprehensive understanding beyond data mining algorithms. It is expected that a review of the data mining systems on different domains will be beneficial, from both system design and implementation perspectives, to users who intend to apply data mining techniques for complete systems.

The aim of this collection is to report the results of mining real world data sets and their associated challenges in a variety of fields. When we posted the call for chapters, we were uncertain what proposals we would receive. We were happy to receive a large variety of proposals and we chose a diverse range of application areas such as software engineering, multimedia computing, biology, clinic study, finance and banking. The types of challenges each chapter addressed were a mix of the expected and unexpected. As expected submissions dealing with well known problems such as inadequate training examples and feature selection, new challenges such as mining multiple *synchronized* sources were explored, as well as the challenges of incorporating domain expertise in data mining process in the form of ontologies. Perhaps the most common trends mentioned in the chapters were the notion of closing the loop in the mining process such that the mining results are able to be fed back into the data set creation and an emphasis of understanding and verification of the data mining results.

Who Should Read This Book

Rather than focusing on an intensive study on data mining algorithms, the focus of this book is the real-world challenges and solutions associated with developing practical data mining systems. The contributors of the book are the data mining practitioners as well as the experts of their own domains, and what is reported here are the techniques they actually use in their own systems. Therefore, data mining practitioners should find this book useful for assisting in the development of practical data mining applications and solving problems raised by different real-world challenges.

We believe this book can stimulate the interests of a variety of audience types such as:

- Academic research scholars with interests in data mining related issues, this book can be a reference for them to understand the realities of real-world data mining applications and motivate them to develop practical solutions.
- General data mining practitioners with focus on knowledge discovery from real-world data, this book can provide guidance on how to design a systematic solution to fulfill the goal of knowledge discovery from their data.
- General audiences or college students who want in-depth knowledge about real-world data mining applications, they may find the examples and experiences reported in the book very useful in helping them bridging the concept of data mining to real-world applications.

Organization of This Book

The entire book is divided into seven sections: Data mining in software quality modeling, knowledge discovery for genetic and medical data, data mining in mixed media data, mining image data repository, data mining and business intelligence, data mining and ontology engineering, and traditional data mining algorithms.

Section I: Data Mining in Software Quality Modeling examines the domain of software quality estimation where the availability of labeled data is severely limited. The core of the proposed study, by Seliya and Khoshgoftaar, is the NASA JP1 dataset with in excess of 10,000 software modules with the aim of predicting if a module is defective or not. Attempts to build accurate models from just the labeled data produce undesirable results, by using semi-supervised clustering and learning techniques, their techniques can improve the results significantly. At the end of the chapter, the authors also explore the interesting direction of including the user in the data mining process via interactive labeling of clusters.

Section II: Knowledge Discovery from Genetic and Medical Data consists of two contributions, which deal with applications in biology and medicine respectively. The chapter by Moore discusses the classical problems in mining biological data: feature selection and weighting. The author studies the problem of epitasis (bimolecular physical interaction) in predicting common human diseases. Two techniques are applied: multifactor dimension reduction and a filter based wrapper technique. The first approach is a classic example of feature selection, whilst the later retains all features but with a probability of being selected in the final classifier. The author then explores how to make use of the selected features to understand why some feature combinations are associated with disease and others are not. In the second chapter, Alvair, Cabrera, Caridi, and Nguyen explore applications of data-mining for pharmaceutical clinical trials, particularly for the purpose of improving clinical trial design. This is an example of what can be referred to as closed loop data mining where the data mining results must be interpretable for better trial design and so on. The authors design a decision tree algorithm that is particularly useful for the purpose of identifying the characteristics of individuals who respond considerably different than expected. The authors provide a detailed case study for analysis of the clinical trials for schizophrenia treatment.

Section III: Data Mining in Mixed Media Data focuses on the challenges of mining mixed media data. The authors, Pan, Yang, Faloutsos, and Duygulu, explore mining from various modalities (aspects) of video clips: image, audio and transcribed text. The benefit of analyzing all three sources together enables finding correlations amongst multiple sources that can be used for a variety of applications. Mixed media data present several challenges such as how to represent features and detect correlations across multiple data modalities. The authors addresses these problems by representing the data as a graph and using a random walk algorithm to find correlations. In particular, the approach requires few parameters to estimate and scales well to large datasets. The results on image captioning indicate an improvement of over 50% when compared to traditional techniques.

Section IV: Mining Image Data Repository discusses various issues in mining image data repositories. The chapter by Perner describes the ImageMinger, the suite of mining techniques specifically for images. A detailed case study for cell classification and in particular the identification of antinuclear autoantibodies (ANA) is also described. The chapter by Zhang, Liu, and Gruenwald discusses the applications of decision trees for remotely sensed image data in order to generate human interpretable rules that are useful for classification. The authors propose a new iterative algorithm that creates a series of linked decision trees. They verify that the algorithm is superior in interpretability and accuracy than existing techniques for Land cover data obtained from satellite images and Urban change data from southern China.

Section V addresses the issues of *Data Mining and Business Intelligence*. Data mining has a long history of being applied in financial applications, Bruckhaus and Olecka in their respective chapters describe several important challenges of the area. Bruckhaus details how to measure the fiscal impact of a predictive model by using simple metrics such as confusion tables. Several counter-intuitive insights are provided such as accuracy can be a misleading measure and an accuracy paradox due to the typical skewness in financial data. The second half of the chapter uses the introduced metrics to quantify fiscal impact. Olecka's chapter deals with the important problem of credit scoring via modeling credit risk. Though this may appear to be a straight-forward classification or regression problem with accurate data, the author actually points out several challenges. In addition to the existing problems such as feature selection and rare event prediction, there are other domain specific issues such as multiple yet overlapping target events (bankruptcy and contractual charge-off) which are driven by different predictors. Details and modeling solutions for predicting expected dollar loss (rather than accuracy) and overcoming sample bias are reported.

Section VI: Data Mining and Ontology Engineering has two chapters, which are contributed by Neaga and Sidhu with collaborators respectively. This section addresses the growing area of applying data mining in areas which are *not* knowledge poor. In both chapters, the authors investigate how to incorporate ontologies into data mining algorithms. Neaga provides a survey of the effect of ontologies on data mining and also the effects of mining on ontologies to create a close-loop style mining process. In particular, the author attempts to answer two explicit questions: How can domain specific ontologies help in knowledge discovery and how can Web and text mining help to build ontologies. Sidhu et al. examine the problem of using protein ontologies for data mining. They begin by describing a well-known protein ontology and then describe how to incorporate this information into clustering. In particular, they show how to use ontology to create an appropriate distance matrix and consequently how to name the clusters. A case study shows the benefits of their approach in using ontologies in general.

The last section, *Section VII: Tradition Data Mining Algorithm*, deals with well known data mining problems but with atypical techniques best suited for specific applications. Hadzic and collaborators use self organized maps to perform outlier detection for applications such as noisy instance removal. Beynon handles the problem of imputing missing values and handling imperfect data by using Dempster-Shafer theory rather than traditional techniques such as expectation maximization typically used in mining. He describes his classification and ranking belief simplex (CaRBS) system and its application to replicate the bank rating schemes of organizations such as Moody's, S&P and Fitch. A case study of how to replicate the ratings of Fitch's individual bank rating is given. Finally, Griffiths and collaborators look at the use of rough set theory to estimating error rates by using leave-one-out, k-fold cross validation and nonparametric bootstrapping. A prototype expert system is utilized to explore the nature of each resampling technique when variable precision rough set theory (VPRS) is applied to an example data set. The software produces a series of graphs and descriptive statistics, which are used to illustrate the characteristics of each technique with regards to VPRS, and comparisons, are drawn between the results.

We hope you enjoy this collection of chapters.

Xingquan Zhu and Ian Davidson

Acknowledgment

We would like to thank all the contributors who produced these articles and tolerated our editing suggestions and deadline reminders.

Xingquan Zhu:
I would like to thank my wife Li for her patience and tolerance of my extra work.

Ian Davidson:
I would like to thank my wife, Joulia, for her support and tolerating my eccentricities.

Section I
Data Mining in Software Quality Modeling

Chapter I
Software Quality Modeling with Limited Apriori Defect Data

Naeem Seliya
University of Michigan, USA

Taghi M. Khoshgoftaar
Florida Atlantic University, USA

ABSTRACT

In machine learning the problem of limited data for supervised learning is a challenging problem with practical applications. We address a similar problem in the context of software quality modeling. Knowledge-based software engineering includes the use of quantitative software quality estimation models. Such models are trained using apriori software quality knowledge in the form of software metrics and defect data of previously developed software projects. However, various practical issues limit the availability of defect data for all modules in the training data. We present two solutions to the problem of software quality modeling when a limited number of training modules have known defect data. The proposed solutions are a semisupervised clustering with expert input scheme and a semisupervised classification approach with the expectation-maximization algorithm. Software measurement datasets obtained from multiple NASA software projects are used in our empirical investigation. The software quality knowledge learnt during the semisupervised learning processes provided good generalization performances for multiple test datasets. In addition, both solutions provided better predictions compared to a supervised learner trained on the initial labeled dataset.

INTRODUCTION

Data mining and machine learning have numerous practical applications across several domains, especially for classification and prediction problems. This chapter involves a data mining and machine learning problem in the context of software quality modeling and estimation. Software measurements and software fault (defect) data have been used in the development of models that predict

Copyright © 2007, IGI Global, distributing in print or electronic forms without written permission of IGI Global is prohibited.

software quality, for example, a software quality classification model (Imam, Benlarbi, Goel, & Rai, 2001; Khoshgoftaar & Seliya, 2004; Ohlsson & Runeson, 2002) predicts the fault-proneness membership of program modules. A software quality model allows the software development team to track and detect potential software defects relatively early-on during development.

Software quality estimation models exploit the software engineering hypothesis that software measurements encapsulate the underlying quality of the software system. This assumption has been verified in numerous studies (Fenton & Pfleeger, 1997). A software quality model is typically built or trained using software measurement and defect data from a similar project or system release previously developed. The model is then applied to the currently under-development system to estimate the quality or presence of defects in its program modules. Subsequently, the limited resources allocated for software quality inspection and improvement can be targeted toward low-quality modules, achieving cost-effective resource utilization (Khoshgoftaar & Seliya, 2003).

An important assumption made during typical software quality classification modeling is that fault-proneness labels are available for all program modules (instances) of training data, that is, supervised learning is facilitated because all instances in the training data have been assigned a quality-based label such as fault-prone (*fp*) or not fault-prone (*nfp*). In software engineering practice, however, there are various practical scenarios that can limit availability of quality-based labels or defect data for all the modules in the training data, for example:

- The cost of running data collection tools may limit for which subsystems software quality data is collected.
- Only some project components in a distributed software system may collect software quality data, while others may not be equipped for collecting similar data.
- The software defect data collected for some program modules may be error-prone due to data collection and recording problems.
- In a multiple release software project, a given release may collect software quality data for only a portion of the modules, either due to limited funds or other practical issues.

In the training software measurement dataset the fault-proneness labels may only be known for some of the modules, that is, labeled instances, while for the remaining modules, that is, unlabeled instances, only software attributes are available. Under such a situation following the typical supervised learning approach to software quality modeling may be inappropriate. This is because a model trained using the small portion of labeled modules may not yield good software quality analysis, that is, the few labeled modules are not sufficient to adequately represent quality trends of the given system. Toward this problem, perhaps the solution lies in extracting the knowledge (in addition to the labeled instances) stored in the software metrics of the unlabeled modules.

The above described problem represents the labeled-unlabeled learning problem in data mining and machine learning (Seeger, 2001). We present two solutions to the problem of software quality modeling with limited prior fault-proneness defect data. The first solution is a semisupervised clustering with expert input scheme based on the *k-means* algorithm (Seliya, Khoshgoftaar, & Zhong, 2005), while the other solution is a semisupervised classification approach based on the expectation maximization (EM) algorithm (Seliya, Khoshgoftaar, & Zhong, 2004).

The semisupervised clustering with expert input approach is based on implementing constraint-based clustering, in which the constraint maintains a strict membership of modules to clusters that are already labeled as *nfp* or *fp*. At the end of a constraint-based clustering run a domain expert is allowed to label the unlabeled clusters, and the semisupervised clustering process is iterated. The EM-based semisupervised classification approach iteratively augments unlabeled program modules with their estimated class labels into the labeled dataset. The class labels of the unlabeled instances are treated as missing data which is estimated by the EM algorithm. The unlabeled modules are added to the labeled dataset based on a confidence in their prediction.

A case study of software measurement and defect data obtained from multiple NASA software projects is used to evaluate the two solutions. To simulate the labeled-unlabeled problem, a sample of program modules is randomly selected from the JM1 software measurement dataset and is used as the initial labeled dataset. The remaining JM1 program modules are treated (without their class labels) as the initial unlabeled dataset. At the end of the respective semisupervised learning approaches, the software quality modeling knowledge gained is evaluated by using three independent software measurement datasets.

A comparison between the two approaches for software quality modeling with limited apriori defect data indicated that the semisupervised clustering with expert input approach yielded better performance than EM-based semisupervised classification approach. However, the former is associated with considerable expert input compared to the latter. In addition, both semisupervised learning schemes provided an improvement in generalization accuracy for independent test datasets.

The rest of this chapter is organized as follows: some relevant works are briefly discussed in the next section; the third and fourth sections respectively present the semisupervised clustering with expert input and the EM-based semisupervised classification approaches; the empirical case study, including software systems description, modeling methodology, and results are presented in the fifth section. The chapter ends with a conclusion which includes some suggestions for future work.

RELATED WORK

In the literature, various methods have been investigated to model the knowledge stored in software measurements for predicting quality of program modules. For example, Schneidewind (2001) utilizes logistic regression in combination with Boolean discriminant functions for predicting *fp* program modules. Guo, Cukic, and Singh (2003) predict *fp* program modules using Dempster-Shafer networks. Khoshgoftaar, Liu and Seliya (2003) have investigated genetic programming and decision trees (Khoshgoftaar, Yuan, & Allen, 2000), among other techniques. Some other works that have focused on software quality estimation include Imam et al. (2001), Suarez and Lutsko (1999) and Pizzi, Summers, and Pedrycz (2002).

While almost all existing works on software quality estimation have focused on using a supervised learning approach for building software quality models, very limited attention has been given to the problem of software quality modeling and analysis when there is limited defect data from previous software project development experiences. In a machine learning classification problem when both labeled and unlabeled data are used during the learning process, it is termed as semisupervised learning (Goldman, 2000; Seeger, 2001). In such a learning scheme the labeled dataset is iteratively augmented with instances (with predicted class labels) from the unlabeled dataset based on some selection measure. Semisupervised classification schemes have been investigated across various domains, including content-based image retrieval (Dong & Bhanu, 2003), human motion and gesture pattern recognition (Wu & Huang, 2000), document categorization (Ghahramani & Jordan, 1994; Nigam & Ghani, 2000), and software engineering (Seliya et al., 2004). Some of the recently investigated techniques for semisupervised classification include the EM algorithm (Nigam, McCallum, Thrun, & Mitchell, 1998), cotraining (Goldman & Zhou, 2000; Mitchell, 1999; Nigam & Ghani, 2000), and support vector machine (Demirez & Bennett, 2000; Fung & Mangasarian, 2001).

While many works in semisupervised learning are geared toward the classification problem, a few studies investigate semisupervised clustering for grouping of a given set of text documents (Zeng, Wang, Chen, Lu, & Ma, 2003; Zhong, 2006). A semisupervised clustering approach has some benefits over semisupervised classification. During the semisupervised clustering process additional classes of data can be obtained (if desired) while the semisupervised classification approach requires the prior knowledge of all possible classes of the data. The unlabeled data may form new classes other than the pre-defined classes for the given data. Pedrycz and Waletzky (1997) investigate semisupervised clustering using fuzzy logic-based clustering for analyzing software reusability. In contrast, this study investigates semisupervised clustering for software quality estimation.

The labeled instances in a semisupervised clustering scheme have been used for initial seeding of the clusters (Basu, Banerjee, & Mooney, 2002), incorporating constraints in the clustering process (Wagstaff & Cardie, 2000), or providing feedback subsequent to regular clustering (Zhong, 2006). The seeded approach uses the labeled data to initialize cluster centroids prior to clustering. The constraint-based approach keeps a fixed-grouping of the labeled data during the clustering process. The feedback-based approach uses the labeled data to adjust the clusters after executing a regular clustering process.

SEMISUPERVISED CLUSTERING WITH EXPERT INPUT

The basic purpose of a semisupervised approach during clustering is to aid the clustering algorithm in making better partitions of instances in the given dataset. The semisupervised clustering approach presented is a constraint-based scheme that uses labeled instances for initial seeding (centroids) of some clusters among the maximum allowable clusters when using *k-means* as the clustering algorithm. In addition, during the semisupervised iterative process a domain (software engineering) expert is allowed to label additional clusters as either *nfp* or *fp* based on domain knowledge and some descriptive statistics of the clusters.

The data in a semisupervised clustering scheme consists of a small set of labeled instances and a large set of unlabeled instances. Let *D* be a dataset of labeled (*nfp* or *fp*) and unlabeled (*ul*) program modules, containing the subsets *L* of labeled modules and *U* of unlabeled modules. In addition, let the dataset *L* consist of subsets *L_nfp* of *nfp* modules and *L_fp* of *fp* modules. The procedure used in our constraint-based semisupervised clustering approach with *k-means* is summarized next:

1. **Obtain initial numbers of *nfp* and *fp* clusters:**
   - An optimal number of clusters for the *nfp* and *fp* instances in the initial labeled dataset are obtained using the C_g criterion proposed by Krzanowski and Lai (1988).
   - Given *L_nfp*, execute the C_g criterion algorithm to obtain the optimal number of *nfp* clusters among $\{1, 2, \ldots, Cin\_nfp\}$ number of clusters, where *Cin_nfp* is the user-defined maximum number of clusters for *L_nfp*. Let *p* denote the obtained number of *nfp* clusters. Given *L_fp*, execute the C_g criterion algorithm to obtain the optimal number of *fp* clusters among $\{1, 2, \ldots, Cin\_fp\}$ number of clusters, where *Cin_fp* is the user-defined maximum number of clusters for *L_fp*. Let *q* denote the obtained number of *fp* clusters.

2. **Initialize centroids of clusters:** Given the maximum number of clusters, C_{max}, allowed during the semisupervised clustering process with *k-means*,
   - The centroids of p clusters out of C_{max} are initialized to centroids of the clusters labeled as *nfp*.
   - The centroids of q clusters out of $\{C_{max} - p\}$ are initialized to centroids of the clusters labeled as *fp*.
   - The centroids of the remaining r (i.e., $C_{max} - p - q$) clusters are initialized to randomly selected instances from U. We randomly select 5 unique sets of r instances each for initializing centroids of the unlabeled clusters. Thus, centroids of the $\{p + q + r\}$ clusters can be initialized using 5 different combinations.
   - The sets of *nfp*, *fp*, and unlabeled clusters are thus,

   $C\_nfp = \{c\_nfp_1, c\_nfp_2, \ldots, c\_nfp_p\}$,
   $C\_fp = \{c\_fp_1, c\_fp_2, \ldots, c\_nfp_q\}$, and
   $C\_ul = \{c\_ul_1, c\_ul_2, \ldots, c\_ul_r\}$ respectively.
3. **Execute constraint-based clustering:**
   - The *k-means* clustering algorithm with the Euclidean distance function is run on D using the initialized centroids for the C_{max} clusters, and under the constraint that *the existing membership of a program module to a labeled cluster remains unchanged.* Thus, at a given iteration during the semisupervised clustering process, if a module already belongs (initial membership or expert-based assignment from previous iterations) to a *nfp* (or *fp*) cluster, then it cannot move to another cluster during the clustering process of that iteration.
   - The constraint-based clustering process with *k-means* is repeated for each of the 5 centroid initializations, and the respective SSE (sum-of-squares-error) values are computed.
   - The clustering result associated with the median SSE value is selected for continuation to the next step. This is done to minimize the likelihood of working with a lucky/unlucky initialization of cluster centroids.
4. **Expert-based labeling of clusters:**
   - The software engineering expert is presented with descriptive statistics of the r unlabeled clusters, and is asked to label them as either *nfp* or *fp*. The specific statistics presented for attributes of instances in each cluster depends on the expert's request, and include data such as minimum, maximum, mean, standard deviation, and so forth.
   - The expert labels only those clusters for which he/she is very confident in the label estimation.
   - If the expert labels at least one of the r (unlabeled) clusters, then go to Step 2 and repeat, otherwise continue.
5. **Stop semisupervised clustering:** The iterative process is stopped when the sets C_nfp, C_fp, and C_ul remain unchanged. The modules in the *nfp* (*fp*) clusters are labeled and recorded as *nfp* (*fp*), while those in the *ul* clusters are not assigned any label. In addition, the centroids of the $\{p + q\}$ labeled clusters are also recorded.

SEMISUPERVISED CLASSIFICATION WITH EM ALGORITHM

The expectation maximization (EM) algorithm is a general iterative method for maximum likelihood estimation in data mining problems with incomplete data. The EM algorithm takes an iterative approach consisting of replacing missing data with estimated values, estimating model parameters, and re-estimating the missing data values. An iteration of EM consists of an E or Expectation step and an M or Maximization step, with each having a direct statistical interpretation.

We limit our EM algorithm discussion to a brief overview, and refer the reader to Little and Rubin (2002) and Seliya et al. (2004) for a more extensive coverage. In our study, the class value of the unlabeled software modules is treated as missing data, and the EM algorithm is used to estimate the missing values. Many multivariate statistical analysis, including multiple linear regression, principal component analysis, and canonical correlation analysis are based on the initial study of the data with respect to the sample mean and covariance matrix of the variables. The EM algorithm implemented for our study on semisupervised software quality estimation is based on maximum likelihood estimation of missing data, means, and covariances for multivariate normal samples (Little et al., 2002).

The E and M steps continue iteratively until a stopping criterion is reached. Commonly used stopping criteria include specifying a maximum number of iterations or monitoring when the change in the values estimated for the missing data reaches a plateau for a specified epsilon value (Little et al., 2002). We use the latter criteria and allow the EM algorithm to converge without a maximum number of iterations, that is, iteration is stopped if the maximum change among the means or covariances between two consecutive iterations is less than 0.0001. The initial values of the parameter set are obtained by estimating means and variances from all available values of each variable, and then estimating covariances from all available pairwise values using the computed means.

Given the *L* (labeled) and *U* (unlabeled) datasets, the EM algorithm is used to estimate the missing class labels by creating a new dataset combining *L* and *U* and then applying the EM algorithm to estimate the missing data, that is, the dependent variable of *U*. The following procedure is used in our EM-based semisupervised classification approach:

1. Estimate the dependent variable (class labels) for the labeled dataset. This is done by treating *L* also as *U*, that is, the unlabeled dataset consists of the labeled instances but without their fault-proneness labels. The EM algorithm is then used to estimate these missing class labels. In our study the *fp* and *nfp* classes are labeled 1 and 0, respectively. Consequently, the estimated missing values will approximately fall within the range 1 and 0.
2. For a given significance level α, obtain confidence intervals for the predicted dependent variable in Step 1. The assumption is that the two confidence interval boundaries delineate the *nfp* and *fp* modules. Record the upper boundary as *ci_nfp* (i.e., closer to 0) and the lower boundary as *ci_fp* (i.e., closer to 1).
3. For the given *L* and *U* datasets, estimate the dependent variable for *U* using EM.
4. An instance in *U* is identified as *nfp* if it's predicted dependent variable falls within (i.e., is lower than) the upper boundary, that is, *ci_nfp*. Similarly, an instance in *U* is identified as *fp* if it's predicted dependent variable falls within (i.e., is greater than) the lower bound, that is, *ci_fp*.
5. The newly labeled instances of *U* are used to augment *L*, and the semisupervised classification procedure is iterated from Step 1. The iteration stopping criteria used in our study is such that if the number of instances selected from *U* is less than a specific number (that is, 1% of initial *L* dataset), then stop iteration.

EMPIRICAL CASE STUDY

Software System Descriptions

The software measurements and quality data used in our study to investigate the proposed semisupervised learning approaches is that of a large NASA software project, JM1. Written in C, JM1 is a real-time ground system that uses simulations to generate certain predictions for missions. The data was made available through the Metrics Data Program (MDP) at NASA, and included software measurement data and associated error (fault or defect) data collected at the function level.

A program module for the system consisted of a function or method. The fault data collected for the system represents, for a given module, faults detected during software development. The original JM1 dataset consisted of 10,883 software modules, of which 2,105 modules had software defects (ranging from 1 to 26) while the remaining 8,778 modules were defect-free, that is, had no software faults. In our study, a program module with no faults was considered *nfp* and *fp* otherwise.

The JM1 dataset contained some inconsistent modules (those with identical software measurements but with different class labels) and those with missing values. Upon removing such modules, the dataset was reduced from 10,883 to 8,850 modules. We denote this reduced dataset as JM1-8850, which consisted of 1,687 modules with one or more defects and 7,163 modules with no defects.

Table 1. Software measurements

Line Count Metrics	Total Lines of Code Executable LOC Comments LOC Blank LOC Code And Comments LOC
Halstead Metrics	Total Operators Total Operands Unique Operators Unique Operands
McCabe Metrics	Cyclomatic Complexity Essential Complexity Design Complexity
Branch Count Metrics	Branch Count

Each program module in the JM1 dataset was characterized by 21 software measurements (Fenton et al., 1997): the 13 metrics as shown in Table 1 and 8 derived Halstead metrics (Halstead length, Halstead volume, Halstead level, Halstead difficulty, Halstead content, Halstead effort, Halstead error estimate, and Halstead program time. We used only the 13 basic software metrics in our analysis. The eight derived Halstead metrics were not used. The metrics for the JM1 (and other datasets) were primarily governed by their availability, internal workings of the projects, and the data collection tools used. The type and numbers of metrics made available were determined by the NASA Metrics Data Program. Other metrics, including software process measurements, were not available. The use of the specific software metrics does not advocate their effectiveness, and a different project may consider a different set of software measurements for analysis (Fenton et al., 1997; Imam et al., 2001).

In order to gauge the performance of the semisupervised clustering results, we use software measurement data of three other NASA projects, KC1, KC2, and KC3, as test datasets. These software measurement datasets were also obtained through the NASA Metrics Data Program. The definitions of what constituted a *fp* and *nfp* module for these projects are the same as those of the JM1 system. A program module of these projects also consisted of a function, subroutine, or method. These three projects were characterized by the same software product metrics used for the JM1 project, and were built in a similar software development organization. The software systems of the test datasets are summarized next:

- The KC1 project is a single CSCI within a large ground system and consists of 43

KLOC (thousand lines of code) of C++ code. A given CSCI comprises of logical groups of computer software components (CSCs). The dataset contains 2107 modules, of which 325 have one or more faults and 1782 have zero faults. The maximum number of faults in a module is 7.

- The KC2 project, written in C++, is the science data processing unit of a storage management system used for receiving and processing ground data for missions. The dataset includes only those modules that were developed by NASA software developers and not commercial-of-the-shelf (COTS) software. The dataset contains 520 modules, of which 106 have one or more faults and 414 have zero faults. The maximum number of faults in a software module is 13.
- The KC3 project, written in 18 KLOC of Java, is a software application that collects, processes, and delivers satellite meta-data. The dataset contains 458 modules, of which 43 have one or more faults and 415 have zero faults. The maximum number of faults in a module is 6.

Empirical Setting and Modeling

The initial *L* dataset is obtained by randomly selecting *LP* number of modules from JM1-8850, while the remaining *UP* number of modules were treated (without their fault-proneness labels) as the initial *U* dataset. The sampling was performed to maintain the approximate proportion of *nfp:fp* = 80:20 of the instances in JM1-8850. We considered different sampling sizes, that is, *LP* = {100, 250, 500, 1000, 1500, 2000, 3000}. For a given *LP* value, three samples were obtained without replacement from the JM1-8850 dataset. In the case of *LP* = {100, 250, 500}, five samples were obtained to account for their relatively small sizes. Due to space consideration, we generally only present results for *LP* = {500, 1000}; however, additional details are provided in (Seliya et al., 2004; Seliya et al., 2005).

When classifying program modules as *fp* or *nfp*, a Type I error occurs when a *nfp* module is misclassified as *fp*, while a Type II error occurs when a *fp* module is misclassified as *nfp*. It is known that the two error rates are inversely proportional (Khoshgoftaar et al., 2003; Khoshgoftaar et al., 2000).

Semisupervised Clustering Modeling

The initial numbers of the *nfp* and *fp* clusters, that is, *p* and *q*, were obtained by setting both *Cin_nfp* and *Cin_fp* to 20. The maximum number of clusters allowed during our semisupervised clustering with *k-means* was set to two values: C_{max} = {30, 40}. These values were selected based on input from the domain expert and reflects a similar empirical setting used in our previous work (Zhong, Khoshgoftaar, & Seliya, 2004). Due to similarity of results for the two C_{max} values, only results for C_{max} = 40 are presented.

At a given iteration during the semisupervised clustering process, the following descriptive statistics were computed at the request of the software engineering expert: minimum, maximum, mean, median, standard deviation, and the 75, 80, 85, 90, and 95 percentiles. These values were computed for all 13 software attributes of modules in a given cluster. The expert was also presented with following statistics for JM1-8850 and the *U* dataset at a given iteration: minimum, maximum, mean, median, standard deviation, and the 5, 10, 15, 20, 25, 30, 35, 40, 45, 55, 60, 70, 75, 80, 85, 90 and 95 percentiles. The extent to which the above descriptive statistics were used was at the disposal of the expert during his labeling task.

Semisupervised Classification Modeling

The significance level used to select instances from the *U* dataset to augment the *L* dataset is set to $\alpha = 0.05$. Other significance levels of 0.01

and 0.10 were also considered; however, their results are not presented as the software quality estimation performances were relatively similar for the different α values. The iterative semisupervised classification process is continued until the number of instances added to *U* is less than 1% of the initial unlabeled dataset.

Table 3. Data performances with unsupervised clustering

Dataset	Type I	Type II	Overall
KC1	0.0617	0.6985	0.1599
KC2	0.0918	0.4151	0.1577
KC3	0.1229	0.5116	0.1594

Semisupervised Clustering Results

The predicted class labels of the labeled program modules obtained at the end of each semisupervised clustering run are compared with their actual class labels. The average classification performance across the different samples for each *LP* and $C_{max} = 40$ is presented in Table 2. The table shows the average Type I, Type II, and Overall misclassification error rates for the different *LP* values. It was observed that for the given C_{max} value, the Type II error rates decreases with an increase in the *LP* value, indicating that with a larger initial labeled dataset, the semisupervised clustering with expert input scheme detects more *fp* modules.

In a recent study (Zhong et al., 2004), we investigated unsupervised clustering techniques on the JM1-8850 dataset. In that study, the *k-means* and *Neural-Gas* (Martinez, Berkovich, & Schulten, 1993) clustering algorithms were used at C_{max} = 30 clusters. Similar to this study, the expert was given descriptive statistics for each cluster and was asked to label them as either *nfp* or *fp*. In (Zhong et al., 2004), the *Neural-Gas* clustering technique yielded better classification results than the *k-means* algorithm.

For the program modules that are labeled after the respective semisupervised clustering runs, the corresponding module classification performances by the *Neural-Gas* unsupervised clustering technique are presented in Table 2. The semisupervised clustering scheme depicts better false-negative error rates (Type II) than the unsupervised clustering method. The false-negative error rates of both techniques tend to decrease with an increase in *LP*. The false-positive error rates (Type I) of both techniques tends to remain relatively stable across the different *LP* values.

A *z-test* (Seber, 1984) was performed to compare the classification performances (populations)

Table 2. Average classification performance of labeled modules with semisupervised clustering.

Sample Size	Semisupervised			Unsupervised		
	Type I	Type II	Overall	Type I	Type II	Overall
100	0.1491	0.4599	0.2058	0.1748	0.5758	0.2479
250	0.1450	0.4313	0.1989	0.1962	0.5677	0.2661
500	0.1408	0.4123	0.1913	0.1931	0.5281	0.2554
1000	0.1063	0.4264	0.1630	0.1778	0.5464	0.2431
1500	0.1219	0.4073	0.1759	0.1994	0.5169	0.2595
2000	0.1137	0.3809	0.1641	0.1883	0.5172	0.2503
2500	0.1253	0.3777	0.1725	0.1896	0.4804	0.2440
3000	0.1361	0.3099	0.1687	0.1994	0.4688	0.2499

of semisupervised clustering and unsupervised clustering. The Overall misclassifications obtained by both techniques are used as the response variable in the statistical comparison at a 5% significance level. The proposed semisupervised clustering approach yielded significantly better Overall misclassifications than the unsupervised clustering approach for *LP* values of 500 and greater.

The KC1, KC2, and KC3 datasets are used as test data to evaluate the software quality knowledge learnt through the semisupervised clustering process as compared to unsupervised clustering with *Neural-Gas*. The test data modules are classified based on their Euclidean distance from centroids of the final *nfp* and *fp* clusters at the end a semisupervised clustering run. We report the averages of the respective number of random samples for *LP* = {500, 1000}. A similar classification is made using centroids of the *nfp* and *fp* clusters labeled by the expert after unsupervised clustering with the *Neural-Gas* algorithm.

The classification performances obtained by unsupervised clustering for the test datasets are shown in Table 3. The misclassification error rates of all test datasets are rather unbalanced with a low Type I error rate and a relatively high Type II error rate. Such a classification is obviously not useful to the software practitioner since among the program modules correctly detected as *nfp* or *fp*, most are *nfp* instances—many *fp* modules are not detected.

Table 4. Average test data performances with semisupervised clustering

Dataset	Type I	Type II	Overall
LP = 500			
KC1	0.0846	0.4708	0.1442
KC2	0.1039	0.3302	0.1500
KC3	0.1181	0.4186	0.1463
LP = 1000			
KC1	0.0947	0.3477	0.1337
KC2	0.1304	0.2925	0.1635
KC3	0.1325	0.3488	0.1528

The average misclassification error rates obtained by the respective semisupervised clustering runs for the test datasets are shown in Table 4. In comparison to the test data performances obtained with unsupervised clustering, the semisupervised clustering approach yielded noticeable better classification performances. The Type II error rates obtained by our semisupervised clustering approach were noticeably lower than those obtained by unsupervised clustering. This was accompanied, however, with higher or similar Type I error rates compared to unsupervised clustering. Though the Type I error rates were generally higher for semisupervised clustering, they were comparable to those of unsupervised clustering.

Semisupervised Classification Results

We primarily discuss the empirical results obtained by the EM-based semisupervised software quality classification approach in the context of a comparison with those of the semisupervised clustering with expert input scheme presented in previous section. The quality-of-fit performances of the EM-based semisupervised classification approach for the initial labeled datasets are summarized in Table 5. The corresponding misclassification error rates for the labeled datasets after the respective EM-based semisupervised classification process is completed are shown in Table 6.

As observed in the Tables 5 and 6, the EM-based semisupervised classification approach improves the overall classification performances for the different *LP* values. It is also noted that the final classification performance is (generally) inversely proportional to the size of the initial labeled dataset, that is, *LP*. This is perhaps indicative of the presence of excess noise in the JM1-

8850 dataset. A further insight into the presence of noise in JM1-8850 in the context of the two semisupervised learning approaches is presented in (Seliya et al., 2004; Seliya et al., 2005).

The software quality estimation performance of the semisupervised classification approach for the three test datasets is shown in Table 7. The table shows the average performance of the different samples for the *LP* values of 500 and 1000. In the case of *LP* = 1000, semisupervised clustering (see previous section) provides better prediction for the KC1, KC2, and KC3 test datasets. The noticeable difference between the two techniques for these three datasets is observed in the respective Type II error rates. While providing relatively similar or comparable Type I error rates, semisupervised clustering with expert input yields much lower Type II error rates than the EM-based semisupervised classification approach.

Table 5. Average (initial) performance with semisupervised classification

LP	Type I	Type II	Overall
100	0.1475	0.4500	0.2080
250	0.1580	0.4720	0.2208
500	0.1575	0.4820	0.2224
1000	0.1442	0.5600	0.2273
1500	0.1669	0.5233	0.2382
2000	0.1590	0.5317	0.2335
3000	0.2132	0.4839	0.2673

Table 6. Average (final) performance with semisupervised classification

LP	Type I	Type II	Overall
100	0.0039	0.0121	0.0055
250	0.0075	0.0227	0.0108
500	0.0136	0.0439	0.0206
1000	0.0249	0.0968	0.0428
1500	0.0390	0.1254	0.0593
2000	0.0482	0.1543	0.0752
3000	0.0830	0.1882	0.1094

Table 7. Average test data performances with semisupervised classification

Dataset	Type I	Type II	Overall
	LP = 500		
KC1	0.0703	0.7329	0.1725
KC2	0.1072	0.4245	0.1719
KC3	0.1118	0.5209	0.1502
	LP = 1000		
KC1	0.0700	0.7528	0.1753
KC2	0.1031	0.4465	0.1731
KC3	0.0988	0.5426	0.1405

For *LP* = 500, the semisupervised clustering with expert input approach provides better software quality prediction for the KC1 and KC2 datasets. In the case of KC3, with a comparable Type I error rate the semisupervised clustering approach provided a better Type II error rate. In summary, the semisupervised clustering with expert input generally yielded better performance than EM-based semisupervised clustering.

We note that the preference of selecting one of the two approaches for software quality analysis with limited apriori fault-proneness data may also be based on criteria other than software quality estimation accuracy. The EM-based semisupervised classification approach requires minimal input from the expert other than incorporating the desired software quality modeling strategy. In contrast, the semisupervised clustering approach requires considerable input from the software engineering expert in labeling new program modules (clusters) as *nfp* or *fp*. However, based on our study it is likely that the effort put into the semisupervised clustering approach would yield fruitful outcome in improving quality of the software product.

CONCLUSION

The increasing reliance on software-based systems further stresses the need to deliver high-quality software that is very reliable during system operations. This makes the task of software quality assurance as vital as delivering a software product within allocated budget and scheduling constraints. The key to developing high-quality software is the measurement and modeling of software quality, and toward that objective various activities are utilized in software engineering practice including verification and validation, automated test case generation for additional testing, re-engineering of low-quality program modules, and reviews of software design and code.

This research presented effective data mining solutions for tackling very important yet unaddressed software engineering issues. We address software quality modeling and analysis when there is limited apriori fault-proneness defect data available. The proposed solutions are evaluated using case studies of software measurement and defect data obtained from multiple NASA software projects, made available through the NASA Metrics Data Program.

In the case when the development organization has experience in developing systems similar to the target project but has limited availability of defect data for those systems, the software quality assurance team could employ either the EM-based semisupervised classification approach or semisupervised clustering approach with expert input. In our comparative study of these two solutions for software quality analysis with limited defect data, it was shown that semisupervised clustering approach generally yielded better software quality prediction that the semisupervised classification approach. However, once again, the software quality assurance team may also want to consider the relatively higher complexity involved in the semisupervised clustering approach when making their decision.

In our software quality analysis studies with the EM-based semisupervised classification and semisupervised clustering with expert input approaches, an explorative analysis of program modules that remain unlabeled after the different semisupervised learning runs provided valuable insight into the characteristics of those modules. A data mining point of view indicated that many of them were likely noisy instances in the JM1 software measurement dataset (Seliya et al., 2004; Seliya et al., 2005). From a software engineering point of view we are interested to learn why those specific modules remain unlabeled after the respective semisupervised learning runs. However, due to the unavailability of other detailed information on the JM1 and other NASA software projects a further in-depth analysis could not be performed.

An additional analysis of the two semisupervised learning approaches was performed by comparing their prediction performances with software quality classification models built by using the C4.5 supervised learner trained on the respective initial labeled datasets (Seliya et al., 2004; Seliya et al., 2005). It was observed (results not shown) that both semisupervised learning approaches generally provided better software quality estimations compared to the supervised learners trained on the initial labeled datasets.

The software engineering research presented in this chapter can lead to further related research in software measurements and software quality analysis. Some directions for future work may include: using different clustering algorithms for the semisupervised clustering with expert input scheme, using different underlying algorithms for the semisupervised classification approach, and incorporating the costs of misclassification into the respective semisupervised learning approaches.

REFERENCES

Basu, S., Banerjee A., & Mooney, R. (2002). Semisupervised clustering by seeding. In *Proceedings of the 19th International Conference on Machine Learning*, Sydney, Australia (pp. 19-26).

Demirez, A., & Bennett, K. (2000). Optimization approaches to semisupervised learning. In M. Ferris, O. Mangasarian, & J. Pang (Eds.), *Applications and algorithms of complementarity*. Boston: Kluwer Academic Publishers.

Dong, A., & Bhanu, B. (2003). A new semisupervised EM algorithm for image retrieval. In *Proceedings of the IEEE International Conference on Computer Vision and Pattern Recognition* (pp. 662-667). Madison, WI: IEEE Computer Society.

Fenton., N. E., & Pfleeger, S. L. (1997). *Software metrics: A rigorous and practical approach* (2nd ed.). Boston: PWS Publishing Company.

Fung, G., & Mangasarian, O. (2001). Semisupervised support vector machines for unlabeled data classification. *Optimization Methods and Software*, *15*, 29-44.

Ghahramani, Z., & Jordan, M. I. (1994). Supervised learning from incomplete data via an EM approach. In J. D. Cowan, G. Tesauro, & J. Alspector (Eds.), *Advances in neural information processing systems* (Vol. 6, pp. 120-127). San Francisco.

Goldman, S., & Zhou, Y. (2000). Enhancing supervised learning with unlabeled data. In *Proceedings of the 17th International Conference on Machine Learning*, Stanford University, CA (pp. 327-334).

Guo, L., Cukic, B., & Singh, H. (2003). Predicting fault prone modules by the dempster-shafer belief networks. In *Proceedings of the 18th International Conference on Automated Software Engineering*, Montreal, Canada (pp. 249-252).

Imam, K. E., Benlarbi, S., Goel, N., & Rai, S. N. (2001). Comparing case-based reasoning classifiers for predicting high-risk software components. *Journal of Systems and Software*, *55*(3), 301-320.

Khoshgoftaar, T. M., Liu, Y., & Seliya, N. (2003). Genetic programming-based decision trees for software quality classification. In *Proceedings of the 15th International Conference on Tools with Artificial Intelligence*, Sacramento, CA (pp. 374-383).

Khoshgoftaar, T. M., & Seliya, N. (2003). Analogy-based practical classification rules for software quality estimation. *Empirical Software Engineering Journal*, *8*(4), 325-350. Kluwer Academic Publishers.

Khoshgoftaar, T. M., & Seliya, N. (2004). Comparative assessment of software quality classification techniques: An empirical case study. *Empirical Software Engineering Journal*, *9*(3), 229-257. Kluwer Academic Publishers.

Khoshgoftaar, T. M., Yuan, X., & Allen, E. B. (2000). Balancing misclassification rates in classification tree models of software quality. *Empirical Software Engineering Journal*, *5*, 313-330.

Krzanowski, W. J., & Lai, Y. T. (1988). A criterion for determining the number of groups in a data set using sums-of-squares clustering. *Biometrics*, *44*(1), 23-34.

Little, R. J. A., & Rubin, D. B. (2002). *Statistical analysis with missing data* (2nd ed.). Hoboken, NJ: John Wiley and Sons.

Martinez, T. M., Berkovich, S. G., & Schulten, K. J. (1993). Neural-gas: Network for vector quantization and its application to time-series prediction. *IEEE Transactions on Neural Networks*, *4*(4), 558-569.

Mitchell, T. (1999). The role of unlabeled data in supervised learning. In *Proceedings of the 6th International Colloquium on Cognitive Science*, Donostia. San Sebastian, Spain: Institute for Logic, Cognition, Language and Information.

Nigam, K., & Ghani, R. (2000). Analyzing the effectiveness and applicability of co-training. In *Proceedings of the 9th International Conference on Information and Knowledge Management*, McLean, VA (pp. 86-93).

Nigam, K., McCallum, A. K., Thrun, S., & Mitchell, T. (1998). Learning to classify text from labeled and unlabeled documents. In *Proceedings of the 15th Conference of the American Association for Artificial Intelligence*, Madison, WI (pp. 792-799).

Nigam, K., McCallum, A. K., Thrun, S., & Mitchell, T. (2000). Text classification from labeled and unlabeled documents using EM. *Machine Learning, 39*(2-3), 103-134.

Ohlsson, M. C., & Runeson, P. (2002). Experience from replicating empirical studies on prediction models. In *Proceedings of the 8th International Software Metrics Symposium*, Ottawa, Canada (pp. 217-226).

Pedrycz, W., & Waletzky, J. (1997a). Fuzzy clustering in software reusability. *Software: Practice and Experience, 27*, 245-270.

Pedrycz, W., & Waletzky, J. (1997b). Fuzzy clustering with partial supervision. *IEEE Transactions on Systems, Man, and Cybernetics, 5*, 787-795.

Pizzi, N. J., Summers, R., & Pedrycz, W. (2002). Software quality prediction using median-adjusted class labels. In *Proceedings of the International Joint Conference on Neural Networks*, Honolulu, HI (Vol. 3, pp. 2405-2409).

Schneidewind, N. F. (2001). Investigation of logistic regression as a discriminant of software quality. In *Proceedings of the 7th International Software Metrics Symposium*, London (pp. 328-337).

Seber, G. A. F. (1984). *Multivariate observations*. New York: John Wiley & Sons.

Seeger, M. (2001). *Learning with labeled and unlabeled data* (Tech. Rep.). Scotland, UK: University of Edinburgh, Institute for Adaptive and Neural Computation.

Seliya, N., Khoshgoftaar, T. M., & Zhong, S. (2004). Semisupervised learning for software quality estimation. In *Proceedings of the 16th IEEE International Conference on Tools with Artificial Intelligence*, Boca Raton, FL (pp. 183-190).

Seliya, N., Khoshgoftaar, T. M., & Zhong, S. (2005). Analyzing software quality with limited fault-proneness defect data. In *Proceedings of the 9th IEEE International Symposium on High Assurance Systems Engineering*, Heidelberg, Germany (pp. 89-98).

Suarez, A., & Lutsko, J. F. (1999). Globally optimal fuzzy decision trees for classification and regression. *Pattern Analysis and Machine Intelligence, 21*(12), 1297-1311.

Wagstaff, K., & Cardie, C. (2000). Clustering with instance-level constraints. In *Proceedings of the 17th International Conference on Machine Learning*, Stanford University, CA (pp. 1103-1110) .

Wu, Y., & Huang, T. S. (2000). Self-supervised learning for visual tracking and recognition of human hand. In *Proceedings of the 17th National Conference on Artificial Intelligence*, Austin, TX (pp. 243-248) .

Zeng, H., Wang, X., Chen, Z., Lu, H., & Ma, W. (2003). CBC: Clustering based text classification using minimal labeled data. In *Proceedings of the IEEE International Conference on Data Mining*, Melbourne, FL (pp. 443-450).

Zhong, S. (2006). Semisupervised model-based document clustering: A comparative study. *Machine Learning, 65*(1), 2-29.

Zhong, S., Khoshgoftaar, T. M., & Seliya, N. (2004). Analyzing software measurement data with clustering techniques. *IEEE Intelligent Systems, 19*(2), 22-27.

Section II

Knowledge Discovery from Genetic and Medical Data

Chapter II
Genome-Wide Analysis of Epistasis Using Multifactor Dimensionality Reduction:
Feature Selection and Construction in the Domain of Human Genetics

Jason H. Moore
Dartmouth Medical School, USA

ABSTRACT

Human genetics is an evolving discipline that is being driven by rapid advances in technologies that make it possible to measure enormous quantities of genetic information. An important goal of human genetics is to understand the mapping relationship between interindividual variation in DNA sequences (i.e., the genome) and variability in disease susceptibility (i.e., the phenotype). The focus of the present study is the detection and characterization of nonlinear interactions among DNA sequence variations in human populations using data mining and machine learning methods. We first review the concept difficulty and then review a multifactor dimensionality reduction (MDR) approach that was developed specifically for this domain. We then present some ideas about how to scale the MDR approach to datasets with thousands of attributes (i.e., genome-wide analysis). Finally, we end with some ideas about how nonlinear genetic models might be statistically interpreted to facilitate making biological inferences.

THE PROBLEM DOMAIN: HUMAN GENETICS

Human genetics can be broadly defined as the study of genes and their role in human biology. An important goal of human genetics is to understand the mapping relationship between interindividual variation in DNA sequences (i.e., the genome) and variability in disease susceptibility (i.e., the phenotype). Stated another way, how does one or more changes in an individual's DNA sequence increase or decrease their risk of

Copyright © 2007, IGI Global, distributing in print or electronic forms without written permission of IGI Global is prohibited.

developing a common disease such as cancer or cardiovascular disease through complex networks biomolecules that are hierarchically organized and highly interactive? Understanding the role of DNA sequences in disease susceptibility is likely to improve diagnosis, prevention and treatment. Success in this important public health endeavor will depend critically on the degree of nonlinearity in the mapping between genotype to phenotype. Nonlinearities can arise from phenomena such as locus heterogeneity (i.e., different DNA sequence variations leading to the same phenotype), phenocopy (i.e., environmentally determined phenotypes), and the dependence of genotypic effects on environmental factors (i.e., gene-environment interactions or plastic reaction norms) and genotypes at other loci (i.e., gene-gene interactions or *epistasis*). It is this latter source of nonlinearity, *epistasis*, that is of interest here. Epistasis has been recognized for many years as deviations from the simple inheritance patterns observed by Mendel (Bateson, 1909) or deviations from additivity in a linear statistical model (Fisher, 1918) and is likely due, in part, to canalization or mechanisms of stabilizing selection that evolve robust (i.e., redundant) gene networks (Gibson & Wagner, 2000; Waddington, 1942, 1957; Proulx & Phillips, 2005).

Epistasis has been defined in multiple different ways (e.g., Brodie, 2000; Hollander, 1955; Philips, 1998). We have reviewed two types of epistasis, biological and statistical (Moore & Williams, 2005). Biological epistasis results from physical interactions between biomolecules (e.g., DNA, RNA, proteins, enzymes, etc.) and occur at the cellular level in an individual. This type of epistasis is what Bateson (1909) had in mind when he coined the term. Statistical epistasis on the other hand occurs at the population level and is realized when there is interindividual variation in DNA sequences. The statistical phenomenon of epistasis is what Fisher (1918) had in mind. The relationship between biological and statistical epistasis is often confusing but will be important to understand if we are to make biological inferences from statistical results (Moore & Williams, 2005).

The focus of the present study is the detection and characterization of statistical epistasis in human populations using data mining and machine learning methods. We first review the concept difficulty and then review a multifactor dimensionality reduction (MDR) approach that was developed specifically for this domain. We then present some ideas about how to scale the MDR approach to datasets with thousands of attributes (i.e., genome-wide analysis). Finally, we end with some ideas about how nonlinear genetic models might be statistically interpreted to facilitate making biological inferences.

CONCEPT DIFFICULTY

Epistasis can be defined as biological or statistical (Moore & Williams, 2005). Biological epistasis occurs at the cellular level when two or more biomolecules physically interact. In contrast, statistical epistasis occurs at the population level and is characterized by deviation from additivity in a linear mathematical model. Consider the following simple example of statistical epistasis in the form of a penetrance function. Penetrance is simply the probability (P) of disease (D) given a particular combination of genotypes (G) that was inherited (i.e., P[D|G]). A single genotype is determined by one allele (i.e., a specific DNA sequence state) inherited from the mother and one allele inherited from the father. For most single nucleotide polymorphisms or SNPs, only two alleles (e.g., encoded by *A* or *a*) exist in the biological population. Therefore, because the order of the alleles is unimportant, a genotype can have one of three values: *AA*, *Aa* or *aa*. The model illustrated in Table 1 is an extreme example of epistasis. Let's assume that genotypes *AA*, *aa*, *BB*, and *bb* have population frequencies of 0.25 while genotypes *Aa* and *Bb* have frequencies

Table 1. Penetrance values for genotypes from two SNPs

	AA (0.25)	*Aa* (0.50)	*aa* (0.25)
BB (0.25)	0	.1	0
Bb (0.50)	.1	0	.1
bb (0.25)	0	.1	0

of 0.5 (values in parentheses in Table 1). What makes this model interesting is that disease risk is dependent on the particular *combination* of genotypes inherited. Individuals have a very high risk of disease if they inherit *Aa* or *Bb* but not both (i.e., the exclusive OR function). The penetrance for each individual genotype in this model is 0.5 and is computed by summing the products of the genotype frequencies and penetrance values. Thus, in this model there is no difference in disease risk for each single genotype as specified by the single-genotype penetrance values. This model is labeled M170 by Li and Reich (2000) in their categorization of genetic models involving two SNPs and is an example of a pattern that is not linearly separable. Heritability or the size of the genetic effect is a function of these penetrance values. The model specified in Table 1 has a heritability of 0.053 which represents a small genetic effect size. This model is a special case where all of the heritability is due to epistasis. As Freitas (2001) reviews this general class of problems has high concept difficulty. Moore (2003) suggests that epistasis will be the norm for common human diseases such as cancer, cardiovascular disease, and psychiatric diseases.

MULTIFACTOR DIMENSIONALITY REDUCTION

Multifactor dimensionality reduction (MDR) was developed as a nonparametric (i.e., no parameters are estimated) and genetic model-free (i.e., no genetic model is assumed) data mining strategy for identifying combinations of SNPs that are predictive of a discrete clinical endpoint (Hahn & Moore, 2004; Hahn, Ritchie, & Moore, 2003; Moore, 2004; Moore et al., 2006; Ritchie, Hahn, & Moore, 2003; Ritchie et al., 2001). At the heart of the MDR approach is a feature or attribute construction algorithm that creates a new attribute by pooling genotypes from multiple SNPs. The process of defining a new attribute as a function of two or more other attributes is referred to as constructive induction or attribute construction and was first developed by Michalski (1983). Constructive induction using the MDR kernel is accomplished in the following way. Given a threshold *T*, a multilocus genotype combination is considered high-risk if the ratio of cases (subjects with disease) to controls (healthy subjects) exceeds *T*, else it is considered low-risk. Genotype combinations considered to be high-risk are labeled G_1 while those considered low-risk are labeled G_0. This process constructs a new one-dimensional attribute with levels G_0 and G_1. It is this new single variable that is assessed using any classification method. The MDR method is based on the idea that changing the representation space of the data will make it easier for a classifier such as a decision tree or a naive Bayes learner to detect attribute dependencies. Open-source software in Java and C are freely available from www.epistasis.org/software.html

Consider the simple example presented above and in Table 1. This penetrance function was used to simulate a dataset with 200 cases (diseased subjects) and 200 controls (healthy subjects) for a total of 400 instances. The list of attributes included the two functional interacting SNPs (SNP1 and SNP2) in addition to three randomly generated SNPs (SNP3 – SNP5). All attributes in these datasets are categorical. The SNPs each have three levels (0, 1, 2) while the class has two levels (0, 1) that code controls and cases. Figure 1a illustrates the distribution of cases (left bars)

Figure 1. (a) Distribution of cases (left bars) and controls (right bars) across three genotypes (0, 1, 2) for two simulated interacting SNPs; (b) distribution of cases and controls across nine two-locus genotype combinations**; (c) an interaction dendrogram summarizing the information gain associated with constructing pairs of attributes using MDR****

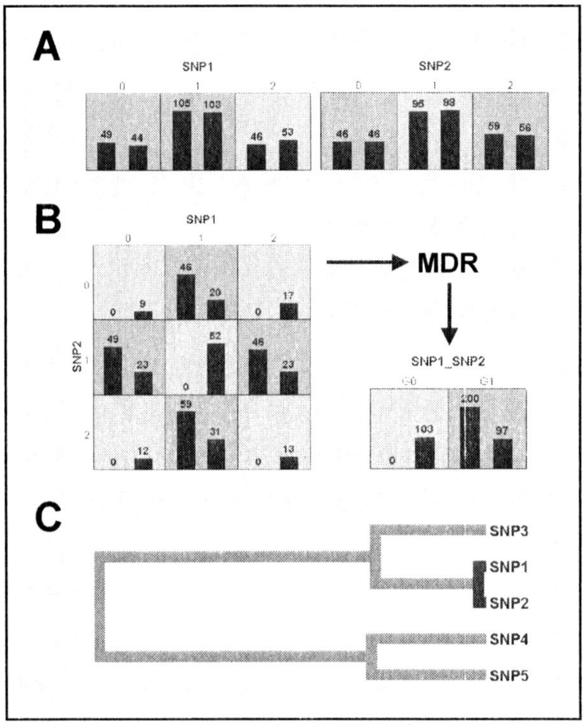

*Note: * The ratio of cases to controls for these two SNPs are nearly identical. The dark shaded cells signify "high-risk" genotypes. ** Considering the two SNPs jointly reveals larger case-control ratios. Also illustrated is the use of the MDR attribute construction function that produces a single attribute (SNP1_SNP2) from the two SNPs. *** The length of the connection between two SNPs is inversely related to the strength of the information gain. Red lines indicate a positive information gain that can be interpreted as synergistic interaction. Brown lines indicate no information gain*

and controls (right bars) for each of the three genotypes of SNP1 and SNP2. The dark-shaded cells have been labeled "high-risk" using a threshold of T = 1. The light-shaded cells have been labeled "low-risk." Note that when considered individually, the ratio of cases to controls is close to one for each single genotype. Figure 1b illustrates the distribution of cases and controls when the two functional SNPs are considered jointly. Note the larger ratios that are consistent with the genetic model in Table 1. Also illustrated in Figure 1b is the distribution of cases and controls for the new single attribute constructed using MDR. This new single attribute captures much of the information from the interaction and could be assessed using a simple naïve Bayes classifier.

The MDR method has been successfully applied to detecting epistasis or gene-gene interactions for a variety of common human diseases including, for example, sporadic breast cancer (Ritchie et al., 2001), essential hypertension (Moore & Williams, 2002; Williams et al., 2004), atrial fibrillation (Moore et al., 2006; Tsai et al., 2004), myocardial infarction (Coffey et al., 2004), type II diabetes (Cho et al., 2004), prostate cancer (Xu et al., 2005), bladder cancer (Andrew et al., 2006), schizophrenia (Qin et al., 2005), and familial amyloid polyneuropathy (Soares et al., 2005). The MDR method has also been successfully applied in the context of pharmacogenetics and toxicogenetics (e.g., Wilke, Reif, & Moore, 2005).

Consider the following case study. Andrew et al. (2006) carried out an epidemiologic study to identify genetic and environmental predictors of bladder cancer susceptibility in a large sample of Caucasians (914 instances) from New Hampshire. This study focused specifically on genes that play an important role in the repair of DNA sequences that have been damaged by chemical compounds (e.g., carcinogens). Seven SNPs were measured including two from the *X-ray repair cross-complementing group 1* gene (*XRCC1*), one from the *XRCC3* gene, two from the *xeroderma pigmentosum group D* (*XPD*) gene, one from the *nucleotide excision repair* gene (*XPC*), and one from the *AP endonuclease 1* gene (*APE1*). Each of these genes plays an important role in DNA repair. Smoking is a known risk factor for bladder cancer and was included in the analysis along with gender and age for a total of 10 attributes. Age was discretized to > or ≤ 50 years.

A parametric statistical analysis of each attribute individually revealed a significant independent main effect of smoking as expected. However, none of the measured SNPs were significant predictors of bladder cancer individually. Andrew et al. (2006) used MDR to exhaustively evaluate all possible two-, three-, and four-way interactions among the attributes. For each combination of attributes a single constructed attribute was evaluated using a naïve Bayes classifier. Training and testing accuracy were estimated using 10-fold cross-validation. A best model was selected that maximized the testing accuracy. The best model included two SNPs from the *XPD* gene and smoking. This three-attribute model had a testing accuracy of 0.66. The empirical p-value of this model was less than 0.001 suggesting that a testing accuracy of 0.66 or greater is unlikely under the null hypothesis of no association as assessed using a 1000-fold permutation test. Decomposition of this model using measures of information gain (see Moore et al., 2006; see below) demonstrated that the effects of the two *XPD* SNPs were non-addtive or synergistic suggestive of nonlinear interaction. This analysis also revealed that the effect of smoking was mostly independent of the nonlinear genetic effect. It is important to note that parametric logistic regression was unable to model this three-attribute interaction due lack of convergence. This study illustrates the power of MDR to identify complex relationships between genes, environmental factors such as smoking, and susceptibility to a common disease such as bladder cancer. The MDR approach works well in the context of an exhaustive search but how does it scale to genome-wide analysis of thousands of attributes?

GENOME-WIDE ANALYSIS

Biological and biomedical sciences are undergoing an information explosion and an understanding implosion. That is, our ability to generate data is far outpacing our ability to interpret it. This is especially true in the domain of human genetics where it is now technically and economically feasible to measure thousands of SNPs from across the human genome. It is anticipated that at least one SNP occurs approximately every 100 nucleotides across the $3*10^9$ nucleotide human genome. An important goal in human genetics is to determine which of the many thousands of SNPs are useful for predicting who is at risk for common diseases. This "genome-wide" approach is expected to revolutionize the genetic analysis of common human diseases (Hirschhorn & Daly, 2005; Wang, Barratt, Clayton, & Todd, 2005) and is quickly replacing the traditional "candidate gene" approach that focuses on several genes selected by their known or suspected function.

Moore and Ritchie (2004) have outlined three significant challenges that must be overcome if we are to successfully identify genetic predictors of health and disease using a genome-wide approach. First, powerful data mining and machine learning methods will need to be developed to statistically model the relationship between combinations of DNA sequence variations and disease susceptibility. Traditional methods such as logistic regression have limited power for modeling high-order nonlinear interactions (Moore & Williams, 2002). The MDR approach was discussed above as an alternative to logistic regression. A second challenge is the selection of genetic features or attributes that should be included for analysis. If interactions between genes explain most of the heritability of common diseases, then combinations of DNA sequence variations will need to be evaluated from a list of thousands of candidates. Filter and wrapper methods will play an important role because there are more combinations than can be exhaustively evaluated. A third challenge is the interpretation of gene-gene interaction models. Although a statistical model can be used to identify DNA sequence variations that confer risk for disease, this approach cannot be translated into specific prevention and treatment strategies without interpreting the results in the context of human biology. Making etiological inferences from computational models may be the most important and the most difficult challenge of all (Moore & Williams, 2005).

Combining the concept difficulty described above with the challenge of attribute selection yields what Goldberg (2002) calls a *needle-in-a-haystack* problem. That is, there may be a particular combination of SNPs that together with the right nonlinear function are a significant predictor of disease susceptibility. However, individually they may not look any different than thousands of other SNPs that are not involved in the disease process and are thus noisy. Under these models, the learning algorithm is truly looking for a genetic needle in a genomic haystack. A recent report from the International HapMap Consortium (Altshuler et al., 2005) suggests that approximately 300,000 carefully selected SNPs may be necessary to capture all of the relevant variation across the Caucasian human genome. Assuming this is true (it is probably a lower bound), we would need to scan $4.5 * 10^{10}$ pair wise combinations of SNPs to find a genetic needle. The number of higher order combinations is astronomical. What is the optimal approach to this problem?

There are two general approaches to selecting attributes for predictive models. The filter approach pre-processes the data by algorithmically or statistically assessing the quality of each attribute and then using that information to select a subset for classification. The wrapper approach iteratively selects subsets of attributes for classification using either a deterministic or stochastic algorithm. The key difference between the two approaches is that the classifier plays no role in selecting which attributes to consider in the filter approach. As Freitas (2002) reviews, the advantage of the filter is speed while the wrapper approach has the potential to do a better job classifying. We discuss each of these general approaches in turn for the specific problem of detecting epistasis or gene-gene interactions on a genome-wide scale.

A FILTER STRATEGY FOR GENOME-WIDE ANALYSIS

There are many different statistical and computational methods for determining the quality of attributes. A standard strategy in human genetics is to assess the quality of each SNP using a chi-square test of independence followed by a correction of the significance level that takes into account an increased false-positive (i.e., type I error) rate due to multiple tests. This is a very efficient filtering method but it ignores the dependencies or interactions between genes. Kira and Rendell (1992) developed an algorithm called Relief that is capable of detecting attribute dependencies. Relief estimates the quality of attributes through a type of nearest neighbor algorithm that selects neighbors (instances) from the same class and from the different class based on the vector of values across attributes. Weights (W) or quality estimates for each attribute (A) are estimated based on whether the nearest neighbor (nearest hit, H) of a randomly selected instance (R) from the same class and the nearest neighbor from the other class (nearest miss, M) have the same or different values. This process of adjusting weights is repeated for m instances. The algorithm produces weights for each attribute ranging from -1 (worst) to +1 (best). The Relief pseudocode is outlined below:

```
set all weights W[A] = 0
for i = 1 to m do begin
        randomly select an instance R_i
        find nearest hit H and nearest miss M
        for A = 1 to a do
                W[A] = W[A] – diff(A, R_i, H)/m
                + diff(A, R_i, M)/m
        end
```

The function diff(A, I_1, I_2) calculates the difference between the values of the attribute A for two instances I_1 and I_2. For nominal attributes such as SNPs it is defined as:

diff(A, I_1, I_2) = 0 if genotype(A, I_1) = genotype(A, I_2),
1 otherwise

The time complexity of Relief is $O(m*n*a)$ where m is the number of instances randomly sampled from a dataset with n total instances and a attributes. Kononenko (1994) improved upon Relief by choosing n nearest neighbors instead of just one. This new ReliefF algorithm has been shown to be more robust to noisy attributes (Kononenko, 1994; Robnik-Šikonja & Kononenko, 2001, 2003) and is widely used in data mining applications.

ReliefF is able to capture attribute interactions because it selects nearest neighbors using the entire vector of values across all attributes. However, this advantage is also a disadvantage because the presence of many noisy attributes can reduce the signal the algorithm is trying to capture. Moore and White (2007a) proposed a "tuned" ReliefF algorithm (TuRF) that systematically removes attributes that have low quality estimates so that the ReliefF values if the remaining attributes can be reestimated. The pseudocode for TuRF is outlined below:

```
let a be the number of attributes
for i = 1 to n do begin
        estimate ReliefF
        sort attributes
        remove worst n/a attributes
end
return last ReliefF estimate for each attribute
```

The motivation behind this algorithm is that the ReliefF estimates of the true functional attributes will improve as the noisy attributes are removed from the dataset.

Moore and White (2007a) carried out a simulation study to evaluate the power of ReliefF, TuRF, and a naïve chi-square test of independence for selecting functional attributes in a filtered subset. Five genetic models in the form of penetrance functions (e.g., Table 1) were generated. Each model consisted of two SNPs that define a nonlinear relationship with disease susceptibility. The heritability of each model was 0.1 which reflects a moderate to small genetic effect size. Each of the five models was used to generate 100 replicate datasets with sample sizes of 200, 400, 800, 1600, 3200 and 6400. This range of sample sizes represents a spectrum that is consistent with small to medium size genetic studies. Each dataset consisted of an equal number of case (disease) and control (no disease) subjects. Each pair of functional SNPs was combined within a genome-wide set of 998 randomly generated SNPs for a total of 1000 attributes. A total of 600 datasets were generated and analyzed.

ReliefF, TuRF and the univariate chi-square test of independence were applied to each of the datasets. The 1000 SNPs were sorted according to their quality using each method and the top 50, 100, 150, 200, 250, 300, 350, 400, 450 and 500 SNPs out of 1000 were selected. From each subset we counted the number of times the two functional SNPs were selected out of each set of 100 replicates. This proportion is an estimate of the power or how likely we are to find the true SNPs if they exist in the dataset. The number of times each method found the correct two SNPs was statistically compared. A difference in counts (i.e., power) was considered statistically significant at a type I error rate of 0.05. Moore and White (2007a) found that the power of ReliefF to pick (filter) the correct two functional attributes was consistently better ($P \leq 0.05$) than a naïve chi-square test of independence across subset sizes and models when the sample size was 800 or larger. These results suggest that ReliefF is capable of identifying interacting SNPs with a moderate genetic effect size (heritability=0.1) in moderate sample sizes. Next, Moore and White (2007a) compared the power of TuRF to the power of ReliefF. They found that the TuRF algorithm was consistently better ($P \leq 0.05$) than ReliefF across small SNP subset sizes (50, 100, and 150) and across all five models when the sample size was 1600 or larger. These results suggest that algorithms based on ReliefF show promise for filtering interacting attributes in this domain. The disadvantage of the filter approach is that important attributes might be discarded prior to analysis. Stochastic search or wrapper methods provide a flexible alternative.

A WRAPPER STRATEGY FOR GENOME-WIDE ANALYSIS

Stochastic search or wrapper methods may be more powerful than filter approaches because no attributes are discarded in the process. As a result, every attribute retains some probability of being selected for evaluation by the classifier. There are many different stochastic wrapper algorithms that can be applied to this problem. Moore and White (2007b) have explored the use of genetic programming (GP). Genetic programming (GP) is an automated computational discovery tool that is inspired by Darwinian evolution and natural selection (Banzhaf, Nordin, Keller, & Francone, 1998; Koza 1992, 1994; Koza, Bennett, Andre, & Keane, 1999; Koza et al., 2003; Langdon, 1998; Langdon & Poli, 2002). The goal of GP is evolve computer programs to solve problems. This is accomplished by first generating random computer programs that are composed of the basic building blocks needed to solve or approximate a solution to the problem. Each randomly generated program is evaluated and the good programs are selected and recombined to form new computer programs. This process of selection based on fitness and recombination to generate variability is repeated until a best program or set of programs is identified. Genetic programming and its many variations have been applied successfully in a wide range of different problem domains including data mining and knowledge discovery (e.g., Freitas, 2002), electrical engineering (e.g., Koza et al., 2003), and bioinformatics (e.g., Fogel & Corne, 2003).

Moore and White (2007b) developed and evaluated a simple GP wrapper for attribute selection in the context of an MDR analysis. Figure 2a illustrates an example GP binary expression tree. Here, the root node consists of the MDR attribute construction function while the two leaves on the tree consist of attributes. Figure 2b illustrates a more complex tree structure that could be implemented by providing additional functions and allowing the binary expression trees to grow beyond one level. Moore and White (2007b) focused exclusively on the simple one-level GP trees as a baseline to assess the potential for this stochastic wrapper approach.

The goal of this study was to develop a stochastic wrapper method that is able to select attributes that interact in the absence of independent main effects. At face value, there is no reason to expect that a GP or any other wrapper method would perform better than a random attribute selector because there are no "building blocks" for this problem when accuracy is used as the fitness measure. That is, the fitness of any given classifier would look no better than any other with just one of the correct SNPs in the MDR model. Preliminary studies by White, Gilbert, Reif, and Moore (2005) support this idea. For GP or any other wrapper to work there needs to be recognizable building blocks. Moore and White (2007b) specifically evaluated whether including pre-processed attribute quality estimates using TuRF (see above) in a multiobjective fitness function improved attribute selection over a random search or just using accuracy as the fitness. Using a wide variety of simulated data, Moore and White (in press) demonstrated that including TuRF scores

Figure 2. (a) Example of a simple GP binary expression with two attributes and an MDR function as the root node; (b) example of what a more complex GP tree might look like

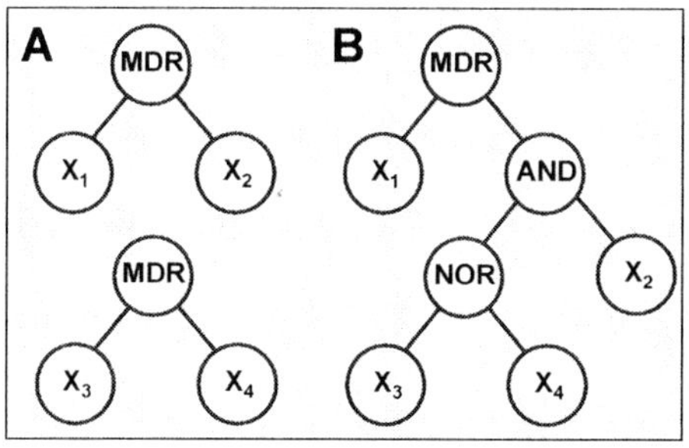

in addition to accuracy in the fitness function significantly improved the power of GP to pick the correct two functional SNPs out of 1000 total attributes. A subsequent study showed that using TuRF scores to select trees for recombination and reproduction performed significantly better than using TuRF in a multiobjective fitness function (Moore & White, 2006).

This study presents preliminary evidence suggesting that GP might be useful for the genome-wide genetic analysis of common human diseases that have a complex genetic architecture. The results raise numerous questions. How well does GP do when faced with finding three, four or more SNPs that interact in a nonlinear manner to predict disease susceptibility? How does extending the function set to additional attribute construction functions impact performance? How does extending the attribute set impact performance? Is using GP better than filter approaches? To what extent can GP theory help formulate an optimal GP approach to this problem? Does GP outperform other evolutionary or non-evolutionary search methods? Does the computational expense of a stochastic wrapper like GO outweigh the potential for increased power? The studies by Moore and White (2006, 2007b) provide a starting point to begin addressing some of these questions.

STATISTICAL AND BIOLOGICAL INTERPRETATION

Multifactor dimensionality reduction is powerful attribute construction approach for detecting epistasis or nonlinear gene-gene interactions in epidemiologic studies of common human diseases. The models that MDR produces are by nature multidimensional and thus diffuct to interpret. For example, an interaction model with four SNPs, each with three genotypes, summarizes 81 different genotype (i.e., level) combinations (i.e., 3^4). How do each of these level combinations relate back to biological processes in a cell? Why are some combinations associated with high-risk for disease and some associated with low-risk for disease? Moore et al. (2006) have proposed using information theoretic approaches with graph-based models to provide both a statistical and a visual interpretation of a multidimensional MDR model. Statistical interpretation should facilitate biological interpretation because it provides a deeper understanding of the relationship between the attributes and the class variable. We describe next the concept of interaction information and how it can be used to facilitate statistical interpretation.

Jakulin and Bratko (2003) have provided a metric for determining the gain in information about a class variable (e.g., case-control status) from merging two attributes into one (i.e., attribute construction) over that provided by the attributes independently. This measure of *information gain* allows us to gauge the benefit of considering two (or more) attributes as one unit. While the concept of information gain is not new (McGill, 1954), its application to the study of attribute interactions has been the focus of several recent studies (Jakulin & Bratko, 2003; Jakulin et al., 2003). Consider two attributes, A and B, and a class label C. Let H(X) be the Shannon entropy (see Pierce, 1980) of X. The information gain (IG) of A, B, and C can be written as (1) and defined in terms of Shannon entropy (2 and 3).

$$IG(ABC) = I(A;B|C) - I(A;B) \quad (1)$$

$$I(A;B|C) = H(A|C) + H(B|C) - H(A,B|C) \quad (2)$$

$$I(A;B) = H(A) + H(B) - H(A,B) \quad (3)$$

The first term in (1), I(A;B|C), measures the *interaction* of A and B. The second term, I(A;B), measures the *dependency* or correlation between A and B. If this difference is positive, then there is evidence for an attribute interaction that cannot be linearly decomposed. If the difference is negative, then the information between A and B is redundant. If the difference is zero, then there is evidence of conditional independence or a mixture of synergy and redundancy. These measures of interaction information can be used to construct interaction graphs (i.e., network diagrams) and an interaction dendrograms using the entropy estimates from Step 1 with the algorithms described first by Jakulin and Bratko (2003) and more recently in the context of genetic analysis by Moore et al. (2006). Interaction graphs are comprised of a node for each attribute with pairwise connections between them. The percentage of entropy removed (i.e., information gain) by each attribute is visualized for each node. The percentage of entropy removed for each pairwise MDR product of attributes is visualized for each connection. Thus, the independent main effects of each polymorphism can be quickly compared to the interaction effect. Additive and nonadditive interactions can be quickly assessed and used to interpret the MDR model which consists of distributions of cases and controls for each genotype combination. Positive entropy values indicate synergistic interaction while negative entropy values indicate redundancy.

Interaction dendrograms are also a useful way to visualize interaction (Jakulin & Bratko 2003; Moore et al., 2006). Here, hierarchical clustering is used to build a dendrogram that places strongly interacting attributes close together at the leaves of the tree. Jakulin and Bratko (2003) define the following dissimilarity measure, D (5), that is used by a hierarchical clustering algorithm to build a dendrogram. The value of 1000 is used as an upper bound to scale the dendrograms.

$$D(A,B) = \begin{cases} |I(A;B;C)|^{-1} & \text{if } |I(A;B;C)|^{-1} < 1000 \\ 1000 & \text{otherwise} \end{cases} \quad (5)$$

Using this measure, a dissimilarity matrix can be estimated and used with hierarchical cluster analysis to build an interaction dendrogram. This facilitates rapid identification and interpretation of pairs of interactions. The algorithms for the entropy-based measures of information gain are implemented in the open-source MDR software package available from www.epistasis.org. Output in the form of interaction dendrograms is provided. Figure 1c illustrates an interaction dendrogram for the simple simulated dataset described above. Note the strong synergistic relationship between SNP1 and SNP2. All other SNPs are independent which is consistent with the simulation model.

SUMMARY

We have reviewed a powerful attribute construction method called multifactor dimensionality reduction or MDR that can be used in a classification framework to detect nonlinear attribute interactions in genetic studies of common human diseases. We have also reviewed a filter method using ReliefF and a stochastic wrapper method using genetic programming (GP) for the analysis of gene-gene interaction or epistasis on a genome-wide scale with thousands of attributes. Finally, we reviewed information theoretic methods to facilitate the statistical and subsequent biological interpretation of high-order gene-gene interaction models. These data mining and knowledge discovery methods and others will play an increasingly important role in human genetics as the field moves away from the candidate-gene approach that focuses on a few targeted genes to the genome-wide approach that measures DNA sequence variations from across the genome.

ACKNOWLEDGMENT

This work was supported by National Institutes of Health (USA) grants LM009012, AI59694, HD047447, RR018787, and HL65234. We thank Mr. Bill White for his invaluable contributions to the methods discussed here.

REFERENCES

Altshuler, D., Brooks L. D, Chakravarti, A., Collins, F. S., Daly, M. J., & Donnelly, P. (2005). International HapMap consortium: A haplotype map of the human genome. *Nature, 437*, 1299-1320.

Andrew, A. S., Nelson, H. H., Kelsey, K. T., Moore, J. H., Meng, A. C., Casella, D. P., et al. (2006). Concordance of multiple analytical approaches demonstrates a complex relationship between DNA repair gene SNPs, smoking, and bladder cancer susceptibility. *Carcinogenesis, 27*, 1030-1037.

Banzhaf, W., Nordin, P., Keller, R. E., & Francone, F. D. (1998). *Genetic programming: An introduction: On the automatic evolution of computer programs and its applications*. San Francisco: Morgan Kaufmann Publishers.

Bateson, W. (1909). *Mendel's principles of heredity*. Cambridge, UK: Cambridge University Press.

Brodie III, E. D. (2000). Why evolutionary genetics does not always add up. In J. Wolf, B. Brodie III, M. Wade (Eds.), *Epistasis and the evolutionary process* (pp. 3-19). New York: Oxford University Press.

Cho, Y. M., Ritchie, M. D., Moore, J. H., Park, J. Y., Lee, K. U., Shin, H. D., et al. (2004). Multifactor-dimensionality reduction shows a two-locus interaction associated with Type 2 diabetes mellitus. *Diabetologia, 47*, 549-554.

Coffey, C. S., Hebert, P. R., Ritchie, M. D., Krumholz, H. M., Morgan, T. M., Gaziano, J. M., et al. (2004). An application of conditional logistic regression and multifactor dimensionality reduction for detecting gene-gene interactions on risk of myocardial infarction: The importance of model validation. *BMC Bioinformatics, 4*, 49.

Fisher, R. A. (1918). The correlations between relatives on the supposition of Mendelian inheritance. *Transactions of the Royal Society of Edinburgh, 52*, 399-433.

Fogel, G. B., & Corne, D. W. (2003). *Evolutionary computation in bioinformatics*. San Francisco: Morgan Kaufmann Publishers.

Freitas, A. (2001). Understanding the crucial role of attribute interactions. *Artificial Intelligence Review, 16*, 177-199.

Freitas, A. (2002). *Data mining and knowledge discovery with evolutionary algorithms*. New York: Springer.

Gibson, G., & Wagner, G. (2000). Canalization in evolutionary genetics: A stabilizing theory? *BioEssays, 22*, 372-380.

Goldberg, D. E. (2002). *The design of innovation*. Boston: Kluwer.

Hahn, L. W., & Moore, J. H. (2004). Ideal discrimination of discrete clinical endpoints using multilocus genotypes. *In Silico Biology, 4*, 183-194.

Hahn, L. W., Ritchie, M. D., & Moore, J. H. (2003). Multifactor dimensionality reduction software for detecting gene-gene and gene-environment interactions. *Bioinformatics, 19*, 376-382.

Hirschhorn, J. N., & Daly, M. J. (2005). Genome-wide association studies for common diseases and complex traits. *Nature Reviews Genetics, 6*, 95-108.

Hollander, W. F. (1955). Epistasis and hypostasis. *Journal of Heredity, 46*, 222-225.

Jakulin, A., & Bratko, I. (2003). Analyzing attribute interactions. *Lecture Notes in Artificial Intelligence, 2838*, 229-240.

Kira, K., & Rendell, L. A. (1992). A practical approach to feature selection. In D. H. Sleeman, & P. Edwards (Eds.), In *Proceedings of the Ninth International Workshop on Machine Learning*, San Francisco (pp. 249-256)

Kononenko, I. (1994). Estimating attributes: Analysis and extension of relief. In *Proceedings of the European Conference on Machine Learning* (pp. 171-182). New York: Springer.

Koza, J. R. (1992). *Genetic programming: On the programming of computers by means of natural selection*. Cambrindge, MA: The MIT Press.

Koza, J. R. (1994). *Genetic programming II: Automatic discovery of reusable programs*. Cambrindge, MA: The MIT Press.

Koza, J. R., Bennett III, F. H., Andre, D., & Keane, M. A. (1999). *Genetic programming III: Darwinian invention and problem solving*. San Francisco: Morgan Kaufmann Publishers.

Koza, J. R., Keane, M. A., Streeter, M. J., Mydlowec, W., Yu, J., & Lanza, G. (2003). *Genetic programming IV: Routine human-competitive machine intelligence*. New York: Springer.

Langdon, W. B. (1998). *Genetic programming and data structures: Genetic programming + data structures = automatic programming!* Boston: Kluwer.

Langdon, W. B., & Poli, R. (2002). *Foundations of genetic programming*. New York: Springer.

Li, W., & Reich, J. (2000). A complete enumeration and classification of two-locus disease models. *Human Heredity, 50*, 334-349.

McGill, W. J. (1954). Multivariate information transmission. *Psychometrica, 19*, 97-116.

Michalski, R. S. (1983). A theory and methodology of inductive learning. *Artificial Intelligence, 20*, 111-161.

Moore, J. H. (2003). The ubiquitous nature of epistasis in determining susceptibility to common human diseases. *Human Heredity, 56*, 73-82.

Moore, J. H. (2004). Computational analysis of gene-gene interactions in common human diseases using multifactor dimensionality reduction. *Expert Review of Molecular Diagnostics, 4*, 795-803.

Moore, J. H., Gilbert, J. C., Tsai, C.-T., Chiang, F. T., Holden, W., Barney, N., et al. (2006). A flexible computational framework for detecting, characterizing, and interpreting statistical patterns of epistasis in genetic studies of human disease susceptibility. *Journal of Theoretical Biology, 241*, 252-261.

Moore, J. H., & Ritchie, M. D. (2004). The challenges of whole-genome approaches to common diseases. *Journal of the American Medical Association, 291*, 1642-1643.

Moore, J. H., & White, B. C. (2007a). *Tuning relieff for genome-wide genetic analysis* (LNCS). New York: Springer.

Moore, J. H., & White, B. C. (2007b). Genome-wide genetic analysis using genetic programming. The critical need for expert knowledge. *Genetic programming theory and practice IV.* New York: Springer.

Moore, J. H., & White, B. C. (2006). Exploiting expert knowledge in genetic programming for genome-wide genetic analysis. *Lecture Notes in Computer Science*. New York: Springer.

Moore, J. H., & Williams, S. W. (2002). New strategies for identifying gene-gene interactions in hypertension. *Annals of Medicine, 34*, 88-95.

Moore, J. H., & Williams, S. W. (2005). Traversing the conceptual divide between biological and statistical epistasis: Systems biology and a more modern synthesis. *BioEssays, 27*, 637-646.

Phillips, P. C. (1998). The language of gene interaction. *Genetics, 149*, 1167-1171.

Proulx, S. R., & Phillips, P. C. (2005). The opportunity for canalization and the evolution of genetic networks. *American Naturalist, 165*, 147-162.

Qin, S., Zhao, X., Pan, Y., Liu, J., Feng, G., Fu, J., et al. (2005). An association study of the N-methyl-D-aspartate receptor NR1 subunit gene (GRIN1) and NR2B subunit gene (GRIN2B) in schizophrenia with universal DNA microarray. *European Journal of Human Genetics, 13*, 807-814.

Ritchie, M. D., Hahn, L. W., & Moore, J. H. (2003). Power of multifactor dimensionality reduction for detecting gene-gene interactions in the presence of genotyping error, phenocopy, and genetic heterogeneity. *Genetic Epidemiology, 24*, 150-157.

Ritchie, M. D., Hahn, L. W., Roodi, N., Bailey, L. R., Dupont, W. D., Parl, F. F., et al. (2001). Multifactor dimensionality reduction reveals high-order interactions among estrogen metabolism genes in sporadic breast cancer. *American Journal of Human Genetics, 69*, 138-147.

Robnik-Sikonja, M., & Kononenko, I. (2001). Comprehensible interpretation of Relief's Estimates. In *Proceedings of the Eighteenth International Conference on Machine Learning*, San Francisco (pp. 433-440).

Robnik-Siknja, M., & Kononenko, I. (2003). Theoretical and empirical analysis of ReliefF and RReliefF. *Machine Learning, 53*, 23-69.

Soares, M. L., Coelho, T., Sousa, A., Batalov, S., Conceicao, I., Sales-Luis, M. L., et al. (2005). Susceptibility and modifier genes in Portuguese transthyretin V30M amyloid polyneuropathy: Complexity in a single-gene disease. *Human Molecular Genetics, 14*, 543-553.

Tsai, C. T., Lai, L. P., Lin, J. L., Chiang, F. T., Hwang, J. J., Ritchie, M. D., et al. (2004). Renin-angiotensin system gene polymorphisms and atrial fibrillation. *Circulation, 109*, 1640-1646.

Waddington, C. H. (1942). Canalization of development and the inheritance of acquired characters. *Nature, 150*, 563-565.

Waddington, C. H. (1957). *The strategy of the genes.* New York: MacMillan.

Wang, W. Y., Barratt, B. J., Clayton, D. G., & Todd, J. A. (2005). Genome-wide association studies: Theoretical and practical concerns. *Nature Reviews Genetics, 6*, 109-118.

White, B. C., Gilbert, J. C., Reif, D. M., & Moore, J. H. (2005). A statistical comparison of grammatical evolution strategies in the domain of human genetics. In *Proceedings of the IEEE Congress on Evolutionary Computing* (pp. 676-682). New York. IEEE Press.

Wilke, R. A., Reif, D. M., & Moore, J. H. (2005). Combinatorial pharmacogenetics. *Nature Reviews Drug Discovery, 4*, 911-918.

Williams, S. M., Ritchie, M. D., Phillips III, J. A., Dawson, E., Prince, M., Dzhura, E., et al. (2004). Multilocus analysis of hypertension: A hierarchical approach. *Human Heredity, 57*, 28-38.

Xu, J., Lowery, J., Wiklund, F., Sun, J., Lindmark, F., Hsu, F.-C., et al. (2005). The interaction of four inflammatory genes significantly predicts prostate cancer risk. *Cancer Epidemiology Biomarkers and Prevention, 14*, 2563-2568.

Chapter III
Mining Clinical Trial Data

Jose Ma. J. Alvir
Pfizer Inc., USA

Javier Cabrera
Rutgers University, USA

Frank Caridi
Pfizer Inc., USA

Ha Nguyen
Pfizer Inc., USA

ABSTRACT

Mining clinical trails is becoming an important tool for extracting information that might help design better clinical trials. One important objective is to identify characteristics of a subset of cases that responds substantially differently than the rest. For example, what are the characteristics of placebo respondents? Who have the best or worst response to a particular treatment? Are there subsets among the treated group who perform particularly well? In this chapter we give an overview of the processes of conducting clinical trials and the places where data mining might be of interest. We also introduce an algorithm for constructing data mining trees that are very useful for answering the above questions by detecting interesting features of the data. We illustrate the ARF method with an analysis of data from four placebo-controlled trials of ziprasidone in schizophrenia.

INTRODUCTION

Data mining is a broad area aimed at extracting relevant information from data. In the 1950s and 60s, J.W. Tukey (1952) introduced the concepts and methods of exploratory data analysis (EDA). Until the early 1980s, EDA methods focused mainly on the analysis of small to medium size datasets using data visualization, data computations and simulations. But the computer revolution created an explosion in data acquisition and in data processing capabilities that demanded the expansion of EDA methods into the new area of data mining. Data mining was created as a large umbrella including simple analysis and visualization of massive data together with more theoretical areas like machine learning or machine vision.

In the biopharmaceutical field, clinical re-

Copyright © 2007, IGI Global, distributing in print or electronic forms without written permission of IGI Global is prohibited.

positories contain large amounts of information from many studies on individual subjects and their characteristics and outcomes. These include data collected to test the safety and efficacy of promising drug compounds, the bases on which a pharmaceutical company submits a new drug application (NDA) to the Food and Drug Administration in the United States. These data may also include data from postmarketing studies that are carried out after the drug has already been approved for marketing. However, in many circumstances, possible hidden relationship and patterns within these data are not fully explored due to the lack of an easy-to-use exploratory statistical tool. In the next sections, we will discuss the basic ideas behind clinical trials, introduce the active region finder methodology and apply it to a clinical problem.

CLINICAL TRIALS

Clinical trials collect large amounts of data ranging from patient demographics, medical history and clinical signs and symptoms of disease to measures of disease state, clinical outcomes and side effects.

Typically, it will take a pharmaceutical company 8 10 years and $800 million to $1.3 billion to develop a promising molecule discovered in the laboratory into a marketed drug (Girard, 2005). To have a medicine approved by the Food and Drug Administration, the sponsoring pharmaceutical company has to take the compound through many development stages (see Figure 1). To obtain final approval to market a drug, it's efficacy, compared to an appropriate control group (usually a placebo group), must be confirmed in at least two clinical trials (U.S. Department of Health and Human Services, FDA, CDER, CBER, 1998). These clinical trials are well-controlled, randomized and double-blind (Pocock, 1999). Briefly, the compound has to show in vitro efficacy and efficacy/safety in animal models. Once approved for testing in humans, the toxicity, pharmacokinetic properties and dosage have to be studied (phase I studies), then tested in a small number of patients for efficacy and tolerability (phase II studies) before running large clinical trials (phase III studies). After the drug is approved for marketing, additional trials are conducted to monitor adverse events, to study the morbidity and mortality, and to market the product (phase IV studies).

In a typical clinical trial, primary and secondary objectives, in terms of the clinical endpoints that measure safety and/or efficacy, are clearly defined in the protocol. Case report forms are developed to collect a large number of observations on each patient for the safety and efficacy endpoints (variables) that are relevant to the primary and secondary objectives of the trial. The statistical methodology and hypothesis to be tested have to be clearly specified in a statistical analysis plan (SAP) prior to the unblinding of the randomization code. The results are summarized in a clinical study report (CSR) in a structured format in the sense that only primary and secondary hypotheses specified in the protocol and SAP will be presented in detail. The discussion section might include some post hoc analyses but generally these additional results do not carry the same weight as the primary/secondary analyses.

The plan of analysis is usually defined in terms of the primary clinical endpoints and statistical analyses that address the primary objective of the trial. Secondary analyses are defined in an analogous manner. *The primary analysis* defines the clinical measurements of disease state along with the appropriate statistical hypotheses (or estimations) and statistical criteria that are *necessary* to demonstrate the primary scientific hypothesis of the trial. *Secondary analyses* are similarly defined to address the secondary scientific hypotheses under study, or to support the primary analysis in the sense of elucidating the primary result or demonstrating robustness of the primary result. Secondary analyses add important information to the study results, but in general positive findings on secondary analyses do not substitute for nonsignificant primary analyses. Often *subgroup analyses* are undertaken to determine if the overall result is consistent across all types of patients or to determine if some subgroups of patients respond differently.

Regulatory agencies usually require that the primary analysis be supplemented with analyses that stratify on some important subgroups of patients, for example, males and females or age categories.

Pharmaceutical companies typically run multiple clinical trials to test compounds that are submitted for approval by the FDA. Individual trials are powered to detect statistically significant differences in the primary test of efficacy within the total study sample. Typically, individual studies are underpowered to detect interactions of treatment with other patient characteristics, except in rare occasions wherein differential efficacy between subgroups is hypothesized *a priori*. No treatment is 100% efficacious and it is reasonable to expect that the effects of treatment could differ among subgroups of individuals. The clinician who prescribes a drug could be better served if information is available regarding the characteristics of individuals who have demonstrated good response to the drug or conversely, who have demonstrated poor response. Individual studies are also typically underpowered to detect statistically significant differences in adverse events that usually occur rarely. Consequently, there is even less power to look for subgroups that are at enhanced risk for adverse events. In order to investigate whether rare but important adverse events occur more frequently with a drug, large long-term clinical trials or open-label studies are undertaken by pharmaceutical companies. These data, along with large clinical databases composed of accumulated clinical trials present an opportunity for developing evidence-based medicine; development teams can apply exploratory data analysis and data mining techniques to enhance understanding of how patients respond to a drug, or to detect signals of potential safety issues, or to inform the design of new studies. Data mining may be a useful tool for finding subgroups of patients with particularly good response to treatment, or for understanding which patients may respond to a placebo. For example, identifying demographic or clinical characteristics that can predict if a patient will respond to placebo would be very useful in designing efficient new trials. Similarly, identifying the characteristics of those patients who respond well or do not respond to drug treatment can help doctors determine the optimal treatment for an individual patient.

Figure 1. Diagram of the drug development process

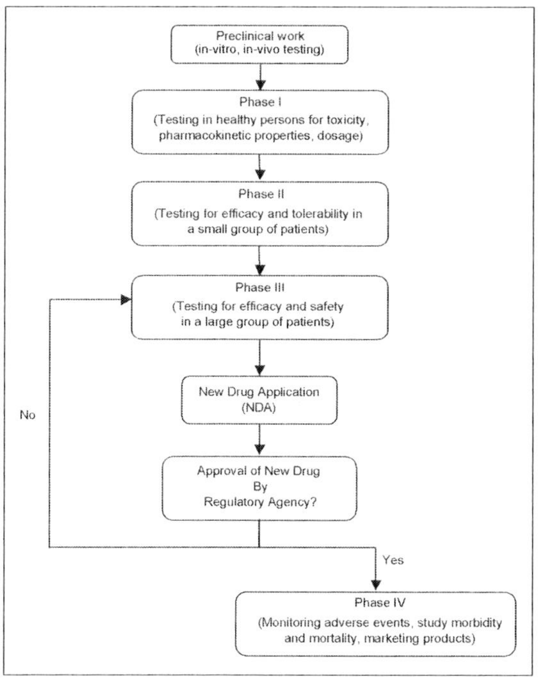

DATA MINING TREES

Classification and regression trees have been the standard data mining methods for many years. An important reference on classification and regression trees is the book by Breiman, Friedman, Olshen and Stone (1984). However, the complexity of the clinical trial databases with potentially thousands of patients and hundreds of features makes it very hard to apply standard

Figure 2. Proportion of placebo responders as a function of a pain score measured at time zero. The interval (a,b) represents the center bucket that was chosen by the ARF algorithm coinciding with the biggest bump in the function. There are other less interesting bumps that are not selected.

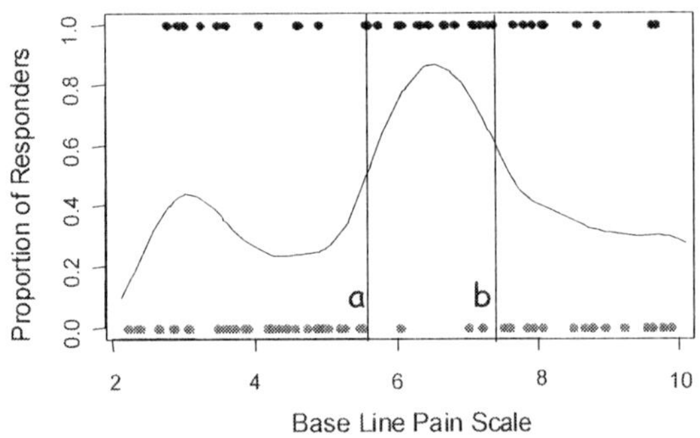

data mining methodology. Standard classification trees produce very large trees that explain all the variation of the response across the entire dataset, and are tedious and difficult to interpret.

An example of this is shown in Figure 2. The graph is a scatter plot of response to treatment Vs initial pain measured on a standard rating scale for a group of individuals who have been administered a placebo. The response to treatment variable takes values 0 for nonresponders and 1 for responders. The pain scale variable takes values from 0 to 10, where 10 means very high pain and 0 means no pain. The smooth curve across the graph represent the average proportion of responders for a given value of the pain scale variable. The important fact on the graph is that there is an interval (a,b) for which proportion of placebo responders is very high. In the rest of the region the curve is still very nonlinear but the information is not so relevant. When the number of observations is very large, the standard tree methods will try to explain every detail of the relationship and make the analysis harder to interpret, when in reality the important fact is very simple.

For this reason we developed the idea of data mining trees. The idea is to build trees that are easier to interpret. The technical details of the algorithm (see Figure 3) can be found in Amaratunga and Cabrera (2004). The important elements of the ARF trees are:

1. **Interval splits:** At each node we split the data into three buckets defined by two cuts (a,b) on the range of a continuous predictor variable X. The main bucket is the central bucket and it is defined by the values of X that fall inside the interval (a,b), namely $a<X<b$. The left bucket is defined by $X<a$ and right bucket is defined by $X>b$. For binary or categorical predictors the node is split into two buckets.
   One great property of interval splits is that it makes trees shorter and less complex. Although binary splits are computationally faster than interval splits, the ARF algorithm solves this problem by reducing the computations of interval splits to a very manageable time
2. **Robust splits:** We achieve robust splits by making the criterion for choosing the optimal split depend only on the data inside the central bucket, unlike CART splits that use the right and left buckets. This is especially useful for the case when the response is numerical because it helps to avoid outliers. For the categorical response case this robustness means that the cuts are independent of the variation between right and left buckets.
3. **Tree sketches:** One of the versions of the data mining tree is a simplified version or sub-tree, which includes only the significant nodes. Significance is calculated according to the criterion explained in item (5) as follows.
4. **Allow for categorical and numerical responses:** There are three kinds of possible responses for clinical trial data:
   - Binary response
   - Categorical response
   - Numeric response
5. **The ARF algorithm for building data mining trees:** The algorithm allows all

the three above cases for the response. The binary response case is the most important case since it will be the basis for the other two cases. As was explained in item (1) above the ARF tree is built by splitting the data into three buckets. The main bucket consists of the observations that fall in the interval (a,b) for some predictor *X*. The criterion that is optimized depends on the proportion $\pi = P(Y=1)$ of the parent bucket and on the proportion $p=P(Y=1|a<X<b)$. Hence the criterion is:

$$A(a,b)=\frac{p-\pi}{\sqrt{\frac{\pi(1-\pi)}{n}}}$$

The interval (a,b) that optimizes the *A* criterion is the optimal split. The optimization occurs over all intervals (a,b) and over all candidate predictors *X* for the split.

The objective criterion *A* could be maximized or minimized. Maximization implies selecting an interval with high *p*, whereas minimization means selecting intervals with low *p*.

In this context a *tree sketch* is a subtree of the main tree containing the root node and all sub-nodes that are deemed *significant*. In order to decide when a node is significant a simulation was performed for many sample sizes and many values of π and the results of the simulation where used to calculate a polynomial approximation that given the parameters N, n, p, and π will decide if the optimal value $A(a,b)$ could happen from a random subset at least 5% of the time. If the probability that $A(a,b)$ could happen by chance is less than 5% then the node is considered *significant* and it becomes part of the *tree sketch*. The subnodes that are at the left and right side of the interval are not evaluated for significance and will not be included on the sketch, but their children could. Nodes that are not *significant* but whose children are *significant* are represented in the tree sketch by empty nodes.

Once the interval split is selected the new buckets, center, right and left buckets are identified and become candidates for further splits.

The process of building the tree stops when the bucket size becomes less than a fixed value n_0. Figure 2 shows an example of a tree *sketch* obtained from the pooled data from four clinical trials of ziprasidone, an antipsychotic drug, in subjects with schizophrenia.

6. **Categorical responses:** A categorical response takes values in a set of categories. We rewrite the response as a set of binary dummy variables and iterate the algorithm over all the responses at each node. To perform a split we select the optimal interval that optimizes the *A* criterion over all responses and all predictors.
7. **Numerical respondent:** If the response is numeric we search for regions of low or high response compared to the mean or median response of the parent bucket.
The *A* criterion is now:

$$A(a,b)=\frac{\bar{y}-\mu}{\frac{\sigma}{\sqrt{n}}},$$

where $\bar{y}$ is the subset mean response and μ and σ are the mean and standard deviation of the response over the parent bucket.
To perform a split we select the optimal interval that optimizes the *A* criterion over all predictors.
8. **ARF report:** The output of the ARF software is summarized in a PDF report containing the following items:

- **Tree sketch**
- **Full tree**
- **Table of results:** A detailed table giving the information of each bucket.
- **Significant subsets:** A list of all the significant subsets according to the A criterion.

Figure 3. Diagram of the ARF algorithm

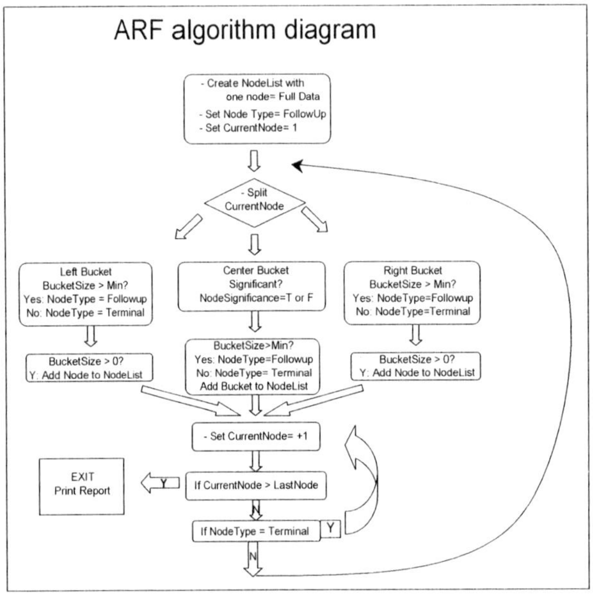

Another example is shown in Figure 4 which shows a CART tree from one of the most standard dataset in machine learning. This is the Pima Indians dataset that was collected from a group of 768 Pima Indian females, 21+ years old many of which tested positive for diabetes (268 tested positive to diabetes). The predictors are eight descriptor variables that are related to pregnancy, racial background, age and other. The tree was built using Splus. The initial tree was about 60 nodes and was quite difficult to read. In order to make it more useful the tree was subsequently pruned using cross-validation. The final result is displayed in Figure 4. We constructed an ARF sketch of the same data and we see that the tree is much smaller and clearer. The ARF tree has a node of 55 observations with 96% rate of diabetes. On the other hand the best node for the CART tree is of 9 observations with 100% diabetes. One might ask how statistically significant are such nodes? The ARF node is very significant because the node size of 55 is very large. However, the node from CART has a high probability of occurring by chance. Suppose that we sample a sequence of 768 independent Bernoulli trials each with a $P(1) = 0.35$ and $P(0) = 0.65$. The probability that the random sequence contains nine consecutive 1s is approximately 4%. If we consider that there are eight predictors and many possible combinations of split we argue that the chances of obtaining a node of nine 1s is quite high. The argument for the ARF tree is that it produces sketches that summarize only the important information and downplay the less interesting information. Also important is the use of statistical significance as a way to make sure the tree sketch does not grow too large.

One could play with the parameters and options of CART to make the CART tree closer to the ARF answers but it will generally require quite a bit of work and the resulting trees are likely to be larger.

CASE STUDY: POOLED DATA FROM FOUR CLINICAL TRIALS OF ZIPRASIDONE

We demonstrate the use of our method to characterize subgroups of good and poor responders in clinical trials, using pooled data from four

Figure 4. CART tree from a group of 768 Pima Indian females, 21+ years old many of which tested positive for diabetes (response 268 tested positive to diabetes)

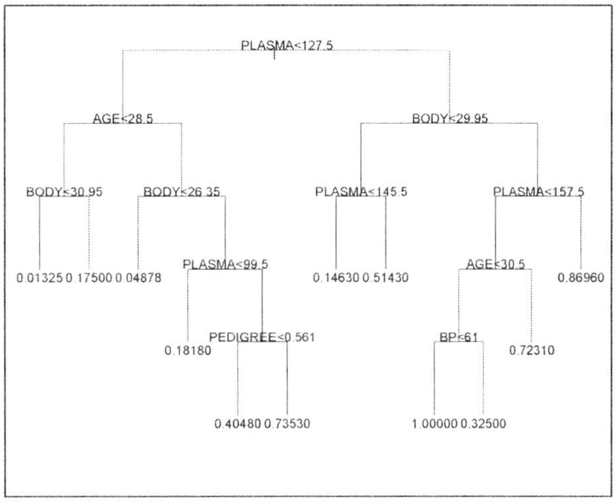

Note: The predictors are eight descriptor variables. The tree was built using Splus and subsequently pruned using cross-validation.

placebo-controlled trials of ziprasidone in schizophrenia (Alvir, Loebel, Lombardo, Nguyen, & Cabrera, 2006; Daniel, Zimbroff, & Potkin, 1999). Schizophrenia is a severe and chronic brain disorder that affects about 1% of the population (Mueser & McGurk, 2004). Symptoms include positive symptoms (hallucinations, delusions and thought disorder), negative symptoms (inability to initiate plans, speak, emote or find pleasure in everyday life), and cognitive deficits (problems with attention, memory, planning and organization).

Ziprasidone belongs to a class of second-generation or atypical antipsychotic drugs used to treat schizophrenia. Unlike older or conventional antipsychotic drugs, atypical drugs have low incidence of tardive dyskinesia, extrapyramidal signs and prolactin elevation, conditions that are commonly associated with the conventional antipsychotic drugs and affect compliance with medication (Kane, 1999). The atypical antipsychotic drugs have also shown efficacy against negative symptoms and cognitive deficits, while conventional antipsychotic drugs have little influence on these. Unlike other atypical drugs, especially olanzapine, ziprasidone does not lead to weight gain and increase in metabolic syndrome (Allison et al., 1999). The FDA approved the oral formulation of ziprasidone for marketing in Feb. of 2001.

Method: Datasets from four short-term randomized, placebo-controlled trials of ziprasidone in patients (n = 951) with acute exacerbation of schizophrenia were pooled for these analyses. The studies included two 4-week trials (protocols 104 and 106) and two 6-week trials (protocols 114 and 115). The dose of ziprasidone ranged from 10 to 200 mg/day. A dose of 10 mg/day is considered therapeutically inefficacious. The daily doses tested against placebo were 10, 40 and 80 for protocol 104, 40 and 120 for protocol 106, 80 and 160 for protocol 114, and 40, 120 and 200 for protocol 115. Males made up 74% of the pooled sample. Smokers comprised 75%. The sample was 65% white, 25% black, and 10% of other racial backgrounds. The sample characteristics are typical of the population available for inclusion into these trials.

The outcome measure was the change from baseline (pretreatment) to the end of study in the brief psychiatric rating scale (BPRS) (Overall & Gorham, 1962) total score, controlling for baseline BPRS score. The last observation was carried

Figure 5. Data mining tree using the ARF algorithm, from the same Pima Indian data as in Figure 4

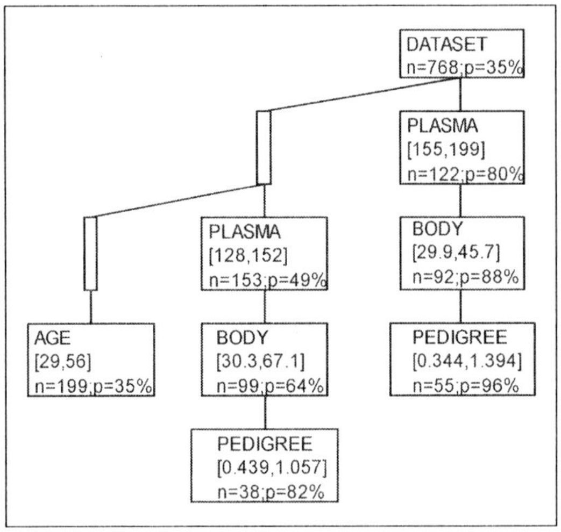

forward for patients who did not complete the entire 4- or 6-week duration of the trial. Because protocols 114 and 115 used the positive and negative syndrome scale (PANSS) (Kay, Fiszbein, & Opler, 1987), a scale that includes the original 18 items in the BPRS, the BPRS total score was derived using these 18 items from the PANSS. Both the BPRS and the PANSS rate items on a seven-point rating scale ranging from absent to extreme.

Predictors [variable names used in the analyses are bracketed] included categorical indicators of sex, race, protocol [STUDNUM], daily dose [DOSE_ZIP] with placebo coded as zero and smoking status [SMOKEYN], as well as measures of age, illness duration in years [DURATILL] and baseline clinical ratings from several standardized instruments. The pretreatment clinical ratings included the clinical global impression of severity of illness [BCGIS] (CGI-S; Guy, 1976, pp. 217-222) ranging from 1 (normal) to 7 (most severely ill). Three symptom scales were derived from the BPRS/PANSS. The positive symptom score [BASEPOS] was the sum of items that measured conceptual disorganization, hallucinatory behavior, unusual thought content and suspiciousness. The depression score [BASEDEP] was the sum of items that measured anxiety, guilt feelings and depressive mood. The anergia score was the sum of items that measured blunted affect, emotional withdrawal and motor retardation. The latter three items are considered "negative" symptoms of schizophrenia. The abnormal involuntary movements scale (AIMS; Guy, 1976, pp. 534-537) measures the amount of involuntary movements manifested by the patients. These movements are part of a syndrome called tardive dyskinesia, a common side effect of older-generation antipsychotic drugs. Patients with spontaneous extrapyramidal symptoms prior to antipsychotic exposure (Chatterjee et al., 1995) and patients who later develop tardive dyskinesia (Chakos et al., 1996) have been reported to be less likely to respond to treatment. The AIMS score [MNAIMS] was derived using the mean of the AIMS total score and the global tardive dyskinesia rating score. The AIMS total score was divided by five so as to render the range similar to that of the global tardive dyskinesia score when computing their mean. For all of the clinical scores we used, higher scores indicate more symptoms and/or poorer function. Table 1 lists descriptive statistics for the predictors used in the analyses, as well as for the raw and residual BPRS change.

Separate trees were produced for good response, as indicated by large reduction in symptoms and poor response, as indicated by small reduction or increase in symptoms.

Results: Dose was the most powerful predictor and produced the first cut in the "good response" tree. Figure 6 presents the results of this analysis. The tree sketch demonstrates the significant nodes while the full tree depicts the entire classification tree. The full table of statistics for the tree and the table listing significant subsets are also provided. The best response noted in the group of 23 patients receiving ziprasidone 120 or 160 mg/day and having a short duration (0-3 years) of illness. Note however that the association of good response with illness duration is not linear because within the 120-160 ziprasidone dose group, the

Table 1. Descriptive statistics of the pooled sample

	Mean	S.D.	Range
BPRS change	-5.1	13.4	-58, 55
Residual BPRS change	0	13.1	-45, 65
Age	38.7	10.1	18, 72
Duration of illness	16.0	9.6	0, 54
Baseline ratings			
BPRS	35.9	11.0	14, 86
Positive Symptoms	12.7	3.4	4, 24
Depression	5.5	3.3	0, 17
CGI-Severity	4.8	0.8	3, 7
Anergia	6.0	3.4	0, 18
AIMS	0.4	0.6	0, 4

group of 20 patients with the longest duration (29-37 years) also responded well. In the other dose groups, the lack of abnormal movements (AIMS scores of 0-0.1) is good, especially in the groups with 0-3 years duration of illness and those with 17-27 years. Note also that among the patients with AIMS scores greater than 0.1, a further split indicates that a group of 25 patients with AIMS scores of 0.6 had good response. Along the same split, a group of patients with AIMS scores of 0.2-0.3 had very poor response, but only six individuals belonged to this node. Four variables that were entered as potential predictors (SEX, RACE, SMOKEYN, BCGIS) were not used in the classification process.

Figure 7 presents the results of analyses that predict poor response. Only the tree sketch and the full tree are shown in Figure 3. The full table of results and table of significant results that are part of the analysis output have been omitted for the sake of brevity. Presence of abnormal movements (MNAIMS) produced the first split in the "poor response" tree (i.e., was the strongest predictor of poor response –). The presence of movements combined with placebo or the ineffective 10 mg. dose of ziprasidone predicts poor response, especially in patients with anergia scores greater than 4. Noteworthy in the "poor response" tree is a tendency for the middle node in splits of three nodes to exhibit the worst response. This is evident in splits along duration of illness, depression, anergia and positive symptoms. The SEX and SMOKEYN variables were entered but not used in the classification process.

Conclusions: ARF analyses successfully identified subgroups with good or poor response and were particularly useful in identifying nonlinear associations between predictors and response.

SOFTWARE

A software package in R that implements data mining trees methodology is available at http://www.rci.rutgers.edu/~cabrera/DM/. The bundle contains the R code and documentation plus example datasets.

The implementation is quite simple and not much knowledge of R is needed to run the ARF methodology. Just put the data on a text file, an MS Excel file saved as ".csv" or a SAS export file. The three data formats are easy to read into R. Within R you need to run two commands. The first one generates the ARF data analysis object. In this example we load a dataset called "hospital" and the response is a categorical variable. The first command specifies the model and the data and creates the ARF object.

```
h.arf = f.arf(SALESC ~ BEDS+OUTV+TRAUMA+
REHAB+FEMUR96,
    data=hospital)
```

The second command generates a summary report of the analysis:

```
f.report(h.arf,file= "hospital.pdf")
```

This report file is a standard PDF file that is read with Adobe Acrobat Reader.

CONCLUSION

Clinical trial data are typically designed to detect clinically and statistically significant differences between the test drug and a comparator drug (usually placebo). These studies usually lack statistical power to detect subgroups with enhanced or poor response to treatment. Since pharmaceutical companies typically need two trials to attain approval from the FDA and generally undertake more than the required two trials, the pooled data from the accumulated trials is available for exploratory analyses and data mining. These data can be supplemented with data from studies, usually larger and longer-term, that are carried out post-approval. We introduced Active Region Finder, a method that builds simple and easily-interpretable data mining trees. This simplicity is due to the concentration on "high activity" areas instead of prediction of the outcome across its entire distribution. Thus this method is exquisitely appropriate when we are asking questions such as "in what subgroups is the test drug highly efficacious?" The example looking at good and poor response in pooled data from four clinical trials of ziprasidone demonstrates a useful application of the method.

REFERENCES

Allison, D. B., Mentore, J. L., Heo, M., Chandler, L. P., Cappelleri, J. C., Infante, M. C., et al. (1999). Antipsychotic-induced weight gain: A comprehensive research synthesis. *A. J. of Psy., 156*, 1686-1696.

Alvir, J., Loebel, A., Lombardo, I., Nguyen, H., & Cabrera, H. (2006, May 20-25). *Identifying subgroups with good and poor response in placebo-controlled trials in schizophrenia.* Poster session presented at the American Psychiatric Association 159th Annual Meeting, Toronto, Canada.

Amaratunga, D., & Cabrera, J. (2004). Mining data to find subsets of high activity. *Journal of Statistical Planning and Inference, 122*, 23-41.

Breiman, L., Friedman, J. H., Olshen, R. A., & Stone, C. J. (1984). *Classification and regression trees.* Belmont, CA: Wadsworth International Group.

Chakos, M. H., Alvir, J. M., Woerner, M. G., Koreen, A., Geisler, S., Mayerhoff, D., et al. (1996). Incidence and correlates of tardive dyskinesia in first episode of schizophrenia. *Arch. G. Psy., 53,* 313-319.

Chatterjee, A., Chakos, M., Koreen, A., Geisler, S., Sheitman, B., Woerner, M., et al. (1995). Prevalence and clinical correlates of extrapyramidal signs and spontaneous dyskinesia in never-medicated schizophrenic patients. *American Journal of Psychiatry, 152*, 1724-1729.

Daniel, D. G., Zimbroff, D. L., Potkin, S. G., et al. (1999). Ziprasidone 80 mg/day and 160 mg/day in the acute exacerbation of schizophrenia and schizoaffective disorder: A 6-week placebo-controlled trial. Ziprasidone Study Group. *Neuropsychopharmacology, 20*, 491-505.

Girard, P. (2005). Clinical trial simulation: A tool for understanding study failures and preventing them. *Basic & Clin. Pharm. & Toxic., 96*, 228-234.

Guy, W. (1976). *Early clinical drug evaluation (ECDEU) manual.* Washington, DC: United States Department of Health, Education, and Welfare.

Kane, J. M. (1999). Schizophrenia: How far have we come? *Current Opinion in Psych., 12*, 17-18.

Kay, S. R., Fiszbein, A., & Opler, L. A. (1987). The positive and negative syndrome scale (PANSS) for schizophrenia. *Schiz. Bulletin, 13*(2), 261-276.

Mueser, K. T., & McGurk, S. R. (2004, June 19). Schizophrenia. *The Lancet, 363*, 2063-2072.

Overall, J. E., & Gorham, D. R. (1962). The brief psychiatric rating scale. *Psychol Rep, 10*, 799-812.

Pocock, S. (1999). *Clinical trials: A practical approach.* London: John Wiley & Sons.

Tukey, J.W. (1962). The future of data analysis. *Annals of Mathematical Statistics, 33*, 1-67.

U.S. Department of Health and Human Services. (1998). *FDA, CDER, CBER. Guidance for industry: Providing clinical evidence of effectiveness for human drug and biological products.* Washington, DC: Author.

Figure 6. Output of results from ARF analysis predicting good response

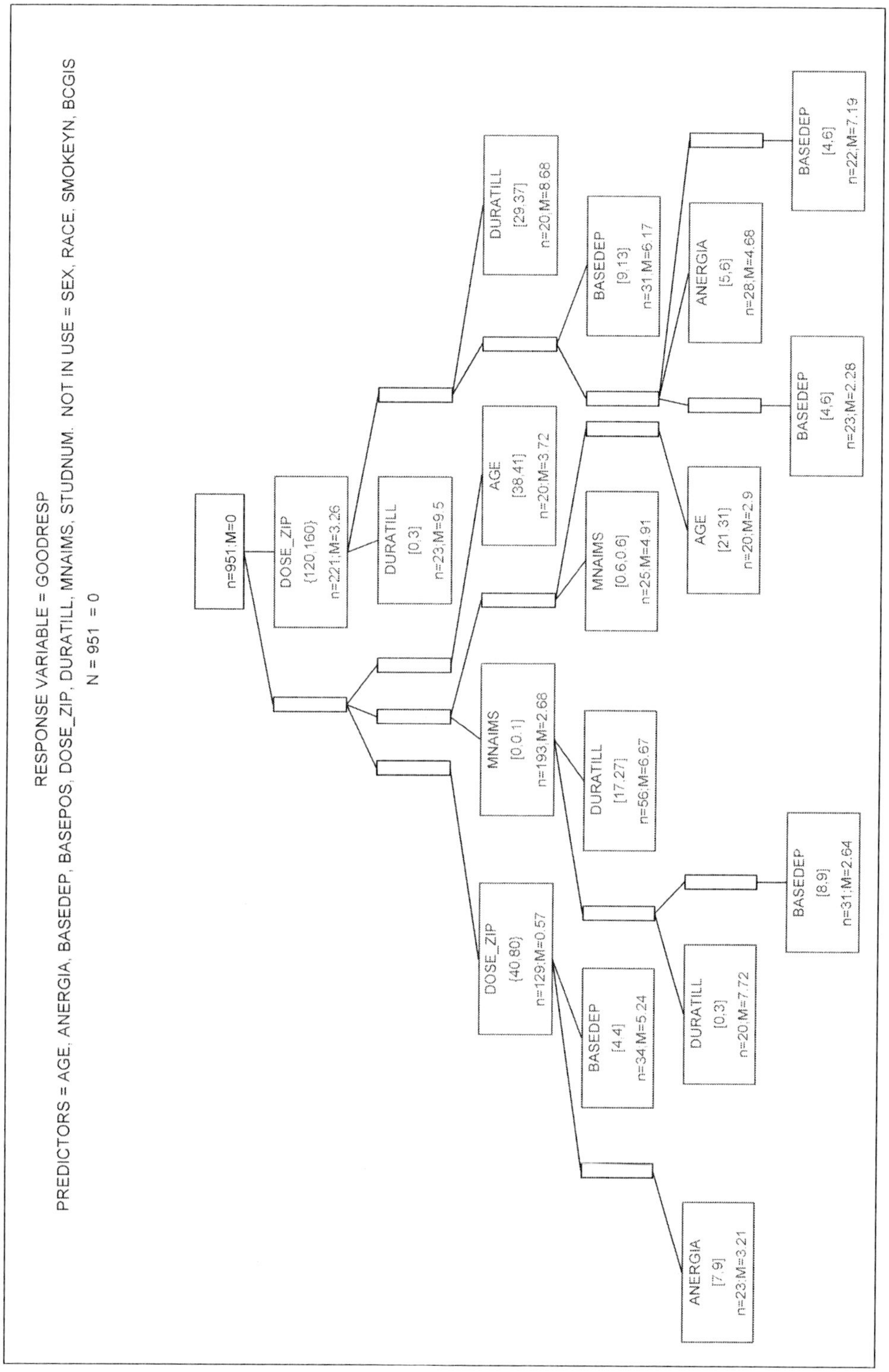

continued on following page

Figure 6. continued

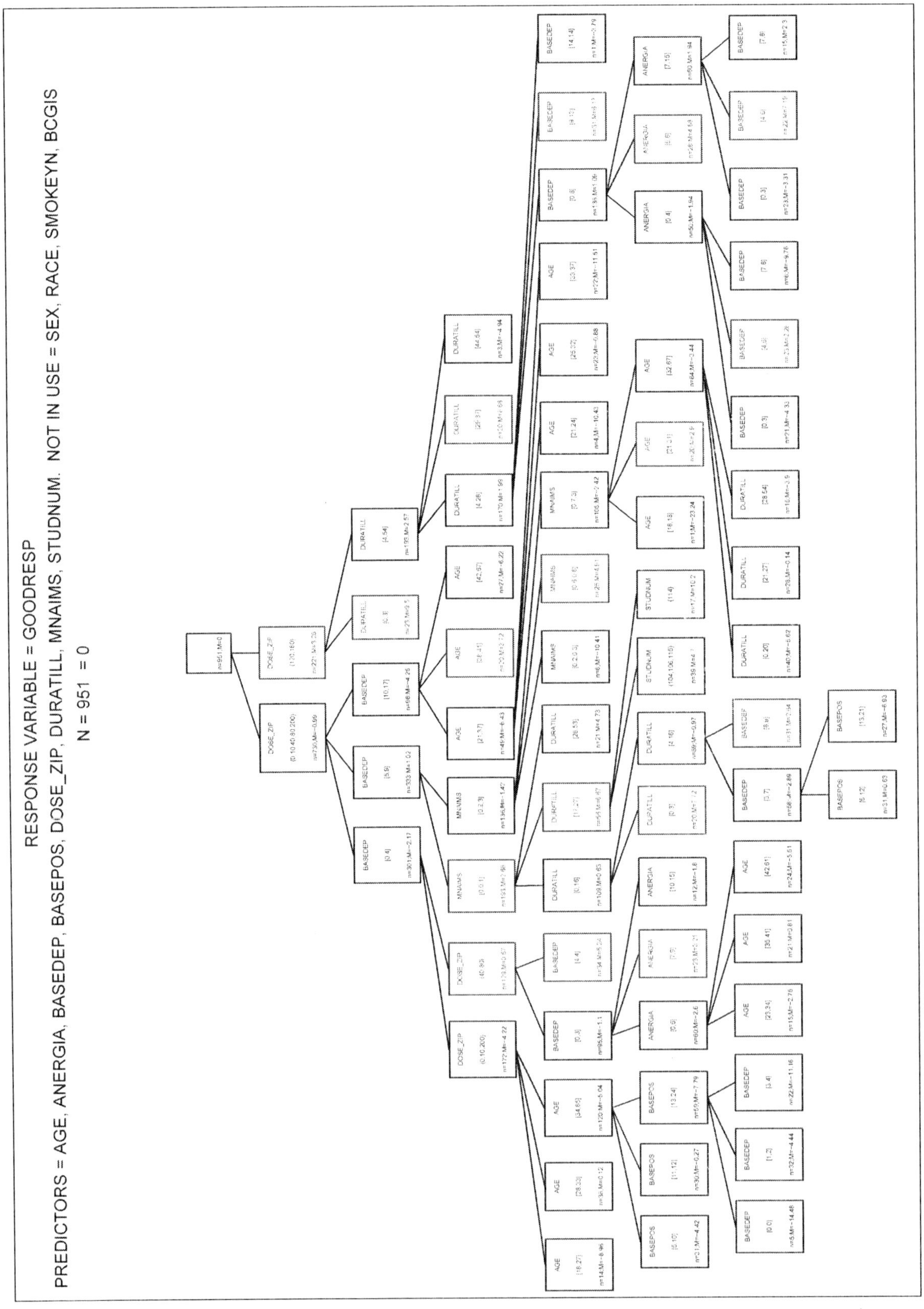

continued on following page

Figure 6. continued

RESPONSE VARIABLE = GOODRESP
PREDICTORS = AGE, ANERGIA, BASEDEP, BASEPOS, DOSE_ZIP, DURATILL, MNAIMS, STUDNUM. NOT IN USE = SEX, RACE, SMOKEYN, BCGIS
N = 951 = 0

	Var	Interval/Subset	%Interval	Crit	Mean	N	Sf	NdTy
M	DOSE_ZIP	{120,160}	23.239	4.486	3.258	221	S	FU
L	DOSE_ZIP	{0,10,40,80,200}	76.761	0	-0.986	730	NS	FU
MM	DURATILL	[0,3]	10.648	3.001	9.501	23	S	TE
MR	DURATILL	[4,54]	20.294	0	2.574	193	NS	FU
LM	BASEDEP	[5,9]	45.616	3.663	1.023	333	NS	FU
LL	BASEDEP	[0,4]	31.651	0	-2.167	301	NS	FU
LR	BASEDEP	[10,17]	10.095	0	-4.255	96	NS	FU
MRM	DURATILL	[29,37]	10.363	2.793	8.678	20	S	TE
MRL	DURATILL	[4,28]	17.876	0	1.988	170	NS	FU
MRR	DURATILL	[44,54]	0.315	0	-4.936	3	NS	TE
LMM	MNAIMS	[0,0.1]	58.663	2.694	2.678	193	S	FU
LMR	MNAIMS	[0.2,3]	14.301	0	-1.422	136	NS	FU
LLM	DOSE_ZIP	{40,80}	42.857	3.563	0.573	129	S	FU
LLL	DOSE_ZIP	{0,10,200}	18.086	0	-4.221	172	NS	FU
LRM	AGE	[38,41]	20.833	2.815	3.718	20	S	TE
LRL	AGE	[21,37]	5.152	0	-6.428	49	NS	FU
LRR	AGE	[42,67]	2.839	0	-6.215	27	NS	TE
MRLM	BASEDEP	[9,13]	18.235	2.567	6.171	31	S	TE
MRLL	BASEDEP	[0,8]	14.511	0	1.09	138	NS	FU
MRLR	BASEDEP	[14,14]	0.105	0	-3.785	1	NS	TE
LMMM	DURATILL	[17,27]	30.108	2.982	6.668	56	S	FU
LMML	DURATILL	[0,16]	11.462	0	0.628	109	NS	FU
LMMR	DURATILL	[28,53]	2.208	0	4.732	21	NS	TE
LMRM	MNAIMS	[0.6,0.6]	18.382	3.031	4.913	25	S	TE
LMRL	MNAIMS	[0.2,0.3]	0.631	0	-10.412	6	NS	TE
LMRR	MNAIMS	[0.7,3]	11.041	0	-2.417	105	NS	FU
LLMM	BASEDEP	[4,4]	26.357	3.505	5.238	34	S	TE
LLML	BASEDEP	[0,3]	9.989	0	-1.096	95	NS	FU
LLLM	AGE	[28,33]	22.093	2.893	0.116	38	NS	TE
LLLL	AGE	[18,27]	1.472	0	-8.957	14	NS	TE
LLLR	AGE	[34,65]	12.618	0	-5.042	120	NS	FU
LRLM	AGE	[25,32]	46.939	2.653	-0.875	23	NS	TE
LRLL	AGE	[21,24]	0.421	0	-10.428	4	NS	TE
LRLR	AGE	[33,37]	2.313	0	-11.507	22	NS	TE
MRLLM	ANERGIA	[5,6]	20.29	2.24	4.678	28	S	TE

continued on following page

Figure 6.continued

RESPONSE VARIABLE = GOODRESP
PREDICTORS = AGE, ANERGIA, BASEDEP, BASEPOS, DOSE_ZIP, DURATILL, MNAIMS, STUDNUM. NOT IN USE = SEX, RACE, SMOKEYN, BCGIS
N = 951 = 0

	Var	Interval/Subset	%Interval	Crit	Mean	N	Sf	NdTy
MRLLL	ANERGIA	[0,4]	5.258	0	-1.94	50	NS	FU
MRLLR	ANERGIA	[7,15]	6.309	0	1.941	60	NS	FU
LMMMM	STUDNUM	{114}	41.071	2.42	10.199	17	NS	TE
LMMML	STUDNUM	{104,106,115}	4.101	0	4.695	39	NS	TE
LMMLM	DURATILL	[0,3]	18.349	3.115	7.716	20	S	TE
LMMLR	DURATILL	[4,16]	9.359	0	-0.965	89	NS	FU
LMRRM	AGE	[21,31]	19.048	2.471	2.902	20	S	TE
LMRRL	AGE	[18,18]	0.105	0	-23.242	1	NS	TE
LMRRR	AGE	[32,67]	8.833	0	-3.435	84	NS	FU
LLMLM	ANERGIA	[7,9]	24.211	2.773	3.205	23	S	TE
LLMLL	ANERGIA	[0,6]	6.309	0	-2.605	60	NS	FU
LLMLR	ANERGIA	[10,15]	1.262	0	-1.798	12	NS	TE
LLLRM	BASEPOS	[11,12]	25	2.835	-0.269	30	NS	TE
LLLRL	BASEPOS	[5,10]	3.26	0	-4.423	31	NS	TE
LLLRR	BASEPOS	[13,24]	6.204	0	-7.795	59	NS	FU
MRLLLM	BASEDEP	[4,6]	46	2.454	2.279	23	S	TE
MRLLLL	BASEDEP	[0,3]	2.208	0	-4.327	21	NS	TE
MRLLLR	BASEDEP	[7,8]	0.631	0	-9.755	6	NS	TE
MRLLRM	BASEDEP	[4,6]	36.667	2.768	7.19	22	S	TE
MRLLRL	BASEDEP	[0,3]	2.419	0	-3.313	23	NS	TE
MRLLRR	BASEDEP	[7,8]	1.577	0	2.298	15	NS	TE
LMMLRM	BASEDEP	[8,9]	34.831	2.343	2.635	31	S	TE
LMMLRL	BASEDEP	[5,7]	6.099	0	-2.89	58	NS	FU
LMRRRM	DURATILL	[21,27]	33.735	2.154	-0.139	28	NS	TE
LMRRRL	DURATILL	[0,20]	4.206	0	-5.621	40	NS	TE
LMRRRR	DURATILL	[28,54]	1.577	0	-3.902	15	NS	TE
LLMLLM	AGE	[35,41]	35	2.474	0.814	21	NS	TE
LLMLLL	AGE	[23,34]	1.577	0	-2.745	15	NS	TE
LLMLLR	AGE	[42,61]	2.524	0	-5.508	24	NS	TE
LLLRRM	BASEDEP	[1,2]	54.237	2.413	-4.436	32	NS	TE
LLLRRL	BASEDEP	[0,0]	0.526	0	-14.475	5	NS	TE
LLLRRR	BASEDEP	[3,4]	2.313	0	-11.162	22	NS	TE
LMMLRLM	BASEPOS	[6,12]	53.448	2.341	0.632	31	NS	TE
LMMLRLR	BASEPOS	[13,21]	2.839	0	-6.933	27	NS	TE

continued on following page

Figure 6. continued

```
                    RESPONSE VARIABLE = GOODRESP
PREDICTORS = AGE, ANERGIA, BASEDEP, BASEPOS, DOSE_ZIP, DURATILL, MNAIMS, STUDNUM.  NOT IN USE = SEX, RACE, SMOKEYN, BCGIS
                          N = 951   = 0

                                            SUBSET  Mean   N
Subset 1          DOSE_ZIP in {120,160} 3.258 221

Subset 2          DOSE_ZIP in {120,160} 9.501  23
                      DURATILL in [0,3]

Subset 3          DOSE_ZIP in {120,160} 8.678  20
                    DURATILL in [29,37]

Subset 4 DOSE_ZIP in {0,10,40,80,200} 2.678 193
                       BASEDEP in [5,9]
                      MNAIMS in [0,0.1]

Subset 5             DOSE_ZIP in {40,80} 0.573 129
                       BASEDEP in [0,4]

Subset 6 DOSE_ZIP in {0,10,40,80,200} 3.718  20
                     BASEDEP in [10,17]
                         AGE in [38,41]

Subset 7          DOSE_ZIP in {120,160} 6.171  31
                     DURATILL in [4,28]
                       BASEDEP in [9,13]

Subset 8 DOSE_ZIP in {0,10,40,80,200} 6.668  56
                       BASEDEP in [5,9]
                      MNAIMS in [0,0.1]
                    DURATILL in [17,27]

Subset 9 DOSE_ZIP in {0,10,40,80,200} 4.913  25
                       BASEDEP in [5,9]
                    MNAIMS in [0.6,0.6]

Subset 10            DOSE_ZIP in {40,80} 5.238  34
                       BASEDEP in [4,4]
```

Figure 7. Output of results from ARF analysis predicting poor response

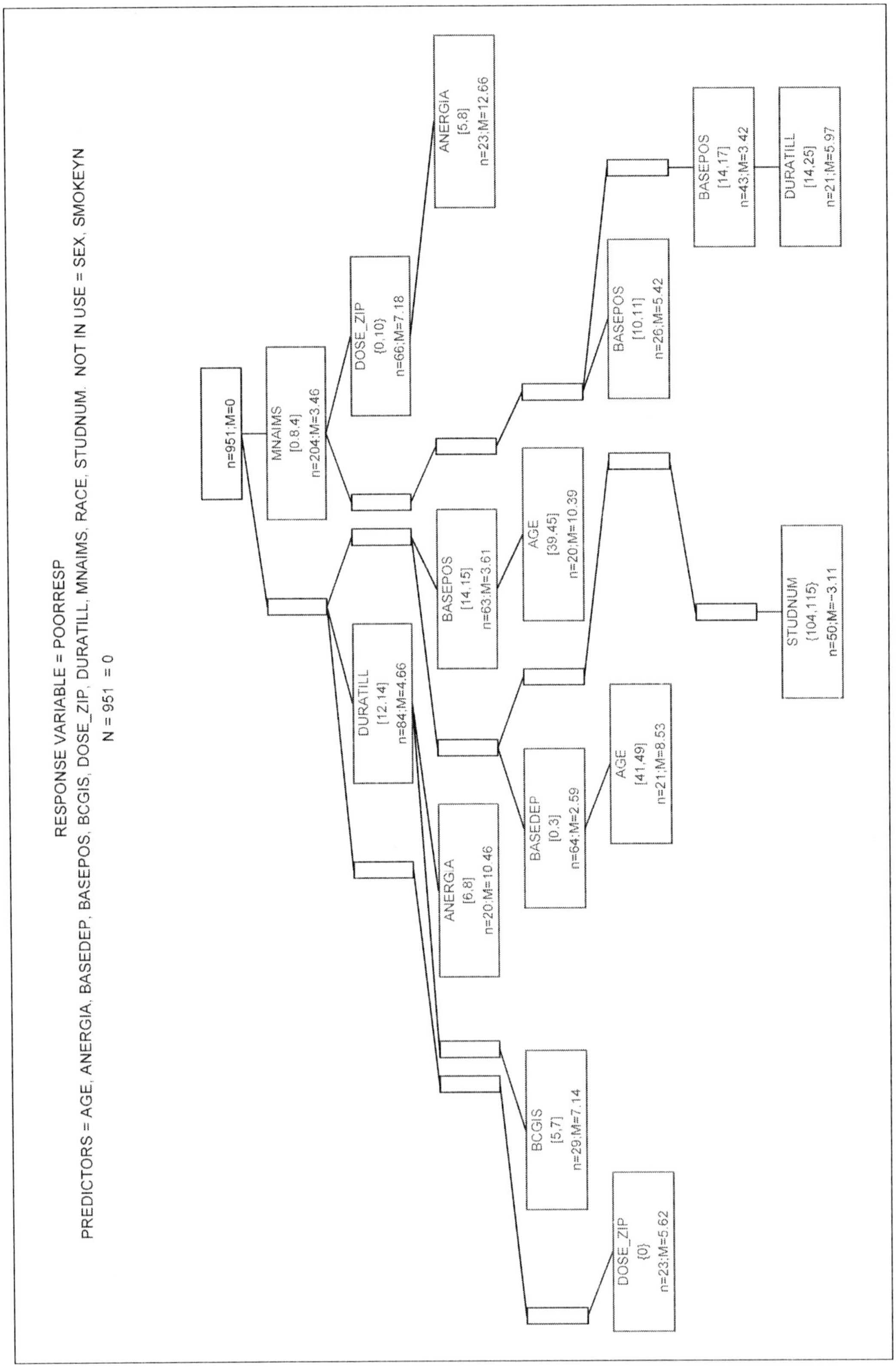

continued on following page

Figure 7. continued

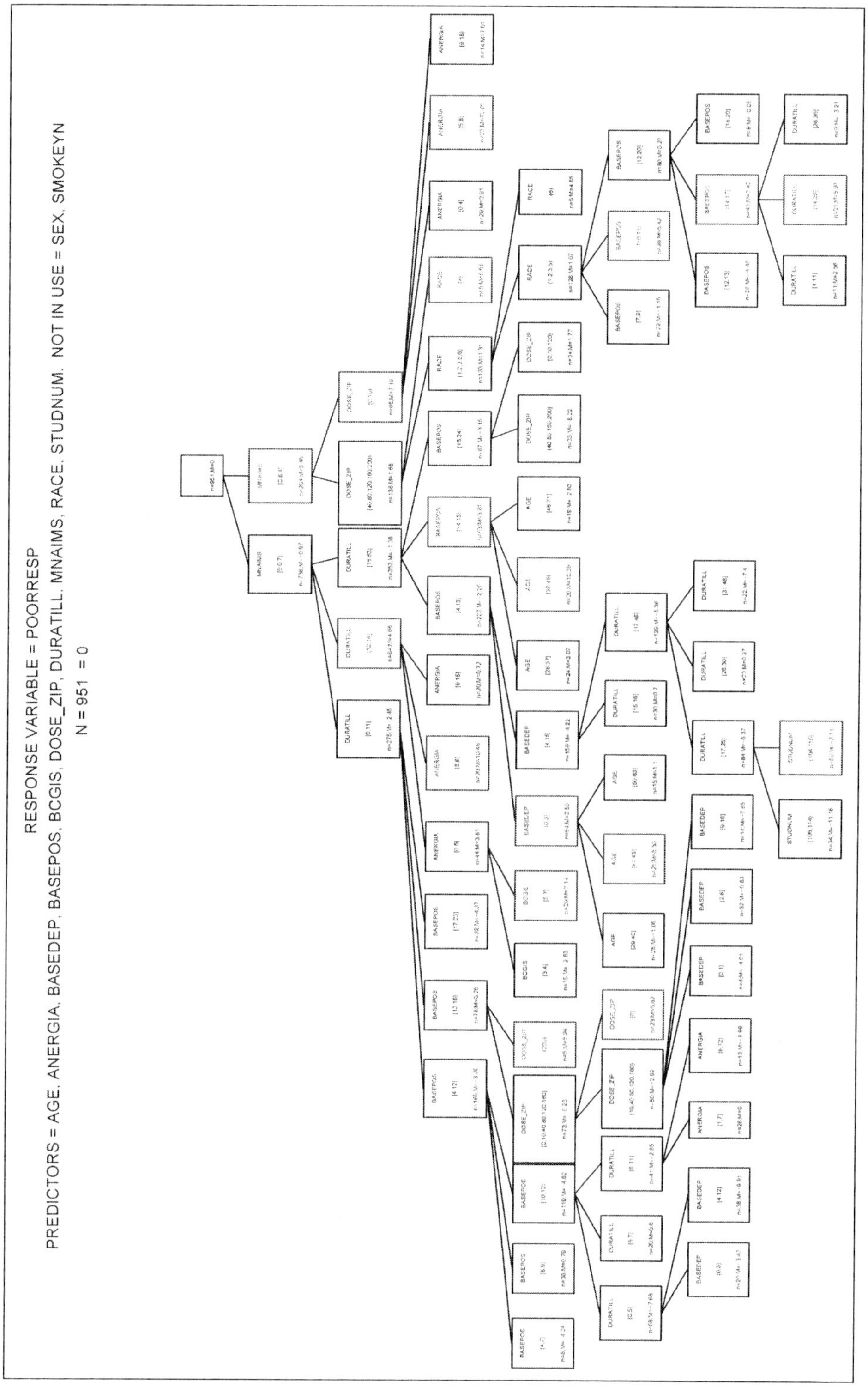

Note: First section is the tree sketch. The second section is a picture of the full tree. We omitted the third and fourth sections.

Section III
Data Mining in Mixed Media Data

Chapter IV
Cross-Modal Correlation Mining Using Graph Algorithms

Jia-Yu Pan
Carnegie Mellon University, USA

Hyung-Jeong Yang
Chonnam National University, South Korea

Christos Faloutsos
Carnegie Mellon University, USA

Pinar Duygulu
Bilkent University, Turkey

ABSTRACT

Multimedia objects like video clips or captioned images contain data of various modalities such as image, audio, and transcript text. Correlations across different modalities provide information about the multimedia content, and are useful in applications ranging from summarization to semantic captioning. We propose a graph-based method, MAGIC, which represents multimedia data as a graph and can find cross-modal correlations using "random walks with restarts." MAGIC has several desirable properties: (a) it is general and domain-independent; (b) it can detect correlations across any two modalities; (c) it is insensitive to parameter settings; (d) it scales up well for large datasets; (e) it enables novel multimedia applications (e.g., group captioning); and (f) it creates opportunity for applying graph algorithms to multimedia problems. When applied to automatic image captioning, MAGIC finds correlations between text and image and achieves a relative improvement of 58% in captioning accuracy as compared to recent machine learning techniques.

Introduction

Advances in digital technologies make possible the generation and storage of large amount of multimedia objects such as images and video clips. Multimedia content contains rich information in various modalities such as images, audios, video frames, time series, and so forth. However, making

Copyright © 2007, IGI Global, distributing in print or electronic forms without written permission of IGI Global is prohibited.

rich multimedia content accessible and useful is not easy. Advanced tools that find characteristic patterns and correlations among multimedia content are required for the effective usage of multimedia databases.

We call a data object whose content is presented in more than one modality a *mixed media* object. For example, a video clip is a mixed media object with image frames, audios, and other information such as transcript text. Another example is a captioned image such as a news picture with an associated description, or a personal photograph annotated with a few keywords (Figure 1). In this chapter, we would use the terms *medium* (plural form *media*) and *modality* interchangeably.

It is common to see correlations among attributes of different modalities on a mixed media object. For instance, a news clip usually contains human speech accompanied with images of static scenes, while a commercial has more dynamic scenes with loud background music (Pan & Faloutsos, 2002). In image archives, caption keywords are chosen such that they describe objects in the images. Similarly, in digital video libraries and entertainment industry, motion picture directors edit sound effects to match the scenes in video frames.

Cross-modal correlations provide helpful hints on exploiting information from different modalities for tasks such as segmentation (Hsu et al., 2004) and indexing (Chang, Manmatha, & Chua, 2005). Also, establishing associations between low-level features and attributes that have semantic meanings may shed light on multimedia understanding. For example, in a collection of captioned images, discovering the correlations between images and caption words could be useful for image annotation, content-based image retrieval, and multimedia understanding.

The question that we are interested in is "*Given a collection of mixed media objects, how do we find the correlations across data of various modalities?*" A desirable solution should be able to include all kinds of data modalities, overcome noise in the data, and detect correlations between any subset of modalities available. Moreover, in

Figure 1. Three sample images: (a),(b) are captioned with terms describing the content; (c) is an image to be captioned. (d)(e)(f) show the regions of images (a)(b)(c), respectively.

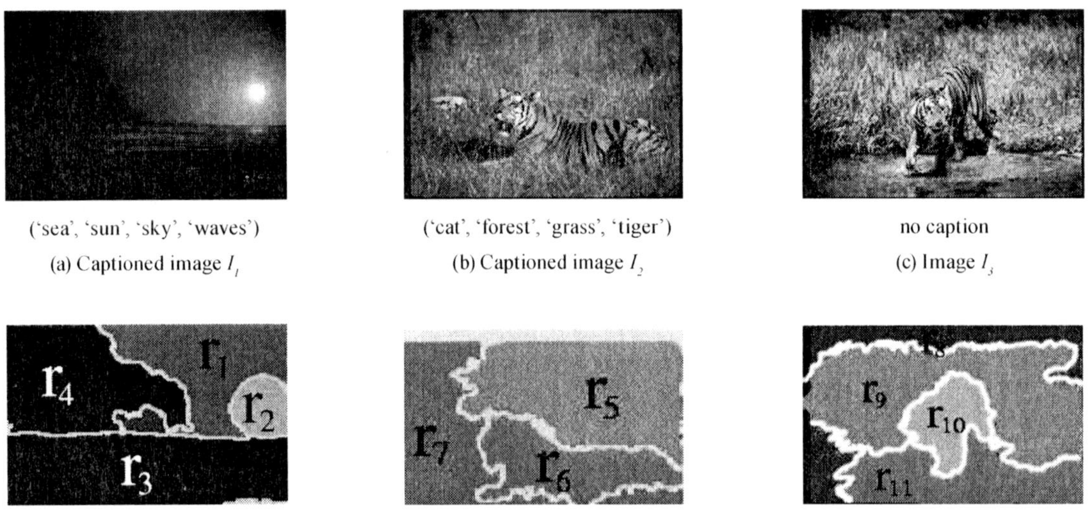

('sea', 'sun', 'sky', 'waves') (a) Captioned image I_1

('cat', 'forest', 'grass', 'tiger') (b) Captioned image I_2

no caption (c) Image I_3

(d) (e) (f)

terms of computation, we would like a method that scales well with respect to the database size and does not require human fine-tuning.

In particular, we want a method that can find correlations among all attributes, rather than just between specific attributes. For example, we want to find not just the image-term correlation between an image and caption terms, but also term-term and image-image correlations, using one single framework. This *any-to-any medium correlation* provides a greater picture of how attributes are correlated, for example, "which word is usually used for images with blue top," "what words have related semantics," and "what objects often appear together in an image."

We propose a novel, domain-independent framework, *MAGIC*, for cross-modal correlation discovery. MAGIC turns the multimedia problem into a graph problem, by providing an intuitive framework to represent data of various modalities. The proposed graph framework enables the application of graph algorithms to multimedia problems.

In particular, MAGIC employs the *random walk with restarts* technique on the graph to discover cross-modal correlations.

In summary, MAGIC has the following advantages:

- It provides a graph-based framework which is domain independent and applicable to mixed media objects which have attributes of various modalities.
- It can detect any-to-any medium correlations.
- It is completely automatic (its few parameters can be automatically preset).
- It can scale up for large collections of objects.

In this study, we evaluate the proposed MAGIC method on the task of *automatic image captioning*. For automatic image captioning, the correlations between image and text are used to predict caption words for an uncaptioned image.

Application 1 (automatic image captioning). *Given a set* $\boldsymbol{I}_{core}$ *of color images, each with caption words, find the best q (say, q=5) caption words for an uncaptioned image* I_{new}.

The proposed method can also be easily extended for various related applications such as captioning images in groups, or retrieving relevant video shots and transcript words.

In the following of this chapter, we will first discuss pervious attempts on multimedia cross-modal correlation discovery. Then, the proposed method, MAGIC, is introduced. We will show that MAGIC achieves a better performance than recent machine learning methods on automatic image captioning (a 58% improvement on captioning accuracy). Several system issues are also discussed and we show that MAGIC is insensitive to parameter settings and is robust to variations in the graph.

RELATED WORK

Multimedia knowledge representation and application have attracted much research attention recently. Mixed media objects provide opportunities for finding correlations between low-level and concept-level features, and multimodal correlations have been shown useful for applications such as retrieval, segmentation, classification, and pattern discovery. In this section, we survey previous work on cross-modal correlation modeling. We also discuss previous work on image captioning, which is the application domain on which we evaluate our proposed model.

Multimedia Cross-Modal Correlation

Combining multimedia correlations in applications leverages all available information and has led to improved performances in segmentation (Hsu et al., 2004), classification (Lin & Hauptmann, 2002; Vries, de Westerveld, & Ianeva, 2004), retrieval (Wang, Ma, Xue, & Li, 2004; Wu, Chang, Chang, & Smith, 2004; Zhang, Zhang, & Ohya, 2004), and topic detection (Duygulu, Pan, & Forsyth, 2004; Xie et al., 2005). One crucial step of fusing multimodal correlations into applications is to detect and model the correlations among different data modalities.

We categorize previous methods for multimedia correlation modeling into two categories: *model-driven* approaches and *data-driven* approaches. A model-driven method usually assumes a certain type of data correlations and focuses on fitting this particular correlation model to the given data. A data-driven method makes no assumption on the data correlations and finds correlations using solely the relationship (e.g., similarity) between data objects.

The model assumed by a model-driven method is usually hand-designed, based on the available knowledge to the domain. Model-driven methods provide a good way to incorporate prior knowledge into the correlation discovery process. However, the quality of the extracted correlations depends on the correctness of the assumed model. On the other hand, the performance of a data-driven method is less dependent on the available domain knowledge, but the ability to incorporating prior knowledge to guide the discovery process is more limited.

Previous model-driven methods have proposed a variety of models to extract correlations from multimodal data. Linear models (Srihari, Rao, Han, Munirathnam, & Xiaoyun, 2000; Li, Dimitrova, Li, & Sethi, 2003) assume that data variables have linear correlations. Linear models are computationally friendly, but may not approximate real data correlations well. More complex statistical models have also been used: for example, the mixture of Gaussians (Vries, Westerveld, et al., 2004), the maximum-entropy model (Hsu et al., 2004), or the hidden Markov model (Xie, Kennedy et al., 2005). Graphical models (Naphade, Kozintsev, & Huang, 2001; Benitez & Chang, 2002; Jeon, Lavrenko, & Manmatha, 2003; Feng, Manmatha, & Lavrenko, 2004) have attracted much attention for its ability to incorporate domain knowledge into data modeling. However, the quality of the graphical model depends on the correctness of the embedded generative process, and sometimes the training of a complex graphical model can be computationally intractable.

Classifier-based models are suitable for fusing multimodal information when the application is data classification. Classifiers are useful in capturing discriminative patterns between different data modalities. To identify multimodal patterns for data classification, one can use either a multimodal classifier which takes a multimodal input, or a metaclassifier (Lin & Hauptmann, 2002; Wu et al., 2004) which takes as input the outputs of multiple unimodal classifiers.

Unlike a model-driven method that fits a prespecified correlation model to the given dataset, a data-driven method finds cross-modal correlations solely based on the similarity relationship between data objects in the set. A natural way to present the similarity relationship between multimedia data objects is using a graph representation, where nodes symbolize objects, and edges (with weights) indicate the similarity between objects.

According to the application domains, different graph-based algorithms have been proposed to find data correlations from a graph representation of a dataset. For example, "spectral clustering" has been proposed for clustering data from different video sources (Zhang, Lin, Chang, & Smith, 2004), as well as for grouping relevant data of different modalities (Duygulu et al., 2004). Link analysis techniques have been used for deriving a multimodal (image and text) similarity function for Web image retrieval (Wang et al., 2004). For these methods, graph nodes are used to represent multimedia objects, and the focus is on finding correlations between data objects. This *object-level graph representation* requires good similarity function between objects (for constructing graph edges) difficult, which is especially hard to obtain for complex multimedia objects.

In this chapter, we introduce MAGIC, a proposed data-driven method for finding cross-modal correlations in general multimedia settings. MAGIC uses a graph to represent the relations between objects and low-level attribute domains. By relating multimedia objects via the constituent single-modal domain tokens, MAGIC does not require object-level similarity functions, which are hard to obtain. Moreover, MAGIC does not need a training phase and is insensitive to parameter settings. Our experiments show that MAGIC can find correlations among all kinds of data modalities, and achieves good performance in real world multimedia applications such as image captioning.

Image Captioning

Although a picture is worth a thousand words, extracting the abundant information from an image is not an easy task. Computational techniques are able to derive low-to-mid level features (e.g., texture and shape) from pixel information, however, the gap still exists between mid-level features and concepts used in human reasoning (Zhao & Grosky, 2001; Sebe, Lew, Zhou, Huang, & Bakker, 2003; Zhang, Zhang, et al., 2004). One consequence of this semantic gap in image retrieval is that the user's need is not properly matched by the retrieved images, and may be part of the reason that practical image retrieval is yet to be popular.

Automatic image captioning, whose goal is to predict caption words to describe image content, is one research direction to bridge the gap between concepts and low-level features. Previous work on image captioning employs various approaches such as linear models (Mori, Takahashi, & Oka, 1999; Pan, Yang, Duygulu, & Faloutsos, 2004), classifiers (Maron & Ratan, 1998), language models (Duygulu, Barnard, de Freitas, & Forsyth, 2002; Jeon et al., 2003; Virga & Duygulu, 2005), graphical models (Barnard et al., 2003; Blei & Jordan, 2003), statistical models (Li & Wang, 2003; Feng et al., 2004; Jin, Chai, & Si, 2004). Interactive frameworks with user involvement have also been proposed (Wenyin et al., 2001).

Most previous approaches derive features from image regions (regular grids or blobs), and construct a model between images and words based on a reference captioned image set. Human annotators caption the reference images. However, we have no information about the association between individual regions and caption words. Some approaches attempt to explicitly infer the correlations between regions and words (Duygulu et al., 2002), with enhancements that take into consideration interactions between neighboring regions in an image (Li & Wang, 2003). Alternatively, there are methods which model the collective correlations between regions and words of an image (Pan, Yang, Faloutsos, & Duygulu, 2004a, 2004b).

Comparing the performance of different approaches is not easy. Although several benchmark datasets are available, not every previous work reports results on the same subset of images. Various metrics, such as accuracy, mean average precision, and term precision and recall, have been used by previous work to measure the performance. Since the perception of an image is subjective, some work also reports user evaluation of the captioning result. In this chapter, the proposed method is evaluated by its performance on image captioning, where the experiments are performed on the same dataset and evaluated using the same performance metric as previous work for fair comparison.

PROPOSED GRAPH-BASED CORRELATION DETECTION MODEL

Our proposed method for mixed media correlation discovery, MAGIC, provides a graph-based representation for multimedia objects with data attributes of various modalities. A technique for finding any-to-any medium correlation, which is based on random walks on the graph, is also proposed. In this section, we explain how to generate the graph representation and how to detect cross-modal correlations using the graph.

Graph Representation for Multimedia

In relational database management systems, a multimedia object is usually represented as a vector of m features/attributes (Faloutsos, 1996). The attributes must be *atomic* (i.e., taking single values) like "size" or "the amount of red color" of an image. However, for mixed media datasets, the attributes can be *set-valued*, such as the caption of an image (a set of words) or the set of regions of an image.

Finding correlations among set-valued attributes is not easy. Elements in a set-valued attribute could be noisy or missing altogether, for example, regions may not be perfectly segmented from an image (noisy regions), and the image caption may be incomplete, leaving out some aspects of the content (noisy captions). Set-valued attributes of an object may have different numbers of elements, and the correspondence between set elements of different attributes is not known. For instance, a captioned image may have unequal numbers of caption words and regions, where a word may describe multiple regions and a region may be described by zero or more than one word. The detailed correspondence between regions and caption words is usually not given by human annotators.

We assume that the elements of a set-valued attribute are tokens drawn from a *domain*. We propose to gear our method toward set-valued attributes, because they include atomic attributes as a special case and also smoothly handle the case of missing values (null set).

Definition 1 (domain and domain token). *The* ***domain*** *D_i of (set-valued) attribute A_i is a collection of atomic values, which we called* ***domain tokens****, which are the values that attribute A_i can take.*

A domain can consist of categorical values, numerical values, or numerical vectors. For example, a captioned image has $m=2$ attributes: The first attribute, "caption," has a set of categorical values (English terms) as its domain; the second attribute, "regions," is a set of image regions, each of which is represented by a p-dimensional vector of p features derived from the region (e.g., color histogram with p colors). As we will describe in the following experimental result section, we extract $p=30$ features from each region. To establish the relation between domain tokens, we assume that we have a similarity function for each domain. Domain tokens are usually simpler than mixed media objects, and therefore, it is easier to define similarity functions on domain tokens than on mixed media objects. For example, for the attribute "caption," the similarity function could be 1 if the two tokens are identical, and 0 if they are not. As for image regions, the similarity function could be the Euclidean distance between the p-dimensional feature vectors of two regions.

Assumption 1. *For each domain D_i ($i=1, ..., m$), we are given a similarity function $Sim_i(*,*)$ which assigns a score to a pair of domain tokens.*

Perhaps surprisingly, with Definition 1 and Assumption 1, we can encompass all the applications mentioned in the introduction. The main idea is to represent all objects and their attributes (domain tokens) as nodes of a *graph*. For multimedia objects with m attributes, we obtain a ($m+1$)-layer graph. There are m types of nodes (one for each attribute),

Figure 2. The MAGIC graph for 3 images in Figure 1. Solid edges: OAV-links; dash edges: NN-links.

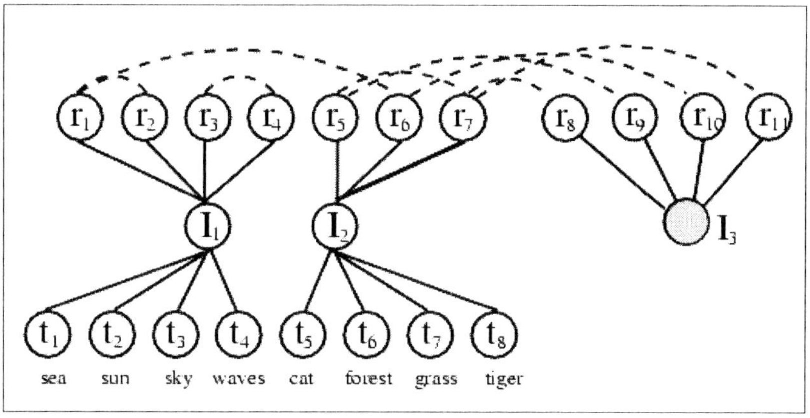

and one more type of nodes for the objects. We call this graph a MAGIC graph (G_{magic}). We put an edge between every object-node and its corresponding attribute-value nodes. We call these edges *object-attribute-value links* (OAV-links).

Furthermore, we consider that two objects are similar if they have similar attribute values. For example, two images are similar if they contain similar regions. To incorporate such information into the graph, our approach is to add edges to connect pairs of domain tokens (attribute values) that are similar, according to the given similarity function (Assumption 1). We call edges that connect nodes of similar domain tokens *nearest-neighbor links* (NN-links).

We need to decide on a threshold for "closeness" when adding NN-links. There are many ways to do this, but we decide to make the threshold adaptive: each domain token is connected to its k nearest neighbors. Computing nearest neighbors can be done efficiently, because we already have the similarity function $Sim_i(*,*)$ for each domain D_i (Assumption 1). In the following section, we will discuss the choice of k, as well as the sensitivity of our results to k.

We illustrate the construction of the MAGIC graph by the following example.

Example 1. *For the three images $\{I_1, I_2, I_3\}$ in Figure 1, the corresponding MAGIC graph (G_{magic}) is shown in Figure 2. The graph has three types of nodes: one for the image objects I_j's (j=1,2,3); one for the regions r_j's (j=1,...,11), and one for the terms $\{t_1,...,t_8\}$ = {sea, sun, sky, waves, cat, forest, grass, tiger}. Solid arcs are the object-attribute-value links (OAV-links). Dashed arcs are the nearest-neighbor links (NN-links), based on some assumed similarity function between regions. There is no NN-link between term-nodes, due to the definition of its similarity function: 1, if the two terms are the same; or 0 otherwise.*

In Example 1, we consider only k = 1 nearest neighbor, to avoid cluttering the diagram. Because the nearest neighbor relationship is not symmetric and because we treat the NN-links as un-directional, some nodes are attached to more than one link. For example, node r_1 has two NN-links attached: r_2's nearest neighbor is r_1, but r_1's nearest neighbor is r_6. Figure 3 shows the algorithm for constructing a MAGIC graph.

We use image captioning only as an illustration: the same graph framework can be generally used for other multimedia problems. For automatic image captioning, we also need to develop a method to find good caption words—words that correlate with an image, based on information in

Figure 3. Algorithm for building the MAGIC graph: $\mathbf{G}_{magic}$ = **buildgraph(O, {D$_1$, ..., D$_m$}, {Sim$_1$, ...,Sim$_m$}, k)**

Input:
1. $\boldsymbol{O}$: a set of n objects (objects are numbered from 1 to n).
2. $\boldsymbol{D}_1, \ldots, \boldsymbol{D}_m$: the domains of the m attributes of the objects in $\boldsymbol{O}$.
3. $Sim_1(*,*), \ldots, Sim_m(*,*)$: the similarity functions of domains $\boldsymbol{D}_1, \ldots, \boldsymbol{D}_m$, respectively.
4. k: the number of neighbors a domain token connects to.

Output:
G_{magic}: a MAGIC graph with a $(m+1)$-layer structure.

Steps:
1. Create n nodes, one for each object. These "object nodes" form the first layer o f nodes.
2. For each domain $\boldsymbol{D}_i$, for i=1,…,m.
   (2.1) Let n_i be the number of tokens in the domain $\boldsymbol{D}_i$.
   (2.2) Create n_i nodes (the token nodes), one for each domain tokens in $\boldsymbol{D}_i$. This is the $(i+1)$-th layer of nodes.
   (2.3) Construct the OAV-links from the object nodes to the token nodes.
   (2.4) Construct the NN-links between the token nodes.
3. Output the final $(m+1)$-layer graph. The final graph has N nodes, where

$$N = n + \sum_{i=1,\ldots,m} n_i \ .$$

Table 1. Summary of symbols used in the chapter

Symbol	Description
N	The number of objects in a mixed media dataset.
M	The number of attributes (domains).
N	The number of nodes in G_{magic}.
E	The number of edges in the graph G_{magic}.
K	Domain neighborhood size: the number of nearest neighbors that a domain token is connected to.
C	The restart probability of RWR (random walk with restarts, RWR).
D_i	The domain of the i-th attribute.
$Sim_i(*,*)$	The similarity function of the i-th domain.
Image captioning	
$\boldsymbol{I}_{core}$	The given captioned image set (the core image set).
$\boldsymbol{I}_{test}$	The set of to-be-captioned (test) images.
I_{new}	An image in $\boldsymbol{I}_{test}$.
G_{core}	The subgraph of G_{magic}, which contains all images in $\boldsymbol{I}_{core}$.
G_{aug}	The augmentation to G_{core}, which contains information of image I_{test}.
GW	The gateway nodes: the set of nodes of G_{core} that are adjacent to G_{aug}.
Random walk with restarts (RWR)	
A	The (column-normalized) adjacency matrix. The (i,j)-element of **A** is $A_{i,j}$.
v_R	The restart vector of the set of query objects $\boldsymbol{R}$, where components correspond to query objects have value 1/|$\boldsymbol{R}$|, while others have value 0).
u_R	The RWR scores of all nodes with respect to the set of query objects $\boldsymbol{R}$.
v_q and u_q	The $\mathbf{v}_R$ and $\mathbf{u}_R$ for the singleton query set $\boldsymbol{R}=\{q\}$.

the G_{magic} graph. For example, to caption the image I_3 in Figure 2, we need to estimate the correlation degree of each term-nodes (t_1, ..., t_8) to node I_3, and the terms that are highly correlated with image I_3 will be predicted as its caption words. The proposed method for finding correlated nodes in the G_{magic} graph is described in the next section.

Table 1 summarizes the symbols we used in the chapter.

Correlation Detection with Random Walks

Our main contribution is to turn the cross-modal correlation discovery problem into a graph problem. The previous section describes the first step of our proposed method: representing set-valued mixed media objects in a graph G_{magic}. Given such a graph with mixed media information, *how do we detect the cross-modal correlations in the graph?*

We define that a node A of G_{magic} is correlated to another node B if A has an "affinity" for B. There are many approaches for ranking all nodes in a graph by their "affinity" for a reference node, for example, electricity-based approaches (Doyle & Snell, 1984; Palmer & Faloutsos, 2003), random walks (PageRank, topic-sensitive PageRank) (Brin & Page, 1998; Haveliwala, 2002; Haveliwala, Kamvar, & Jeh., 2003), hubs and authorities (Kleinberg, 1998), elastic springs (Lovász, 1996), and so on. Among them, we propose to use *random walk with restarts* (RWR) for estimating the affinity of node B with respect to node A. However, the specific choice of method is orthogonal to our framework.

The "random walk with restarts" operates as follows: To compute the affinity $u_A(B)$ of node B for node A, consider a random walker that starts from node A. The random walker chooses randomly among the available edges every time, except that, before he makes a choice, he goes back to node A (restart) with probability c. Let $u_A(B)$ denote the steady state probability that our random walker will find himself at node B. Then, $u_A(B)$ is what we want, the affinity of B with respect to A. We also call $u_A(B)$ the *RWR score* of B with respect to A. The algorithm of computing RWR scores of all nodes with respect to a subset of nodes $\boldsymbol{R}$ is given in Figure 4.

Definition 2 (RWR score). *The RWR score, $u_A(B)$, of node B with respect to node A is the steady state probability of node B, when we do the random walk with restarts from A, as defined above.*

Let $\mathbf{A}$ be the adjacency matrix of the given graph G_{magic}, and let $A_{i,j}$ be the (i,j)-element of $\mathbf{A}$. In our experiments, $A_{i,j}$=1 if there is an edge between nodes i and j, and $A_{i,j}$=0 otherwise. To

Figure 4. Algorithm for computing random walks with restart: $\boldsymbol{u}_R = \boldsymbol{RWR}(\mathbf{G}_{magic}, \boldsymbol{R}, c)$

Input:
1. G_{magic}: a G_{magic} graph with N nodes (nodes are numbered from 1 to N).
2. $\boldsymbol{R}$: the set of restart nodes. (Let $|\boldsymbol{R}|$ be the size of $\boldsymbol{R}$.)
3. c: the restart probability.

Output:
$\mathbf{u_R}$: a N-by-1 vector of the RWR scores of all N nodes, with respect to $\boldsymbol{R}$.

Steps:
1. Let $\mathbf{A}$ be the adjacency matrix of G_{magic}. Normalize the columns of $\mathbf{A}$ and make each column sum up to 1.
2. $\mathbf{v_R}$ is the N-by-1 restart vector, whose i-th element $\mathbf{v_R}(i)$ is $1/|\boldsymbol{R}|$, if node i is in $\boldsymbol{R}$; otherwise, $\mathbf{v_R}(i)=0$.
3. Initialize $\mathbf{u_R} = \mathbf{v_R}$.
4. While($\mathbf{u_R}$ has not converged)
   4.1 Update $\mathbf{u_R}$ by $\mathbf{u_R} = (1\text{-}c)\mathbf{A}\,\mathbf{u_R} + c\,\mathbf{v_R}$.
5. Return the converged $\mathbf{u_R}$.

perform RWR, columns of the matrix **A** are normalized such that elements of each column sum up to 1. Let $\mathbf{u}_q$ be a vector of RWR scores of all N nodes with respect to a restart node q, and $\mathbf{v}_q$ be the "restart vector," which has all N elements zero, except for the entry that corresponds to node q, which is set to 1. We can now formalize the definition of the RWR score as follows:

Definition 3 (RWR score computation). The N-by-1 steady state probability vector $\mathbf{u}_q$, which contains the RWR scores of all nodes with respect to node q, satisfies the following equation:

$$\mathbf{u}_q = (1\text{-}c)\mathbf{A}\ \mathbf{u}_q + c\ \mathbf{v}_q,$$

where c is the restart probability of the RWR from node q.

The computation of RWR scores can be done efficiently by matrix multiplication (Step 4.1 in Figure 4). The computational cost scales linearly with the number of elements in the matrix **A**, that is , the number of graph edges determined by the given database. We keep track of the L_l distance between the current estimate of $\mathbf{u}_q$ and the previous estimate, and we consider the estimation of $\mathbf{u}_q$ *converges* when this L_l distance is less than 10^{-9}. In our experiments, the computation of RWR scores converges after a few (~10) iterations (Step 4 in Figure 4) and takes less than five seconds. Therefore, the computation of RWR scales well with the database size. Moreover, MAGIC is modular and can continue improve its performance by including the best module (Kamvar, Haveliwala, Manning, & Golub, 2003; Kamvar, Haveliwala, & Golub, 2003) for fast RWR computation.

The RWR scores specify the correlations across different media and could be useful in many multimedia applications. For example, to predict the caption words for image I_3 in Figure 1, we can compute the RWR scores $\mathbf{u}_{I3}$ of all nodes and report the top few (say, 5) term-nodes as caption words for image I_3. Effectively, MAGIC exploits the correlations across images, regions and terms to caption a new image.

The RWR scores also enable MAGIC to detect any-to-any medium correlation. In our running example of image captioning, an image is captioned with the term nodes of highest RWR scores. In addition, since all nodes have their RWR scores, other nodes, say image nodes, can also be ranked and sorted, for finding images that are most related to image I_3. Similarly, we can find the most relevant regions to image I_3. In short, we can restart from any subset of nodes, say term nodes, and derive term-to-term, term-to-image, or term-to-*any* correlations. We will discuss more on this in the experimental result section. Figure 5 shows the overall procedure of using MAGIC for correlation detection.

Figure 5. Steps for correlation discovery using MAGIC. Functions "buildgraph()" and "RWR()" are given in Figure 3 and Figure 4, respectively.

Step 1: Identify the objects $\boldsymbol{O}$ and the m attribute domains $\boldsymbol{D}_i$, $i=1,...,m$.
Step 2: Identify the similarity functions $Sim_i(*,*)$ of each domain.
Step 3: Determine k: the neighborhood size of the domain tokens. (Default value $k=3$.)
Step 4: Build the MAGIC graph,
  G_{magic} = buildgraph($\boldsymbol{O}$, $\{\boldsymbol{D}_1, ..., \boldsymbol{D}_m\}$, $\{Sim_1(*,*), ..., Sim_m(*,*)\}$, k).
Step 5: Given a query node $\boldsymbol{R}=\{q\}$ (q could be an object or a domain token),
  (Step 5.1) Determine the restart probability c. (Default value $c=0.65$.)
  (Step 5.2) Compute the RWR scores: $\mathbf{u_R}$ = RWR(G_{magic}, $\boldsymbol{R}$, c).
Step 6: Objects and domain tokens with high RWR scores are considered correlated to q.

APPLICATION: AUTOMATIC IMAGE CAPTIONING

Cross-modal correlations are useful for many multimedia applications. In this section, we present results of applying the proposed MAGIC method to automatic image captioning. Intuitively, the cross-modal correlations discovered by MAGIC are used in the way that an image is captioned automatically with words that correlate with the image content.

We evaluate the quality of the cross-modal correlations identified by MAGIC in terms of captioning accuracy. We show experimental results to address the following questions:

- **Quality:** Does MAGIC predict the correct caption terms?
- **Generality:** Beside the image-to-term correlation for captioning, can MAGIC capture any-to-any medium correlation?

Our results show that MAGIC successfully exploits the image-to-term correlation to caption test images. Moreover, MAGIC is flexible and can caption multiple images as a group. We call this operation "*group captioning*" and present some qualitative results.

For detecting any-to-any medium correlations, we show that MAGIC can also capture same-modal correlations such as the term-term correlations: that is, "given a term such as 'sky,' find other terms that are likely to correspond to it." Potentially, MAGIC is also capable of detecting other correlations such as the reverse captioning problem: that is, "given a term such as 'sky,' find the regions that are likely to correspond to it." In general, MAGIC can capture any-to-any medium correlations.

Dataset

Given a collection of captioned images $\boldsymbol{I}_{core}$, how do we select caption words for an uncaptioned image I_{new}? For automatic image captioning, we propose to caption I_{new} using the correlations between caption words and images in $\boldsymbol{I}_{core}$.

In our experiments, we use the same 10 sets of images from Corel that are also used in previous work (Duygulu et al., 2002; Barnard et al. 2003), so that our results can be compared to the previous results. In the following, the 10 captioned image sets are referred to as the "001," "002," ..., "010" sets. Each of the 10 datasets has around 5,200 images, and each image has about 4 caption words. These images are also called the *core images* from which we try to detect the correlations. For evaluation, each dataset is accompanied with a non-overlapping test set $\boldsymbol{I}_{test}$ of around 1,750 images for evaluating the captioning performance. Each test image has the ground truth caption.

Similar to previous work (Duygulu et al,. 2002; Barnard et al., 2003), each image is represented by a set of image regions. Image regions are extracted using a standard segmentation tool (Shi & Malik, 2000), and each region is represented as a 30-dimensional feature vector. The regional features include the mean and standard deviation of RGB values, average responses to various texture filters, its position in the entire image layout, and some shape descriptors (e.g., major orientation and the area ratio of bounding region to the real region). Together, regions extracted from an image form a set-valued attribute "regions" of the object "image." In our experiments, an image has 10 regions on average. Some examples of image regions are shown in Figure 1 (d), (e), and (f).

The exact region segmentation and feature extraction details are *orthogonal* to our approach—any published segmentation methods and feature extraction functions (Faloutsos, 1996) will suffice. All our MAGIC method needs is a black box that will map each color image into a set of zero or more feature vectors.

We want to stress that there is no given information about which region is associated with which term—all we know is that a set of regions co-occurs with a set of terms in an image. That is, no alignment information between individual regions and terms is available.

Therefore, a captioned image becomes an object with two set-valued attributes: "regions" and "terms." Since the regions and terms of an image are correlated, we propose to use MAGIC to detect this correlation and use it to predict the missing caption terms correlated with the uncaptioned test images.

Constructing the MAGIC Graph

The first step of MAGIC is to construct the MAGIC graph. Following the instructions for graph construction in Figure 3, the graph for captioned images with attributes "regions" and "terms" will be a 3-layer graph with nodes for images, regions and terms. To form the NN-links, we define the distance function (Assumption 1) between two regions (tokens) as the L_2 norm between their feature vectors. Also, we define that two terms are similar if and only if they are identical, that is, no term is any other's neighbor. As a result, there is no NN-link between term nodes.

For results shown in this section, the number of nearest neighbors between attribute (domain) tokens is k=3. However, as we will show later in the experimental result section, the captioning accuracy is insensitive to the choice of k. In total, each dataset has about 50,000 different region tokens and 160 words, resulting in a graph G_{magic} with about 55,500 nodes and 180,000 edges. The graph based on the core image set $\boldsymbol{I}_{core}$ captures the correlations between regions and terms. We call such graph the "*core*" *graph*.

How do we caption a new image, using the information in a MAGIC graph? Similar to the core images, an uncaptioned image I_{new} is also an object with set-valued attributes: "regions" and "caption," where attribute "caption" has null value. To find caption words correlated with image I_{new}, we propose to look at regions in the core image set that are similar to the regions of I_{new}, and find the words that are correlated with these core image regions. Therefore, our algorithm has two main steps: finding similar regions in the core image set (augmentation) and identifying caption words (RWR). Next, we define "core graph," "augmentation" and "gateway nodes," to facilitate the description of our algorithm.

Definition 4 (core graph, augmentation, and gateway nodes). *For automatic image captioning, we define the* ***core*** *of the graph* G_{magic}, G_{core}, *be the subgraph that constitutes information of the given captioned images* $\boldsymbol{I}_{core}$. *The graph* G_{magic} *for captioning a test image* I_{new} *is an* ***augmented graph****, which is the core* G_{core} *augmented with the region-nodes and image-node of* I_{new}. *The augmentation subgraph is denoted as* G_{aug}, *and hence the overall* $G_{magic}=G_{core}\cup G_{aug}$. *The nodes of the core subgraph* G_{core} *that are adjacent to the augmentation* G_{aug} *are called the* ***gateway*** *nodes,* ***GW****.*

As an illustration, Figure 2 shows the graph G_{magic} for two core (captioned) images $\boldsymbol{I}_{core}=\{I_1, I_2\}$ and one test (to-be-captioned) image $\boldsymbol{I}_{test}=\{I_3\}$, with the parameter for NN-links k=1. The core subgraph G_{core} contains region nodes $\{r_1, ..., r_7\}$, image nodes $\{I_1, I_2\}$, and all the term nodes $\{t_1, ..., t_8\}$. The augmentation G_{aug} contains region nodes $\{r_8, ..., r_{11}\}$ and the image node $\{I_3\}$ of the test image. The gateway nodes $\boldsymbol{GW} = \{r_5, r_6, r_7\}$ that bridge subgraphs G_{core} and G_{aug} are the nearest neighbors of the test image's regions $\{r_8, ..., r_{11}\}$.

In our experiments, the gateway nodes are always region-nodes in G_{core} that are the nearest neighbors of test image's regions. Different test images have different augmented graphs and gateway nodes. However, since we will caption only one test image at a time, we will use the symbols

Figure 6. The proposed steps for image captioning, using the MAGIC framework

Input:
1. The core graph G_{core}, an image I_{new} to be captioned.
2. g: The number of caption words we want to predict for I_{new}.

Output: Predicted caption words for I_{new}.

Steps:
1. Augment the image node and region nodes of I_{new} to the core graph G_{core}.
2. Do RWR from the image node of I_{new} on the augmented graph G_{magic} (Algorithm 4).
3. Rank all term nodes by their RWR scores.
4. The g top-ranked terms will be the output - the predicted caption for I_{new}.

G_{aug} and ***GW*** to represent the augmented graph and gateway nodes of the test image in question.

To sum up, for image captioning, the proposed method first constructs the core graph G_{core}, according to the given set of captioned images $\boldsymbol{I}_{core}$. Then, each test image I_{new} is captioned one by one, in two steps: augmentation and RWR. In the augmentation step, the G_{aug} subgraph of the test image I_{new} is connected to G_{core} via the gateway nodes - the k nearest neighbors of each region of I_{new}. In the RWR step, we do RWR on the whole augmented graph $G_{magic}=G_{core} \cup G_{aug}$, restarting from the test image-node, to identify the correlated words (term-nodes). The g term-nodes with highest RWR scores will be the predicted caption for image I_{new}. Figure 6 gives the details of our algorithm for image captioning.

Captioning Accuracy

We measure captioning performance by the captioning accuracy. The captioning accuracy is defined as the fraction of terms correctly predicted. Following the same evaluation procedure as that in previous work (Duygulu et al., 2002; Barnard et al., 2003), for a test image which has g ground-truth caption terms, MAGIC will also predict g terms. If p of the predicted terms are correct, then the captioning accuracy acc on this test image is defined as:

$$acc = p/g.$$

The average captioning accuracy acc_{mean} on a set of T test images is defined as:

$$acc_{mean} = \frac{1}{T}\sum_{i=1}^{T} acc_i,$$

where acc_i is the captioning accuracy on the i-th test image.

Figure 7 shows the average captioning accuracy on the 10 image sets. We compare our results with the method in (Duygulu et al., 2002), which considers the image captioning problem as a statistical translation modeling problem and solves it using expectation-maximization (EM). We refer to their method as the "EM" approach. The x-axis groups the performance numbers of MAGIC (white bars) and EM (black bars) on the 10 datasets. On average, MAGIC achieves captioning accuracy improvement of 12.9 percentage points over the EM approach, which corresponds to a relative improvement of 58%.

The EM method assumes a generative model of caption words given an image region. The model assumes that each region in an image is considered separately when the caption words for an image are "generated." In other words, the model does not take into account the potential correlations among the "same-image regions"—regions from a same image. On the other hand, MAGIC incorporates such correlations, by connecting nodes of the "same-image regions" to the same image node in the MAGIC graph. Ignoring the correlations between "same-image regions" could be a reason why the EM method performs not as good as MAGIC.

We also compare the captioning accuracy with even more recent machine vision methods: the hierarchical aspect models method ("HAM") and the latent dirichlet allocation model ("LDA") (Barnard et al., 2003). The methods HAM and LDA are applied to the same 10 Corel datasets, and the average captioning accuracy (averages over the test images) from each set is computed. We summarize the overall performances of a method by taking the mean and variance of the 10 average captioning accuracy values on the 10 datasets. Figure 8 compares MAGIC with LDA and HAM, in terms of the mean and variance of the average captioning accuracy over the 10 datasets. Although both HAM and LDA improve on the EM method, they both lose to our generic MAGIC approach (35%, vs. 29% and 25%). It is also interesting that MAGIC gives significantly lower variance, by roughly an order of magnitude: 0.002 vs. 0.02 and 0.03. A lower variance indicates that the proposed MAGIC method is more robust to variations among different datasets.

The EM, HAM, and LDA methods all assume a generative model on the relationship among image regions and caption words. For these models, the quality of the data correlations depends on how good the assumed model matches the real data characteristics. Lacking correct insights to the behavior of a dataset when designing the model may hurt the performance of these methods.

Unlike EM, HAM, and LDA, which are methods specifically designed for image captioning, MAGIC is a method for general correlation detection. We are pleasantly surprised that a generic method like MAGIC could outperform those domain-specific methods.

Figure 9 shows some examples of the captions given by MAGIC. For the test image I_3 in Figure 1, MAGIC captions it correctly (Figure 9a). In Figure 9b, MAGIC surprisingly gets the seldom-used word "mane" correctly; however, it

Figure 7. Comparing MAGIC to the EM method. The parameters for MAGIC are c=0.66 and k=3. The x-axis shows the 10 datasets, and the y-axis is the average captioning accuracy over all test images in a set.

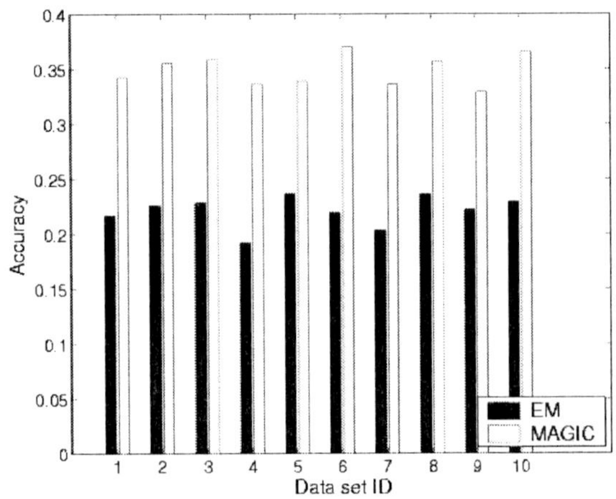

Figure 8. Comparing MAGIC with LDA and HAM. The mean and variance of the average accuracy over the 10 Corel datasets are shown at the y-axis - LDA: (μ, σ2)=(0.24,0.002); HAM: (μ, σ^2)=(0.298,0.003); MAGIC: (μ, σ^2)=(0.3503, 0.0002). μ: mean average accuracy. σ^2: variance of average accuracy. The range of the error bars at the top of each bar is 2σ.

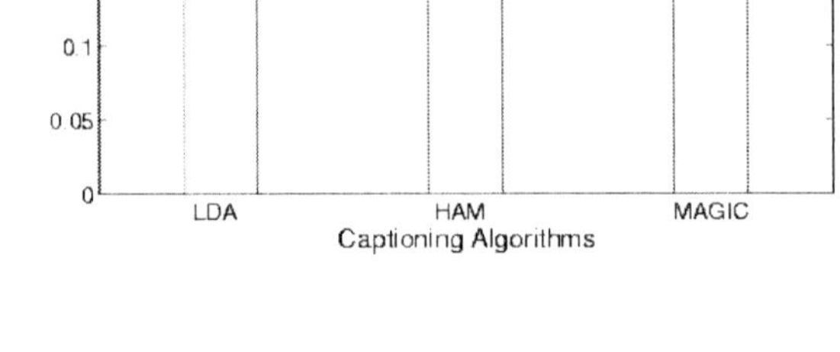

Figure 9. Image captioning examples: For MAGIC, terms with highest RWR scores are listed first

	(a)	(b)	(c)
Truth	cat, grass, tiger, water	mane, cat, lion, grass	sun, water, tree, sky
MAGIC	grass, cat, tiger, water	lion, grass, cat, mane	tree, water, buildings, sky

mixes up "buildings" with "tree" for the image in Figure 9c.

Generalization

MAGIC treats information from all media uniformly as nodes in a graph. Since all nodes are basically the same, we can do RWR and restart from any subset of nodes of any medium, to detect any-to-any medium correlations. The flexibility of our graph-based framework also enables novel applications, such as captioning images in groups (*group captioning*). In this subsection, we show results on (a) detecting the term-to-term correlation in image captioning datasets, and (b) group captioning.

Our image captioning experiments show that MAGIC successfully exploits the image-to-term correlation in the MAGIC graph (G_{magic}) for image captioning. However, the MAGIC graph G_{magic} contains correlations among all media (image, region, and term), not just between images and terms. To show how well MAGIC works on discovering correlations among all media, we design an experiment to extract the term-to-term correlation in the graph G_{magic} and identify correlated captioning terms.

We use the same 3-layer MAGIC core graph G_{core} constructed in the previous subsection for automatic image captioning (Figure 2). Given a query term t, we use RWR to find other terms correlated with it. Specifically, we perform RWR, restarting from the query term(-node). The terms whose corresponding term-nodes receive high RWR scores are considered correlated with the query term.

Table 2 shows the top 5 terms with the highest RWR scores for some query terms. In the table, each row shows a query term at the first column, followed by the top 5 correlated terms selected by MAGIC (sorted by their RWR scores). The selected terms have meanings that are semantically related with the query term. For example, the term "branch," when used in image captions, is strongly related to forest- or bird- related concepts. MAGIC shows exactly this, correlating "branch" with terms such as "birds," "owl," and "nest."

Another subtle observation is that our method does not seem to be biased by frequently appeared words. In our collection, the terms "water" and "sky" appear more frequently in image captions, that is, they are like terms "the" and "a" in normal English text. Yet, these frequent terms do *not* show up too often in Table 2, as a correlated term of a query term. It is surprising, given that we do nothing special when using MAGIC: no tf/idf weighting, no normalization, and no other domain-specific analysis. We just treat these frequent terms as nodes in our MAGIC graph, like any other nodes.

Another advantage of the proposed MAGIC method is that it can be easily extended to caption a group of images, considering the whole group at once. This flexibility is due to the graph-based framework of MAGIC, which allows augmentation of multiple nodes and doing RWR from any subset of nodes. To the best of our knowledge, MAGIC is the first method that is capable of doing group captioning.

Application 2 (group captioning). *Given a set* I_{core} *of captioned images and a (query) group of uncaptioned images* $\{I'_1, ..., I'_t\}$*, find the best g (say, g=5) caption words to assign to the group.*

Possible applications for group captioning include video segment captioning, where a video segment is captioned according to the group of keyframes associated with the segment. Since keyframes in a video segment are usually related, captioning them as a whole can take into account the inter-keyframe correlations, which are missed if each keyframe is captioned separately. Accurate captions for video segments may improve performances on tasks such as video retrieval and classification.

The steps to caption a group of images are similar to those for the single-image captioning outlined in Figure 6. A core MAGIC graph is still used to capture the mixed media information of a given collection of captioned images. The different steps for doing group captioning are: First, instead of augmenting the single query image to the core and restarting from it, we augment all t images in the query group $\{I'_1, ..., I'_t\}$ to the core. Then, the RWR step is performed by randomly restarts from one of the images in the group (i.e., each of the t query image has probability $1/t$ to be the restart node).

Figure 10 shows the result of using MAGIC for captioning a group of three images. MAGIC finds reasonable terms for the entire group of images: "sky," "water," "tree," and "sun." Captioning multiple images as a group takes into consideration the correlations between different images in the group, and in this example, this helps reduce the scores of irrelevant terms such as "people." In contrast, when we caption these images individually, MAGIC selects "people" as caption words for images in Figure 10(a) and (b), which do not contain people-related objects.

Table 2. Correlated terms of some query terms

Query term	1	2	3	4	5
branch	birds	night	owl	nest	Hawk
bridge	water	arch	sky	stone	Boats
cactus	saguaro	desert	sky	grass	Sunset
car	tracks	street	buildings	turn	prototype
f-16	plane	jet	sky	runway	Water
market	people	street	food	closeup	buildings
mushrooms	fungus	ground	tree	plants	Coral
pillars	stone	temple	people	sculpture	Ruins
reefs	fish	water	ocean	coral	Sea
textile	pattern	background	texture	designs	close-up

SYSTEM ISSUES

MAGIC provides an intuitive framework for detecting cross-modal correlations. The RWR computation in MAGIC is fast and it scales linearly with the graph size. For example, a straightforward implementation of RWR can caption an image in less than five seconds.

In this section, we discuss system issues such as parameter configuration and fast computation. In particular, we present results showing:

- MAGIC is insensitive to parameter settings.
- MAGIC is modular that we can easily employ the best module to date to speedup MAGIC.

Optimization of Parameters

There are several design decisions to be made when employing MAGIC for correlation detection: *what should be the values for the two parameters: the number of neighbors k of a domain token, and the restart probability c of RWR?* And, *should we assign weights to edges, according to the types of their end points?* In this section, we empirically show that the performance of MAGIC is insensitive to these settings, and provide suggestions on determining reasonable default values.

We use automatic image captioning as the application to measure the effect of these parameters. The experiments in this section are performed on the same 10 captioned image sets ("001", ..., "010") described in previous sections, and we measure how the values of the parameters, such as k, c, and the weights of the links of the MAGIC graphs, effect the captioning accuracy.

Number of Neighbors *k*. The parameter k specifies the number of nearest domain tokens to which a domain token connects via the NN-links. With these NN-links, objects having little difference in their attribute values will be closer to each other in the graph, and therefore, are considered more correlated by MAGIC. For $k = 0$, all domain tokens are considered distinct; for larger k, our application is more tolerant to the difference in attribute values.

We examine the effect of various k values on image captioning accuracy. Figure 11 shows the captioning accuracy on the dataset "006," with the restart probability $c = 0.66$. The captioning accuracy increases as k increases from $k = 1$, and reaches a plateau between $k = 3$ and 10. The

Figure 10. Group captioning by MAGIC: Caption terms with highest RWR scores are listed first

	(a)	(b)	(c)
Truth	sun, water, tree, sky	sun, clouds, sky, horizon	sun, water
MAGIC	sky, water, tree, sun		

plateau indicates that MAGIC is insensitive to the value of k. Results on other datasets are similar, showing a plateau between $k = 3$ and 10.

In hindsight, with only $k = 1$, the collection of regions (domain tokens) is barely connected, missing important connections and thus leading to poor performance on detecting correlations. At the other extreme, with a high value of k, everybody is directly connected to everybody else and there is no clear distinction between really close neighbors or just neighbors. For a medium value of k, the NN-links apparently capture the correlations between the close neighbors and avoid noise from remote neighbors. Small deviations from that value make little difference, which is probably because that the extra neighbors we add (when k increases), or those we retained (when k decreases), are at least as good as the previous ones.

Restart Probability *c*. The restart probability c specifies the probability to jump back to the restarting node(s) of the random walk. Higher value of c implies giving higher RWR scores to nodes closer in the neighborhood of the restart node(s). Figure 12 shows the image captioning accuracy of MAGIC with different values of c. The dataset is "006," with the parameter $k=3$. The accuracy reaches a plateau between $c = 0.5$ and 0.9, showing that the proposed MAGIC method is insensitive to the value of c. Results on other datasets are similar, showing a plateau between $c = 0.5$ and 0.9.

For Web graphs, the recommended value for c is typically $c = 0.15$ (Haveliwala et al., 2003). Surprisingly, our experiments show that this choice does not give good performance. Instead, good quality is achieved for $c = 0.6 \sim 0.9$. Why is this discrepancy?

We conjecture that what determines a good value for the restart probability is the diameter of the graph. Ideally, we want our random walker to have a nontrivial chance to reach the outskirts

Figure 11. The plateau in the plot shows that the captioning accuracy is insensitive to value of the number of nearest neighbors k. Y-axis: Average accuracy over all test images of dataset "006". The restart probability is c=0.66.

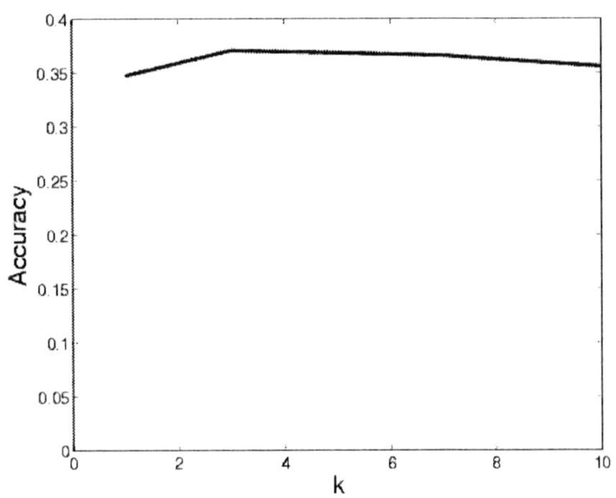

Figure 12. The plateau in the plot shows that the captioning accuracy is insensitive to value of the restart probability c. Y-axis: Average accuracy over all images of dataset "006." The number of nearest neighbors per domain token (region) is k = 3.

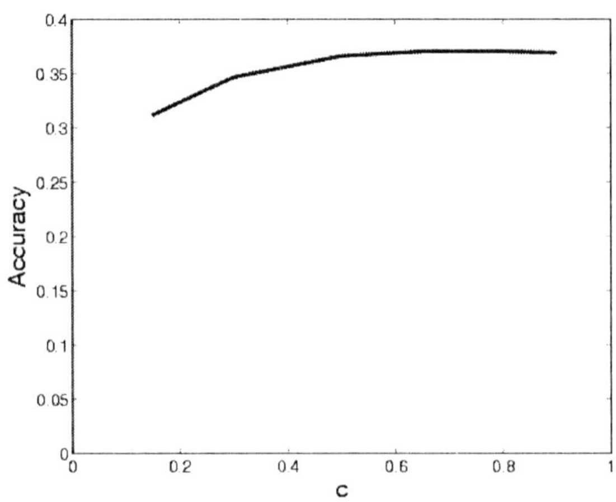

of the whole graph. If the diameter of the graph is d, the probability that the random walker (with restarts) will reach a point on the periphery is proportional to $(1-c)^d$, that is , the probability of not restarting for d consecutive moves.

For the Web graph, the diameter is estimated to be $d = 19$ (Albert, Jeong, & Barabasi, 1999). This implies that the probability $p_{periphery}$ for the random walker to reach a node in the periphery of the Web graph is roughly:

$$p_{periphery} = (1-c)^{19} = (1-0.15)^{19} = 0.045 \ .$$

In our image captioning experiments, we use graphs that have three layers of nodes (Figure 2). The diameter of such graphs is roughly $d = 3$. If we demand the same $p_{periphery} = 0.045$, then the c value for our 3-layer graph would be:

$$(1-0.15)^{19} = (1-c)^3,$$
$$\Rightarrow c = 0.65,$$

which is much closer to our empirical observations. Of course, the problem requires more careful analysis—but we are the first to show that $c = 0.15$ is not always optimal for random walk with restarts.

Link weights. MAGIC uses a graph to encode the relationship between mixed media objects and their attributes of different media. The OAV-links in the graph connect objects to their domain tokens (Figure 2). To give more attention to an attribute domain D, we can increase the weights of OAV-links that connect to the tokens of domain D. *Should we treat all media equally, or should we weight OAV-links according to their associated domains? How should we weight the OAV-links? Could we achieve better performance on weighted graphs?*

We investigate how the change on link weights influences the image captioning accuracy. Table 3 shows the captioning accuracy on dataset "006" when different weights are assigned on the OAV-links to regions (weight w_{region}) and those to terms (w_{term}). Specifically, the elements $A_{i,j}$ of the adjacency matrix **A** will now take values w_{region} or w_{term}, besides values 0 and 1, depending on the type of link $A_{i,j}$ corresponds to. For all cases, the number of nearest neighbors is $k = 3$ and the restart probability is $c = 0.66$. The case where $(w_{region}, w_{term}) = (1,1)$ is that of the unweighted graph, and is the result we reported in Figure 7. As link weights vary from 0.1, 1 to 10, the captioning accuracy is basically unaffected. The results on other datasets are similar—captioning accuracy is at the same level on a weighted graph as on the unweighted graph.

This experiment shows that an unweighted graph is appropriate for our image captioning application. We speculate that an appropriate weighting for an application depends on properties such as the number of attribute domains (i.e., the number of layers in the graph), the average size of a set-valued attribute of an object (such as, average number of regions per image), and so on. We plan to investigate more on this issue in our future work.

Speedup Graph Construction by Approximation

The proposed MAGIC method encodes a mixed media dataset as a graph, and employs the RWR algorithm to find cross-modal correlations. The construction of the G_{magic} graph is intuitive and straightforward, and the RWR computation is light and linear to the database size. One step that is relatively expensive is the construction of NN-links in a MAGIC graph.

When constructing the NN-links of a MAGIC graph, we need to compute the nearest neighbors for every domain token. For example, in our image captioning experiments, to construct the NN-links among region-nodes, k-NN searches are performed about 50,000 times (one for each region token) in the 30-dimensional region-feature space.

In MAGIC, the NN-links are proposed to capture the similarity relation among domain tokens. The goal is to associate similar tokens to each other, and therefore, it could be suffice to have the NN-links connect to neighbors that are close enough, even if they are not exactly the closest ones. The approximate nearest neighbor search is usually faster, by trading accuracy for speed. The interesting questions are: *How much speedup could we gain by allowing approximate NN-links? How much is the performance reduction by approximation?*

For efficient nearest neighbor search, one common way is to use a spatial index, such as R^+-tree (Sellis, Roussopoulos, & Faloutsos, 1987), to find exact nearest neighbors in logarithmic time. Fortunately, MAGIC is modular and we can pick the best module to perform each step. In our experiments, we use the approximate nearest neighbor searching (ANN) (Arya, Mount, Netanyahu, Silverman, & Wu, 1998), which supports both exact and approximate nearest neighbor search. ANN estimates the distance to a nearest neighbor up to $(1+\varepsilon)$ times of the actual distance: $\varepsilon=0$ means exact search with no approximation; bigger ε values give rougher estimation.

Table 4 lists the average wall clock time to compute the top 10 neighbors of a region in the 10 Corel image sets of our image captioning experiments. The table shows the efficiency/accuracy trade off on constructing the NN-links among image regions. In an approximate nearest neighbor search, the distance to a neighboring

Table 3. Captioning accuracy is insensitive to various weight settings on OAV-links to the two media: region (weight w_{region}) and term (w_{term}).

	w_{region}		
w_{term}	**0.1**	**1**	**10**
0.1	0.370332	0.371963	0.370812
1	0.369900	0.370524	0.371963
10	0.368969	0.369181	0.369948

Table 4. The efficiency/accuracy trade off of constructing NN-links using an approximate method (ANN). $\varepsilon=0$ indicates the exact nearest neighbor computation. Elapse time: average wall clock time for one nearest neighbor search. Speedup: the ratio of the time of sequential search (SS) and that of an ANN search. The error is measured as the percentage of mistakes made by approximation on the k nearest neighbors. The symbol "-" means zero error.

	Approximate Nearest Neighbor Search			Sequential search (SS)
	$\varepsilon=0$	$\varepsilon=0.2$	$\varepsilon=0.8$	
Elapse time (msec.)	3.8	2.4	0.9	46
Speedup to SS	12.1	19.2	51.1	1
Error (in top k=10)	-	0.0015%	1.67%	-
Error (in top k=3)	-	-	0.46%	-

region is approximated to within (1+ε) times of the actual distance. The speedup of using the approximate method is compared to the sequential search method (SS). In our experiments, the sequential search method is implemented in C++ and compiled with the code optimization, using the command "g++ -O3."

Compared to the sequential search, the speedup of using the ANN method increases from 12.1 to 51.1, from the exact search (ε=0) to a rough approximation of (ε=0.8). For the top k = 3 nearest neighbors (the setting used in most of our experiments), the error percentage is at most 0.46% for the roughest approximation, which is equivalent to making one error in every 217 NN-links.

We conduct experiments to investigate the effect on captioning accuracy from using the approximate NN-links. In general, the small differences on NN-links due to approximation do not change the characteristic of the MAGIC graph significantly, and has limited affect on the performance of image captioning (Figure 13). At the approximation level ε = 0.2, we achieve a speedup of 19.1 times and surprisingly that no error is made on the NN-links in the MAGIC graph, and therefore the captioning accuracy is the same as exact computation. At the approximation level ε = 0.8, which gives an even better speedup of 51.1 times, the average captioning accuracy decreases by just 1.59 percentage point (averaged over the 10 Corel image sets). Therefore, by using an approximate method, we can significantly reduce the time to construct the MAGIC graph (up to 51.1 times speedup), with almost no decrease on the captioning accuracy.

CONCLUSION

Mixed media objects such as captioned images or video clips contain attributes of different modalities (image, text, or audio). Correlations across different modalities provide information about the multimedia content, and are useful in applications ranging from summarization to semantic captioning. In this chapter, we develop MAGIC, a graph-based method for detecting cross-modal correlations in mixed media dataset.

There are two challenges in detecting cross-modal correlations, namely, representation of attributes of various modalities and the detection of correlations among any subset of modalities. MAGIC turns the multimedia problem into a graph problem, and provides an intuitive solution that easily incorporates various modalities. The graph framework of MAGIC creates opportunity for applying graph algorithms to multimedia problems. In particular, MAGIC finds cross-modal correlations using the technique of random walk with restarts (RWR), which accommodates set-valued attributes and noise in data with no extra effort.

We apply MAGIC for automatic image captioning. By finding robust correlations between text and image, MAGIC achieves a relative improvement by 58% in captioning accuracy as compared

Figure 13. Speeding up NN-links construction by ANN (with ε=0.8) reduces captioning accuracy by just 1.59% on the average. X-axis: 10 datasets. Y-axis: average captioning accuracy over test images in a set. In this experiment, the parameters are c=0.66 and k=3.

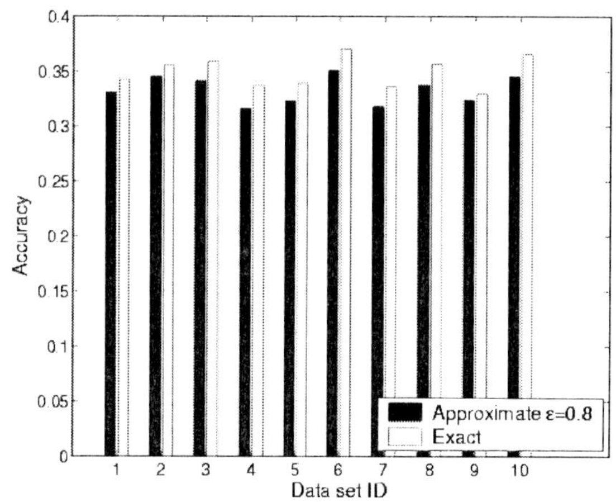

to recent machine learning techniques (Figure 8). Moreover, the MAGIC framework enables novel data mining applications, such as *group captioning* where multiple images are captioned simultaneously, taking into account the possible correlations between the multiple images in the group (Figure 10).

Technically, MAGIC has the following desirable characteristics:

- It is domain independent: The $Sim_i(*,*)$ similarity functions (Assumption 1) completely isolate our MAGIC method from the specifics of an application domain, and make MAGIC applicable to detect correlations in all kinds of mixed media datasets.
- It requires no fine-tuning on parameters or link weights: The performance is not sensitive to the two parameters—the number of neighbors k and the restart probability c, and it requires no special weighting scheme like tf/idf for link weights.
- Its computation is fast and scales up well with the database/graph size.
- It is modular and can easily incorporate recent advances in related areas (e.g., fast nearest neighbor search) to improve performance.

We are pleasantly surprised that such a domain-independent method, with no parameters to tune, outperforms some of the most recent and carefully tuned methods for automatic image captioning. Most of all, the graph-based framework proposed by MAGIC creates opportunity for applying graph algorithms to multimedia problems. Future work could further exploit the promising connection between multimedia databases and graph algorithms for other data mining tasks, including multimodal event summarization (Pan, Yang, & Faloutsos, 2004) or outlier detection, that require the discovery of correlations as its first step.

REFERENCES

Albert, A., Jeong, H., & Barabasi, A.-L. (1999). Diameter of the World Wide Web. *Nature, 401*, 130-131.

Arya, S., Mount, D. M., Netanyahu, N. S., Silverman, R., & Wu, A. Y. (1998). An optimal algorithm for approximate nearest neighbor searching. *Journal of the ACM, 45*, 891-923.

Barnard, K., Duygulu, P., Forsyth, D. A., de Freitas, N., Blei, D. M., & Jordan, M. I. (2003). Matching words and pictures. *Journal of Machine Learning Research, 3*, 1107-1135.

Benitez, A. B., & Chang, S.-F. (2002). Multimedia knowledge integration, summarization and evaluation. In *Proceedings of the 2002 International Workshop on Multimedia Data Mining in conjunction with the International Conference on Knowledge Discovery and Data Mining (MDM/KDD-2002)*, Edmonton, Alberta, Canada (pp.39-50).

Blei, D. M., & Jordan, M.I. (2003). Modeling annotated data. In *Proceedings of the 26th Annual International ACM SIGIR Conference on Research and Development in Information Retrieval* (pp.127-134).

Brin, S., & Page, L. (1998). The anatomy of a large-scale hypertextual Web search engine. In *Proceedings of the Seventh International Conference on World Wide Web*, Brisbane, Australia (pp.107-117).

Chang, S.-F., Manmatha, R., & Chua, T.-S. (2005). Combining text and audio-visual features in video indexing. In *Proceedings of the 2005 IEEE International Conference on Acoustics, Speech, and Signal Processing (ICASSP 2005)*, Philadelphia (pp. 1005-1008).

Doyle, P. G., & Snell, J. L. (1984). *Random walks and electric networks.* Mathematical Association of America.

Duygulu, P., Barnard, K., de Freitas, J. F. G., & Forsyth, D. A. (2002). Object recognition as machine translation: Learning a lexicon for a fixed image vocabulary. In *Proceedings of the Seventh European Conference on Computer Vision (ECCV 2002)* (LNCS 2353, pp. 97-112). Springer-Verlag.

Duygulu, P., Pan, J.-Y., & Forsyth, D. A. (2004). Towards auto-documentary: Tracking the evolution of news stories. In *Proceedings of the Annual International ACM Conference on Multimedia*, New York (pp. 820-827).

Faloutsos, C. (1996). *Searching multimedia databases by content.* Kluwer Academic Publishers.

Feng, S. L., Manmatha, R., & Lavrenko, V. (2004). Multiple Bernoulli relevance models for image and video annotation. In *Proceedings of the 2004 IEEE Computer Society Conference on Computer Vision and Pattern Recognition (CVPR 2004)* (pp.1002-1009).

Haveliwala, T., Kamvar, S., & Jeh, G. (2003). *An analytical comparison of approaches to personalizing PageRank* (Tech. Rep. No. 2003-35). Stanford University, CA: InfoLab.

Haveliwala, T. H. (2002). Topic-sensitive PageRank. In *Proceedings of the 11th International Conference on World Wide Web*, Honolulu, HI (pp. 517-526).

Hsu, W., Kennedy, L., Huang, C.-W., Chang, S.-F., Lin, C.-Y., & Iyengar, G. (2004). News video story segmentation using fusion of multi-level multi-modal features in TRECVID 2003. In *Proceedings of the 2004 IEEE International Conference on Acoustics, Speech, and Signal Processing (ICASSP 2004)*, Montreal, Quebec, Canada (pp. 645-648).

Jeon, J., Lavrenko, V., & Manmatha, R. (2003). Automatic image annotation and retrieval using cross-media relevance models. In *Proceedings of the 26th Annual International ACM SIGIR Conference on Research and Development in Information Retrieval*, Toronto, Canada (pp. 119-126). New York: ACM Press.

Jin, R., Chai, J. Y., & Si, L. (2004). Effective automatic image annotation via a coherent language model and active learning. In *Proceedings of the 12th Annual ACM international Conference on Multimedia*, New York (pp. 892-899).

Kamvar, S. D., Haveliwala, T. H., & Golub, G. H. (2003). Adaptive methods for the computation of PageRank. In *Proceedings of the International Conference on the Numerical Solution of Markov Chains (NSMC)* (pp. 31-44).

Kamvar, S. D., Haveliwala, T. H., Manning, C. D., & Golub, G. H. (2003). Extrapolation methods for accelerating PageRank computations. In *Proceedings of the 12th International Conference on World Wide Web*, Budapest, Hungary (pp. 261-270).

Kleinberg, J. (1998). Authoritative sources in a hyperlinked environment. In *Proceedings of the 9th Annual ACM-SIAM Symposium on Discrete Algorithms*, San Francisco. (pp. 668-677)

Li, D., Dimitrova, N., Li, M., & Sethi, I. K.. (2003). Multimedia content processing through cross-modal association. In *Proceedings of the Eleventh ACM International Conference on Multimedia*, Berkeley, CA (pp. 604-611).

Li, J., & Wang , J. Z. (2003). Automatic linguistic indexing of pictures by a statistical modeling approach. *IEEE Transactions on Pattern Analysis and Machine Intelligence, 25,* 1075-1088.

Lin, W.-H., & Hauptmann, A. (2002). News video classification using SVM-based multimodal classifiers and combination strategies. In *Proceedings of the 10th Annual ACM International Conference on Multimedia*, Juan-les-Pins, France (pp. 323-326).

Lovász, L. (1996). Random walks on graphs: A survey. *Combinatorics, Paul Erdös is Eighty, 2,* 353-398.

Maron, O., & Ratan, A. L. (1998). Multiple-instance learning for natural scene classification. In *Proceedings of the Fifteenth International Conference on Machine Learning* (pp. 341-349).

Mori, Y., Takahashi, H., & Oka, R. (1999). Image-to-word transformation based on dividing and vector quantizing images with words. In *Proceedings of the First International Workshop on Multimedia Intelligent Storage and Retrieval Management*, Orlando, FL.

Naphade, M. R., Kozintsev, I., & Huang, T. (2001). Probabilistic semantic video indexing. In T. K. Leen, T. G., Dietterich, & V. Tresp (Eds.), *Advances in Neural Information Processing Systems, Papers from Neural Information Processing Systems (NIPS)*, Denver, CO (Vol. 13, pp. 967-973). MIT Press.

Palmer, C. R., & Faloutsos, C. (2003). Electricity based external similarity of categorical attributes. In *Proceedings of the 7th Pacific-Asia Conference on Knowledge Discovery and Data Mining (PAKDD 2003)*, Seoul, South Korea (pp. 486-500).

Pan, J.-Y., & Faloutsos, C. (2002). VideoCube: A novel tool for video mining and classification. In *Proceedings of the Fifth International Conference on Asian Digital Libraries (ICADL 2002)*, Singapore (pp. 194-205).

Pan, J.-Y., Yang, H.-J., Duygulu, P., & Faloutsos, C. (2004). Automatic image captioning. In *Proceedings of the 2004 IEEE International Conference on Multimedia and Expo (ICME 2004)*, Taipei, Taiwan (pp. 1987-1990).

Pan, J.-Y., Yang, H., & Faloutsos, C. (2004). MMSS: Multi-modal story-oriented video summarization. In *Proceedings of the Fourth IEEE International Conference on Data Mining (ICDM 2004)*, Brighton, UK (pp. 491-494).

Pan, J.-Y., Yang, H.-J., Faloutsos, C., & Duygulu, P. (2004a). Automatic multimedia cross-modal correlation discovery. In *Proceedings of the 10th ACM SIGKDD International Conference on Knowledge Discovery and Data Mining*, Seattle, WA (pp. 653-658).

Pan, J.-Y., Yang, H.-J., Faloutsos, C., & Duygulu, P.(2004b). GCap: Graph-based automatic image captioning. In *Proceedings of the 2004 Conference on Computer Vision and Pattern Recognition Workshop (CVPRW 2004)* (p. 146).

Sebe, N., Lew, M. S., Zhou, X. S., Huang, T. S., & Bakker, E. M. (2003). The state of the art in image and video retrieval. In *Proceedings of the International Conference on Image and Video Retrieval (CIVR'03)*, Urbana, IL (pp. 1-8).

Sellis, T. K., Roussopoulos, N., & Faloutsos, C. (1987). The R^+-tree: A dynamic index for multi-dimensional objects. In *Proceedings of the 12th International Conference on Very Large Data Bases* (pp. 507-518).

Shi, J., & Malik, J. (2000). Normalized cuts and image segmentation. *IEEE Transactions on Pattern Analysis and Machine Intelligence, 22*, 888-905.

Srihari, R. K., Rao, A., Han, B., Munirathnam, S., & Xiaoyun, W. (2000). A model for multimodal information retrieval. In *Proceedings of the 2000 IEEE International Conference on Multimedia and Expo (ICME 2000)* (pp. 701-704).

Virga, P., & Duygulu, P. (2005). Systematic evaluation of machine translation methods for image and video annotation. In *Proceedings of the Fourth International Conference on Image and Video Retrieval (CIVR 2005)*, Singapore (pp. 174-183).

Vries, A. P., de Westerveld, T. H. W., & Ianeva, T. (2004). Combining multiple representations on the TRECVID search task. In *Proceedings of 2004 IEEE International Conference on Acoustics, Speech, and Signal Processing (ICASSP 2004)*, Montreal, Quebec, Canada (pp. 1052-1055).

Wang, X.-J., Ma, W.-Y., Xue, G.-R., & Li, X. (2004). Multi-model similarity propagation and its application for Web image retrieval. In *Proceedings of the 12th Annual ACM International Conference on Multimedia*, New York (pp. 944-951).

Wenyin, L., Dumais, S.T., Sun, Y.F., Zhang, H.J., Czerwinski, M.P., Field, B., et al. (2001). Semi-automatic image annotation. In *Proceedings of the 8th IFIP TC.13 Conference on Human-Computer Interaction (INTERACT 2001).*

Wu, Y., Chang, E. Y., Chang, K. C.-C., & Smith, J. R. (2004). Optimal multimodal fusion for multimedia data analysis. In *Proceedings of the 12th Annual ACM International Conference on Multimedia*, New York (pp. 572-579).

Xie, L., Kennedy, L., Chang, S.-F., Divakaran, A., Sun, H., & Lin, C.-Y. (2005). Layered dynamic mixture model for pattern discovery in asynchronous multi-modal streams. In *Proceedings of the 2005 IEEE International Conference on Acoustics Speech and Signal Processing (ICASSP 2005)*, Philadelphia (pp. 1053-1056).

Zhang, D.-Q., Lin, C.-Y., Chang, S.-F., & Smith, J. R. (2004). Semantic video clustering across sources using bipartite spectral clustering. In *Proceeding of 2004 IEEE Conference on Multimedia and Expo (ICME 2004)*, Taipei, Taiwan (pp. 117-120).

Zhang, Z., Zhang, R., & Ohya, J. (2004). Exploiting the cognitive synergy between different media modalities in multimodal information retrieval. In *Proceedings of the 2004 IEEE International Conference on Multimedia and Expo (ICME 2004)*, Taipei, Taiwan (pp. 2227-2230).

Zhao, R., & Grosky, W. I. (2001). Bridging the semantic gap in image retrieval. In T. K. Shih (Ed.), *Distributed multimedia databases: Techniques and applications* (pp. 14-36).

Section IV
Mining Image Data Repository

Chapter V
Image Mining for the Construction of Semantic-Inference Rules and for the Development of Automatic Image Diagnosis Systems

Petra Perner
Institute of Computer Vision and Applied Computer Sciences (IBal), Germany

ABSTRACT

This chapter introduces image mining as a method to discover implicit, previously unknown and potentially useful information from digital image and video repositories. It argues that image mining is a special discipline because of the special type of data and therefore, image-mining methods that consider the special data representation and the different aspects of image mining have to be developed. Furthermore, a bridge has to be established between image mining and image processing, feature extraction and image understanding since the later topics are concerned with the development of methods for the automatic extraction of higher-level image representations. We introduce our methodology, the developed methods and the system for image mining which we successfully applied to several medical image-diagnostic tasks.

INTRODUCTION

The increasing number of digital-image and video repositories have made image mining an important task. Image mining means a process of nontrivial extraction of implicit, previously unknown and potentially useful information from image databases. The application of image min-

Copyright © 2007, IGI Global, distributing in print or electronic forms without written permission of IGI Global is prohibited.

ing will help to get some additional knowledge about specific features of different classes and the way in which they are expressed in the image. This method can elicit nonformalized expert knowledge; it can automatically create effective models for decision-making, and can help to find some inherent non-evident links between classes and their imaging in the picture. It can help to get some nontrivial conclusions and predictions on the basis of image analysis. The new knowledge obtained as a result of data analysis in the database can enhance the professional knowledge of the expert or the user of the image-database. This knowledge can also be used for teaching novices or can support image analysis and diagnosis by the expert. It can be used for semantic annotation of digital visual content to enable sophisticated semantic querying of the media in terms familiar to the user's domain, whilst also ensuring that the information and knowledge have a much greater chance of being discovered and exploited by services, agents and applications on the Web.

An additional advantage of image-mining application in decision-making of medical or other tasks is on the long-run the opportunity of creating fully automatic image-diagnosis systems that could be very important and useful in the case of lacking knowledge for decision-making.

In this chapter we present our methods and methodology for performing image mining. We describe the recent state of the art in image mining, the questions that can be answered by applying image-mining methods to image databases, and the problems concerned with image mining. A design of image-mining tools is considered followed by a presentation of our methods and the developed tool for image mining. A methodology for image mining that was created and tested in the task of Hep-2 cell analysis is described. Finally, we summarize our experience in applications of image-mining methodology in different medical tasks, such as pre-clinical diagnosis of peripheral lung cancer on the basis of lung tomograms, lymph-node diagnosis and investigation of breast diseases in MRI and the inspection of microscopic images of cell-based assays. Conclusions and plans for future work are given at the end of this chapter.

BACKGROUND

As in data mining, we can classify image mining into two main problem types: prediction and knowledge discovery. While prediction is the strongest goal, knowledge discovery is the weaker approach and usually occurs prior to prediction. In prediction we want to discover a model that allows us, based on the model, to predict new data in the respective classes. In knowledge discovery we want to discover similar groups of database entries, frequent patterns, and deviations from a normal status or just relations among the database entries.

Image mining differs from data mining in respect of the data and the nature of the data. The raw image is of 2-dimensional or 3-dimensional numerical data type. Videos are temporal sequences of numerous 2-d images. The image information can be represented by the 2-d or 3-d image matrix itself, by low-level features such as edges, blobs and regions, or by high-level features that allow a human to semantically understand the image content. The different data types in which an image or an image sequence can be represented and the resulting need for special methods and techniques offer a data-type dimension to data mining and make image mining a specific field.

Consequently, image mining can be applied to all the different data representations of an image. Which of the data representations is used, usually depends on the question under study. If we mine our images for knowledge that can be used to construct a fully automatic image-interpretation system, we have different questions to answer: We have to mine the images for regions-of-interest and separate them from the background of the image. Once we have found these regions we need to mine them for distinguishing features and later on we are interested in discovering rules that allow us to classify these regions into different patterns. Based on all this information discovered we might be able to build an automatic image-interpretation system.

In video mining it is of interest to detect scenes, group them into similar groups or detect events. These three main tasks require a specific image-mining procedure applicable to videos.

Unlike in other fields we can only do this automatically if we have proper automatic information-extracting methods. This brings us to the topics of image processing, feature extraction and image understanding. Image mining is closely related to these topics and will only succeed if a bridge can be established between image mining and these topics.

All the above mentioned questions can inherently suffice in other applications. The problem of searching the regions of special visual attention or interesting patterns in a large set of images has been studied for medical CT and MRI image sets in Megalooikonomou, Davatzki, and Herskovits (1999) and Eklund, You, and Deer (2000) or in satellite images (Burl & Lucchetti, 2000). Usually, experienced experts have discovered this information. However, the amount of images, which is being created by modern sensors, makes the development of methods necessary that can tackle this task for the expert. Therefore, standard primitive features able to describe the visual changes in the image background are being extracted from the images, and the significance of these features is being tested by a sound statistical test (Burl & Lucchetti, 2000; Megalooikonomou, Davatzki, & Herskovits, 1999).

Clustering is applied in order to explore the images seeking similar groups of spatial connected components (Zaiane & Han, 2000) or similar groups of objects (Eklund, You, & Deer, 2000). Association rules are used for finding significant patterns in the images (Burl & Lucchetti, 2000). A method for obtaining the principal objects, characters and scenes in a video by measuring the reoccurrence of spatial configurations of viewpoint invariant features is described in Sivic and Zisserman (2004). How to discover the editing patterns of videos from different editors with data mining and to use the discovered rules for editing new video material is described in Matsuo, Amano, and Uehara (2002). Multilevel sequential association mining is applied to explore associations among the audio and visual cues in Zhu, Wu, Elmagardmid, Feng, and Wu (2005). The associations are classified by assigning each of them with a class label. Their appearances in the video is recognized and used to construct video indices. A method for unsupervised classification of events in multi-camera indoors surveillance video by applying self-organizing map (SOM) is described in Petrushin (2005).

The measurement of image features in these regions or patterns provides the basis for pattern recognition and image classification. Computer-vision researches are conducted to create proper models of objects and scenes, to obtain image features and to develop decision rules that allow one to analyze and interpret the observed images. Computer-assisted diagnosis methods of image processing, segmentation, and feature measurements are successfully used for this purpose (Kehoe & Parker, 1991; Perner, 1998; Schröder, Niemann, & Sagerer, 1988).

The basic research of image mining and machine learning in pattern recognition deals with a wide spectrum of different problems that need to be solved for image mining. The developed methods reach from learning local structural features by a multiscale relevance function (Palenichka & Volgin, 1999) to the construction of artificial neural nets for estimating the local mean grey value for image processing (Jahn, 1999) or for model selection and fitting if the models are linear manifolds and data points distribute to the union of a finite number of linear data points (Imiya & Oatani, 2001). Multiple classifier systems and case-based reasoning (Perner, 1998, 2005;

Schmidt & Gierl, 2001) are further approaches for prediction models. Case-based reasoning methods for image segmentation (Perner, 1999) as well as for the recognition of similar video scenes (Zhu, Wu, Elmagardmid, Feng, & Wu, 2005) have been developed. Multiple classifier systems can be designed by applying unsupervised learning to ensure that the multiple classifiers works efficiently by making independent errors (Giacinto & Roli, 1999). First-order rule induction (Malerba, Esposito, Lanza, & Lisi, 2001) is applied for the recognition of morphological patterns based on symbolic terms in topographic maps. Methods for clustering with relevance feedback (Bhanu & Dong, 2001) have been developed to overcome the gap between low-level visual features and human high-level concepts and rule-based ensembles are applied to solve regression problems (Indurkhya & Weiss, 2001). The incremental appearance of most media is now considered by incremental clustering techniques (Bougila & Ziou, 2005; Jänichen & Perner, 2005). Sampling schedules for face recognition and finger print recognition based on neural nets that are adaptive to the data and allow using only a portion of data from a huge dataset for the development of recognition models are developed in Satyanarayana and Davidson (2005). These few examples show that image mining is still a basic research topic with a lot of different subtopics, but on the other hand systems for image mining are needed that can be used in practice.

The mining process is often done bottom-up. As many numerical features as possible are extracted from the images, in order to achieve the final goal—the classification of the objects (Fischer & Bunke, 2001; Perner, Zscherpel, & Jacobsen, 2001). However, such a numerical approach usually does not allow the user to understand the way in which the reasoning process has been achieved.

The second approach to pattern recognition and image classification is an approach based on the symbolic description of images made by the expert (Perner, 2000). This approach can present to the expert in an explicit form the way in which the image has been interpreted. The experts having the domain knowledge usually prefer the second approach.

Normally simple numerical features are not able to give a description of complex objects and scenes. They can be described by an expert with the help of non-formalized symbolic descriptions, which reflect some gestalt in the expert domain knowledge. This task of semantic tagging becomes more popular since such descriptions enable sophisticated semantic querying of the media in terms familiar to the user's domain, whilst also ensuring that the information and knowledge have a much greater chance of being discovered and exploited by services, agents and applications on the Web. In contrast to that it is also the basis for the development of automatic image interpretation systems.

One problem is how to find out the relevant descriptions of the object (or the scene) for its interpretation and how to construct a proper procedure for the extraction of these features. This top-down approach is the more practical approach for most applications. However, the symbolic description of images and feature estimation face numerous difficulties:

1. A skilled expert knows how to interpret the image, but often has no well-defined vocabulary to describe the objects, visual patterns and gestalt variances, which are standing behind the expert's diagnostic decisions. When the expert is asked to make this knowledge explicit, the expert usually cannot specify and verbalize it.
2. Although numerous efforts are going on to develop such a vocabulary for specific medical tasks (for example, the ACR-BIRADS-code has been constructed for image analysis in mammography) and MPEG-7 standard (Martinez, 2001) is used for ontology-based annotations of natural images, the problem

of the difference between "displaying and naming" still exists.

3. A developed description language will differ for example from medical school to medical school and as a result the obtained symbolical description of image features by a human will be expert-dependent and subjective.
4. Besides this, the developed vocabulary usually consists of a large number of different symbolic features (image attributes) and feature values. It is not clear a-priori whether all the attributes included into the vocabulary are necessary for the diagnostic reasoning process. To select the necessary and relevant features would make the reasoning process more effective.

We propose a methodology of image mining that allows one to learn a compact vocabulary for the description of objects and to understand how this vocabulary is used for diagnostic reasoning or in semantic-inference rules of semantic tagging. Besides that we also use basic image features that have been calculated from the image. This methodology can be used for a wide range of image-diagnostic tasks and semantic annotations.

Developed methodology takes into account the recent status of the art in image analysis and feature extraction and combines it with new methods of data mining. It allows us to extract quantitative information from the image and when possible combine it with subjectively determined diagnostic features, and then to mine this information for the relevant diagnostic knowledge acquisition by objective methods such as data mining.

Our methodology should help to solve some cognitive, theoretical and practical problems:

1. It will reproduce and display a decision model of an expert for specific task solutions.
2. It will show the pathway of human reasoning and classification. Image features will be discovered which are basic for correct decision-making by the expert.
3. A developed model will be used as a tool to support the decision-making of a human who is not an expert in a specific field of knowledge. It can be used for teaching novices, as well as for semantic image retrieval.

The application of data mining will help to get some additional knowledge about specific features of different classes and the way in which they are expressed in the image. It could help to find some inherent non-evident links between classes and their imaging in the picture that could be used to make some nontrivial conclusions and predictions on the basis of elicited knowledge.

DESIGN CONSIDERATIONS

Besides the development of new methods for image mining, there is a need for systems that can support a user at all steps of an image-mining task. We developed a tool for data mining which was to meet several requirements:

1. The tool had to be applicable for a wide range of image-diagnostic tasks and image modalities that occur for example in medical practice. It was to be used for semantic annotation of large image contents for image retrieval.
2. It should allow the users to develop their own symbolic descriptions of images in the terms which are appropriate to the specific diagnostic task.
3. Users should have a possibility for updating or adding features according to new images or a diagnostic problem.
4. It should support the user in the analysis and interpretation of images; for example, in the evaluation of new imaging devices and radiographic materials.
5. It should assist the user in learning a proper prediction model based on different methods

that are applicable for different data-type characteristics.

6. It should support the user in finding groups of features, objects or relations by proper clustering methods.

Taking into account these criteria and the recent state-of-the-art in image analysis, we provided an opportunity for semiautomatic image processing and analysis to enhance imaging of diagnostically important details in the image and measure some image features directly in the image and by this way to support the user by the analysis of images. The user has to have the possibility to interact with the system in order to adapt the results of image processing.

This image-processing unit should provide extraction of such low-level features as blobs, regions, ribbons, lines and edges. On the basis of these low-level features we are able to calculate then some high-level features to describe the image. Besides that, the image-processing unit should allow evaluation of some statistical image properties, which might give valuable information for the image description.

However, some diagnostically important features, such as "irregular structure inside the nodule," "tumor" are not so-called low-level features. They present some gestalts of expert domain knowledge. Development of an algorithm for extraction of such image features can be a complex or even unsolvable problem. So we identify different ways of representing the contents of an image that belongs to different abstraction levels (see Figure 1). We can describe an image:

- By statistical properties (i.e., that is, the lowest abstraction level)
- By low-level features and their statistical properties such as regions, blobs, ribbons,

Figure 1. Overview on image descriptions based on different abstraction levels

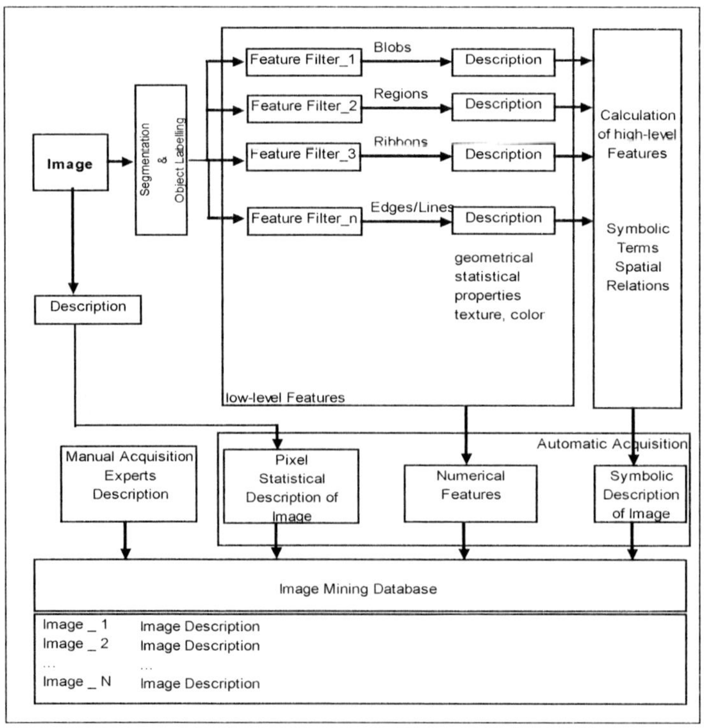

edges and lines (this is the next higher abstraction level)
- By high-level or symbolic features that can be obtained from the low-level features
- By an expert's symbolic description, which is the highest abstraction level

The image-processing unit combined with the data-evaluation unit should allow a user to learn the relevant diagnostic features and effective models for the image interpretation. Therefore, the system as a whole should meet the following criteria:

1. Support the medical person as much as possible by the extraction of the necessary image details (region of interest).
2. Fulfill measurement of the feature values directly in the image when possible.
3. Display the interesting image details to the expert.
4. Store in a database the measured feature values as well as the subjective description of images by the expert.
5. Import these data from the database into the data-mining unit.

SYSTEM DESCRIPTION

Overall System Architecture

Figure 2 shows a scheme of the tool *ImageMiner Version 2.1.* There are two main parts in the tool:

- The online part that is comprised of the image analysis (Figure 3) and the image interpretation part
- The off-line part that is comprised of the database and the data-mining and knowledge discovery part (Figure 4)

The tool is written in C++ and runs under Windows NT. These two units communicate over a database of image descriptions which is created in the frame of the image-processing unit. This database is the basis for the image-mining unit.

The online part can automatically detect the objects, extract image features from the objects and classify the recognized objects into the respective classes based on the previously stored decision rules. The interface between the offline and the online part is the database where images and calculated image features are stored. The off-line part can mine the images for a prediction

Figure 2. Architecture of an image mining tool

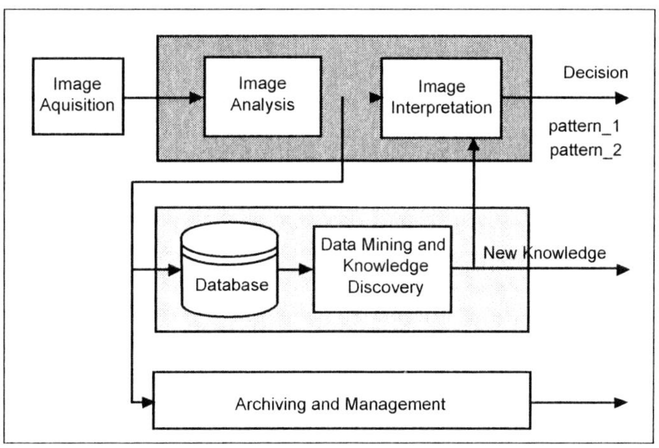

Figure 3. (a)-(f) Image analysis unit for the extraction of the image descriptions

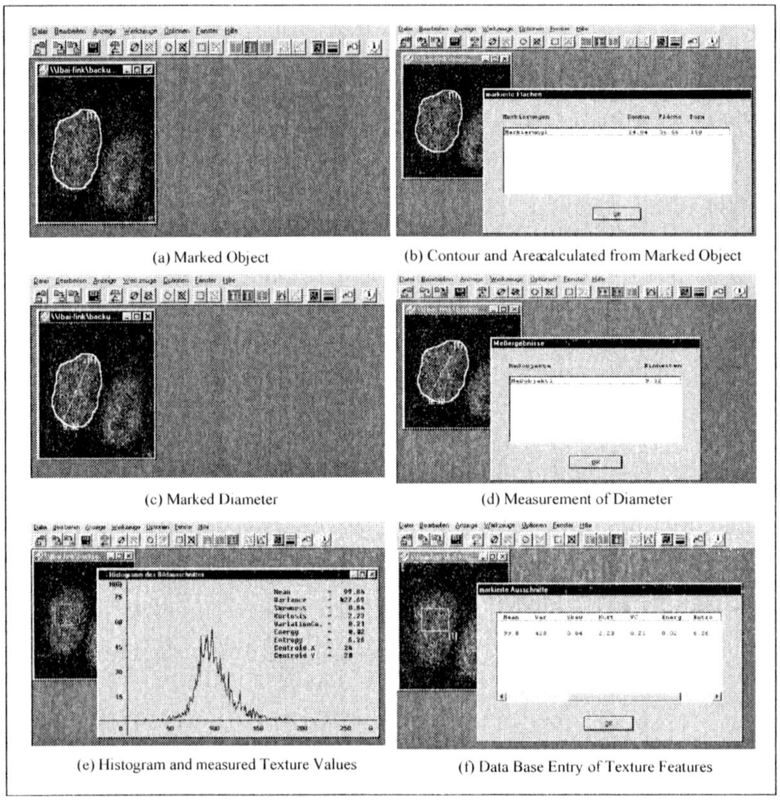

(a) Marked Object

(b) Contour and Areacalculated from Marked Object

(c) Marked Diameter

(d) Measurement of Diameter

(e) Histogram and measured Texture Values

(f) Data Base Entry of Texture Features

model or discover new groups of objects, features or relations. These similar groups can be used for learning the classification model or just for understanding the domain. In the latter case the discovered information is displayed to the user on the terminal of the system. Once a new prediction model has been learnt, the rules are inserted into the image interpretation part for further automatic interpretation after approval of the user.

Besides that there is an archiving and management part that controls the whole system and stores information for long-term archiving.

Images can be processed automatically or semi-automatically. In the first case a set of images specified by the expert is automatically segmented into the background and objects of interest and for all these objects features based on the feature-extracting procedures installed in the system are automatically calculated. In this way as many features as possible are calculated, regardless of whether they make sense for a specific application or not. This requires feature-subset selection methods later on. In the second case, an image from the image archive is selected by the expert and then displayed on the monitor (Figure 3). In order to perform image processing an expert communicates with a computer. In this mode he has the option to calculate features based on the feature-extracting procedures and/or insert symbolic features based on his expert knowledge. In both modes the features are stored into the database.

CBR Image Segmentation

To ensure that the system is as flexible as possible we have installed a case-based image-segmentation procedure (Perner, 1999) into our image-analysis part.

The CBR-based image segmentation consists of a case base in which formerly processed cases are stored. A case comprises image information, non-image information (e.g., image acquisition parameters, object characteristics, and so on), and image-segmentation parameters. The task is now to find the best segmentation for the current image by looking in the case base for similar cases. Similarity determination is based on both non-image information and image information. The evaluation unit will take the case with the highest similarity score for further processing. If there are two or more cases with the same similarity score, the case that appear first will be taken. After the closest case has been chosen, the image-segmentation parameters associated with the selected case will be given to the image-segmentation unit, and the current image will be segmented. Images having similar image characteristics will show similar good segmentation results when the same segmentation parameters are applied to these images.

This procedure finds the objects-of-interest in the image and labels them. In the automatic mode the labeled objects are automatically calculated and given to the image-interpretation part, whilst in the off-line mode the found object is displayed on a monitor to the user.

Feature Extraction

The expert can calculate image features for the labeled objects. These features are composed of statistical gray level features, the object contour, square, diameter, shape (Zamperoni, 1996) and a novel texture feature that is flexible enough to describe different textures on objects (Perner, Perner, & Müller, 2002). The expert evaluates or calculates image features and stores their values in a database of image features. Each entry in the database presents features of the object of interest. These features can be numerical (calculated on the image) and symbolical (determined by the expert as a result of image reading by the expert). In the latter case the expert evaluates object features according to the attribute list, which has to be specified in advance for object description, or is based on a visual ontology available for visual content description. Then the expert feeds these values into the database.

When the expert has evaluated a sufficient number of images, the resulting database can be used for the mining process.

Decision Tree Induction Unit

The stored database can easily be loaded into the image mining tool (Figure 4).

The tool fulfills a decision-tree induction as well as case-based reasoning and clustering. Decision-tree induction allows one to learn a set of rules and basic features necessary for decision-making in a specified diagnostic task. The induction process does not only act as a knowledge-discovery process, it also works as a feature selector, discovering a subset of features that is the most relevant to the problem solution.

Decision trees partition decision space recursively into sub-regions based on the sample set. By this way the decision trees recursively break down the complexity of the decision space. The outcome has a format which naturally presents the cognitive strategy that can be used for the human decision-making process.

For any tree all paths lead to a terminal node, corresponding to a decision rule that is a conjunction (AND) of various tests. If there are multiple paths for a given class, then the paths represent disjunctions (ORs).

The developed tool allows choosing different kinds of methods for feature selection, feature discretization, pruning of the decision tree and evaluation of the error rate. It provides an entropy-based measure, a gini-index, gain-ratio and chi square method for feature selection (Perner, 2002).

The following methods for feature discretization are provided: cut-point strategy, chi-merge

Figure 4. Tool ImageMiner Version 2.1

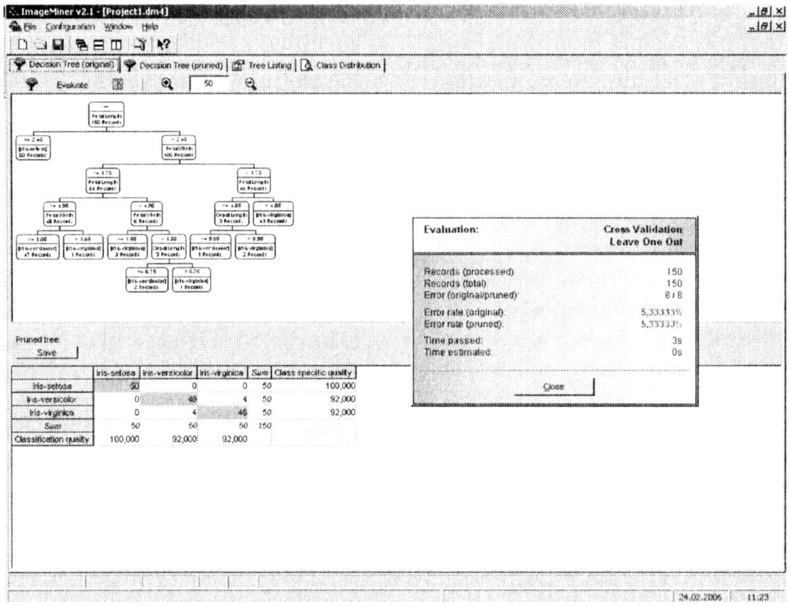

discretization, minimum description-length-principal based discretization method and lvq-based method (Perner, 2002). These methods allow one to make discretization of the feature values into two and more intervals during the process of decision-tree building. Depending on the chosen method for attribute discretization, the result will be a binary or n-ary tree, which will lead to more accurate and compact trees.

The *ImageMiner* allows one to chose between cost-complexity pruning, error-reduction-based methods and pruning by confidence-interval prediction. The tool also provides functions for outlier detections.

To evaluate the obtained error rate one can choose test-and-train and n-fold cross validation. Missed values can be handled by different strategies (Perner, 2002).

The user selects the preferred method for each step of the decision tree induction process. After that the induction experiment can start on the acquired database. A resulting decision tree will be displayed to the user. The user can evaluate the tree by checking the features used in each node of the tree and comparing them with his/her domain knowledge.

Once the diagnosis knowledge has been learnt, the rules are provided either in txt-format or XML format for further use in the image-interpretation system or the expert can use the diagnosis component of the *ImageMiner tool* for interactive work. It has a user-friendly interface and is set up in such a way that non-computer specialists can handle it very easily.

Case-Based Reasoning Unit

Decision trees are difficult to utilize in domains where generalized knowledge is lacking. But often there is a need for a prediction system even though there is not enough generalized knowledge. Such a system should (a) solve problems using the already stored knowledge and (b) capture new knowledge making it immediately available to solve the next problem. To accomplish these tasks case-based reasoning is useful. Case-based reasoning explicitly uses past cases from the domain expert's successful or failing experiences.

Therefore, case-based reasoning can be seen as a method for problem solving as well as a method to capture new experience in incremental fashion and make it immediately available for problem solving. It can be seen as a learning and knowledge-discovery approach, since it can capture from new experience some general knowledge such as case classes, prototypes and some higher level concept. We find these methods especially applicable for inspection and diagnosis tasks (Perner, 2006). In the case of these applications people rather store prototypical images into a digital image catalogues than a large set of different images.

We have developed a unit for our *ImageMiner* that can perform similarity determination between cases, as well as prototype selection and feature weighting[Cheng, 1974]. We call $x_n \in \{x_1, x_2, ..., x_n\}$ a nearest-neighbor to x if $\min d(x_i, x) = d(x_n', x)$, where i=1,2,...,n. The instance x is classified into category C_n, if x_n is the nearest neighbor to x and x_n belongs to class C_n.

In the case of the k-nearest neighbor we require k-samples of the same class to fulfil the decision rule. As a distance measure we use the Euclidean distance. Prototype Selection from a set of samples is done by Cheng's algorithm (Cheng, 1974). Suppose a training set T is given as $T = \{t^1, ..., t^m\}$. The idea of the algorithm is as follows: We start with every point in T as a prototype. We then successively merge any two closest prototypes p^1 andm p^2 of the same class by a new prototype p if the merging will not downgrade the classification of is patterns in T. The new prototype p may simply be the average vector of p^1 and p^2. We continue the merging process until the number of incorrect classifications of patterns in T starts to increase.

The wrapper approach (Wetterschererk & Aha, 1995) is used for selecting a feature subset from the whole set of features. This approach conducts a search for a good feature subset by using the k-NN classifier itself as an evaluation function. The 1-fold cross validation method is used for estimating the classification accuracy and the best-first search strategy is used for the search over the state space of possible feature combination. The algorithm terminates if we have not found an improved accuracy over the last k search states. The feature combination that gave the best classification accuracy is the remaining feature subset. After we have found

Figure 5. Concept hierachy for 2-D forms of biological objects

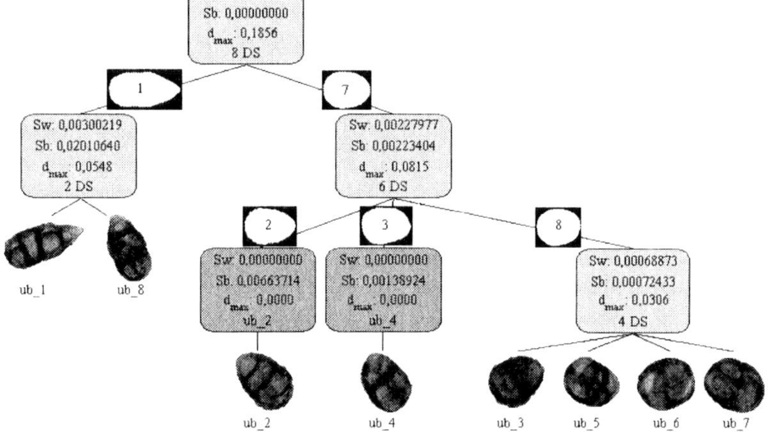

Figure 6. Procedure of the image mining process

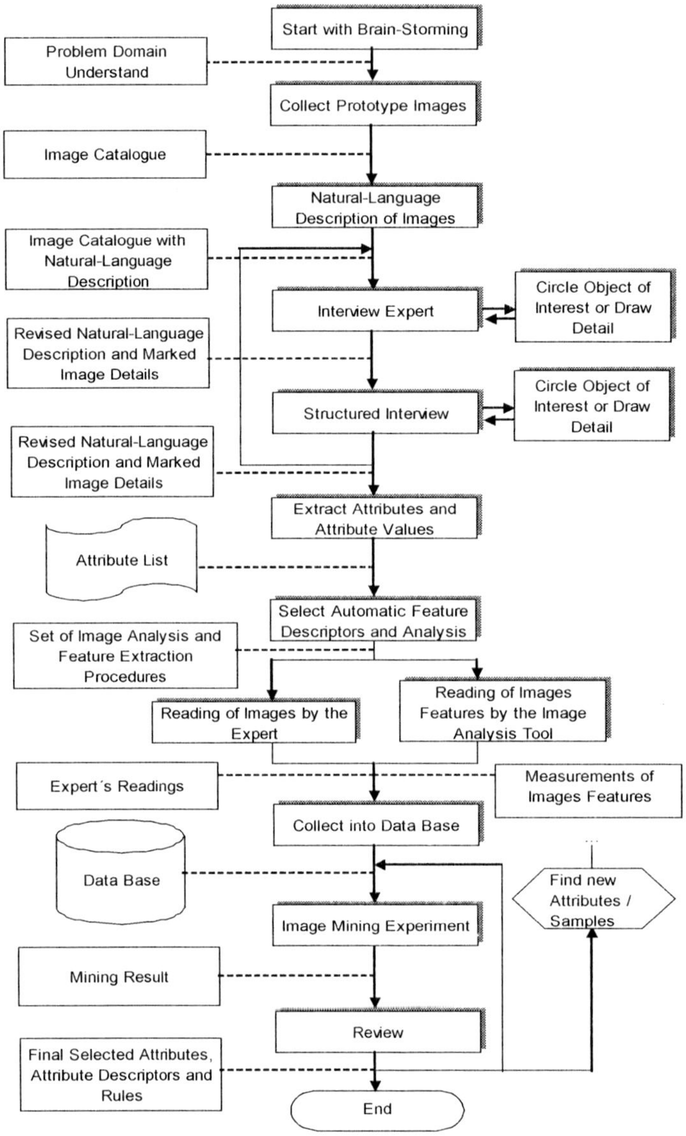

the best feature subset for our problem, we try to further improve our classifier by applying a feature weighting technique.

The weights of each feature w_i are changed by a constant value δ:w_i:=$w_i \pm \delta$. If the new weight causes an improvement of the classification accuracy, then the weight will be updated accordingly; if not, the weight will remain as it is. After the last weight has been tested the constant δ will be divided into half and the procedure repeats. The procedure terminates if the difference between the classification accuracy of two iterations is less than a predefined threshold.

Conceptual Clustering

The intention of clustering is to find groups of similar cases among the data according to the observation. This can be done based on one feature or a feature combination. The resulting groups give an idea how data fit together and how they can be classified into interesting categories.

Classical clustering methods only create clusters but do not explain why a cluster has been established. Conceptual clustering methods build clusters and explain why a set of objects forms a cluster. Thus, conceptual clustering is a type of learning by observations and it is a way of summarizing data in an understandable manner (Fisher, 1987; Gennari, Langley, & Fisher, 1989). In contrast to hierarchical clustering methods, conceptual clustering methods build the classification hierarchy not only based on merging two groups. The algorithmic properties are flexible enough to dynamically fit the hierarchy to the data. This allows incremental incorporation of new instances into the existing hierarchy and updating this hierarchy according to the new instance.

A concept hierarchy is a directed graph in which the root node represents the set of all input instances and the terminal nodes represent individual instances. Internal nodes stand for sets of instances attached to the nodes and represent a super-concept. The super-concept can be represented by a generalized representation of this set of instances such as the prototype, the mediod or a user-selected instance. Therefore a concept C, called a class, in the concept hierarchy is represented by an abstract concept description and a list of pointers to each child concept $M(C)=\{C_1, C_2, ..., C_i, ..., C_n\}$, where C_i is the child concept, called subclass of concept C.

Our conceptual clustering algorithm presented here is based on similarities (Jänichen & Perner, 2006; Perner, 2003). Due to its concept description, it explicitly supplies for each cluster a general-

Figure 7. Image catalogue and expert's description

Class	Image	Description
Fine Speckled 200 000	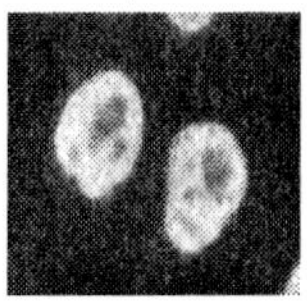	Smooth and uniform fluorescence of the nuclei Nuclei sometimes dark Chromosomes fluoresced weak up to extreme intensive
Fine dotted (speckled) nuclei fluorescence 320 200		Dense fine speckled fluorescence Background diffuse fluorescent
Homogeneous Nuclear 100 000	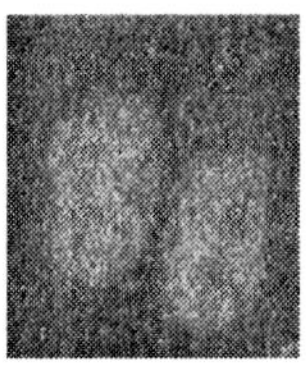	A uniform diffuse fluorescence of the entire nucleus of interphase cells. The surrounding cytoplasm is negative.
...	...	...
Centromere 500 000	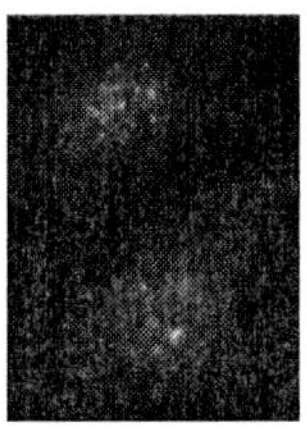	Nuclei weak uniform or fine granular, poor distinction from background

ized shape case which represents this group and a measure for the degree of its generalization. The result will be a sequence of partitions (concept hierarchy), where the root node contains the complete set of input cases and hence it follows that this node is represented by the most generalized case. The nodes in lower hierarchy levels are comprised of fewer cases (at least one) and are more specific.

In addition to *create* and *add*, we also introduced the operators *split* and *merge* into the algorithm. We prefer to apply these local operators because they preserve the incremental fashion of the algorithm. Order dependency also becomes decreased sufficiently, even it is not guaranteed that the local changes have a sufficiently strong effect on the global data.

The algorithm implements a top-down method. Initially the concept hierarchy only consists of an empty root node. A new case is placed into the actual concept hierarchy level by level, beginning with the root node until a terminal node is reached. In each hierarchy level one of these four different kinds of operations is performed:

- The new case is incorporated into an existing child node.
- A new empty child node is created where the new case is incorporated.
- Two existing nodes are merged to form a single node where the new case is incorporated.
- An existing node is split into its child nodes.

The new case is tentatively placed into the next hierarchy level by applying all of these operations. Finally that operation is performed which gives the best score to the partition according to the evaluation criteria. A proper utility function prefers compact and well- separated clusters. These are clusters with small inner-cluster variances and high inter-class variances. Thus we calculate the score of a partition comprised of the clusters $\{X_1, X_2, \ldots X_m\}$ by: $SCORE = \frac{1}{m}\sum_{i=1}^{m} p_i\,(SB_i - SW_i)$, where m is the number of clusters in this partition, p_i is the relative frequency of the i-th cluster, SB_i is the inter-cluster variance and SW_i is the inner-cluster variance of the i-th cluster. The normalization according to m is necessary to compare partitions of different size. The relative frequency p_i of the i-th cluster is: $p_i = \frac{n_i}{n}$, where n_i is the number of cases in the i-th cluster and n is the number of cases in the parent node. The inter-cluster variance of a cluster X is calculated by: $SB_X = \frac{1}{n_X}\sum_{i=1}^{n_X} d(x_i, \bar{\mu}_P)^2$, where $\bar{\mu}_P$ is the cluster centre of the parent node and x_i are the instances in all child nodes.

The output of our algorithm for applying eight exemplary shape cases of fungal strain *Ulocladium Botrytis* is shown in Figure 5. On the top level the root node is shown which comprises of all input cases. Successively the tree is partitioned into nodes until each input case forms its own cluster.

The main advantage of our conceptual clustering algorithm is that it brings along a concept description. Thus, in comparison to agglomerative clustering methods, it is easy to understand why a set of cases forms a cluster. During the clustering process the representative case, and also the variances and maximum distances in relation to this representative case are calculated, since they are part of the concept description. The algorithm is of incremental fashion, because it is possible to incorporate new cases into the existing learnt hierarchy.

THE OVERALL IMAGE MINING PROCEDURE

The whole procedure for image mining is summarized in Figure 6. It is partially based on our developed methodology for image-knowledge engineering (Perner, 1994). The process can be divided into five major steps: (1) brain storming, (2) interviewing process, (3) collection of image descriptions into the data base, (4) mining experiment and (5) review.

Brain storming is the process of understanding the problem domain and identifying the important knowledge pieces on which the knowledge-engineering process will focus.

For the interviewing process we used our developed methodology for image-knowledge engineering described in Perner (1994) in order to elicit the basic attributes as well as their attribute values. Then the proper image processing and feature-extraction algorithms are identified for the automatic extraction of the features and their values.

Table 1. Attribute list

Attribute	Code	Attribute Values
Interphase Cells	0	Undefined
	1	Fine speckled
	2	homogeneous
	3	Coarse Speckled
	4	Dense fine speckled Fluorescence
Nucleoli	0	Undefined
	1	Dark area
	2	fluoresce
Background	0	Undefined
	1	Dark
	2	Fluorescence
Chromosomes	0	Undefined
	1	Fluorescence
	2	Dark
Cytoplasm	0	Undefined
	1	Speckled Fluorescence
Classes	100 000	Homogeneous
	100 320	Homogeneous fine speckled
	200 000	Nuclear
	320 000 320 200	Fine speckled Fine speckled nuclear

Based on these results we then collected into the data base image readings done by the expert and done by the automatic image-analysis and feature-extraction tool. The resulting data base is the basis for our mining experiment. The error rate of the mining result was then determined based on sound statistical methods such as cross validation. The error rate as well as the rules were then reviewed together with the expert and depending on the quality of the results the mining process stops or goes into a second trail, starting either at the top with eliciting new attributes or at a deeper level, for example with reading new images or incorporating new image-analysis and feature-extraction procedures. The incorporation of new image-analysis and feature-extraction procedures seems to be an interactive and iterative process at the moment, since it is not possible to provide ad-hoc sufficient image-analysis procedures for all image features and details appearing in the real world. The mining procedure stops as soon as the expert is satisfied with the results.

A CASE STUDY

The Application

We will describe the usage of the image-mining tool based on the task of HEp-2 cell classification. HEp-2 cells are used for the identification of antinuclear autoantibodies (ANA). They allow the recognition of over 30 different nuclear and cytoplasmic patterns which are given by upwards of 100 different autoantibodies. The identification of these patterns has up to now been done manually by a human inspecting the slides with the help of a microscope. The lacking automation of this technique has resulted in the development of alternative techniques based on chemical reac-

Figure 8. Excerpt from database

Class	Contour (Kontur)	Area	Shape Factor (Form)	MEAN	VAR	SKEW	CURT	VC	ENERGY	...	NUCLEOLI	CHROMO	CYTOPLA (Zytopla)	Background (Hintergrund)	
100000	14,3734	14,3189	144,2812	87,1507	244,3043	1,1233	7,5139	0,1793	0,0209	...	1	1	0	1	
100320	10,3675	7,2986	147,2687	144,6974	282,0444	-0,6999	2,4243	0,1161	0,0238	...	1	0	0	0	
320200	11,9142	9,4348	150,4512	132,5286	675,6562	0,1685	-0,5039	0,1961	0,0119	...	2	0	0	1	
200000	9,0332	5,2114	156,5795	94,5199	1400,9983	0,6564	-0,3728	0,3960	0,0100	...	2	0	0	1	
...	...	...	...	...	...	...	...	...	...	...	...	...	...	...	

Figure 9. Decision tree obtained from expert's readings

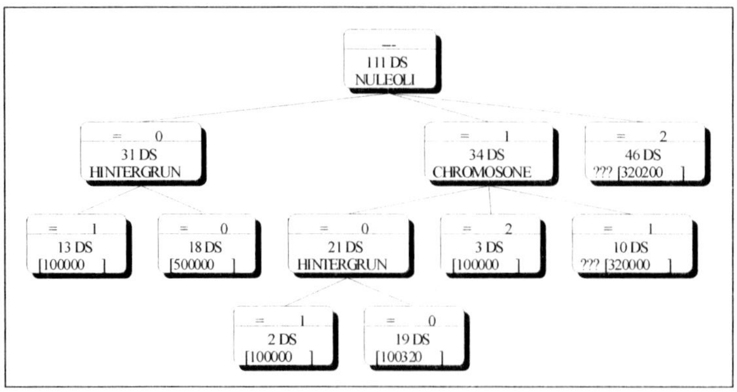

tions, which do not have the discrimination power of the ANA testing. An automatic system would pave the way for a wider use of ANA testing.

Recently, the various HEp-2 cell images occurring in medical practice are being collected into a data base at the university hospital of Leipzig. The images were taken by a digital image-acquisition unit consisting of a microscope AXIOSKOP 2 from Carl Zeiss Jena, coupled with a color CCD camera Polariod DPC. The digitized images were of 8-bit photometric resolution for each color channel with a per pixel spatial resolution of 0.25 μm. Each image was stored as a color image on the hard disk of the PC but is transformed into a gray-level image before being used for automatic image analysis.

The scope of our work was to mine these images for proper classification knowledge, so that it can be used in medical practice for diagnosis or for teaching novices. Besides that it should give us the basis for the development of an automatic image-diagnosis system.

Our experiment was supported by an immunologist who is an expert in the field and acts as a specialist to other laboratories in case of diagnostically complex cases.

Brainstorming and Image Catalogue

First, we started with a brain storming process that helped us to understand the expert's domain and to identify the basic pieces of knowledge. We could identify mainly four pieces of knowledge: Hep-2 cell atlas, the expert, slide preparation and a book describing the basic parts of a cell and their appearance.

Then the expert collected prototype images for each of the six classes appearing most frequently in his daily practice. The expert wrote down a natural-language description for each of these images. As a result we obtained an image cataloge having a prototype image for each class and associated to each image is a natural-language description of the expert (see Figure 7).

Interviewing Process

Based on these image descriptions we started our interviewing process. First, we only tried to understand the meaning of the expert description in terms of image features. We let the individual circle the interesting object in the image to understand the meaning of the description. After having done this, we went into a structured interviewing process asking for specific details such as: "Why do you think this object is *fine-speckled* and the other one is not. Please describe the difference between these two." It helped us to verify the expert description and to make the object features more distinct.

Finally, we could extract from the natural-language description the basic vocabulary (attributes and attribute values, see Table 1) and associate the meaning to each attribute.

In a last step we reviewed the chosen attributes and the attribute values with the expert and found a common agreement on the chosen terms. The result was an attribute list which is the basis for the description of object details in the images. Furthermore, we identified from the whole set of feature descriptors the set of a feature descriptors which might be useful for the objective measurement of image features. In our case we found that describing the cells by their boundary and calculating the size and the contour of the cell might be appropriate. The different descriptors of the nuclei of the cells might be sufficiently described by the texture descriptor of our image-analysis tool.

Collection of Image Descriptions into the Data Base

Now we could start to collect a data base of image descriptions based on these attributes and attribute values as well as on feature measurements calculated with the help of the image-analysis tool. For our experiment we used a dataset of 110 images.

The dataset contained 6 classes, each equally distributed. For each class we had 20 images. The expert used the image-analysis tool shown in Figure 3 and displayed one after another each image from our data base. He watched the images on display and described the image content on the basis of our attribute list and fed the attribute values into the data base. Besides that he marked the objects of interest in the image on display and used the necessary feature descriptors selected during the interviewing process and provided by the image-analysis unit to measure the image features such as size, contour, and texture. The resulting values for these features are automatically fed into the data base and stored together with the expert's image description into the data base (see Figure 8).

The Image Mining Experiment

The collected dataset was then given to the tool *ImageMiner*. The decision-tree induction algorithm that showed the best results on this dataset is based on the entropy-criterion for the attribute selection, cut-point strategy for the attribute discretization and minimal error-reduction pruning. We carried out three experiments. First, we learnt a decision tree only based on the image reading by the expert, then learnt a decision tree only based on the automatic calculated images features, and finally, we learnt a decision tree based on a data base containing both feature descriptions. The resulting decision tree for the expert's reading is shown in Figure 9 and the resulting decision tree for the expert's reading together with the measured image features is shown in Figure 10. We do not show the tree for the measured image features, since the tree is too complex. The error rate was evaluated by leave-one-out cross-validation.

The error rate of the decision trees from the first two experiments is higher than the error rate made by the expert (see Table 2). None of the trees, whether based on the expert's reading or based on the measured image features, give a sufficiently low error rate. Only the combined data base from the expert's reading and measured image features gives us an error rate that comes close to an expert's error rate.

Review

The tree created based on the image readings from the expert has an error rate of 27.9% (see Table 2). Under the assumption that the class labels represent the true class (gold standard), we can only conclude that there is a knowledge gap. There must be some hidden knowledge which the expert is using during decision making, but the expert could not make this knowledge explicit during the interviewing process. Here we have an example for the problem "difference between showing and naming" mentioned in the second section. However, the expert's error rate is also high.

Table 2. Error rate for decision trees obtained from the different databases

	Error Rate		
Data Set	**Expert**	**Unpruned Tree**	**Pruned Tree**
Original Data Set	25 %		
Expert Readings		27 %	27 %
Automatic Feature Analysis		27 %	27 %
Combined Data Set		6,9 %	6,9 %

Our first objection was: Is the assumption that the class label is the true class label true or not? As far as we know the chemical investigation of the serum which was used to determine the gold standard does not so accurately discriminate between the different classes.

The experiment based on the features automatically measured in the images gives us no better results. The resulting tree is very bushy and deep and uses almost all attributes.

Only the combination between the expert's readings and the readings by the image-analysis unit shows us reasonable results. The feature nucleoli is the most important feature and the correct description of the nucleoli will improve the results dramatically. During the image-analysis phase we did not describe this object separately. The hope was that the texture descriptor for the whole cell is sensitive enough to model the different visual appearances of the different cells. The experiment shows that only the combination of basic image descriptors from the image analysis with expert reading gave sufficient results. Therefore, we believe that our first objection concerning the true class label does not hold any more. We rather think that in order to improve the accuracy of the classifier we must find a good feature descriptor for the different appearances of the object nucleoli.

LESSONS LEARNED

We have found out that our methodology of data mining allows a user to learn the decision model and the relevant diagnostic features. A user can independently use such a methodology of data mining in practice. The user can easily perform different experiments until the user is satisfied with the result. By practicing this, the user can explore the application and find out the connection between different knowledge pieces.

However, some problems should be taken into account for the future system design.

As we have already pointed out in a previous experiment (Perner, 2000), an expert tends to specify symbolic attributes by means of a large number of attribute values. For example in this experiment the expert specified for the attribute "margin" 15 attribute values such as "non-sharp," "sharp," "non-smooth," smooth," and so on. A large number of attribute values will result in small sub-sample sets soon after the tree-building

Figure 10. Decision tree obtained from expert's readings and image readings

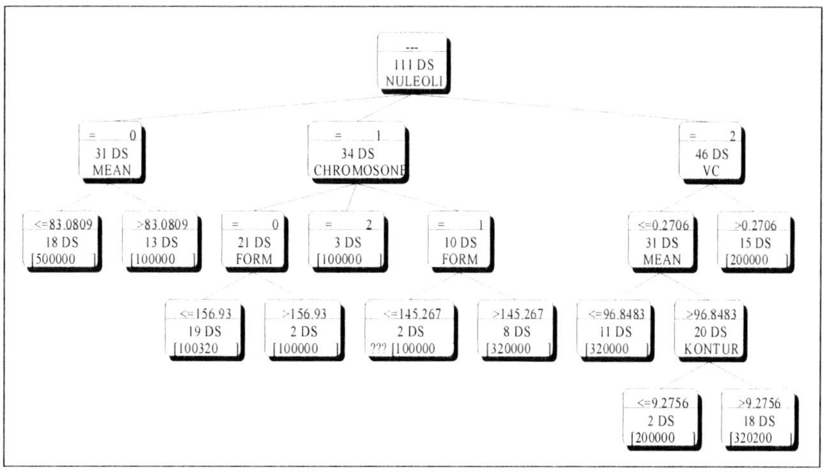

process started. It will result in a fast termination of the tree-building process. This is also true for small sample sets that are usual in medicine. Therefore, a careful analysis of the attribute list should be done after the physician has specified it.

During the process of building the tree, the algorithm picks the attribute with the best attribute-selection criteria. If two attributes have both the same value, the one that appears first in the attribute list will be chosen. That might not always be the attribute the expert himself would choose. In order to avoid this problem, we think that in this case we should allow the expert to choose manually the attribute that the expert prefers. We expect that this procedure will bring the resulting decision model closer to the expert's ones.

The developed image-analysis tool allows extracting image features (see the fourth section). It supported the analysis and exploration of other image-diagnosis tasks, such as the analysis of sheep follicle and lymph nodule analysis. It proved to be very useful for the analysis of microscopic images of different cell-based assays. New applications might require further feature descriptors. Therefore the image-analysis tool must have an open architecture that allows incorporating new feature descriptors into the tool.

The described method of image mining had been applied to a wide range of applications. This includes the analysis of sheep follicle based on a texture descriptor, evaluation of imaging effects of radiopaque material for lymph-nodule analysis, mining knowledge for IVF therapy, transplantation medicine, and inspection of microscopic images of cell-based assays and for the diagnosis of breast carcinoma in MR images. In all these tasks we did not have a well-trained expert. These were new tasks and reliable decision knowledge had not been built up in practice yet. The physicians did the experiments by themselves. They were very happy with the obtained results, since the learnt rules gave them deeper understanding of their problems and helped to predict new cases. It helped the physicians to explore their data and inspired them to think about new improved ways of diagnosis. In some of the tasks we were able to build an automatic image-interpretation system based on the discovered visual features and knowledge.

Compared to our first version of the image-mining tool the new features of case-based image segmentation, case-based reasoning and clustering gave a new flexibility to the image mining process depending on the characteristics of the data of the particular application. The clustering method allowed discovering new groups according to the considered observation(s) that could be used further for the construction of the prediction model. Case-based image segmentation gave the flexibility needed to discover objects of interest in different image modalities and qualities. In the case of rare data or image catalogues case-based reasoning was the right method to construct a decision model and acquire new images in incremental fashion.

CONCLUSION AND FURTHER WORK

In this chapter we have presented our methods and the methodology for image mining. Based on that, we built our system *ImageMiner Version 2.1.* This tool has shown excellent performance for a wide range of image-mining tasks. The basis for the image mining experiment is a sufficiently large database with images, feature description and/or expert descriptions. Such databases result for example from the broad use of image databases in many fields.

We were able to learn the important attributes needed for image interpretation and to understand the way in which these attributes were used for decision-making by applying data-mining methods to the database of image descriptions. We showed how the domain vocabulary should be set up to get good results and which techniques should be used in order to check the reliability of the chosen features.

The explanation capability of the induced tree was reasonable. The attributes included into the tree represented the expert knowledge. Finally, we can say that image-archiving systems in a combination with image-mining methods open a possibility for advanced computer-assisted diagnosis-system development.

We have recently been going on to apply the system to video microscopy and develop more feature extractions and image-mining procedures that can further support the image-mining process.

REFERENCES

Bhanu, B., & Dong, A. (2001). Concepts learning with fuzzy clustering and relevance feedback. In P. Perner (Ed.), *Machine learning and data mining in pattern recognition* (pp. 102-116). Berlin; Heidelberg: Springer-Verlag.

Bouguila, N., & Ziou, D. (2005). MML-based approach for finite dirichlet mixture estimation and selection. In P. Perner (Ed.), *Machine learning and data mining in pattern recognition* (pp. 42-52). Berlin; Heidelberg: Springer-Verlag.

Burl, M. C., & Lucchetti, D. (2000) Autonomous visual discovery. In B. V. Dasarathy (Ed.), *Data mining and knowledge discovery: Theory, tools, and technology, Proceedings of SPIE* (Vol. 4057, pp. 240-250).

Chang, C. L. (1974). Finding prototypes for nearest neighbor classifiers. *IEEE Transactions on Computers, C-23*(11), 1179-1184.

Eklund, P. W., You, J., & Deer, P. (2000). *Mining remote sensing image data: An integration of fuzzy set theory and image understanding techniques for environmental change detection*. In B. V. Dasarathy (Ed.), Data mining and knowledge discovery: Theory, tools, and technology, Proceedings of SPIE (Vol. 4057, pp. 265-273).

Fisher, D. H. (1987). Knowledge acquisition via incremental conceptual clustering. *Machine Learning, 2*(2), 139-172.

Fischer, S., & Bunke, H. (2001). Automatic identification of diatoms using decision forests. In P. Perner (Ed.), *Machine learning and data mining in pattern recognition* (pp. 173-183). Berlin; Heidelberg: Springer-Verlag.

Gennari, J. H., Langley, P., & Fisher, D. H. (1989). Models of incremental concept formation. *Artificial Intelligence, 40*(1-3), 11-61.

Giacinto, G., & Roli, F. (1999). Automatic design of multiple classifier systems by unsupervised learning. In P. Perner & M. Petrou (Eds.), *Machine learning and data mining in pattern recognition* (pp. 131-143). Berlin; Heidelberg: Springer-Verlag.

Imiya, A., & Ootani, H. (2001). PCA-based model selection and fitting for linear manifolds. In P. Perner (Ed.), *Machine learning and data mining in pattern recognition* (pp. 278-292). Berlin; Heidelberg: Springer-Verlag.

Indurkhya, N., & Weiss, S. M. (2001). Rule-based ensemble solutions for regression. In P. Perner (Ed.), *Machine learning and data mining in pattern recognition* (pp. 62-72). Berlin; Heidelberg: Springer-Verlag.

Jahn, H. (1999). Unsupervised learning of local mean gray values for image processing. In P. Perner & M. Petrou (Eds.), *Machine learning and data mining in pattern recognition* (pp. 64-74). Berlin; Heidelberg: Springer-Verlag.

Jänichen, S., & Perner, P. (2006). Conceptual clustering and case generalization of 2-dimensional forms. *International Journal of Computational Intelligence, 22*(3-4), 177-193.

Kehoe, A., & Parker, G. A. (1991). An IKB defect classification system for automated industrial radiographic inspection. *IEEE Expert Systems, 8*, 149-157.

Malerba, D., Esposito, F., Lanza, A., & Lisi, F. A. (2001). First-order rule induction for the recognition of morphological patterns in topographic maps. In P. Perner & M. Petrou, (Eds.), *Machine learning and data mining in pattern recognition* (pp. 88-101). Berlin; Heidelberg: Springer Verlag.

Matsuo, Y., Amano, M., & Uehara, K. (2002). Mining video editing rules in video streams. *ACM Multimedia*, 255-258.

Martinez, J. (2001). *Overview of the MPEG-7 Standard* (version 5.0), ISO/IEC JTC1/SC29/WG11 N4031, Singapore. Retrieved October 19, 2006, from http://www.cselt.it/mpeg/standards/mpeg-7/mpeg-7.htm

Megalooikonomou, K., Davatzikos, C., & Herskovits, E. (1999). Mining lesion-defect associations in a brain image database. In *Proceedings from the International Conference Knowledge Discovery and Data Mining (KDD99)*, San Diego, CA (pp. 347-351).

Palenichka, R. M., & Volgin, M. A. (1999). Extraction of local structural features in images by using a multi-scale relevance function. In P. Perner & M. Petrou (Eds.), *Machine learning and data mining in pattern recognition* (pp. 87-102). Berlin; Heidelberg: Springer-Verlag.

Perner, P. (1994). A knowledge-based image inspection system for automatic defect recognition, classification, and process diagnosis. *International Journal on Machine Vision and Applications, 7*, 135-147.

Perner, P. (1998). Case-based reasoning for the low-level and high-level unit of an image interpretation system. In S. Singh (Ed.), *Advances in pattern recognition* (pp. 45-54). Berlin; Heidelberg: Springer-Verlag.

Perner, P. (1999). An architeture for a CBR image segmentation system. *Engineering Applications of Artificial Intelligence, 12*(6), 749-759.

Perner, P. (2000). Mining knowledge in medical image databases. In B. V. Dasarathy (Ed.), *Data mining and knowledge discovery: Theory, tools, and technology, Proceedings of SPIE* (Vol. 4057, pp. 359-369).

Perner, P., Zscherpel, U., & Jacobsen, C. (2001). A comparison between neural networks and decision trees based on data from industrial radiographic testing. *Pattern Recognition Letters, 2*, 47-54.

Perner, P., Perner, H., & Müller, B. (2002). Mining knowledge for Hep-2 cell image classification. *Journal Artificial Intelligence in Medicine, 26*, 161-173.

Perner, P. (2002). *Data mininig on multimedia data.* Berlin; Heidelberg: Springer-Verlag.

Perner, P. (2003). Incremental learning of retrieval knowledge in a case-based reasoning system. In K. D. Ashley & D. G. Bridge (Eds.), *Case-based reasoning—Research and development* (pp. 422-436). London: Springer-Verlag.

Perner, P. (2005). Case-based reasoning for image analysis and interpretation. In C. H. Chen & P. S. P. Wang (Eds.), *Handbook of pattern recognition and computer vision* (3rd ed., pp. 95-114). World Scientific Publishing.

Perner, P. (in press). A comparative study of catalogue-based classification. In *Proceedings ECCR 2006.* Berlin; Heidelberg.

Petrushin, V. A. (2005). Mining rare and frequent events in multi-camera surveillance video using self-organizing maps. In *Proceedings of KDD2005* (pp. 794-800).

Satyanarayana, A., & Davidson, I. (2005). A dynamic adaptive sampling algorithm (DASA) for real world applications: Finger print recognition and face recognition. In M.-S. Hacid, N. V. Murray, Z. W. Ras, & S. Tsumoto (Eds.), *Foundations of intelligent systems* (pp. 631-640). New York: Springer-Verlag.

Schmidt, R., & Gierl, L. (2001). Temporal abstraction and case-based reasoning for medical course data: Two prognostic applications. In P. Perner (Ed.), *Machine learning and data mining in pattern recognition* (pp. 23-33). Berlin; Heidelberg: Springer Verlag.

Schröder, S., Niemann, H., & Sagerer, G. (1988). Knowledge acquisition for a knowledge-based image analysis system. In J. Bosse & B. Gaines (Eds.), *Proceedings of the European Knowledge-Acquisition Workshop EKAW 88*, Sankt Augustin.

Sivic, J., & Zisserman, A. (2004). Video data mining using configurations of viewpoint invariant regions. *Computer Vision and Pattern Recognition, 1*, 488-495.

Wettschereck, D., & Aha, D. W. (1995). Weighting features. In M. M. Veloso & A. Aamodt (Eds.), Case-based reasoning research and development (pp. 347-358). Berlin; Heidelberg: Springer-Verlag.

Zhu, X., Wu, X., Elmagarmid, A. K., Feng, Z., & Wu, L. (2005). Video data mining: Semantic indexing and event detection from the association perspective. *IEEE Transaction on Knowledge and Data Engineering, 17*(5), 665-677.

Zaiane, O. R., & Han, J. (2000) Discovery spatial associations in image. In B. V. Dasarathy (Ed.), *Data mining and knowledge discovery: Theory, tools, and technology* (pp. 138-148).

Zamperoni, P. (1996). Feature extraction. In H. Maitre & J. Zinn-Justin (Eds.), *Progress in picture processing* (pp. 121-184). Elsevier Science.

Chapter VI
A Successive Decision Tree Approach to Mining Remotely Sensed Image Data

Jianting Zhang
University of New Mexico, USA

Wieguo Liu
University of Toledo, USA

Le Gruenwald
University of Oklahoma, USA

ABSTRACT

Decision trees (DT) has been widely used for training and classification of remotely sensed image data due to its capability to generate human interpretable decision rules and its relatively fast speed in training and classification. This chapter proposes a successive decision tree (SDT) approach where the samples in the ill-classified branches of a previous resulting decision tree are used to construct a successive decision tree. The decision trees are chained together through pointers and used for classification. SDT aims at constructing more interpretable decision trees while attempting to improve classification accuracies. The proposed approach is applied to two real remotely sensed image datasets for evaluations in terms of classification accuracy and interpretability of the resulting decision rules.

INTRODUCTION

Compared with statistical and neural/connectionist approaches to classification of remotely sensed image data, decision trees (DT) have several advantages. First of all, there is no presumption of data distribution in DT. Second, since DT adopts a divide-and-conquer strategy, it is fast in training and execution. Most importantly, the resulting classification rules are presented in a tree form. Paths from the root to leaf nodes can easily be transformed into decision rules (such as

Copyright © 2007, IGI Global, distributing in print or electronic forms without written permission of IGI Global is prohibited.

if *a*>10 and *b*<*20* then Class 3), which is suitable for human interpretation and evaluation. In the past years, DT has gained considerable research interests in analysis of remotely sensed image data, such as automated knowledge-base building from remote sensing and GIS data (Huang & Jensen, 1997), land cover classification (Friedl & Brodley, 1997), soil salinity analysis (Eklund, Kirkby, & Salim, 1998), change detection in an urban environment (Chan, Chan, & Yeh, 2001), building rule-based classification systems for remotely sensed images (Lawrence & Wright, 2001) and knowledge discovery from soil maps (Qi & Zhu, 2003). In particular, DT has been employed for global land cover classifications at 8km spatial resolution (De Fries, Hansen, Townshend, & Sohlberg, 1998) using NOAA AVHRR data. Interestingly, DT has also been adopted as the primary classification algorithm to generate global land cover maps from NASA MODIS data (Friedl et al., 2002) where spatial and radiometric attributes have been significantly improved.

In ideal situations, each leaf node contains a large number of samples, the majority of which belongs to one particular class called the dominating class of that leaf node. All samples to be classified that fall into a leaf node will be labeled as the dominating class of that leaf node. Thus the classification accuracy of a leaf node can be measured by the number of the actual samples of the dominating class over all the samples in its leaf node. However, when there are no dominating classes in the leaf nodes, class labels are assigned based on simple majority vote and, hence, the decision tree nodes have low classification accuracy.

While DT has gained considerable applications, the resulting decision trees from training datasets could be complex due to the complex relationship between features and classes. They are often the mixtures of the branches with high and low classification accuracies in an arbitrary manner and are difficult for human interpretation. In this study, we propose to apply DT multiple times to a training dataset to construct more interpretable decision trees while attempting to improve classification accuracy. The basic idea is to keep classification branches of a resulting decision tree that have high classification accuracy while combining samples that are classified under branches with low classification accuracy into a new training dataset for further classifications. The process is carried out in a successive manner and we term our approach as successive decision tree (SDT). For notation purposes, we also term classic DT as CDT.

The heuristics behind the expectation that SDT can increase classification accuracy are based on the following observation. There are samples in a multi-class training dataset, although their patterns may be well perceived by human, they are small in sizes and are often assigned to various branches during the classification processes according to information entropy gain or gain ratio criteria. At some particular classification levels, the numbers of the samples may be below predefined thresholds in decision tree branches to be qualified as a decision tree leaf node with high classification accuracy, thus the splitting processes stop and they are treated as noises. On the other hand, if we combine these samples into a new dataset, since the distribution of the new dataset may be significantly different from the original one, meaningful classification rules may be derived in a new decision tree from the new dataset. By giving some samples a second chance to be correctly classified, the overall accuracy may be improved. The heuristics will be further illustrated through an example in "The Method" section.

The proposed SDT method is different from existing meta-learning approaches that are applied to DT, such as the boosting (Freund & Schapire, 1997) DT approach (Friedl, Brodley, & Strahler, 1999; Pal & Mather, 2003). Boosting DT gives higher weights to the samples that have been misclassified in a previous process but uses all the samples in all the classification processes. Boosting DT does not aim at generating interpretable decision rules. In contrast, the proposed SDT approach generates compact decision rules from decision tree branches with high classification accuracy; only samples that cannot be generalized by decision rules with high classification accuracy are combined for further classifications. By saying "generalize" we mean fitting samples into the leaf nodes of decision tree branches (i.e., decision rules).

This chapter is arranged as follows. In the section "The Method," we present the proposed SDT approach which begins with a motivating example and is followed by the algorithm description. In "Experiments," we test SDT using two real remotely sensed datasets and demonstrate SDT's capability in generating compact classification rules and improving classification accuracy. "Discussion" is dedicated to the discussions of several parameters involved in SDT. Finally, the last section is "Summary and Conclusion."

THE METHOD

In this section, we will first introduce the principles of decision tree using the example shown in Figure 1. We then use the example to demonstrate the effectiveness of the proposed SDT approach and finally we present the algorithm.

The Decision Tree Principle

The decision tree method recursively partitions the data space into disjoint sections using impurity measurements (such as information gain and gain ratio). For the sake of simplicity, binary partition of feature space is adopted in implementations, such as J48 in WEKA (Witten & Frank, 2000). Let $f(C_i)$ be the count of class i before the partition and $f(C_i^1)$ and $f(C_i^2)$ be the counts of class i in each of the two partitioned sections, respectively. Further let C be the total number of classes, $n=\sum_{i=1}^{C} f(c_i)$, $n_1=\sum_{i=1}^{C} f(c_i^1)$, and $n_2=\sum_{i=1}^{C} f(c_i^2)$, then the information entropy before the partition is defined as $e=-\sum_{i=1}^{C}\frac{f(c_i)}{n}*\log(\frac{f(c_i)}{n})$. Correspondingly the entropies of the two partitions are defined as $e_1=-\sum_{i=1}^{C}\frac{f(c_i^1)}{n_1}*\log(\frac{f(c_i^1)}{n_1})$ and $e_2=-\sum_{i=1}^{C}\frac{f(c_i^2)}{n_2}*\log(\frac{f(c_i^2)}{n_2})$, respectively. The overall entropy after the partition is defined as the weighted average of e_1 and e_2, that is,

$$entropy\_partition=\frac{n_1}{n}*e_1+\frac{n_2}{n}*e_2$$

The information gain then can be defined as:

$$entropy\_gain=e-entropy\_partition$$

The gain ratio is defined as:

$$gain\_ratio=\frac{entropy\_gain}{entropy\_partition}$$

For the example shown in Figure 1a, there are 24 samples in the two dimensional data space (x,y) and 3 classes represented as the black circle, square and triangle, the sizes of which are 10, 10 and 4, respectively. We use x and y as two features for classification. For notational convenience, the pure regions in the data space are numbered 1 though 8 as indicated by the white circles in Figure 1a.

Suppose the minimum number of samples in each of the decision tree branches is four. The largest information gain is obtained when partitioned at $x\leq3$ (root partition) according to the partition principle. For the left side of the root partition, the largest information gain is obtained when partitioned at $y\leq3$ where the top part is a pure region which does not require any further partition. Unfortunately, the three classes have equal portions in the lower part of the partition (x≤3, y≤3) and the further partitions at (x≤1, y≤3) and (x≤2, y≤3) result in the same information gain. The similar situation happens to the right part of the root partition (x>3).

If we prune the resulting decision tree and only keep the partition at the root, then any samples in section x≤3 will be classified as class 1 (represented as black circles in Figure 1a), with a classification accuracy of 8/12=67% since the dominating class 1 has 8 samples while there are 12 samples in section x≤3. However, if we prune the resulting decision tree at level 2, then any samples in section x≤3 and y≤3 will be assigned to one of the three classes arbitrarily chosen. The classification accuracy in the resulting section will be only 2/6=33%. The same low classification accuracy also happens to the samples in section 4≤x<6 and y≤3 if pruned at level 2. In the meantime, the decision rule (2<x≤4, 2<y≤4)➔class 3 (represented as black triangles) with 100% classification accuracy is missed in CDT.

The Motivating Example

In Figure 1, if we determine that the two level-2 sections (1≤x<4, 1≤y<3) (i.e., the combinations of regions 3, 4 and 5) and (4≤x<6 and 1≤y<3) (i.e., the combinations of regions 6, 7 and 8) do not meet our classification accuracy expectation, they can be removed from the resulting decision tree (T_1), and the samples that fall into the sections can be combined into a new dataset for further classification. The new resulting decision tree (T_2) can successfully find the decision rule (2<x≤4, 2<y≤4)➔class 3 (represented as black triangles) that is missed by the CDT approach. The extra cost of the SDT approach is to have the nodes in T_1 that represent the sections with low classification accuracies point to the root of T_2, which is rather simple in programming languages (such as Java or C/C++). In this chapter, we use T_i' to denote the modified decision tree of T_i. All T_i' form a tree chain and we term it as SDT chain. Note that the last decision tree in a

Figure 1. Example to illustrate the CDT and SDT approaches: (a) sample data, (b) resulting CDT tree, (c) resulting SDT tree

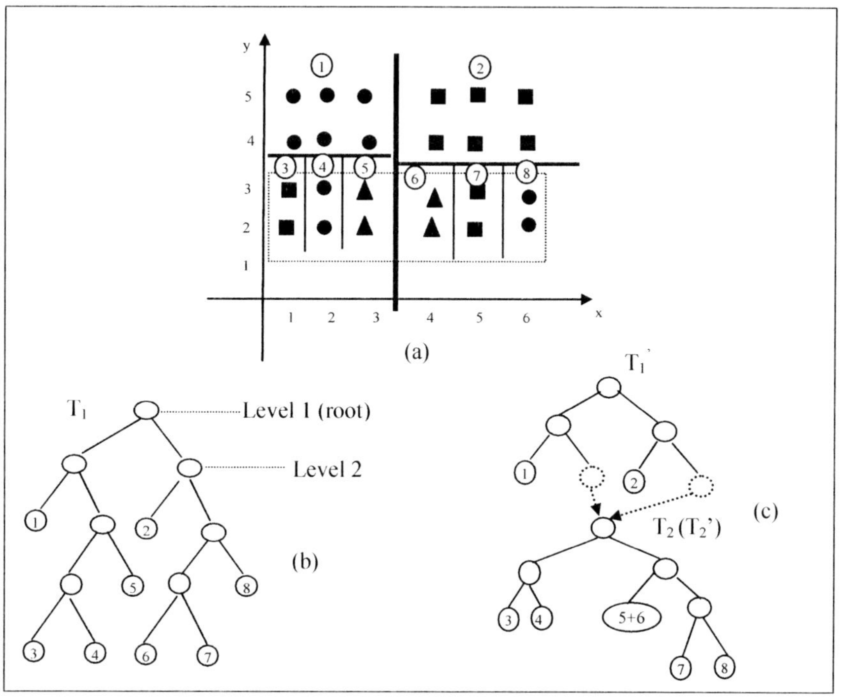

SDT chain (T_k') is the same as its corresponding original decision tree (T_k) since no modification is performed. In Figure 1c, T_2' is the same as T_2 since it is the last decision tree in the SDT tree chain and no branches are removed any more. We next compare CDT and SDT approaches based on the example in terms of classification accuracy and tree interpretability.

To comply with the practices in classifying remotely sensed image data, we measure the classification accuracy based on the percentage of testing samples that are correctly classified using the resulting classic decision tree (CDT) or tree chain (SDT). For testing the example in Figure 1, we use the training dataset also as the testing dataset since all the samples have been used as the training data (we will use separate training and testing data in the experiments using real datasets). We measure the classification accuracy as the ratio of number of correctly classified samples over the number of samples under a decision tree node (leaf or non-leaf). In the example, if we set the minimum number of objects to 2, both SDT and CDT achieve 100% accuracy. However, if we set the minimum number of objects to 4, CDT achieves 16/24=66.7% accuracy and SDT achieve 20/24=83.3% accuracy. The corresponding resulting DTs and accuracies of their leaf nodes are shown in Figure 2. From the results we can see that SDT achieves much higher accuracy than CDT (83.3% vs. 67.7%). Meanwhile, more tree nodes with dominating classes, that is, more meaningful decision rules, are discovered.

To the best of our knowledge, there are no established criteria to evaluate the interpretability of decision trees. We use the number of leaves and the number of nodes (tree size) as the measurements of the compactness of a decision tree. We assume that a smaller decision tree can be better interpreted. For the full CDT tree and SDT tree shown in Figure 1, CDT has 8 leaves and 15 nodes. By omitting the nodes that only have a pointer (or a virtual node), the first level of SDT tree has 2 leaves and 5 nodes and the second level of SDT tree has 5 leaves and 9 nodes. Each of the two trees is considerably smaller than the CDT tree. While we recognize that there are multiple trees in a SDT tree chain, we argue that, based on our experiences, multiple smaller trees are easier to interpret than a big tree.

In addition, contrary to CDT trees where branches are arranged in the order of construction without considering their significances, the resulting SDT trees naturally leveraged decision branches with high classification accuracy to the

Figure 2. Accuracy evaluations of the example resulting (a) CDT tree, (b) SDT tree

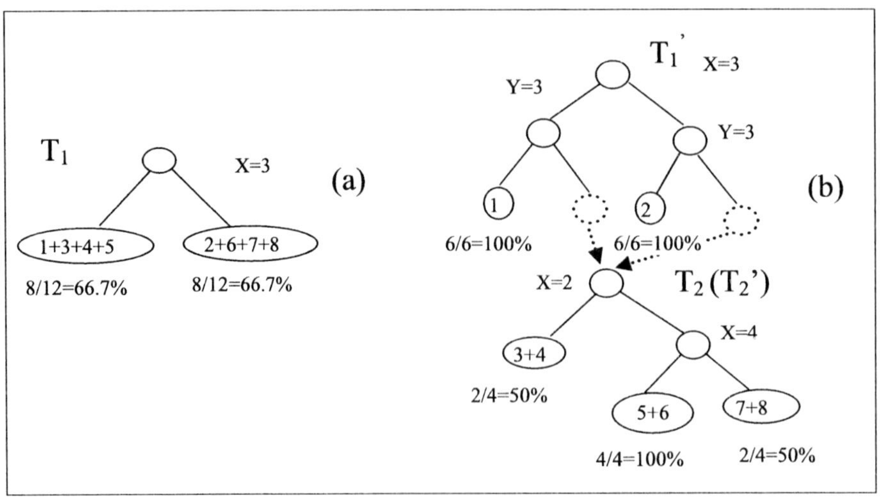

top and can catch user's attention immediately. Figure 3 shows the resulting CDT and SDT trees in text format corresponding to those of Figure 1(b) and 1(c). The dots ("...") in Figure 3 (b) denote the pointers to the next levels of the SDT tree. We can see that the two most significant decision rules (x<=3, y>3)→1 and (x>3, y>3)→2 are buried in the CDT tree while they are correctly identified in the first decision tree of the SDT tree chain and presented to users at the very beginning of the interpretation process.

While not being able to show the advantages in terms of classification accuracy and tree interpretability at the same time, the motivating example demonstrates the ideas of our proposed approach. By removing decision tree branches with low classification accuracies, combining the training samples under the branches into a new dataset and then constructing a new decision tree from the derived dataset, we can build a decision tree chain efficiently by successively applying the decision tree algorithm on the original and derived datasets. The resulting decision tree chain potentially has the advantages of being simple in presentation forms, having higher classification accuracy and sorting decision rules according to their significances for easy user interpretations. We next present the SDT approach as a set of algorithms. The algorithms are implemented in the WEKA open source data mining toolkit (Witten et al., 2000).

Figure 3. Resulting trees in text format of the example (a) CDT tree, (b) SDT tree

```
x <= 3
| y <= 3
| | x <= 1: 2 (2.0)
| | x > 1
| | | x <= 2: 1 (2.0)
| | | x > 2: 3 (2.0)
| y > 3: 1 (6.0)
x > 3
| y <= 3
| | x <= 4: 3 (2.0)
| | x > 4
| | | x <= 5: 2 (2.0)
| | | x > 5: 1 (2.0)
| y > 3: 2 (6.0)
```

(a)

```
x <= 3
| y <= 3 ...
| y > 3: 1 (6.0)
x > 3
| y<=3 ...
| y > 3: 2 (6.0)
```

```
x <= 1: 2 (2.0)
x > 1
| x <= 4
| | x <= 2: 1 (2.0)
| | x > 2: 3 (4.0)
| x > 4
| | x <= 5: 2 (2.0)
| | x > 5: 1 (2.0)
```

(b)

The Algorithm

The SDT algorithm adopts the same divide-and-conquer strategy and can use the same information entropy measurements for partitioning as those of the CDT algorithms. Thus the structure of the SDT algorithm is similar to that of CDT. The overall control flow of SDT is shown in Figure 4. The algorithm repeatedly calls Build_Tree to construct decision trees while combing samples that cannot be generalized into new datasets (D) for further classifications. SDT will terminate under three conditions: (1) the predefined maximum number of classifications (i.e., the length of the SDT tree chain) is reached, (2) the number of samples to be used to construct a decision tree is below a predefined threshold, and (3) the newly combined dataset is the same as the one in the previous classification, which means no samples can be used to generate meaningful decision rules during this round. In all the three cases, if there are still samples that need to be classified, they are sent to CDT for final classification.

The function Build_Tree (Figure 5) recursively partitions a dataset into two and builds a decision tree by finding a partition attribute and its partition value that gives the largest information gain. There are several parameters used in function Build_Tree. Min_obj1 specifies the number of samples to determine whether the branches of a decision tree should be considered to stop or continue partitioning. min_obj2 specifies the minimum number of samples for a branch to be qualified as having high classification accuracy. Min_accuracy specifies the percentage of samples of the dominating classes. While the purposes of setting min_obj1 and min_accuracy are clear, the purpose of setting min_obj2 is to prevent generating small branches with high classification accura-

Figure 4. Overall control flow of SDT algorithm

Algorithm SDT (P, *max_cls, min_obj, min_obj1, min_obj2, min_accuracy*)
Inputs:

- A training sample table (*P*) with *N* samples, each sample has *M* attributes (number of bands of the image to classify) and a class label
- Two global thresholds: number of maximum classifier (*max_cls*), the minimum number of samples needed to add a new DT to the SDT chain (*min_obj*)
- Three thresholds local to each DT in a SDT chain: the number of samples to determine whether the branches of a DT should be considered to stop or continue partitions (*min_obj1*), the minimum number of samples in a branch (*min_obj2*), and the percentage of the samples of a class in branches that can be considered as dominating (*min_accuracy*)

Output:

- A chain of successive decision trees begins with tree *T*

1. Set loop variable *i*=1
2. Set data set *D*=*P*, tree *T*=NULL, tree *root*=NULL
3. Do while (*i*< *max_cls*)
   a. Set data set *D'*={}
   b. Call *T'*=*Build_Tree* (*i, D, D',min_obj1, min_obj2, min_accuracy*)
   c. If (*T* is not NULL)
      i. Call *Chain_Tree*(*T, T'*)
      ii. *T*=*T'*
   d. Else
      root=*T'*
   e. If (*D'*==*D* || |*D'*|< *min_obj*) then break
   f. *D*=*D'*
   g. *i*=*i*+1
4. If |*D*|>0
   a. Call *T'*=*Classic_DT*(*D*)
   b. Call *Chain_Tree*(*T*,*T'*)
5. Return *root*

Figure 5. Algorithm Build_Tree

Algorithm *Build_Tree* (*seq, D, D', min_obj1, min_obj2, min_accuracy*)
Inputs:

- *Seq*: sequence number of the DT in the SDT chain
- *D'*: new data set combining ill-classified samples
- *D, min_obj1, min_obj2, min_accuracy*: same as in function *SDT* in Fig. 4

Output:

- The *seq*[th] decision tree in the SDT chain

1. Let *num_corr* be the number of samples of the dominating class
2. if(|*D*|< *min_obj1*[*seq*])
   a. If (*num_corr*>|*D*|* *min_accuracy*[*seq*]) and |*D*|> *min_obj2*[*seq*])
      i. Mark this branch as high accuracy branch (no need for further partition) and assign the label of the dominating class to the branch
      ii. Return NULL
   b. Else
      i. Mark this branch as low accuracy branch
      ii. Merge *D* into *D'*
      iii. Return NULL
3. else
   a. if (*num_corr*>|*D*|* *min_accuracy*[*seq*])
      i. Mark this branch as high accuracy branch (no need for further partition) and assign the label of the dominating class to the branch
      ii. Return NULL

//begin binary partition

4. For each of the attributes of *D*, find partition value using *entropy_gain* or *gain_ratio*
5. Find the partitioning attribute and its partition value that has largest *entropy_gain* or *gain_ratio*
6. Divide *D* into two partitions according to the partition value of the attribute, *D1* and *D2*
7. Allocate the tree structure to *T*
8. *T.left_child*= *Build_Tree*(*seq*+1,*D1, D', min_obj1, min_obj2, min_accuracy*)
9. *T.right_child*= *Build_Tree*(seq+1,*D2, D', min_obj1, min_obj2, min_accuracy*)
10. return *T*

cies in hope that the samples that fall within the branches can be used to generate more significant decision rules by combining with similar samples in the other branches. For example, in Figure 1a, region 5 and region 6, although both have only two samples of the same class, can be combined to generate a more significant branch in a new decision tree as shown in Figure 1c.

Build_Tree stops under three conditions. The first condition is that the number of samples in the dataset is below min_obj1, and there is a dominating class in the dataset (the ratio of the number of dominating samples to the number of samples is greater than min_accuracy), and the number of the samples is above min_obj2, then this branch has high classification accuracy and no further classification is necessary. The second condition is that the number of samples in the dataset is below min_obj1, and either the branch does not have a dominating class or the number of samples is below min_obj2, then the samples will be sent to further classification in the next decision tree in the SDT tree chain and this tree building process is stopped. The third condition is that the number of samples in the dataset is above min_obj1 and there is a dominating class in the dataset, then this branch also has high classification accuracy and no further classification is necessary. Guidelines to choose the values of these parameters are discussed in the section "Choosing Parameters."

Function Chain_Tree is relatively simple (Figure 6). Given a decision tree T, it recursively finds the branches that are removed due to low classification accuracy (or ill-classification branch) and makes the branches pointing to the new decision tree (c.f., Figure 1).

Given the first decision tree (T) of a SDT tree chain, the algorithm for classifying an instance I is given in Figure 7 which is a combination of recursive and chain-following procedures.

Figure 6. Algorithm Chain_Tree

```
Algorithm Chain_Tree (T,T')
Input:
•   Two successive decision trees T and T'

1.  If T is a leaf node
      If T is marked as a low classification confidence node
        i.Set T.next=T'
        ii.Return
2.  if(T.left_child is not NULL)
        Chain_Tree(T.left_child,T')
3.  if(T.right_child is not NULL)
        Chain_Tree(T.right_child,T')
```

Figure 7. Algorithm Classify_Instance

```
Algorithm Classify_Instance (T, I)
Input:
•   A SDT begins with decision tree T
•   An instance I with M attributes
Output:
•   Class label of I

 1.  If T is a leaf node
     a. If T is marked as a high classification confidence node
           i.  Assign the class label of T to I
           ii.   Return
     b.    Else if T is marked as a low classification confidence node
             Return Classify_Instance (T.next, I)
 2.  Else
     a. Let A be the partitioning attribute and V be the partition value
     b. If(I[A]<=V) then
           Return Classify_Instance(T.left_child, I)
     c. Else
           Return Classify_Instance(T.right_child, I)
```

Starting from the root of T, it uses the partitioning attribute and the partition value to decide whether to go to the left or right branches of T. This procedure is carried out recursively until a leaf node is reached. If the leaf node represents a branch with high classification accuracy then the class label of the branch will be assigned to the instance; otherwise the branch will point to the next decision tree in the SDT tree chain and the classification will be passed to the next decision tree by following the link.

EXPERIMENTS

We report the experimental results from two real remote sensing image datasets: the land cover dataset and the urban change detection dataset. For each experiment, we report the data source, thresholds used in the experiment, the comparisons of the accuracies and the interpretability of the decision trees result from J48 implementation of CDT (Witten et al., 2000) and SDT. Note that we use separate datasets for training and testing when measuring classification accuracy according to practices in remotely sensed image classification.

The first dataset is relatively simple with a small number of class labels. Since its classification accuracy using CDT is already high and the space to improve classification accuracy is limited, the primary purpose of the experiment is to demonstrate the SDT's capability to generate compact decision trees for easier interpretations. The second dataset is relatively complex with a large number of classes. Due to the complexities of the datasets and the resulting decision trees, it is impossible to present and visually examine the results and, thus, our focus on the second experiment is classification accuracy. Since the primary purpose is to compare the two methods, CDT and SDT, in terms of accuracy and interpretability, the presentations of final classified images are omitted.

Experiment 1: Land Cover Data Set

The dataset is obtained from LandSat ETM+ 7 satellite and was acquired on August 31, 2002. It covers the coast area in the greater Hanoi-Red River Delta region of northern Vietnam. Six bands are used and there are six classes: mangrove, aquaculture, water, sand, ag1 and ag2. We evenly divide the 3262 samples into training and testing datasets. The training parameters are shown in Table 1 and the classification accuracies of SDT are shown in Table 2. Note that the last decision tree is a classic decision tree (c.f., Figure 4) and its parameters are set by J48 defaults. In Table 2, DT# means the sequence number of a decision tree in its SDT tree chain, "Last" means the last decision tree in the SDT tree chain. The overall accuracy is computed as the ratio of the number of correctly classified samples by all the decision trees in the SDT tree chain over the number of samples to be classified. The resulting decision trees of CDT and SDT are shown in Figure 8. The default values for the required parameters in J48 are used for constructing the CDT tree except that the minNumObj is changed from 2 to 10 to accommodate the resulting tree in one page for illustration purposes.

The overall accuracy of SDT is 90.56%, which is about 2% higher than that of CDT (88.78%). The first decision tree in the SDT tree chain, which has 12 leaf nodes (rules), generalized 67.7% of the total samples with more than 96% purity. The numbers of leaves and the tree sizes of the five decision trees in the SDT tree chain are listed in Table 3. From the table we can see that the number of leaves and the tree size in each of the decision trees of the SDT tree chain is significantly smaller than that of the CDT decision tree. Visual examinations indicate that the resulting smaller decision trees of the SDT tree chain are significantly easier to interpret than the big CDT decision tree (c.f., Figure 8). This experiment shows that while SDT may not be able to improve classification accuracies signifi-

Table 1. SDT parameters for land cover data set

DT #	min_accuracy	Min-NumObj1	Min-NumObj2
0	0.95	30	20
1	0.90	25	15
2	0.85	20	10
3	0.80	15	5

Table 2. SDT classification results for land cover data set

DT #	#of samples to classify	# of correctly classified samples	Accuracy (%)
0	1089	1047	96.14
1	196	175	89.26
2	100	89	89.00
3	97	75	77.32
Last	149	91	61.07
Overall	1631	1477	90.56

Table 3. Comparisons of decision trees from SDT and CDT for land cover data set

DT #	# of Leaves	Tree Size
0	12	40
1	8	28
2	6	23
3	7	20
Last	11	21
CDT	35	69

cantly when CDT already has high classification accuracy, it has the capability to generate more compact and interpretable decision trees.

Experiment 2: Urban Change Detection Data Set

The dataset consists of 6222 training samples and 1559 testing samples. Each sample has 12 attributes: 6 bands from a TM image during winter time (December 10, 1988) and 6 bands from another TM image during spring time (March 3, 1996), both from a southern China region located between 21° N and 23° N and crossed by the Tropic of Cancer (Seto & Liu, 2003). The resulting decision trees are too complex to present in this chapter due to space limitation. The parameters and classification accuracies of SDT are shown in Table 4 and Table 5, respectively. The overall accuracy of SDT is 80.24%, which is more than 4% higher than that of CDT (76.01%), a significant improvement.

Similar to experiment 1, we also list the numbers of leaves and tree sizes of the decision trees of the SDT and CDT in Table 4. The number of leaves and tree sizes in the SDT tree are reduced even further: they are only about 1/10 of those of the CDT. Even the totals of the numbers of leaves and tree sizes in the five decision trees in the SDT tree chain are only about half of those of the CDT. While it is possible to prune a CDT to reduce its number of leaves and tree size, usually this can only be achieved at the cost of classification accuracy, which is not desirable in the application context. On the other hand, the SDT approach

Figure 8. Decision trees from CDT and SDT for the land cover data set

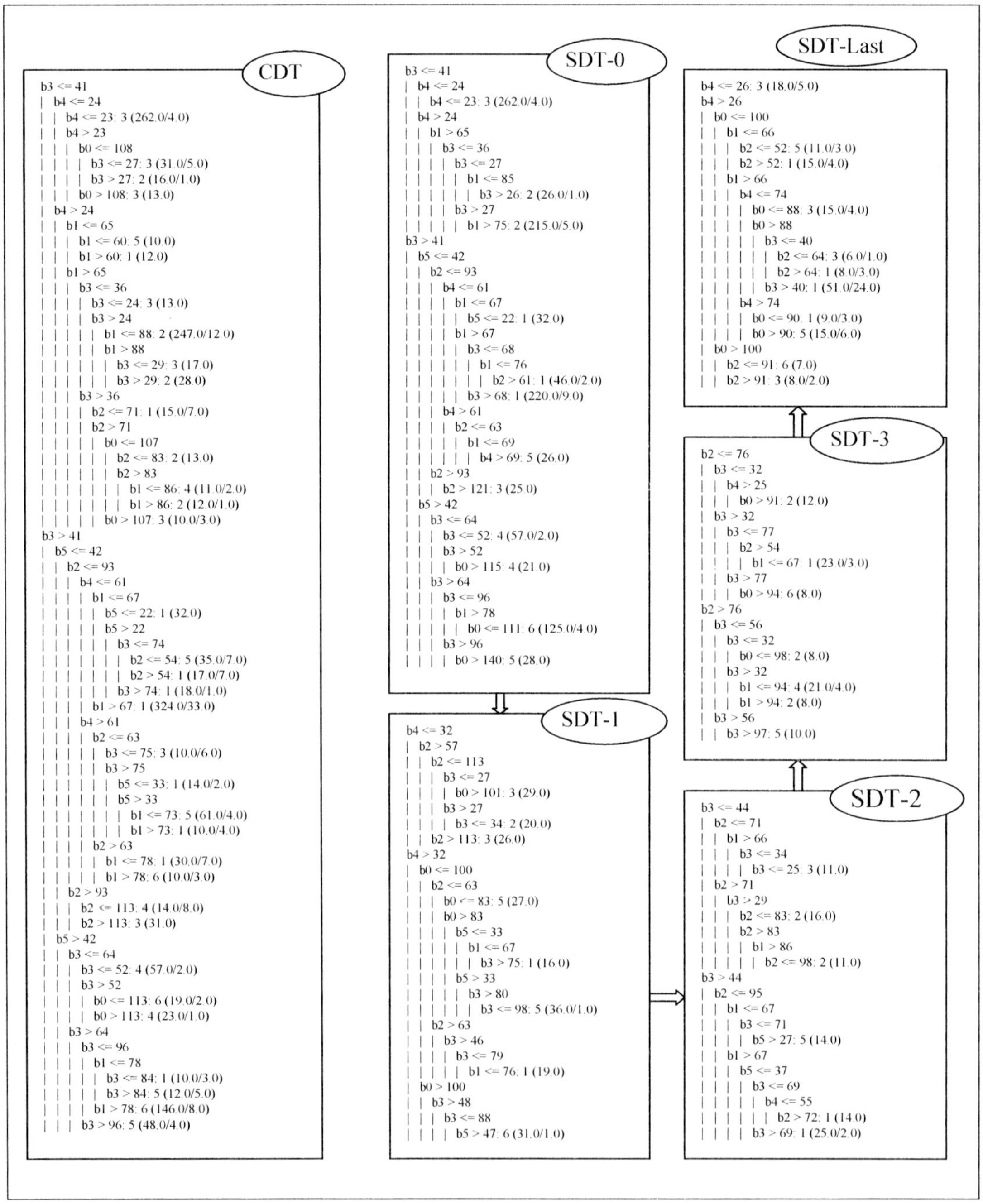

Table 4. SDT parameters for urban change detection data set

DT #	min_accuracy	Min-NumObj1	Min-NumObj2
0	0.95	50	20
1	0.85	40	15
2	0.75	30	10
3	0.65	20	5

Table 5. SDT classification results for urban change detection data set

DT #	#of samples to classify	# of correctly classified samples	Accuracy(%)
0	968	892	92.15
1	266	160	60.15
2	171	107	62.57
3	130	86	66.15
Last	24	6	25.00
Overall	1559	1251	80.24

Table 6. Comparisons of decision trees from SDT and CDT for urban change data set

DT #	# of Leaves	Tree Size
0	31	104
1	22	71
2	18	61
3	25	55
Last	10	19
CDT	284	567

reduces the number of leaves and tree size while increasing classification accuracy.

DISCUSSION

Limitations of SDT

The proposed SDT approach does have a few limitations. First, although the two experiments show favorable increases of classification accuracy, there is no guarantee that the SDT can always increase classification accuracy. This is especially true when the CDT already has high classification accuracy. In this case, the first decision tree in a SDT tree chain has the capability to generalize most of the samples. The samples fed to the last decision tree of the SDT tree chain are likely to be mostly noise samples and cannot be generalized well by the last decision tree in the SDT tree chain. Depending on the setting of the thresholds used in SDT, the SDT may achieve lower classification accuracies. However, we argue that the importance of improving classification accuracy decreases as the classification accuracy increases and the interpretability of resulting decision trees increases. In this respect, the SDT is still valuable in finding significant classification rules from the CDT which could be too complex for direct human interpretation. The second major limitation is that, there are five parameters, which can affect SDTs classification accuracies and structures of decision trees in the SDT tree chain, need to be fine tuned. This will be discussed in details in the next sub-section. Finally, the SDT approach inherits several disadvantage of the CDT, such as being hungry for training samples due to its divide-and-conquer strategy. For training datasets with a small number of samples but with complex classification patterns, the classification of the SDT may not be as good as those of connectionist approaches, such as neural network.

Choosing Parameters

There are five parameters used in the SDT approach: the maximum number of classifiers (max_cls), the minimum number of samples needed to add a new decision tree to the SDT tree chain (min_obj), the number of samples to determine whether the branches of a decision tree should be considered to stop or continue partitioning (min_obj1), the minimum number of samples (min_obj2) and the percentage (min_accuracy) of the samples of a class in branches that can be considered as dominating (c.f., Figure 4 and Section 2.3). As pointed out, max_cls and min_obj are global and the rest three parameters are local to each of the decision trees in a SDT tree chain.

The most significant parameter might be the min_accuracy values of each decision tree in a SDT tree chain. If the first few min_accuracy values are set to high percentages, many branches in the corresponding decision trees will not be able to be qualified as high classification accuracy and samples that fall within these branches will need to be fed to the next decision trees, which in turn requires larger max_cls to deplete all significant decision rules. On the other hand, using higher min_accuracy values generate decision branches that are higher in classification accuracies and smaller in numbers.

For min_obj1 and min_obj2, it is clear that min_obj1 needs to be greater than min_obj2. The larger min_obj1, the earlier to check whether to further partition a decision tree branch. Once the number of samples is below min_obj1, the branch will be either marked as having high classification accuracy or marked as need to be processed in the next decision tree of the SDT tree chain, depending on min_accuracy and min_obj2. A larger min_obj1, together with a higher min_accuracy, will let SDT to find larger decision branches that are high in classification accuracy and smaller in number, and are more likely to send samples to the next decision trees of the SDT tree chain, which in turn requires larger max_cls to deplete all significant decision rules. For example, considering a dataset that consists of 100 samples and can be partitioned into 2 sections, each has 50 samples. Assume min_accuracy=0.95. If there are 94 samples of dominating classes and the two sections with each having 48 and 46 samples of dominating classes, respectively. If min_obj1 = 100, then all the samples will be sent to the next decision tree in the SDT tree chain. On the other hand, if min_obj1 = 50, then only the samples of one of the branches needs to be sent to the next decision tree in the SDT tree chain. With a reduced min_accuracy of the next decision tree in the SDT tree chain, these samples alone may be generalized as a significant decision rule. Consider another scenario where min_accuracy = 0.90, the branch will be marked as having high classification accuracy and no samples will be sent to the next decision tree in the SDT tree chain.

The parameter min_obj2 is more related to determining the granularity of "noises" in a particular decision tree. A smaller min_obj2 means that fewer branches, the samples of which are almost of the same class (>min_accuracy) but are small in size, will be considered as unclassifiable in the current decision tree and sent to the next decision tree in the SDT tree chain. This also means that the number of decision trees in the SDT chain is smaller but the number of branches in each of the DTs is larger. Some of the bottom level branches generalize only a small number of samples.

The two global parameters, min_obj and max_cls, are used to determine when to terminate the SDT algorithm. They play less significant roles than min_obj1, min_obj2 and min_accuracy. If min_obj is set to smaller values, the first one or two decision trees will be able to generalize most of the samples into decision rules and no significant decision rules can be generalized from the samples combined from their ill-classified branches (i.e., terminate condition 3). In this case, the SDT algorithm terminates but does not involve min_obj and max_cls. Most likely, min_obj is involved in terminating the SDT algorithm only when most of the samples are generalized by the previous decision trees and only very few samples are needed to be sent to the next decision tree in the SDT chain while max_cls has not been reached yet (i.e., terminate condition 2). Max_cls becomes a constraint only when users intend to generate fewer rules but with high classification accuracies by using larger min_obj, min_obj2 and min_accuracy values (i.e., terminate condition 1).

Finally we provide the following guidelines in setting the parameter values based on our experiences.

- max_cls: 5-10
- min_obj: min{50, 5% of number of training samples}
- For two successive decision trees in the SDT chain, min_obj1[i]>min_obj1[i+1], min_obj2[i]>min_obj2[i+1], min_accuracy[i]>min_accuracy[i+1]. We recommend using min_obj1[i+1]=0.8* min_obj1[i], min_obj2[i] =0.8*min_obj2[i+1] and min_accuracy[i+1]=min_obj1[i]-5% as the initial values for further manual adjustments.
- For each of the decision trees in the SDT chain, min_obj1> min_obj2. We recommend using min_obj1=2.5*min_obj2 as the initial values for further manual adjustments.

SUMMARY AND CONCLUSION

In this study we proposed a successive decision tree (SDT) approach to generating decision rules from training samples for classification of remotely sensed images. We presented the algorithm and discussed the selection of parameters needed for SDT. The two experiments using ETM+ land cover dataset and TM urban change detection dataset show the effectiveness of the proposed SDT approach. The classification accuracy increases slightly in the land cover classification experiment where the classification accuracies are already high for CDT. The classification accuracy in the urban change detection experiment increases about 4% which is considerably significant. In addition, in both experiments, each of the decision trees in the SDT chains is considerably more compact than the decision trees generated by CDT. This gives users an easier interpretation of classification rules and may possibly associate machine learning rules with physical meanings.

REFERENCES

Chan, J. C. W., Chan, K. P., & Yeh, A. G. O. (2001). Detecting the nature of change in an urban environment: A comparison of machine learning algorithms. *Photogrammetric Engineering and Remote Sensing, 67*(2), 213-225.

De Fries, R. S., Hansen, M., Townshend, J. R. G., & Sohlberg, R. (1998). Global land cover classifications at 8 km spatial resolution: The use of training data derived from Landsat imagery in decision tree classifiers. *International Journal of Remote Sensing, 19*(16), 3141-3168.

Eklund, P. W., Kirkby, S. D., & Salim, A. (1998). Data *mining and soil salinity analysis. International Journal of Geographical Information Science, 12*(3), 247-268.

Freund, Y., & Schapire, R. E. (1997). A decision-theoretic generalization of on-line learning and an application to boosting. *Journal of Computer and System Sciences, 55*(1), 119-139.

Friedl, M. A., & Brodley, C. E. (1997). Decision tree classification of land cover from remotely sensed data. *Remote Sensing of Environment, 61*(3), 399-409.

Friedl, M. A., Brodley, C. E., & Strahler, A. H. (1999). Maximizing land cover classification accuracies produced by decision trees at continental to global scales. *IEEE Transactions on Geoscience and Remote Sensing, 37*(2), 969-977.

Friedl, M. A., McIver, D. K., Hodges, J. C. F., Zhang, X. Y., Muchoney, D., Strahler, A. H., et al. (2002). Global land cover mapping from MODIS: Agorithms and early results. *Remote Sensing of Environment, 83*(1-2), 287-302.

Huang, X. Q., & Jensen, J. R. (1997). A machine-learning approach to automated knowledge-base building for remote sensing image analysis with GIS data. *Photogrammetric Engineering and Remote Sensing, 63*(10), 1185-1194.

Lawrence, R. L., & Wright, A. (2001). Rule-based classification systems using classification and regression tree (CART) analysis. *Photogrammetric Engineering and Remote Sensing, 67*(10), 1137-1142.

Pal, M., & Mather, P. M. (2003). An assessment of the effectiveness of decision tree methods for land cover classification. *Remote Sensing of Environment, 86*(4), 554-565.

Qi, F., & Zhu, A. X. (2003). Knowledge discovery from soil maps using inductive learning. International *Journal of Geographical Information Science, 17*(8), 771-795.

Seto, K. C., & Liu, W. G. (2003). Comparing ARTMAP neural network with the maximum-likelihood classifier for detecting urban change. *Photogrammetric Engineering and Remote Sensing, 69*(9), 981-990.

Witten, I. H., & Frank, E. (2000). *Data mining: Practical machine learning tools with Java implementations.* San Francisco: Morgan Kaufmann.

Section V

Data Mining and Business Intelligence

Chapter VII
The Business Impact of Predictive Analytics

Tilmann Bruckhaus
Numetrics Management Systems, USA

ABSTRACT

This chapter examines the business impact of predictive analytics. It argues that in order to understand the potential business impact of a predictive model, an organization must first evalute the model with technical metrics, and then interpret these technical metrics in terms of their financial business impact. This chapter first reviews a set of technical metrics which can assist in analyzing model quality. The remaining portion of the chapter then shows how to combine these technical metrics with financial data to study the economic impact of the model. This know-how is used to illustrate how a business can choose the best predictive model from among two or more candidate models. The analysis techniques presented are illustrated by various sample models from the domains of insurance fraud prevention and predictive marketing.

INTRODUCTION

Metrics of financial business impact such as ROI and net profit are the key to success with predictive analytics in real world applications. Yet, current practices do not focus on such metrics and instead employ what may be termed "technical metrics." As we will see, technical metrics tell an organization little about whether a predictive model will benefit the organization. This chapter will review these topics, explain the difference between financial business impact metrics and technical metrics, and show how financial business impact metrics can be calculated with little effort. Throughout the chapter, we will illustrate the use of technical and financial business impact metrics with running examples in the areas of insurance fraud prevention and predictive marketing.

Copyright © 2007, IGI Global, distributing in print or electronic forms without written permission of IGI Global is prohibited.

The academic community has created an awesome arsenal of tremendously useful machine learning algorithms. However, when working with predictive modeling technology, the needs in academia and the commercial sector are different. The academic community strives to bring about and demonstrate algorithmic improvements, whereas the business community must generate financial profits. Algorithms are often designed by researchers to work across a wide variety of application areas. This makes it difficult to analyze the financial business impact because financial impacts vary greatly from one business context to the next. Because of this difficulty, and in order to allow for objective analysis of algorithms, a variety of benchmark datasets have been established. New algorithms are tested against these benchmarks, and researchers have developed metrics for analyzing model quality which can be applied in the absence of financial considerations. When data mining algorithms are then transferred into the business community the same technical metrics are transferred along with the algorithms. Practitioners in the business world are then able to evaluate predictive models developed with the available technical metrics. The dilemma is that, as we will see, these technical metrics do not answer the one question business practitioners need to answer: will this model have a beneficial impact on my business?

There are many types and versions of technical metrics of the quality of predictive models. Some of these are *accuracy, precision, top k precision, false alarms, recall, sensitivity, missed alarms, specificity, selectivity*, and we will review each of these in turn. As we introduce some of these technical metrics we will describe how each metric can be useful in a business context. Another group of technical metrics of model quality are based on graphical analysis of model performance, such as lift chart, gain chart, and even measurements of the size of the area under a geometric curves known as receiver operating characteristic (ROC). These chart-based metrics are out of the scope of this chapter and the reader is referred to other texts on data mining for more information on these. Some good texts on data mining technology are Berry and Linoff (1997), Han and Kamber (2005), Mitchell (1997), Quinlan (1993), Soukup and Davidson (2002), and Witten and Frank (2005).

Table 1. Overview of sample models discussed in this chapter; the calculation and meaning of the data presented will be discussed in the following sections

	Outcome Distribution and Information Entropy	Accuracy	Precision	Recall	Model Strategy
M_1^{Fraud}	Skewed H(X)=0.021	98.0%	40.0%	66.7%	Maximize business impact
M_2^{Fraud}	Skewed H(X)=0.021	98.5%	undefined	0.0%	Always predict negative
M_3^{Fraud}	Balanced H(X)=1.0	50.0%	undefined	0.0%	Always predict negative
M_4^{Fraud}	Skewed H(X)=0.021	50.0%	1.5%	50.0	Predict randomly
M_5^{Fraud}	Skewed H(X)=0.021	98.5%	100.0%	.7%	Maximize precision

After exploring these technical metrics we will turn to the analysis of the financial business impact of predictive models. We will show how an organization can collect required data, compute the expected financial impact for a given model, determine whether a model in question will benefit or harm an organization, and select the best model from a selection of alternative candidate models. Nonprofit organizations face a somewhat different situation in that they are not focused on financial profits. Therefore, nonprofits may find it harder to apply financial impact evaluation techniques. However, it appears that when non-profits apply predictive analytics it is often in areas which are indeed also measured in dollars and cents, such as when predictive marketing technology is used for selecting contacts for mailing requests for donations, or when the United States Internal Revenue Service (IRS) uses predictive analytics to select tax returns for audits. In other cases it may be possible to translate specific objectives into dollar terms, or to use non-financial metrics of organizational impact. For example, a quantitiative value could be assigned to different levels of member satisfaction, or to citizen health.

As we review technical metrics of the quality of predictive models we will consider a variety of sample models and calculate various quality metrics for each. Table 1 serves as a reference point for this set of sample models.

TECHNICAL METRICS

There are two key steps to analyzing the business impact of predictive models: first, understanding technical metrics of model quality, and second, interpreting technical metrics with respect to business impact. In the remainder of this chapter, we will first review technical metrics, and then describe how these metrics can be used for busines impact analysis.

The Table of Confusion

Before we turn to the various technical metrics, we must study the table of confusion which is the basis for several technical metrics. The table of confusion consists of two rows and two columns that compare true outcomes for cases to predicted outcomes. Customarily, the terms "positive" and "negative" are used to distinguish the two possible true outcomes, as well as for distinguishing the two possible predicted outcomes. The true outcomes are referred to as "positive cases" and "negative cases," whereas predictions are classified as "positive predictions" and "negative predictions." The terms "positive" and "negative" can be confusing at times. For example, in a manufacturing quality control procedure the goal may be to predict defective parts to prevent shipping these, and in this application, defective parts are usually labeled as "positive cases" although the term defect clearly has a negative connotation. The reasoning behind this convention is that positive cases and positive predictions relate to situations where a case or a prediction belongs to the abnormal or unusual class that the analyst is trying to identify.

All of the technical metrics reviewed here are derived from four basic metrics: *true negatives*, *true positives*, *false positives*, and *false negatives*. A table which shows these four metrics is known as a "*table of confusion*," "*truth table*," or "*evaluation matrix*." As shown in the Table 2, the terms *true negatives*, *false positives*, *false negatives*, and *true positives* are usually abbreviated as *TN*, *FP*, *FN*, and *TP*. In statistics, false positives are known as *type I errors*, and false negatives are known as *type II errors*. In manufacturing applications the terms *manufacturer's risk* and *consumer's risk* relate to quality control procedures where gadgets that are predicted to be defective are scrapped by the manufacturer while items thought to be functional are shipped to the consumer. The term manufac-

Table 2. Table of confusion: Shown are the four fundamental technical metrics of quality for predictive models; they are identified by their common abbreviation, their formal name, and any other commonly used names

	Predicted Negative	**Predicted Positive**
Negative Cases	TN True Negatives	FP False Positives Type I Error
Positive Cases	FN False Negatives Type II Error False Alarms Manufacturer's Risk	TP True Positives

turer's risk refers to cases where the manufacturer scraps false positives and so incurs an unnecessary loss. In other words, the manufacturer carries the risk for false positives. Conversely, when a false negative part is shipped then the consumer will receive a faulty part, and the consumer carries the risk associated with false negatives. As a matter of convention it is helpful to follow some formatting guidelines when creating a table of confusion. The rows show *truth* and the columns show *predictions*, and in rows and columns the negative cases come first, followed by the positive cases. This convention facilitates reading the table of confusion at a glance by making it easier to locate cells of interest. The standardized format is also helpful in remembering that type I errors are shown in the upper row and type II errors in the lower table row.

To create a table of confusion, the true outcome as well as the predicted outcome for each case must be known. Typically, it is costly to determine the true outcome for a large number of cases. In order to to understand why this is so, note that the task of determining true outcomes can be accomplished in one of two ways, depending on the nature of the business process. Either each case must be evaluated manually, or each case must be tracked to record its eventual outcome. For example, in an insurance fraud prediction application the true outcome as to the potential fraudulent nature of each case may never become known unless it is investigated by an expert. On the other hand, in a predictive marketing application, manual investigation of each case is not a practical option, and instead one must wait until each recipient of a mailing has either responded or not responded. For this reason, it is helpful to define a positive outcome with a time limit. For example: "A marketing mailing case is considered positive if the recipient responds to the mailing within 30 days, else it is considered negative." In the marketing case, assessing the truth of each case will therefore involve waiting and tracking the outcome for each case, while in the insurance fraud case the assessment of truth involves manual evaluation. Either option is expensive in a business context, and when considering a predictive analytics project the cost of creating such a historical dataset should be estimated and taken into account as part of the business case.

A table of confusion provides information on one specific predictive model in a specific business context, and once the true outcome of each case is known one needs to score all cases with the predictive model in question. Based on the resulting predictions, the numbers of true negatives, false positives, false negatives and true positives are tallied up, and inserted into the table of confusion. Let us look at an *insurance fraud prevention* example to illustrate this

Table 3. Table of confusion for fraud model M_1^{Fraud}

	Predicted Negative	Predicted Positive
Negative Cases	9,700	150
Positive Cases	50	100

analysis. Consider a predictive model for predicting fraudulent claims in an insurance company. In total, 10,000 insurance claims are considered. The true outcome of each case was determined by way of a manual investigation by fraud experts, and the predicted outcome was determined by scoring each case with a predictive model. Now, the business impact and the quality of the predictive model are to be analyzed with the help of a table of confusion. The resulting numbers are as follows. Of the 10,000 cases studied, 9,850 cases were not fraudulent while the remaining 150 cases were determined as fraudulent. The predictive model predicted "*no fraud*" for 9,750 cases and "*fraud*" for the other 250 cases. After comparing truth and prediction for each case it is found that there were 9,700 true negative cases where the model correctly predicted "no fraud." There were also 100 cases where the model correctly predicted "fraud." On the other hand, the model incorrectly predicted "fraud" for 150 false positive cases, and "no fraud" for 50 false negative cases. Next, let us see what we can learn about business impact and the quality of this predictive model by looking at technical metrics.

The Accuracy Paradox

Accuracy is often the starting point for analyzing the quality of a predictive model, and accuracy is also probably the first term that comes to mind when non-experts think about how to evaluate the quality of a prediction. As shown below, accuracy measures the ratio of correct predictions over the total number of cases evaluated. In our example from above this computes to 9,800 correct predictions out of 10,000 cases, or 98.0% for model M_1^{Fraud}.

Formula 1. Definition of Accuracy

$$A(M) = \frac{TN + TP}{TN + FP + FN + TP}$$

Formula 2. Accuracy of Model M_1^{Fraud}

$$A(M_1^{Fraud}) = \frac{9,700 + 100}{9,700 + 150 + 50 + 100} = 98.0\%$$

What about the business relevance of accuracy? Surprisingly, this is a difficult question. It seems obvious that the ratio of correct predictions over all cases should be a key metric for determining the business impact of a predictive model. Yet, the value of the accuracy metric is dubious as we will see next. It is often trivially easy to create a predictive model with high accuracy and such models can be useless despite high accuracy. Similarly, when comparing the business impact of two alternative predictive models, it may well be the less accurate model that is more beneficial to the organization.

A simple example illustrates the issues associated with the accuracy metric. Consider again the Insurance Fraud example where an insurance is faced with fraudulent claims. The insurance analyzes each claim to predict and prevent paying out settlements on fraudulent claims. In our example, fewer than 1 in 50 claims is fraudulent. The insurance has devised a predictive model M_1^{Fraud} that predicts fraud with some degree of accuracy for a sample dataset of 10,000 claims. All 10,000 cases in the validation sample have

Table 4. Table of confusion for fraud model M_2^{Fraud}: This is the trivial always-predict-negative model, and its surprisingly high accuracy is 98.5%; this level of accuracy can be reached by such a trivial model because the distribution of cases is highly skewed

	Predicted Negative	Predicted Positive
Negative Cases	9,850	0
Positive Cases	150	0

been carefully checked and it is known which cases are fraudulent. To analyze the quality of the model the insurance uses the table of confusion introduced above. With an accuracy of 98.0%, model M_1^{Fraud} appears to perform fairly well. The manifestation of the accuracy paradox for this example lies in the fact that accuracy can be easily improved to 98.5% by always predicting "no fraud." The table of confusion and the accuracy for this trivial always-predict-negative model are in Table 4 and Formula 3.

Formula 3. Accuracy for Model M_2^{Fraud}

$$A(M_2^{Fraud}) = \frac{9,850 + 0}{9,850 + 0 + 150 + 0} = 98.5\%$$

Model M_2^{Fraud} reduces the rate of inaccurate predictions from 2% to 1.5%. This is an apparent improvement of 25%. Although the new model M_2^{Fraud} shows fewer incorrect predictions and markedly improved accuracy, as compared to the original model M_1^{Fraud}, the new model is obviously useless. The alternative model M_2^{Fraud} does not offer any value to the insurance company for preventing fraud, and clearly, the less accurate model is more useful than the more accurate model. The inescapable conclusion is that high accuracy is not necessarily an indicator of high model quality, and therein lies the Accuracy Paradox of predictive analytics. High accuracy does not necessarily lead to desirable business outcomes, and model improvements should not be measured in terms of accuracy gains. It may go too far to say that accuracy is irrelevant for assessing business benefits but I advise against using accuracy when evaluating predictive models.

The inefficiency of the accuracy measure has long been recoginzed by the machine learning community, and specialized techniques have been integrated directly into so called *cost-sensitive* machine learning algorithms. A more detailed review of cost-sensitive machine learning algorithms is beyond the scope of this chapter, because here we focus on the evaluation of the business impact of predictive models rather than on the algorithms used to create such models. For more information on cost-sensitive learning in machine learning algorithms see Breiman (1996); Bruckhaus, Ling, Madhavji, and Sheng (2004); Chawla, Japkowicz, and Kolcz (2004); Domingos (1999); Drummond and Holte (2003); Elkan (2001); Fan, Stolfo, Zhang, and Chan (1999); Fayyad, Piatetsky-Shapiro, Smyth, and Uthurusamy (1996); Freund and Schapire (1996); Japkowicz (2001); Joshi, Agarwal, and Kumar (2001); Ling and Li (1998); Ling, Yang, Wang, and Zhang (2004); Niculescu-Mizil and Caruana (2001); Ting (2002); Weiss and Provost (2003); and Zadrozny, Langford, and Abe (2003).

The Perils of Skew

Why is it so easy to create a predictive model with seemingly desirable accuracy for our Insurance Fraud example? Consider that a trivial "always predict negative" model only achieves a high level of accuracy because the distribution of cases is highly skewed to negative cases. In other words, the accuracy of such a trivial model is governed by the skew of the distribution of outcomes in favor of the predicted outcome. In contrast to this, a balanced distribution which has an equal number of positive and negative cases cannot be accurately predicted with the trivial always-predict-negative model. Such always-predict-negative or always-predict-positive models achieve an accuracy of only 50% for balanced distributions. Tables 5 , 6, and 7 and Formulas 4, 5, 6, and 7 illustrate this situation. First, consider the highly skewed distribution of the Insurance Fraud example shown in Table 5. Table 6 provides data on the number of cases and the percentage of cases for an alternate, balanced distribution for the Insurance Fraud example.

Now consider a trivial always-predict-negative model M_3^{Fraud} applied to the alternate, balanced distribution for the insurance fraud example. The table of confusion, Table 7, illustrates that half of the predictions are correct and half are incorrect, leading to an accuracy of only 50%.

Formula 4. Accuracy for Model M_3^{Fraud}

$$A(M_3^{Fraud}) = \frac{5,000 + 0}{5,000 + 0 + 5,000 + 0} = 50\%$$

A good measure of skew for a binary distribution is information entropy. The more skewed the binary distribution the lower its information entropy. For applications where outcomes are evenly distributed, information entropy is 1.0, and it is not possible to achieve high accuracy with a trivial model which always predicts "no fraud." The same is true for a similar trivial model which always predicts "fraud." Information entropy for the original distribution of the insurance fraud example is 0.021, indicating a highly skewed distribution. By comparison, the alternate, balanced distribution yields an information entropy of 1.0. Accuracy should only be used as a measure of model quality when the distribution of cases is evenly split between positive and negative cases, and the utility of accuracy measurements for judging model quality declines rapidly with

Table 5. Distribution of outcomes for insurance fraud example: The distribution is highly skewed

	Number of Cases	Percentage of Cases
Negative Cases	9,850	98.5%
Positive Cases	150	1.5%

Table 6. Alternate, balanced distribution of outcomes for model M_3^{Fraud} in the insurance fraud example

	Number of Cases	Percentage of Cases
Negative Cases	5,000	50.0%
Positive Cases	5,000	50.0%

Table 7. Table of confusion for fraud model M_3Fraud

	Predicted Negative	Predicted Positive
Negative Cases	5,000	0
Positive Cases	5,000	0

declining information entropy. The definition of information entropy, along with its graph, and the calculation of information entropy for the skewed and balanced distributions are provided in Formula 5, 6, and 7, and in Figure 1.

Formula 5. Definition of Information Entropy

$$H(X) = -\sum_{i=1}^{n} p(i)\log_2 p(i)$$

Formula 6. Information entropy for the orginial distribution of cases in the Insurance Fraud example

$$H(X_1^{Fraud}) = -(0.985 * \log_2(0.985) + 0.015 * \log_2(0.015)) = 0.021$$

Figure 1. Information entropy graph: For our discussion, information entropy is a measure of skew of the distribution of positive and negative cases. Information entropy peaks for distributions without skew where positive and negative cases are evenly distributed, P(X)=0.5. For skewed distributions with P(X) ≠ 0.5, information entropy declines at increasing rate.

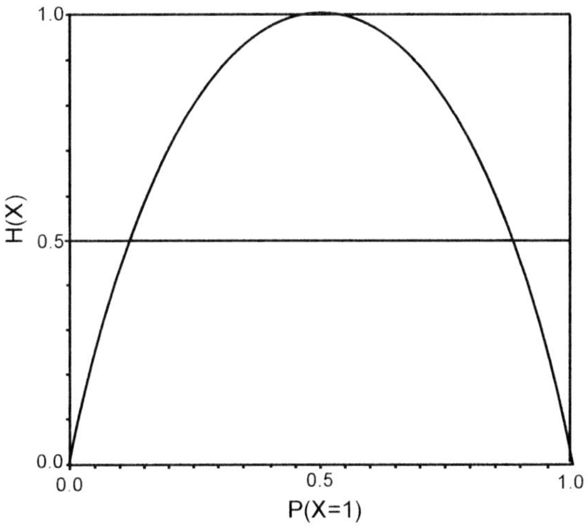

Formula 7. Information entropy for alternate distribution of cases in the Insurance Fraud example

$$H(X_2^{Fraud}) = -(0.5 * \log_2(0.5) + 0.5 * \log_2(0.5)) = 1.0$$

We have seen that accuracy is only a good indicator of model quality when the distribution of outcomes is balanced and information entropy is 1.0 or close to that value. How likely is it to find applications with a balanced distribution of outcomes? Quite unlikely. Applications of predictive analytics abound where the distributions of outcomes is highly skewed. Fraud typically occurs in a small minority of cases, few contacts respond to marketing campaigns, rarely do debtors default on their loans, telecommunications customer infrequently "churn" and cancel their telephone service contracts, and only some of the people who call into call centers respond to cross and up-selling offers. Due to the preponderance of highly skewed outcome distributions in business applications of predictive modeling, accuracy should probably not be used for model quality assessment. Reports of high accuracy in business applications should be viewed with healthy skepticism, and the skew of the outcome distribution must be considered to understand the significance of any reported accuracy measurements.

Achieving Efficiency Through Precision

Having reviewed the unfortunate reality that accuracy is not a good metric of model quality for skewed distributions, let us turn to more useful metrics of model quality. As we look at *precision* we will find it to be a more reliable tool for evaluating model quality. In fact, precision is the first metric that should be considered for evaluating model quality for highly skewed distributions because it can help resolve the accuracy paradox. Precision is also known as *positive predictive value*, and as shown in Formulas 8 and 9, it measures the ratio of true positive predictions over the total number of positive predictions.

Formula 8. Definition of Precision

$$P(M) = \frac{TP}{FP + TP}$$

With our example data, this gives us 100 true positives out of 250 positive predictions, yielding a precision of 40%. An precision of 40% may appear low at first glance. Less than half of the positive predictions are correct, and after all, when tossing a coin and placing a random bet on the outcome one has a 50% chance of guessing right. However, when the skew of the distribution of outcomes in the insurance fraud example is taken into account it becomes apparent that the performance of the predictive model M_1^{Fraud} is quite impressive.

Formula 9. Precision for Model M_1^{Fraud}

$$P(M_1^{Fraud}) = \frac{100}{150 + 100} = 40.0\%$$

Let's look at a model M_4^{Fraud} which picks outcomes at random, fill in the table of confusion for such a model and evaluate its accuracy and precision. The table of confusion for M_4^{Fraud} shows 4,925 true negatives, 4,925 false positives, 75 false negatives, and 75 true positives. Accuracy and precision for this random model are 50% and 1.5% respectively. The high quality of model M_1^{Fraud} becomes apparent when the precisions for the two models are compared. The precision of model M_1^{Fraud} of 40% is 26 times improved over the precision of the random model M_4^{Fraud} of 1.5%.

Formula 10. Accuracy for random model M_4^{Fraud}

$$A(M_4^{Fraud}) = \frac{4{,}925 + 75}{4{,}925 + 4{,}925 + 75 + 75} = 50.0\%$$

Formula 11. Precision for random model M_4^{Fraud}

$$P(M_4^{Fraud}) = \frac{75}{4{,}925 + 75} = 1.5\%$$

Precision is useful to the business user because it measures how often the user will be successful when acting on all positive predictions. For example, in our Insurance Fraud scenario the insurance may decide to have a team of specialists investigate each insurance claim that is predicted to be fraudulent by a predictive model. With a precision of 40% the specialists investigating these high-risk claims can be expected to successfully discover a fraudulent claim in 40% of the cases they investigate, and in the remaining 60% of the cases their investigation will conclude that the claim was not fraudulent. It is clear that higher precision will translate to savings because the insurance employs or contracts specialists at significant costs, and when precision is high they will spend less time on non-fraud cases. Since the investigation of non-fraud cases does not lead to any savings, lower precision diminishes the benefits the insurance receives from the predictive model and from the investigative activities of their fraud experts.

A situation similar to the Accuracy Paradox has been described in medicine where medical tests such as blood tests are used to assess the risk

Table 8. Table of confusion for random model M_4^{Fraud}

	Predicted Negative	Predicted Positive
Negative Cases	4,925	4,925
Positive Cases	75	75

of disease. Think of Table 3 from the Insurance Fraud example as relating to such a medical test. Then, imagine a patient receiving news from the doctor that the test came out positive. The doctor also shares that the accuracy of the test is 98.5% but he assures that there is only a 40% chance of having the disease. To most people, this may be puzzling. It seems that there should now be a 98.5% risk of having the disease. However, based on the concept of precision it is quite obvious that only 40% of those patients who receive a positive test result actually have the disease.

All examples reviewed so far illustrate that precision is a better indicator of model quality than accuracy. This is so because precision is a metric of how much an organization can trust a positive prediction. Another way of looking at precision is to consider it a measure of efficiency. Merriam Webster defines efficiency as "effective operation as measured by a comparison of production with cost," and there is a clear correspondence between this definition of efficiency and the definition of precision (http://www.m-w.com, 2007). The "production," or output, of the fraud prevention procedure is proportional to the number of detected fraudulent cases, which in turn is given by the number of true positives. Therefore, there is a correspondence between the nominators in the definition of precision, and in the definition of efficiency. Likewise, there is a congruence in the denominators, as positive predictions are a measure of "cost." We had already seen that the cost of the fraud avoidance procedure is proportional to the number of positive predictions. And so there is a match between the dictionary definition of efficiency and the definition of precision.

However, there are limitations that come along with the advantages of precision measurement. Precision does not tell the organization how well the model is able to catch all the positive cases. To illustrate this point, consider a model that has perfect precision but only catches one of the 150 positive cases from the insurance fraud example. The table of confusion for such a "hole in one" model M_5^{Fraud} shows 9,850 true negatives, 0 false positives, 149 false negatives, and 1 true positive case. Since all of the positive predictions are correct the precision of model M_5^{Fraud} is 100%. As one might expect, there is a complementary metric that helps us expose that, although this model has "perfect" precision, it is not a perfect model overall. In fact, model M_5^{Fraud} does not catch many of the positive cases at all, and the metric that exposes this weakness is the *recall* or *sensitivity* metric.

Formula 12. Precision for Model M_5^{Fraud}

$$P(M_5^{Fraud}) = \frac{1}{0+1} = 100.0\%$$

A metric that is closely related to precision is *top-k precision*. Top-k precision is defined identically to precision, except that only the top k predictions are taken into consideration. Top-k precision is often used in the field of information retrieval. For example, an Internet search engine may retrieve one million pages for a certain query out of a pool of billions of pages. Now, the precision metric assesses the percentage of these one million retrieved documents that are relevant to the query. However, users likely do not care about the precision of a search result that delivers a million pages. Therefore, information retrieval analysts may want to look instead at only the top 10 pages returned by the search engine. With k set to 10 the top-k precision is then the percentage of those 10 documents which are relevant to the query.

Another metric that is similar and complementary to precision is the *false alarm rate*, or *false positive rate*. The false alarm rate is complementary to precision because it is also a ratio of positive predictions. The false alarm rate is defined as false positives over positive predictions. Therefore, it is possible to calculate the false alarm rate by subtracting precision from 1.0. The false alarm rate measures the proportion of waste associated with actions taken on positive

Table 9. Table of confusion for model M_5^{Fraud}: This is a "hole in one" model with 100% precision but only 0.7% recall

	Predicted Negative	Predicted Positive
Negative Cases	9,850	0
Positive Cases	149	1

predictions. In the case of the insurance fraud example, model M_1^{Fraud} yields a false alarm rate of 60% and therefore expenses, such as investigating high-risk claims, can be expected to include 60% overhead cost of the investigation efforts without uncovering fraud. In other words, 60% of the investigation effort is wasted. One business application of predictive modeling where the term "waste" may be even more fitting is predictive marketing where mailings are sent to all contacts corresponding to positive predictions. Mailings that do not lead to a response can be considered wasted. The false alarm rate is therefore considered a measure of waste.

Formula 13. Definition of False Alarm Rate

$$FalseAlarmRate(M) = \frac{FP}{FP + TP}$$

Formula 14. False Alarm Rate for Model M_1^{Fraud}

$$FalseAlarmRate(M_1^{Fraud}) = \frac{150}{150 + 100} = 60.0\%$$

Recall Delivers Effectiveness

The metric *recall* measures the effectiveness of a predictive model. In other words, it measures how many of the positive cases are correctly classified as positive predictions. As shown next, recall is defined as true positives over all positive cases, and the recall of our initial insurance fraud model M_1^{Fraud} is 100 true positives out of 150 positive cases, or 66.7%.

Formula 15. Definition of Recall

$$R(M) = \frac{TP}{FN + TP}$$

Formula 16. Recall for Model M_1^{Fraud}

$$R(M_1^{Fraud}) = \frac{100}{50 + 100} = 66.7\%$$

For our insurance company this means that the manual evaluation of each positive prediction can be expected to identify 2 out of every 3 fraudulent claims. If there is currently no process in place for investigating cases with high fraud risk then the company can reduce instances of pay-out on fraudulent cases by 66.7%. On the other hand, if checking of high-risk cases is already practiced then a possible improvement in effectiveness must be measured in terms of the improvement of recall. As we have seen above, the price of such a reduction is determined by the precision of the model. Armed with knowledge about accuracy, precision, and recall we can answer three conspicuous questions about the fraud prevention model M_1^{Fraud}. The first question is "how many of the predictions are correct?," and we can use accuracy to compute the answer: "98.0% of all predictions are correct." The second question is "how many fraudulent cases are caught?" This question is answered with the help of the recall metric, and the answer is: "66.7% of fraudulent cases are caught." Third, and finally, we would like to ask "how many of the investigated cases are fraudulent?" The answer is provided by the precision metric, and we can respond: "40.0% of the investigated cases are fraudulent."

In contrast to a recall of 66.7% for the original model M_1^{Fraud}, the recall for our "perfect precision" model M_5^{Fraud} is only 1 true positive case out of 150 positive cases, or 0.7%. If model M_5^{Fraud} is to be deployed then the insurance company will only be able to reduce payouts on fraudulent claims by 0.7%. Model M_5^{Fraud} is inexpensive to deploy because of its high precision but its potential to reduce fraud is low. In other words, whereas efficiency is high, effectiveness is low for model M_5^{Fraud}.

Formula 17. Recall for Model M_5^{Fraud}

$$R(M_5^{Fraud}) = \frac{1}{149+1} = 0.7\%$$

We had seen that precision and false alarm rate are two complementary metrics, and another such pair of complementary metrics exists in recall and *missed alarm rate*. The missed alarm rate is defined as the ratio of false negatives to positive cases. Missed alarm rate and recall are complementary in the sense that they respectively measure the two subsets of positive cases: false negatives and true positives. Because of their complementary nature the sum of missed alarm rate and recall is invariably one hundred percent. The missed alarm rate of model M_1^{Fraud} is 50 false negatives out of 150 positive cases, or 33.3%, which together with the recall of 66.7% adds up to 100.0%. The missed alarm rate can be used to measure risk in business applications, and a missed alarm rate of 33.3% in the insurance fraud example can be interpreted as the risk of fraudulent claims going undetected. Generally, the higher the missed alarm rate, the higher the risk of missing fraudulent claims. Extreme cases of missed alarm rate are models M_2^{Fraud} and M_3^{Fraud} which are both always-predict-negative models. These models suffer a missed alarm rate of 100% because they do not produce any alarms that flag cases as positive predictions. Model M_4^{Fraud} which makes predictions at random has a 50% missed alarm rate because all positive cases are scored randomly as either positive or negative, and this results in half of the positive cases being missed. The "hole-in-one" model M_5^{Fraud} which only makes a single, correct positive prediction misses 149 of the 150 positive cases and yields a 99.3% missed alarm rate. The observation that the high precision (100.0%) of this model goes along with a high missed alarm rate (99.3%) is evidence of the general trade off between achieving a high precision and preventing a high missed alarm rate.

Formula 18. Definition of Missed Alarm Rate

$$MissedAlarmRate(M) = \frac{FN}{FN+TP}$$

Formula 19. Missed Alarm Rate for model M_1^{Fraud}

$$MissedAlarmRate(M_1^{Fraud}) = \frac{50}{50+100} = 33.3\%$$

From the above review of recall it becomes apparent that there is a delicate balance between precision and recall that affects the business impact of predictive modeling, and we will investigate that trade-off later in this chapter. For now, we will continue our tour of technical metrics.

Specificity Enables Economy

The metric *specificity* is another analytic tool that is based on the table of confusion. The definition of specificity mirrors the definition of recall, but while recall considers the correctness of predictions for positive cases, specificity considers the correctness of predictions for negative cases. The insurance fraud prediction model M_1^{Fraud} produces 9,700 true negatives and 50 false positives which results in a specificity of 9,700 out of 9,750, or 99.5%. How does specificity relate to business impact? Consider the insurance fraud prevention procedure where cases scored as high-risk are investigated by insurance fraud experts. If customers of the insurance company are to be inconvenienced in the process of investigation, then specificity is a measure of how often honest customers must endure unnecessary hassles in the course of this procedure. The denominator of specificity is the number of negative cases, in other words, the number of legitimate claims. The nominator, on the other hand, quantifies how many claims, out of this pool of legitimate claims, are not to be investigated because they were correctly classified as not fraudulent by the predictive model. In general, the higher the specificity of the model the fewer resources will be expended unnecessarily on negative cases that were incorrectly flagged as positive predictions. And so, specificity can be interpreted as a measure of economy.

Formula 20. Definition of Specificity

$$Sp(M) = \frac{TN}{TN + FP}$$

Formula 21. Specificity of model M_1^{Fraud}

$$Sp(M_1^{Fraud}) = \frac{9,700}{9,700 + 50} = 99.5\%$$

Specificity for the always-predict-negative model M_2^{Fraud} is 100.0%. Since there are no positive predictions there are no cases where negative cases are incorrectly predicted positive, leading to perfect specificity. The same holds for model M_3^{Fraud} which is also an always-predict-negative model, and for any other model with zero false positives such as the hole-in-one model M_5^{Fraud}. The model which provides random predictions, model M_4^{Fraud}, has a specificity of only 50.0%, and it matches our intuitive understanding of the term "unspecific" when we say that this random model provides unspecific predictions.

Formula 22. Specificity for model M_2^{Fraud}

$$Sp(M_2^{Fraud}) = \frac{9,850}{9,850 + 0} = 100.0\%$$

Formula 23. Specificity for model M_4^{Fraud}

$$Sp(M_4^{Fraud}) = \frac{4,925}{4,925 + 4,925} = 50.0\%$$

Oversights Cause Exposure

The three last metrics reviewed operated on specific rows or columns of the table of confusion. Precision operates on the cells in the right-hand column of the table of confusion (when the formatting convention suggested above is followed). This right-hand column shows counts of the true outcomes for all positive predictions. The recall metric operates on the cells of the lower row of the table of confusion which shows the predicted values for positive cases. And finally, the specificity metric operates on the upper row of the table of confusion which tallies up predictions for negative cases. Literature does not appear to provide any metric which operates on the left column of the table of confusion which lists the number of positive and negative cases for all negative predictions. Regardless of this lack of an established metric, an analysis of negative predictions is useful for analyzing the model quality. After all, when considering a set of negative predictions, it is useful to know whether a model is lax or negligent by incorrectly assigning negative predictions to many positive cases, or whether the model is correctly classifying negative cases.

One possible reason for the lack of an established metric for negative predictions may be be the difficulty of naming such a metric. A reasonable choice may be the term *exposure*. One inconsistency that comes with the name "exposure," however, lies in the fact that precision, recall and specificity use the number of correct predictions (true positives or true negatives) as the nominator of a ratio. The negative connotation of the term "exposure" on the other hand implies that the nominator is false negatives which is the count of incorrect predictions. So then, let us define exposure as the ratio of false negatives to negative predictions. Exposure measures the rate of oversights, or omissions among the negative predictions, and a model with high exposure will expose the user organization to high risk of missing positive cases among the negative predictions. In the insurance fraud example, model M_1^{Fraud} allows an exposure of 50 false negatives out of 9,750 negative predictions, or 0.5%. In the insurance fraud example this can be interpreted as 0.5% of those cases that are not investigated being fraudulent.

Formula 24. Definition of Exposure

$$E(M) = \frac{FN}{TN + FN}$$

Formula 25. Exposure for model M_1^{Fraud}

$$E(M_1^{Fraud}) = \frac{50}{9,700 + 50} = 0.5\%$$

Model M_2^{Fraud} which is an always-predict-negative model with a skewed distribution of outcomes has an exposure of 150 false negatives out of 10,000, or 1.5%, which is three times higher than the exposure rate of model M_1^{Fraud}. In contrast, when considering the balanced outcome distribution of model M_3^{Fraud} we calculate an exposure rate of 5,000 false negatives out of 10,000 cases, or 50.0%. The model M_4^{Fraud} which assigns predictions at random bears an exposure of 75 out of 5,000, or 1.5%. Finally, the "hole-in-one" model M_5^{Fraud} tolerates an essentially identical exposure of 149 false negatives out of 10,000, or 1.49%.

Selectivity Focuses Effort

Selectivity is defined differently from the last few metrics we have reviewed. With the exception of accuracy all of the metrics discussed above operated on just one row or just one column of the table of confusion. Selectivity on the other hand compares the number of positive predictions to the total number of cases. Selectivity is thus a measure how many cases are selected by the model as positive. One could also think of it as a measure of how "trigger happy" the model is. The selectivity of model M_1^{Fraud} from the fraud insurance example is measured as 250 positive predictions out of 10,000 cases, or 2.5%. When considering the fraud prevention practice which investigates all positive predictions it becomes clear that selectivity is a measure of effort. The insurance company can estimate the expected effort for investigating high-risk claims by multiplying the expected case load by the selectivity of the fraud prediction model that will be used.

Formula 26. Definition of Selectivity

$$Se(M) = \frac{FP + TP}{TN + FP + FN + TP}$$

Formula 27. Selectivity for model M^{1Fraud}

$$Se(M_1^{Fraud}) = \frac{100 + 150}{9,700 + 100 + 50 + 150} = 2.5\%$$

It is immediately obvious that all of the always-predict-negative models we have considered exhibit a selectivity of 0.0% because these models do not make any positive predictions. In other words, false positives and true positives are zero for any always-predict-negative model. Therefore, selectivity is zero for M_2^{Fraud} and M_3^{Fraud}. It is similarly intuitive that selectivity for model M_4^{Fraud} which picks predictions at random is 50.0%, since positive and negative predictions are chosen with equal probability. Lastly, model M_5^{Fraud}, the "hole-in-one" model which makes only one single (correct) positive prediction has a selectivity of 1 out of 10,000, or 0.01%.

Review of Technical Metrics

The table of confusion relates predictions to case outcomes by classifying the predictions for all cases as either true negative, false positive, false negative, or true positive. An organization can learn about model quality and business impact by tracking the number of cases of each type. To do so, the number of correct or incorrect predictions can be related to other quantities, and the two fundamental view points are to consider either cases or predictions. Business is primarily affected by the true outcomes for each case, and thus denominators of business impact metrics are the number positive and negative cases. Conversely, model quality can be characterized by analyzing the correctness of model predictions, and thus, denominators of model quality metrics are the numbers of positive or negative predictions.

Precision measures the rate of correct predictions for positive predictions, whereas exposure measure the rate of incorrect predictions for negative predictions. And so precision and exposure are complementary *measures of model quality.* Similarly, specificity measures the rate of correct predictions for negative cases, while recall measures the rate of correct predictions for positive cases. Specificity and recall are thus *measures of business impact.* The false-alarm-rate and missed-alarm-rate metrics are variations of the precision and recall metrics, respectively, however with a view to the incorrect predictions in the nominator instead of gauging correct predictions. Above, we laid out the table of confusion with predicted outcomes listed across the columns and true outcomes along the rows. If this convention is followed then measures of model quality consider the columns of the table of confusion, and measures of business impact operate on the rows of the table of confusion. In addition to these row and column ratios there are also metrics which measure overall model characteristics by relating data across all rows and columns to each other. Selectivity is one such metrics with assesses the bias of a model to make positive predictions. Lastly accuracy measures the rate of correct predictions across all cases.

Each of these metrics has a distinct purpose in analyzing the utility of a predictive model in a business application. Precision measures the *efficiency* of positive predictions, whereas exposure measures the rate of *oversight* among negative predictions. Recall considers the business impact in terms of the *effectiveness* of catching positive cases, and specificity measures the business impact in terms of the *economy* of correctly classifying negative cases which do not require action. The false-alarm-rate measures *waste*, the opposite of efficiency, and the missed-alarm-rate measures *risk*, the flip side of effectiveness. Lastly, selectivity relates to the *effort* required to act on positive predictions. Tables 10 and 11 summarize this review of technical metrics. Table 10 identifies each technical metric and lists its formula, description and business use. Table 11 shows the body cells of the table of confusion, labeled TN, FP, FN, and TP, and shows four technical metrics along with their formula next to the column or row that each metric analyzes. That is, precision is shown next to the column listing FP and TP because precision is calculated based on these two data points. Recall is listed next to the row showing FN and TP, and so forth for exposure and specificity.

For an empirical evaluation and comparison of various different technical metrics, see Caruana and Niculescu-Mizil (2004). This paper reviews the following nine technical metrics of model quality: accuracy, lift, f-score, area under the ROC curve, average precision, precision/recall break-even point, squared error, cross entropy, and probability calibration.

BUSINESS IMPACT ANALYSIS

When organizations adopt predictive analytics they need to understand the potential business impact of predictive models. To do so, an organization must first evalute the model with technical metrics, and then interpret these technical metrics in the light of financial business impact. In the first part of this chapter we have introduced a set of technical metrics which can assist in analyzing model quality. The remaining portion of this chapter now shows how to combine technical metrics with financial business data to examine the business impact of predictive models. This know-how is then used to illustrate how a business can choose the best predictive model from among two or more candidate models.

Model Benefit and Model Comparison

It may appear as though the various technical metrics of model quality introduced above are sufficient for analyzing model benefit and for selecting the best model from a set of alternatives. However, this is not so. Although all the technical metrics discussed above certainly provide interesting insights about model quality and business impact, they cannot answer the most fundamental questions a business must ask when deploying predictive models: can a given predictive model benefit the organization, and which of two given models provides more benefits? An example may help to illustrate this point. Let's go back to our first insurance fraud example model M_1^{Fraud}. The technical metrics of model quality and business impact are shown again below. Based on these technical metrics, it is not possible to know whether this model would be useful and help the insurance company save costs related to fraud. Now, to complicate matters further, an alternate model M_6^{Fraud} has been devised, and its technical metrics are also included in the below table. The analyst can glean that there are certain trade-offs to be had between model M_1^{Fraud} and model M_6^{Fraud}, but the analyst cannot tell which model will provide greater benefits to the organization.

These metrics provide the insurance with a significant amount of information about the performance of both models and how they differ. Every one of the technical metrics has changed. There are 200 fewer true negatives, 200 more false positives, 25 fewer false negatives, and 25 more true positives. Based on these changes in the table of confusion accuracy declines by 1.75%, precision declines by 13.7% (leading to an increase of the false alarm rate by the same amount), and recall

Table 10. Overview of technical metrics

	Formula	Discription	Business Use
Accuracy	$\frac{TN+TP}{TN+FP+FN+TP}$	Rate of correct predictions.	(Avoid)
Precision	$\frac{TP}{FP+TP}$	Measures prediction quality: rate of correct positive predictions.	Efficiency
Recall	$\frac{TP}{FN+TP}$	Measures business impact: rate of correctly predicted positive cases.	Effectiveness
Specificity	$\frac{TN}{TN+FP}$	Measure business impact: rate of correctly predicted negative cases.	Economy
Exposure	$\frac{FN}{TN+FN}$	Measures prediction quality: rate of incorrect negative predictions.	Oversight
Selectivity	$\frac{FP+TP}{TN+FP+FN+TP}$	Rate of positive predictions.	Effort
False Alarm Rate	$\frac{FP}{FP+TP}$	Measures prediction quality: rate of incorrect positive predictions.	Waste
Missed Alarm Rate	$\frac{FN}{FN+TP}$	Measures business impact: rate of incorrectly predicted negative cases.	Risk

Table 11. Overview of technical metrics based on the table of confusion

	Specificity $= \frac{TN}{TN+FP}$		
Exposure $= \frac{FN}{TN+FN}$	TN	*FP*	*Precision* $= \frac{TP}{FP+TP}$
	FN	TP	
	Recall $= \frac{TP}{FN+TP}$		

increases by 16.6% (leading to a decrease of the missed alarm rate by the same amount). Finally, specificity declines by 3.1%, exposure declines by 0.24%, and selectivity increases by 2.25%. None of this helps the insurance determine whether either model should be deployed for investigating high-risk claims, or which of these two models will lead to greater financial returns. Clearly, to answer these questions, we must broaden our view of model quality to address financial considerations. Expanding the analysis of model quality to the financial domain is actually quite simple. The formulas are straight forward and easy to understand and compute. The most difficult task of the financial business impact analysis may be to obtain the cost and benefit figures which are needed as inputs to the analysis.

Financial Business Impact Drivers

The impact of a predictive model is driven largely by a small set of factors. The first such financial factor is either *event cost*, if predicting an adverse event such as fraud, or *event benefit* if predicting a beneficial event such as a response to a marketing campaign. In the machine learning literature it is the custom to speak of cost and to represent benefits as negative costs to simplify the discussion, and we will adopt this practice here and denote event cost by $C(E)$. The second factor to consider is the *risk* or *probability*, denoted by p, of the predicted event occurring. Risk is a number between 0.0% and 100.0%, and it can be assessed using a calibration procedure that transforms scores from the predictive model into probabilities, or risks. The risk can then be used to derive the *expected cost*, by multiplying risk and event cost. Typically, a prediction is made for the purpose of determining whether the predicted risk is sufficiently high to merit taking an *action* of some kind. For example, in our Insurance Fraud example, the insurance takes action to investigate high-risk claims. Similarly, a marketing department may want to take the action of sending a mailing to a contact if the probability, or "risk," is high that this contact might respond to the mailing. The cost of this action, $C(A)$, or *action cost*, is the third factor that goes into our financial business impact analysis. Lastly, a second probability has to be considered, and this is the probability that action will lead to the desired result. This probability characterizes the *effectiveness* of the action, and it is denoted

Table 12. Table of confusion for fraud model M_6^{Fraud}

	Predicted Negative	**Predicted Positive**
Negative Cases	9,500	350
Positive Cases	25	125

Table 13. Technical metrics for models M_1^{Fraud} and M_6^{Fraud}

	M_1^{Fraud}	M_6^{Fraud}
True Negatives	9,700	9,500
False Positives	150	350
False Negatives	50	25
True Positives	100	125
Accuracy	98.0%	96.25%
Precision	40.0%	26.3%
Recall	66.7%	83.3%
Specificity	99.5%	96.4%
Exposure	0.5%	0.26%
Selectivity	2.5%	4.75%
False Alarm Rate	60.0%	73.7%
Missed Alarm Rate	33.3%	16.7%

by *E*. By further multiplying the expected cost by the effectiveness of taking action we can calculate the *expected benefit* of taking action.

The *expected financial impact* of taking action on a given case can now be calculated by subtracting the action cost from the expected benefit of taking action. The reasoning behind this calculation is simple. If the organization is certain that the predicted event will occur if it does not take action, and if the organization is certain that taking action will prevent the event, then the expected benefit is the avoided entire cost of the event *C*(*E*). Since the organization cannot generally be certain that the event will occur one must multiply the cost of the event by the probability of the event to arrive at the expected cost of the event. Following the same logic the analyst must again multiply the expected cost of the event by the probability of preventing the event by taking action, *E*. With this, the analyst arrives at the expected benefit of taking action. Finally, the analyst subtracts the cost of taking action from the expected benefit to arrive at the expected financial business impact of taking action. Below, these formulas and the four factors of financial analysis of business impact are summarized and illustrated for the insurance fraud and predictive marketing applications.

Formula 28. Definition of the expected financial impact of taking action for an individual case with rik p.

$$E(I) = C(E) * p * E - C(A)$$

Case Risk and Action Effectiveness

In this approach to the financial analysis of business impact, there is a distinction between two probabilities. The first probability is the risk of a case being a positive case. And the second probability is the effectiveness of taking action, that is, the probability that taking action can bring about a benefit for a positive case. Making this distinction allows for some flexibility in defining the target variable for predictive modeling. For example, in a predictive marketing application the organization may have available one of two kinds of historical data. Either it may have available information on which contacts have historically replied to mailings, but not all of the replies may have resulted in purchases and revenue. Or the organization may have available data on which mailings have resulted in incremental revenue that can be traced back to the mailing. In the former case the organization will need to break down the analysis into the probability of responses and the effectiveness of converting responses to payments. In the latter case, the organization can predict the probability (referred to as "risk") of the desired outcome directly, and in that case, the effectiveness of taking action, *E*, can be set to 1.0. If risk and effectiveness are to be considered separately, as in the former case, then the risk can be quantified by a predictive model, whereas the effectiveness figure may come from an analysis of the business process.

Similarly, in the insurance fraud example, the available historical data may identify either claims that appeared to be fraudulent after investigation, or cases where payment was avoided. In the first case where data identifies only the outcome of the investigation it may be appropriate to differentiate between the probability of a positive investigation result and a positive business outcome. If the business outcome is not directly predicted by the model then that should be considered in the financial analysis. For instance, a simple low-cost investigation may have been applied to determine the fraudulent nature of claims in the historical data, whereas in order to deny payment a more thorough investigation may be needed. In some cases where payment is initially denied the claimant may also challenge the insurance in a court of law resulting in additional cost and lowering the probability of the desired business outcome of reducing costs.

These considerations may appear complex. However, when an organization pursues predictive analytics it is likely that the organization will discover that the historical data that are available from records and archives do not directly provide information about the pursued business outcome. Similarly, an organization may decide to create a historical dataset by analyzing every case for a set period of time to determine its outcome, or to analyze a statistical sample. When this approach is selected it may be impractical, or prohibitively expensive to analyze each case to determine the business outcome of interest with certainty. The distinction between case risk and action effectiveness allows the organization to analyze both aspects separately, and to roll them up into a comprehensive analysis of financial impact.

Case Analysis and Data Set Analysis

There is some versatility in the presented techniques for analyzing the financial business impact because they can be applied to either a single case, or to an entire dataset. The analysis of individual cases is at the heart of any predictive analytics capability. After all, conducting business requires handling each situation case by case. And this is where predictive analytics can offer information about risks and opportunities tailored for each specific case. Each call coming into a call center

Table 14. Summary of business impact drivers

		Insurance Fraud	Predictive Marketing
C(E)	Event Cost	The average cost incurred by the insurance per undected fraudulent claim, not taking into consideration any prevention cost. The average claim amount per fraudulent claim may be a good initial aproximation.	It is more intuitive to consider the "Event Benefit", and this is the average financial benefit of a contact responding to a mailing. The average revenue per response may be a good initial approximation.
P	Risk	The risk that a specific claim is fraudulent, based on the score produced by the predictive model.	It is more intuitive to consider "risk" as "probability", and this is the probability that a specific contact will respond to a mailing.
C(A)	Action Cost	The cost of taking action to prevent the event. The estimated average cost of investigating a claim may be a good approximation.	The cost of taking action to bring the event about. The estimated average cost of sending one mailing to one contact may be a good approximation.
E	Action Effectiveness	For a fraudulent claim, the probability that payment can be prevented by taking action. A good approximation may take into account the probability of preventing payment on claims considered fraudulent, such as risks of law suites, odds of winning such suites and other related considerations.	For a response to a marketing campaign, the probability that payment will be received. A good approximation may take into account the probability of the response form containing the necessary information, that suffinient funds are available to transact the payment, and that the purchase is not subsequently cancelled.

will generally have a different probability of succeeding with an offer to up-sell or cross-sell. And each claim received by an insurance company must be analyzed individually by a predictive model in order to provide guidance to the insurance where fraud investigations are most beneficial. Therefore, the risk, or probability, p, that is predicted by a model will generally have a different value for each case analyzed.

How about the other factors in the financial analysis discussed above? Should the event cost $C(E)$, action cost $C(A)$, and effectiveness E also be analyzed for each specific case? For practical reasons and cost considerations it may be best to use average figures rather then case specific figures. As an organization embarks on implementing predictive analytics it may be too ambitious to attempt to estimate event cost, action cost and effectiveness on a case by case basis, and that is the approach we suggest here. Yet, it would certainly be beneficial if these factors could be estimated accurately for each case. It may be possible to define different types of cases and to use different event cost, action cost, and effectiveness data for each type. Or, it may be possible to create a set of predictive models which predict event cost, action cost and effectiveness, in addition to case risk. However, a description of how to implement such a capability is beyond the scope of this chapter. Therefore, we will assume that averages are used, and this is also the reason why we use capital letters to denote event cost $C(E)$, action cost $C(A)$, and effectiveness E, whereas we use a lower case letter to denote the case risk p. That is, capital letters refer to data about the entire dataset, and lower case letters refer to data about specific cases.

Then, if an organization uses averages one might anticipate that questions and concerns may arise when such an average may be obviously inappropriate for a specific case in question. For instance, in the insurance fraud example, it may be obvious to users of a predictive capability that the average cost of investigating a claim may be unrealistic for both extremely large and very small claims. Similarly, the effectiveness of taking action to prevent payment once a claim is believed to be fraudulent may be lower or higher than the average effectiveness E, depending on the details of the claim.

The financial analysis of business impact described here can be applied on a case-by-case basis because it is tailored to each case by way of incorporating the case-specific risk p. A decision to take action can then be guided by the expected financial business impact of taking action. Additionally, the expected financial impact of taking action can be rolled up to the dataset level. At that level, the organization can then juxtapose various policies it may consider by comparing different ways of rolling up the expected impact. In some cases, the analysis of profit may assume that currently no procedure is in place to predict and prevent the adverse events of interest. If on the other hand, there is a pre-existing procedure in place then an analysis of net profit may be more appropriate. This can be accomplished by subtracting the profit generated by the pre-existing procedure from the profit that is expected from deploying the new predictive model.

Other variations on the analysis concern the inclusion and exclusion of cases from the financial impact analysis. For instance, by summing the expected impact over all cases in the dataset, the organization can analyze the impact of a policy to take action on every single case. A complementary method of rolling up case level impact data is to sum only over those cases that have a positive expected business impact, and this figure can provide information about a policy to take action when the expected financial impact of taking action is positive. If the organization is currently taking action on all cases then the benefit of deploying the predictive model along with a new policy can be calculated by subtracting the expected impact of the new policy from that for the old policy, taking into account the expected financial benefit of acting on different subsets of claims. Similar comparisons with other variations of policies can also be made. For example, the organization may not have been taking action on any cases, or only cases that meet specific criteria may have been acted upon. An insurance company may have investigated only claims that exceed a certain dollar amount, say $10,000, and a comparison between this policy and a risk-prediction-based policy is possible. Variations on a risk-prediction-based policy may also be considered. For example, an insurance may decide to only investigate claims with a predicted financial business benefit of greater than $3,000, so as to limit the size of the team of fraud experts who must investigate high-risk claims.

These analysis techniques can be applied with slight variations depending on whether the organization is interested in profit, net profit, or return-on-investment (ROI). Profit is calculated as shown above, which involves several steps. As a first step, a dataset is assembled that is representative of the time period in question, such as a fiscal month, quarter or year. The analysis of financial business impact is applied using event cost, action cost and effectiveness data, as well as the data from the table of confusion. The result of the analysis is the profit of applying the evaluated predictive model. If an ROI figure is needed, then the profit or net profit, which ever is more appropriate, must be divided by the cost of implementing the new model-based procedure. When calculating ROI it is necessary to proceed with caution to prevent any double counting of costs or benefits. Specifically, the analyst must avoid to include the cost of taking action on positive predictions, because this cost has already been accounted for in the profit analysis.

Calculating Business Impact and Selecting Models

For the analysis of business impact on the level of entire datasets, the business impact of a model, $I(M)$, is the expected avoided cost minus the cost of taking action across all cases. The organization can expect to avoid the cost of the adverse event for a fraction of all true positive predictions, and this fraction is quantified by the effectiveness, E, of the prevention procedure the organization implements. The cost of taking action, on the other hand, is incurred for each of the positive predictions. The resulting formula for computing the expected business benefit on the dataset level is shown in Formula 29.

Formula 29. Definition of the expected financial business impact, I, of predictive model M

$$I(M) = TP * C(E) * E - (FP + TP) * C(A)$$

Let us apply this analysis to two example applications, the insurance fraud example and a predictive marketing example. Both examples will differ in their underlying cost data. The cost of an event, in the case of Insurance Fraud, is the cost of paying out on a fraudulent claim. Let us assume this cost to be $C(E) = \$100,000$. The cost of taking action is related to investigating each case that is predicted positive. There may also be other related costs included in the cost of taking action, such as the expected cost of litigation and so forth. Let us set this cost of taking action to $C(A) = \$1,000$. The third parameter for the Insurance Fraud example is the effectiveness of preventing pay-out on claims which were predicted and confirmed as fraudulent through an investigation. For our analysis, let us set effectiveness to $E = 80\%$.

Furthermore, for the predictive marketing example, let us consider a telecommunications company which sends marketing collateral in the mail to those contacts which were predicted as potential responders by a predictive model. Because this situation involves different economic considerations we will deal with costs and effectiveness rates that differ in magnitude from those we assumed for the insurance fraud example. For the case of predictive marketing, the benefit of a positive event is related to purchases made by contacts who have received marketing materials. Although this is a benefit rather than a cost we will use the same terminology as in the insurance fraud example and set the "cost of the event" to $C(E) = \$1,000$. The cost of taking action is related to the cost of printing and distributing marketing materials, and other such costs as credit checks and processing may also be included. Let's set this cost of taking action to $C(A) = \$10$. Lastly, let's set the effectiveness in the predictive marketing example to $E = 3\%$, denoting that only a small fraction of those who respond to the marketing campaign actually follow through with a purchase and payment.

Now, let's organize these figures in a table and compute the expected business impact of deploying models M_1^{Fraud} and M_6^{Fraud} in the insurance fraud scenario, and models M_1^{Mktg} and M_6^{Mktg} in the predictive marketing scenario. Let's further assume that models M_1^{Fraud} and M_1^{Mktg} have identical technical metrics, and that the same is true for models M_6^{Fraud} and M_6^{Mktg}. It becomes apparent that in one of the four cases considered, where model M_6^{Mktg} is deployed, there is actually a negative business impact from deploying the predictive model amounting to a loss of \$1,000. Model M_6^{Fraud} which has identical technical metrics leads to a positive business benefit of \$9,525,000 which proves that it is impossible to judge model benefit based on technical metrics alone. The same model, with identical technical metrics leads to a loss in one business scenario but to a profit in a different scenario. Moreover, selecting a model for best business impact is also impossible based on technical metrics alone. Model M_6^{Fraud} with a business benefit of \$9,525,000 is superior to model M_1^{Fraud} with a business benefit of \$7,750,000. However, model M_6^{Mktg} delivers a negative business impact of \$1,000 and is therefore inferior to model M_1^{Mktg} which provides a positive business impact of \$500. We conclude that although technical metrics do not change, the best choice of model may change when the business context changes.

In this discussion of financial business impact analysis, we have focused primarily on analyzing positive predictions. We have assumed that there is an action cost for all positive predictions and that there is an event cost which can be avoided for true positive predictions. Although beyond the scope of this chapter, more generally, it is possible to expand the analysis of financial business impacts by also considering similar cost and benefit data for negative predictions.

SUMMARY AND CONCLUSION

In this chapter we have explored the analysis of model quality and business impact. We introduced the table of confusion which breaks down cases into true negatives, false positives, false negatives, and true positives, based on how positive and negative cases coincide with positive and negative predictions. We then investigated the accuracy paradox and learned that accuracy can be a misleading measure of model quality because less accurate models may provide more benefits to a business than more accurate models. We proceeded to show how skew in the distribution of positive and negative cases can lead to this accuracy paradox, and concluded that accuracy is a metric of dubious utility for analyzing model quality in a business setting. We next reviewed a variety of other technical metrics which can be used to assess various aspects of model quality and business impact such as precision which measures efficiency, recall (effectiveness), specificity (economy), exposure (oversight), selectivity (effort), false-alarm-rate (waste) and missed-alarm-rate (risk).

Unfortunately, these commonly used metrics provide results which are not obviously connected to financial business goals. In a general sense then, although the tremendous potential value

Table 15. Analyzing business benefit and selecting the best model; two models are used in two different contexts, and business benefit and model selection depend on cost data

	M_1^{Fraud}	M_6^{Fraud}	M_1^{Mktg}	M_6^{Mktg}
C(E)	$100,000	$100,000	$1,000	$1,000
C(A)	$1,000	$1,000	$10	$10
E	80%	80%	3%	3%
TN	9,700	9,500	9,700	9,500
FP	150	350	150	350
FN	50	25	50	25
TP	100	125	100	125
Cases	10,000	10,000	10,000	10,000
Profit	$7,750,000	$9,525,000	$500	-$1,000

of predictive analytics is quite obvious, it is not clear how to quantify the financial business value of a given predictive model in a specific business environment, based on technical metrics alone. Therefore, following the review of technical metrics, we moved on to analyze whether a given predictive model can benefit an organization, and how an organization can choose among multiple alternative predictive models. We learned that costs are a key consideration to answering these questions and that technical metrics are agnostic to cost data. In order to overcome this limitation, we developed metrics of financial business impact and compared the performance of various sample models. We also discussed the analysis of business impact for a single case, as compared to analyzing the business impact for an entire dataset, and outlined how an organization may use both types of analysis. Since it is often difficult or expensive to obtain true case outcomes for extensive historical datasets, we also provided a technique for connecting available case outcome data to business outcomes by making a distinction between case risk and effectiveness of a prevention procedure. Taken together, these techniques provide a potent tool set for analyzing the business impact of predictive models in the business context.

The most pertinent conclusions from our tour of the business impacts of predictive analytics is that, first, accuracy measurements may be misleading and should best be avoided in favor of alternative metrics such as precision and recall. Second, technical metrics alone cannot be used to determine whether a given predictive model can benefit or harm an organization, and cost data must be taken into account to investigate business benefits. And third, in order to select among alternative predictive models the analyst must again take into account cost data because technical metrics cannot generally be used to select the best model from within a set of alternative models.

REFERENCES

Berry, M. J. A., & Linoff, G. (1997). *Data mining techniques: For marketing, sales, and customer support*. John Wiley & Sons.

Breiman, L. (1996). Bagging predictors. *Machine Learning 24*(2), 123-140.

Bruckhaus, T., Ling, C. X., Madhavji, N. H., & Sheng, S. (2004). *Software escalation prediction with data mining.* Paper presented at the Workshop on Predictive Software Models (PSM 2004), A STEP Software Technology & Engineering Practice.

Caruana, R., & Niculescu-Mizil, A. (2004, August 22-25). Data mining in metric space: An empirical analysis of supervised learning performance criteria. In *Proceedings of the Tenth ACM SIGKDD International Conference on Knowledge Discovery and Data Mining,* Seattle, WA.

Chawla, N. V., Japkowicz, N., & Kolcz, A. (Eds.). (2004). Special Issue on Learning from Imbalanced Datasets. *SIGKDD, 6*(1).

Domingos, P. (1999). MetaCost: A general method for making classifiers cost-sensitive. In *Proceedings of the Fifth International Conference on Knowledge Discovery and Data Mining* (pp.155-164). ACM Press.

Drummond, C., & Holte, R. C. (2003). *C4.5, class imbalance, and cost sensitivity: Why under-sampling beats over-sampling.* Paper presented at the Workshop on Learning from Imbalanced Datasets II.

Elkan, C. (2001). The foundations of cost-sensitive learning. In *Proceedings of the International Joint Conference of Artificial Intelligence (IJCAI 2001)* (pp. 973-978).

Fan, W., Stolfo, S. J., Zhang, J., & Chan, P. K. (1999). AdaCost: Misclassification cost-sensitive boosting. In *Proceedings of the Sixteenth International Conference on Machine Learning* (pp. 97-105).

Fayyad, U., Piatetsky-Shapiro, G., Smyth, P., & Uthurusamy, R. (Eds). (1996). *Advances in knowledge discovery and data mining.* AAAI/MIT Press.

Freund, Y., & Schapire, R. E. (1996). Experiments with a new boosting algorithm. In *Proceedings of International Conference on Machine Learning (ICML)* (pp.148-156).

Han, J., & Kamber, M. (2005). *Data mining: Concepts and techniques* (The Morgan Kaufmann Series in Data Management Systems, 2nd ed.).

Japkowicz, N. (2001). Concept-learning in the presence of between-class and within-class imbalances. In *Proceedings of the Fourteenth Conference of the Canadian Society for Computational Studies of Intelligence (AI'2001).*

Joshi, M. V., Agarwal, R. C., & Kumar, V. (2001). Mining needles in a haystack: Classifying rare classes via two-phase rule induction. In *Proceedings of the SIGMOD'01 Conference on Management of Data.*

Ling, C. X., & Li, C. (1998). Data mining for direct marketing: Specific problems and solutions. In *Proceedings of the Fourth International Conference on Knowledge Discovery and Data Mining (KDD-98)* (pp. 73-79).

Ling, C. X., Yang, Q., Wang, J., & Zhang, S. (2004). Decision trees with minimal costs. In *Proceedings of International Conference on Machine Learning (ICML).*

Mitchell, T. (1997). *Machine learning* (1st ed.). McGraw-Hill.

Niculescu-Mizil, A., & Caruana, R. (2001). Obtaining calibrated probabilities from boosting. *AI Stats.*

Quinlan, J. R. (1993). *C4.5: Programs for machine learning.* Morgan Kaufmann.

Soukup, T., & Davidson, I. (2002). *Visual data mining: Techniques and tools for data visualization and mining.* Wiley & Sons.

Ting, K. M. (2002). An instance-weighting method to induce cost-sensitive trees. *IEEE Transactions on Knowledge and Data Engineering, 14*(3), 659-665.

Webster, M. (2007). http://www.m-w.com

Weiss, G., & Provost, F. (2003). Learning when training data are costly: The effect of class distribution on tree induction. *Journal of Artificial Intelligence Research, 19*, 315-354.

Witten, I. H., & Frank, E. (2005). *Data mining: Practical machine learning tools and techniques* (2nd ed.). San Francisco: Morgan Kaufmann.

Zadrozny, B., Langford, J., & Abe, N. (2003). Cost-sensitive learning by cost-proportionate example weighting. In *Proceedings of International Conference of Data Mining (ICDM).*

Chapter VIII
Beyond Classification:
Challenges of Data Mining for Credit Scoring

Anna Olecka
D&B, USA

ABSTRACT

This chapter will focus on challenges in modeling credit risk for new accounts acquisition process in the credit card industry. First section provides an overview and a brief history of credit scoring. The second section looks at some of the challenges specific to the credit industry. In many of these applications business objective is tied only indirectly to the classification scheme. Opposing objectives, such as response, profit and risk, often play a tug of war with each other. Solving a business problem of such complex nature often requires a multiple of models working jointly. Challenges to data mining lie in exploring solutions that go beyond traditional, well-documented methodology and need for simplifying assumptions; often necessitated by the reality of dataset sizes and/or implementation issues. Examples of such challenges form an illustrative example of a compromise between data mining theory and applications.

INTRODUCTION: PRACTITIONER'S LOOK AT DATA MINING

"Knowledge discovery in databases is the non-trivial process of identifying valid, novel, potentially useful, and ultimately understandable patterns in data" (Fayyad, Piatetsky-Shapiro, & Smyth, 1996).

This basic KDD definition has served well as a foundation of this field during its early explosive growth. For today's practitioner, however, let us consider some small modifications: *novel* is not a necessity, but the patterns must be not only *valid* and *understandable* but also *explainable*.

Copyright © 2007, IGI Global, distributing in print or electronic forms without written permission of IGI Global is prohibited.

[...] process of identifying ***valid, useful, understandable and explainable*** *patterns in data.*

A *data mining* practitioner does not set out to look for patterns hoping their practitioners discoveries might become useful. A goal is typically defined beforehand, and is usually driven by an existing business problem. Once the goal is known, a search begins. This search is guided by a need to best solve the business problem. Any patterns discovered, as well as any subsequent solutions, need to be understandable in the context of the business domain. Furthermore, they need to be acceptable to the owner of the business problem.

Successes of data mining over the last decade, paired with a rapid growth of commercially available tools as well as a supportive IT infrastructure, have created a hunger in the business community for employing data mining techniques to solve complex problems.

Problems that were once the sole domain of top researchers and experts can be now solved by a lay practitioner with the aid of commercially available software packages. With this new ability to tackle modeling problems in-house, our appetites and ambitions have grown; we now want to undertake increasingly complex business issues using data mining tools. In many of these applications, a business objective is tied to the classification scheme only indirectly. Solving these complex problems often requires multiple models working jointly or other solutions that go beyond traditional, well documented techniques. Business realities, such as data availability, implementation issues, and so forth, often dictate simplifying assumptions. Under these conditions, data mining becomes a more empirical than scientific field: in the absence of a supporting theory, a rigorous proof is replaced with pragmatic, data driven analysis and meticulous monitoring and tracking of the subsequent results.

This chapter will focus on business needs of risk assessment for new accounts acquisition. It presents an illustrative example of a compromise between data mining theory and its real life challenges. The section "Data Mining for Credit Decisioning" outlines credit scoring background and common practice in the U.S. financial industry. The section titled "Challenges for Data Miner" addresses some of the specific challenges in credit model development.

DATA MINING FOR CREDIT DECISIONING

In today's competitive world of financial services, companies strive to derive every possible advantage by mining information from vast amounts of data. Account level scores become drivers of a strong analytic environment. Within a financial institution, there are several areas of data mining applications:

- Response modeling applied to potential prospects can optimize marketing campaign results, while controlling acquisition costs.
- Customer's propensity to accept a new product offer (cross-sell) aids business growth.
- Predicting risk, profitability, attrition and behavior of existing customers can boost portfolio performance.
- Behavioral models are used to classify credit usage patterns. Revolvers are customers who carry balances from month to month, Rate Surfers shop for introductory rates to park their balance and move on once the intro period ends. Convenience Users tend to pay their balances every month. Each type of customer behavior has a very different impact on profitability. Recognizing those patterns from actual usage data is important. But the real trick is in predicting which pattern a potential new customer is likely to adopt.

- Custom scores are also developed for fraud detection, collections, recovery, and so forth.
- Among the most complex are models predicting risk level of prospective customers. Credit cards lose billions of dollars annually in credit losses incurred by defaulted accounts. There are two primary components of credit card losses: bankruptcy and contractual charge-off. The former is a result of a customer filing for bankruptcy protection. The latter involves a legal regulation, where banks are required to "write off" (charge-off) balances which remained delinquent for certain period. Length of this time period varies for different type of loan. Credit cards in the U.S. charge-off accounts 180 days past due.

According to national level statistics, credit losses for credit cards exceed marketing and operating expenses combined. Annualized net dollar losses, calculated as a ratio of charge-off amount to outstanding loan amount, varied between 6.48% in 2002 and 4.03% in 2005 (U.S. Department of Treasury, 2005). $35 billion was charged-off by the U.S. credit card companies in 2002 (Furletti, 2003). Even a small lift provided by a risk model translates into million dollar savings in future losses.

Generic risk scores, such as FICO, can be purchased from credit bureaus. But in an effort to gain a competitive edge, most financial institutions build custom risk scores in-house. Those scores use credit bureau data as predictors, while utilizing internal performance data and data collected through application forms.

Brief History of Credit Scoring

Credit scoring is one of the earliest areas of financial engineering and risk management. Yet if you google the term *credit risk*, you are likely to come up with a lot of publications on portfolio optimization and not much on credit scoring for consumer lending. Perhaps due to this scarcity of theoretical work, or maybe because of the complexity of the underlying problems, credit scoring is still largely an empirical field.

Early lending decisions were purely judgmental and localized. If a friendly local banker deemed you to be credit worthy, you got your loan. Even after credit decisions moved away from local lenders, the approval process remained largely judgmental. First credit scoring models were introduced in late 1960s in response to growing popularity of credit cards and an increasing need for automated decision making. They were proprietary to individual creditors and built on that creditors' data. Generic risk scores were pioneered in the following decade by Fair Isaac, a consulting company founded by two operations research scientists, Bill Fair and Earl Isaac. The FICO risk score was introduced by Fair Isaac and became credit industry standard by the 1980s. Other generic scores followed, some developed by Fair Isaac, others by competitors, but FICO remains the industry staple.

Availability of commercial data mining tools, improved IT infrastructure and the growth of credit bureaus make it possible today to get the best of both worlds: custom, in-house models, built on pooled data reflecting individual customer's credit history and behavior across all creditors. Custom scores improve quality of a portfolio by booking higher volumes of higher quality accounts. To close the historic circle, however, judgmental overrides of automated solutions are also sought to provide additional, human insight based, lift.

New Account Acquisition Process

Two types of risk models are used in a pre-screen credit card mailing campaign. One, applied at a pre-screen stage, prior to mailing the offer, eliminates the most risky prospects, those not likely to be approved. The second model is used to score incoming applications. Between the two risk models, other scores may be applied as well, such as response, profitability, and so forth. Some binary rules (judgmental criteria) may also be used in addition to the credit scores. For example, very high utilization of existing credit or lack of credit experience might be used to eliminate a prospect or decline an applicant.

Data

Performance information comes from bank's own portfolio. Typical target classes for risk scoring are those with high delinquency levels (60+ days past due, 90+ days past due, etc.) or those who have defaulted on their credit card debt.

Additional data comes from a credit application: income, home ownership, banking relationships, job type and employment history, balance transfer request (or lack of it), and so forth.

Credit bureaus provide data on customers' behavior based on reporting from all creditors. They include credit history, type and amount of credit available, credit usage, and payment history. Bureau data arrives scrubbed clean, making it easy to mine. Missing values are rare. Matching to the internal data is simple, because key customer identifiers have long been established. But the timing of model building (long observation windows) causes loss of predictive power. Furthermore, the bureau attributes tend to be noisy and highly correlated.

Modeling Techniques

In-house scoring is now standard for all but the smallest of financial institutions. This is possible because of readily available commercial software packages. Another crucial factor is existence of IT implementation platforms. The main advantage of in-house scoring is a rapid development of proprietary models and a quick implementation. This calls for standard, tried and true techniques. Not often companies can afford the time and resources for experimenting with methods that would require development of new IT platforms.

Statistical techniques were the earliest employed in risk model development and remain dominant to this day. Early approaches involved discriminant analysis, Bayesian decision theory and linear regression. The goal was to find a classification scheme which best separates the "goods" from the "bads." That led to a more natural choice for a binary target—the logistic regression.

The logistic regression is by far the most common modeling tool, a benchmark that other techniques are measured against. Among its strengths are: flexibility, ease of finding robust solutions, ability to assess the relative importance of attributes in the model, as well as the statistical significance and the confidence intervals for model parameters.

Other forms of nonlinear regression, namely probit and tobit, are recognized as powerful enough to make their way into commercial statistical packages, but never gained the popularity that logistic regression enjoys.

A standout tool in credit scoring is a decision tree. Sometimes trees are used as a stand alone classification tool. More often, they aid exploratory data analysis and feature selection. Trees also are perfectly suitable as a segmentation tool. The popularity of decision trees is well deserved; they combine strong theoretical framework with ease of use, visualization and intuitive appeal.

Multivariate adaptive regression splines (MARS), a nonparametric regression technique, proved extremely successful in practice. MARS determines a data driven transformation for each attribute, by splitting the attribute's values into segments and constructing a set of basis functions and their coefficients. The end result is a piecewise linear relationship with the target. MARS produces robust models and handles with ease non-monotone relationships between the predictor variables and the target.

Clustering methods are often employed for segmenting population into behavioral clusters.

Early non-statistical techniques involved linear and integer programming. Although these are potent and robust separation techniques, they are far less intuitive and computationally complex. They never took root as a stand alone tool for credit scoring. With very few exceptions, neither did genetic algorithms.

This is not so for neural networks models. Their popularity has grown, and they have found their way into commercial software packages. Neural networks have been successfully employed in behavioral scoring models and response modeling. They have one drawback when it comes to credit scoring, however. Their non-linear interactions

Chart 1.

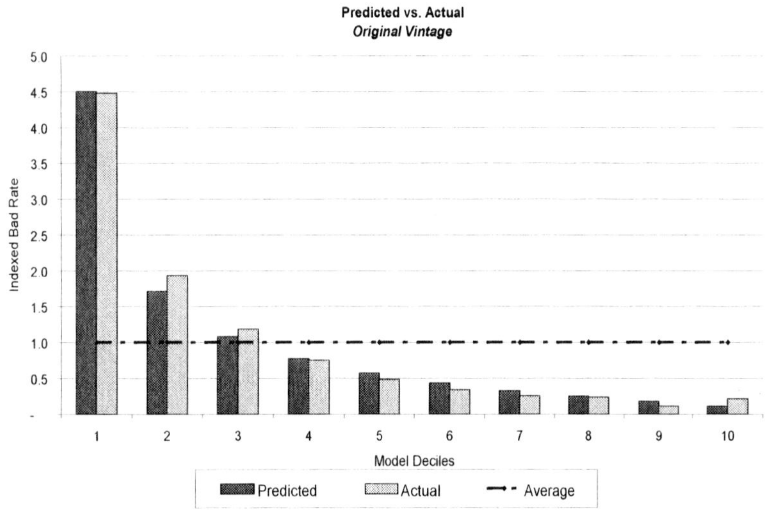

Chart 2.

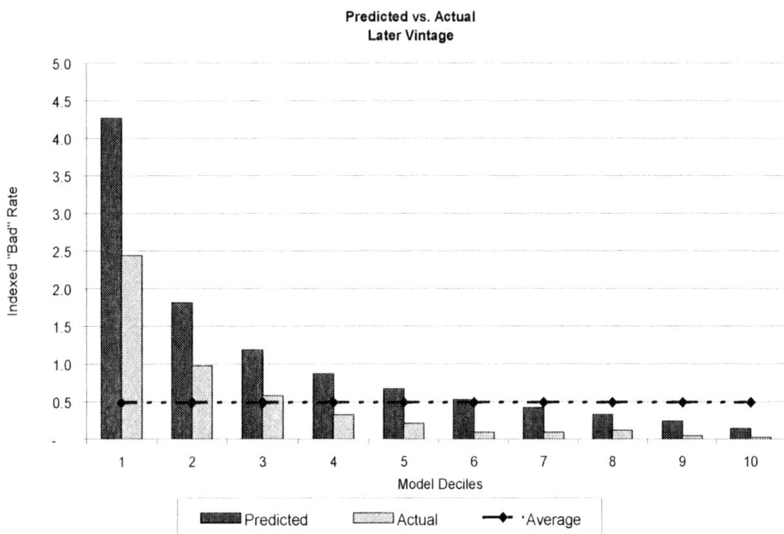

both with the target and between attributes (one attribute contributing to several network nodes, for example) are difficult to explain to the end-user, and would make it impossible to justify resulting credit decisions.

There are promising attempts to employ other techniques. In an emerging trend to employ the survival analysis, models estimate WHEN a customer will default, rather than predicting IF a customer will default. Markov chains and Bayesian networks have also been successfully used in risk and behavioral models.

Forms of Scorecards

Credit scoring models estimate probability of an individual falling into the bad category during a pre-defined time window. The final the output of a risk model is often the default probability.

This format supports loss forecasting and is employed when we are confident in a model's ability to accurately predict bad rates for a given population. Population shifts, policy changes and other factors may cause risk models to over- or under-predict individual and group outcomes. This does not automatically render a risk model useless, however. Chart 1 shows model performance on the original vintage. To protect proprietary data, bad rates have been shown as indices, in proportion to the population average. The top decile of the model has bad rate 4.5 times the average for this group. Chart 2 shows another cohort scored with the same model. In this population average bad rate is only half of the original rate, so the model over-predicts. Nevertheless, it rank orders risk equally well. The bad rate in the top decile is almost five times the average for this group.

Another common form of credit scorecards is built on a point-based system, by creating a linear function of log (odds). The slope of this function is a constant factor which can be distributed through all bins of each variable in the model to allocate "weights."

Table 1 shows an example of a point based, additive scorecard. After adding scores in all categories we arrive at the numerical value (score) for each applicant. This format of a credit score is simple to interpret and can be easily understood by non-technical personnel. A well known and widely utilized case of an additive scorecard is FICO.

Table 1.

Additive Scorecard Example (*)

Predictive Characteristics	Interval (Bin)	Point Values
Monthly income	Missing	0
	< $1,000	-75
	$1,001 - $2,999	0
	$3,000+	40
Time at residence in months	Missing	0
	1-15	-50
	16-60	-22
	61-139	40
	140+	80
Ratio of satisfactory to total trades	<45	-60
	46-70	-32
	71-90	0
	90+	80
Credit utilization (balance to limit)	<20%	100
	21-50	78
	51-75	0
	76+	-72
Age of oldest trade in months	<15	-145
	16-48	0
	49-74	35
	75+	72

(*)Example from a training manual, not real data

Model Quality Assessment

The first step in evaluating any (binary) classifier is confusion matrix (sometimes called a contingency table) represents classification decisions for a test dataset. For each classified record there are four possible outcomes. If the record is bad and it is classified as positive (bad), it is counted as a true positive; if it is classified as negative (good), it is counted as a false negative. If the record is good and it is classified as negative (good), it is counted as a true negative; if it is classified as positive(bad), it is counted as a false positive. Table 2 shows the confusion matrix scheme.

Several performance metrics common in the data mining industry are calculated from the confusion matrix.

Table2.

		True Outcome	
		Bad	**Good**
Predicted Outcome	**Bad**	True Positive TP	False Positive FP
	Good	False Negative FN	True Negative TN
Column Totals		**P = Total Bads**	**N = Total Goods**

Precision = TP/(TP+FP)
Accuracy = (TP +TN)/(P + N)
Error Rate = (FP + FN)/(P + N)
tp_rt = TP/P
fp_rt = FP/N

Credit risk community recognized early on that the top three metrics are not good evaluation tools for scorecards. As is usually the case with modeling of rare events, the misclassification rates are too high to make accuracy a goal. In addition, those metrics are highly sensitive to changes in class distributions. Several empirical metrics have taken root instead.

Prior to selecting an optimal classifier (i.e., threshold), model's strength is evaluated on the entire dataset. First we make sure that it rank-orders the bads on selected level aggregate (deciles, percentiles, etc.). If a fit is required, we compare the predicted performance to the actual. Chart 1 and Chart 2 above illustrate rank-order and fit assessment by model decile.

Data mining industry standard for model performance assessment is the ROC analysis. On an ROC curve the hit rate (true positive rate) and false alarm rate (false positive rate) are plotted on a two-dimensional graph. This is a great visual tool to assess model's predictive power. It is also a great tool to compare performance of several models on the same dataset. Chart 3 shows the ROC curves for three different risk models. Higher true positive rate for the same false positive rate represents superior performance. Model 1 clearly dominates Model 2 as well as the benchmark model.

A common credit industry metric related to the ROC curve, is the Gini coefficient. It is calculated as twice the area between the diagonal and the curve (Source: Banasik, Crook, & Thomas 2005).

Chart 3.

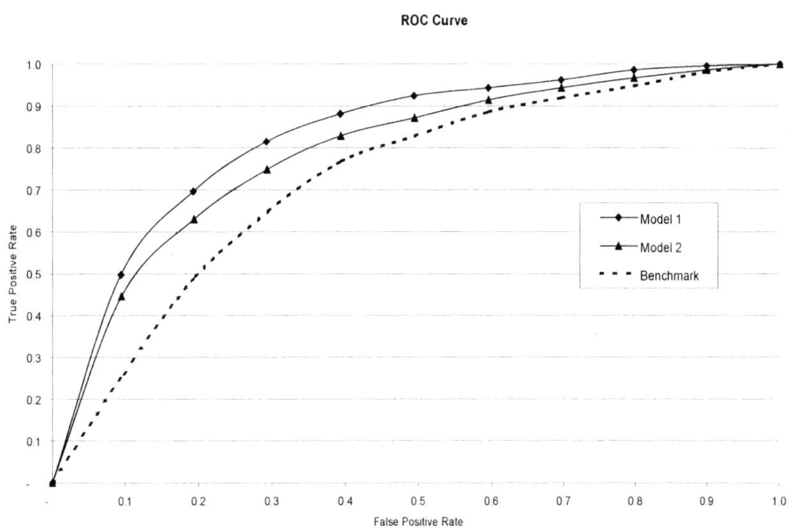

The higher the value of the coefficient the better performance of the model.

In case of a risk model, the ROC curve resembles another data mining standard—the gains curve. On a gains curve the cumulative percent of "hits" is plotted against the cumulative percent of the population. Chart 4 shows the gains chart for the same three models. The cumulative percent of hits (charge-offs) is equivalent to the true positive rate. The cumulative percent of population is close to the false positive rate, because, as a consequence of highly imbalanced class distribution, the percentage of false positives is very high.

A key measure in model performance assessment is its ability to separate classes. A typical approach to determine class separation considers "goods" and "bads" as two separate distributions. Several techniques have been developed to measure their separation.

Early works on class separation in credit risk models used standardized distance between means of the empirical densities of good and bad populations. It's a metric derived from the Mahalanobis distance (Duda, Hart, & Stork, 2001). In it's general form the squared Mahalanobis distance is defined as:

$$r^2 = (\mu_1 - \mu_2)^T \Sigma^{-1}((\mu_1 - \mu_2)$$

where μ_1, μ_2 are means of the respective distributions and Σ is a covariance matrix.

In case of one-dimensional distributions with equal variance, the Mahalanobis distance is calculated as a difference of the two means divided by the standard deviation.

$$r = | \mu_1 - \mu_2 | / \sigma$$

If the variances are not equal, which is typically the case in good and bad classes, the distance is standardized by dividing by the pooled variance.

$$\sigma = ((N_G \sigma_G^2 + N_B \sigma_B^2) / (N_G + N_B))^{½}$$

Chart 5 shows empirical distributions of a risk score on good and bad population.

Chart 6 shows the same distributions smoothed.

Chart 4.

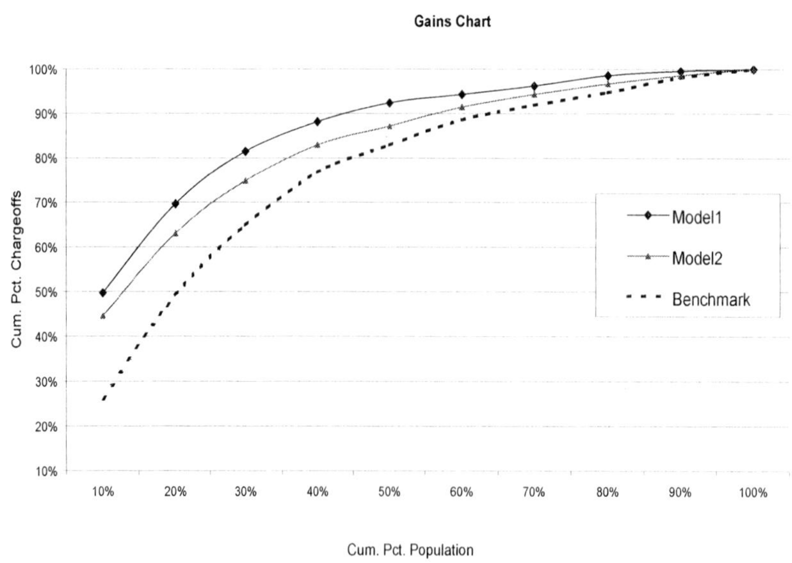

Chart 5.

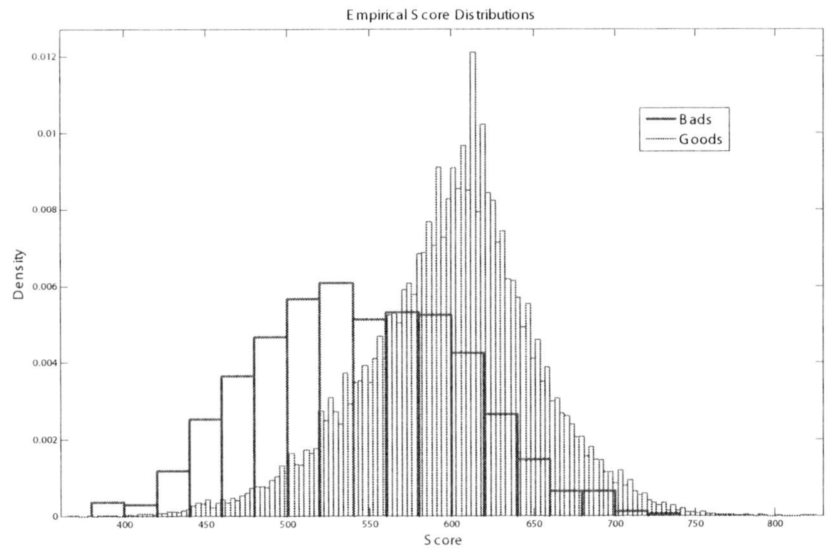

Chart 6.

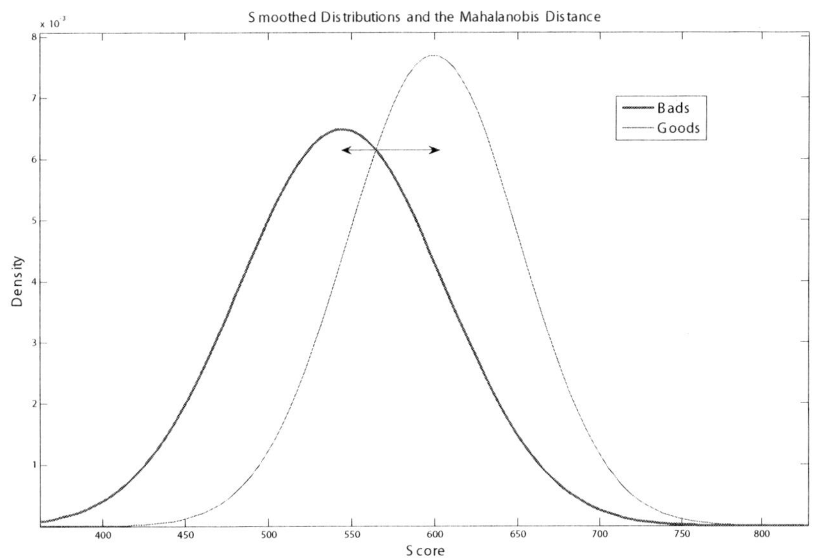

While the concept of Mahalanobis distance is visually appealing and intuitive, the need for normalization makes its calculations tedious and not very practical.

The credit industry's favorite separation metric is the Kolmogorov-Smirnov (K-S) statistic. The K-S statistic is calculated as the maximum distance between cumulative (empirical) distributions of goods and bads (Duda et al., 2001).If the cumulative distributions of goods and bads, as rank ordered by the score under consideration, are respectively is $F_G(x)$ and $F_B(x)$ then:

K-S distance = $| F_G(x) - F_B(x) |$

K-S statistic is the maximum K-S distance across all values of the score. The larger K-S statistic, the better separation of goods and bads has been accomplished by the score.

Chart 7 shows the cumulative distributions of the above scores, and the K-S distance.

K-S is a robust metric and it proved simple and practical, especially for comparing models built on the same dataset. It enjoys tremendous popularity in the credit industry. Unfortunately, the K-S statistic, like its predecessor Mahalanobis, tends to be most sensitive in the center of the distribution whereas the decisioning region (and the likely threshold location) is usually in the tail.

Typically, model performance is validated on a holdout sample. Techniques of cross-validation, such as k-fold, jackknifing, or bootstrapping are employed if datasets are small.

The model selected still needs to be validated on the out-of-time dataset. This is a crucial step in selecting a model that will perform well on new vintages. Credit populations evolve continually with marketplace changes. New policies impact class distribution and credit quality of incoming vintages.

Threshold Selection

The next step is the cutoff (threshold) selection. A number of methods have been proposed for optimization of the threshold selection, from introducing cost curves (Drummond & Holte, 2002, 2004), to employing OR techniques which support additional constraints (Olecka, 2002).

Chart 7.

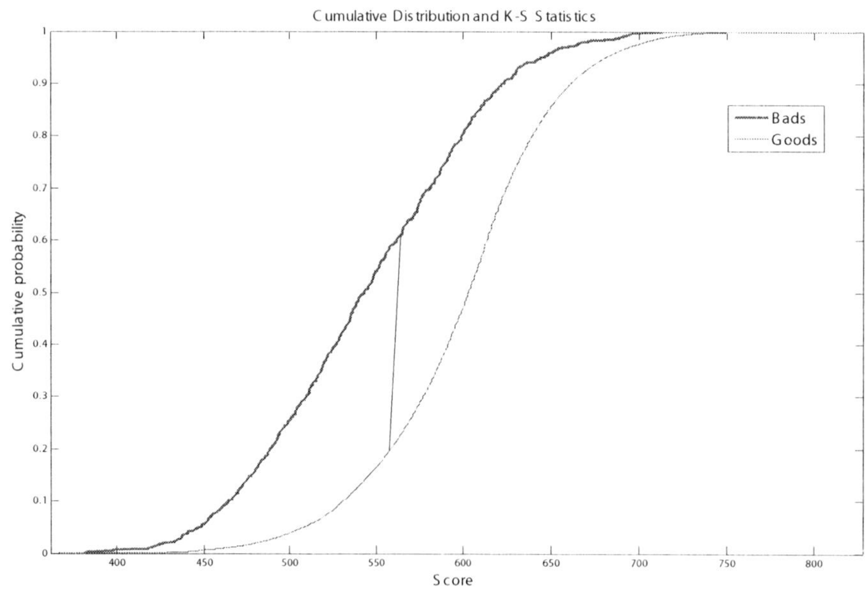

Broadly accepted, flexible classifier selection tool is ROCCH (ROC convex hull) introduced by Provost and Fawcett (2001). This approach introduced a hybrid classifier forming a boundary of a convex hull in the ROC space (fp_rt, tp_rt). Expected cost is defined based on fixed costs of each error type.

The cost line "slides" upwards, until hits the boundary of the convex hull. The tangent point minimizes the expected cost and represents optimal threshold. In this approach, the optimal point can be selected in real time, at each run of the application, based on the costs and the current class distribution. The sliding cost lines and the optimal point selection have been illustrated in Chart 8.

Unfortunately, this flexible approach does not translate well into the reality of lending institutions. Due to regulatory requirements, the lending criteria need to be clear cut and well documented. Complexity of factors affecting score cuts selection precludes static costs assignments and makes dynamic solutions difficult to implement. More importantly, the true class distribution on a group of applicants is not known, since performance has been observed only on the approved accounts.

Chief among the challenges of threshold selection, is striking a balance between the risk exposure, approval rates and cost of a marketing campaign. More risky prospects usually generate better response rate. Cutting risk too deep will adversely impact the acquisition costs. Threshold selection is a critical analytic task which determines company's credit policy. In practice it becomes a separate data mining undertaking. It involves exploration of various "what if" scenarios and evaluating numerous cost factors, such as risk, profitability, expected response and approval rates, determining swap-in and swap-out volumes and so forth. In many cases, population will be segmented and separate cut-offs applied to each segment.

An interesting approach to threshold selection, based on the efficient frontier methodology, has been proposed by Oliver and Wells (2001).

Ongoing Validation, Monitoring, and Tracking

In words of Dennis Ash, at the Federal Reserve Forum on Consumer Credit Risk Model Validation: "The scorecards are old when they are first put in. Then they are used for 5-10 years" (Burns & Ody, 2004).

Chart 8.

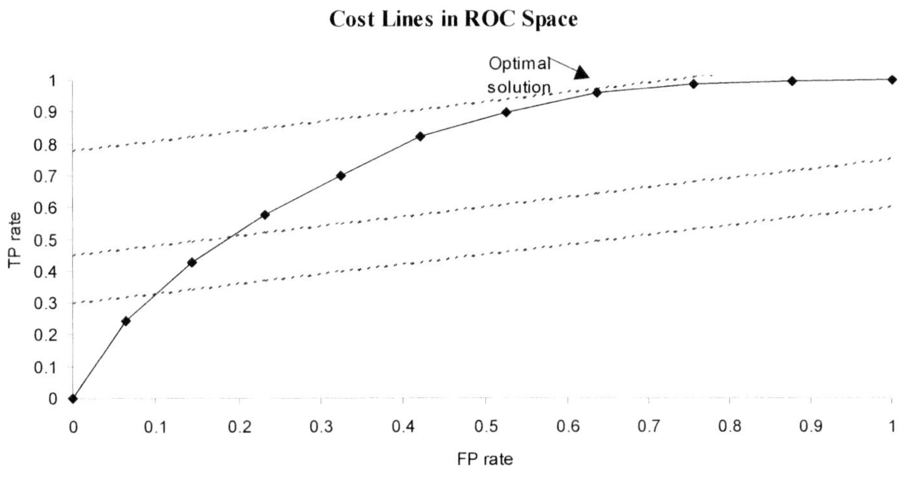

With the 18-24 month observation window, attributes used in the model are at least two years old. In that time not only the attributes get "stale," but populations coming through the door can evolve, due to changing economic conditions and our own evolving policies.

It is imperative that the models used for managing credit losses undergo continuous re-evaluation on new vintages. In addition, we need to monitor distribution of key attributes and the score itself for incoming vintages as well as early delinquencies of young accounts. This will ensure early detection of a population shift, so that models can be recalibrated or rebuilt.

Some companies implement score monitoring program in the quality control fashion, ensuring that mean scores do not cross over pre-determine variance. Others rely on a χ^2 type calculated metric known as stability index (SI). SI measures how well the newly scored population fits into deciles established by the original population.

Let $s_0 = 0, s_1, s_2, \ldots s_{10} = s_{max}$ are bounds determined by the score deciles in the original population. Record x with a score x_s falls into the i'th decile if $s_{i-1} < x_s < s_i$. Ideally we would like to see in each score interval close to the original 10% of individuals. The divergence from the original distribution is calculated as:

$$SI = \Sigma_{i=1...10} ((F_i / M - 0.1) * (\log(10 * F_i / M)))$$

where $F_i = |\{x: s_{i-1} < x_s < s_i\}|$ and M = size of the new sample.

It is generally accepted that SI > 0.25 indicates significant departure from the original distribution and a need for a new model. SI > 0.1 indicates a need for further investigation (Crook, Edelman, & Thomas, 2002). One can perform similar analysis on score components to find out which attributes caused the shift.

CREDIT SCORING CHALLENGES FOR DATA MINER

In some aspects data mining for credit card risk is easier than in other applications. Data have been scrubbed clean, management is already convinced of value of analytic solutions and support infrastructure is in place. Still, many of the usual data mining challenges are present, from unbalanced data, to multi-colinearity of predictors. Other challenges are unique to the credit industry.

Target Selection and Other Data Challenges

We need to provide business with a tool to manage credit losses. Precise definition of target behavior and dataset selection is crucial and can actually be quite complicated. This challenge is no different than in other business oriented settings. But credit specific realities provide a good case in point of complexity of the target selection step.

Suppose the goal is to target charge-offs, the simplest of all "bad" metrics. What time window should be selected for observation of the target behavior? It needs to be long enough to accumulate sufficient bad volume. But if it is too long, the present population may be quite different than the original one. Most experts agree on 18-24 month performance time horizon for prime credit card portfolio and 12 months for sub-prime lending. A lot can change in such a long time: from internal policies to economic conditions and changes in the competitive marketplace.

Once the "bads" are defined, who is classified as "goods"? What to do with delinquent accounts for example? And what about accounts which had been "cured" due to collections activity but are still more likely than average to charge-off in the end? Sometimes these decisions depend on modeler's ability to recognize such cases in the databases. Subjective approvals, for example, that is accounts approved by manual overrides, may behave differently than the rest of the portfolio, but we may not be able to identify them in the portfolio.

Feature selection always requires careful screening process. When it comes to credit decisioning models, however, compliance considerations take priority over modeling ones. Financial industry is required to comply with stringent legal regulations. Models driving credit approvals need to be transparent. Potential rejection reasons must be clearly explainable and within legal framework. Factors such as prospect's age, race, gender, or neighborhood cannot be used to decline credit, no matter how predictive they are. Subsequently, they cannot be used in a decisioning model, regardless of their predictive power.

Challenges in feature selection are amplified by extremely noisy data. Most credit bureau attributes are highly correlated. Just consider a staple foursome of attributes: number of credit cards, balances carried, total credit lines, and utilization. With such obvious dependencies, it takes a skillful art to navigate traps of multicollinearity.

A risk modeler also needs to make sure that variables selected have weights aligned with the risk direction. Attributes with non-monotone relationships with the target pose another challenge. Chart 9 demonstrates one such example.

Bad rate clearly grows with increasing utilization of the existing credit. Except for those with 0% utilization. This is because credit utilization for an individuals with no credit card is zero. They may have bad credit rating or are just entering the credit market. Either case makes them more risky than average. We could find a transformation to smooth out this "bump." But while technically simple, this might cause difficulties in model application. The underlying reason for risk level is different in this group than in the high utilization group.

We could use a dummy variables to separate the non-users. If that group is small, however, our dummy variable will not enter the model and some of the information value from this attribute will be lost.

Segmentation Challenge

If the non-users population in the above example is large enough, we can segment-out the non-users and build a separate scorecard for that segment. Non-users are certain to behave very differently than experienced credit users and should be considered a separate sub-population. Need for segmentation is well recognized in credit scor-

Chart 9.

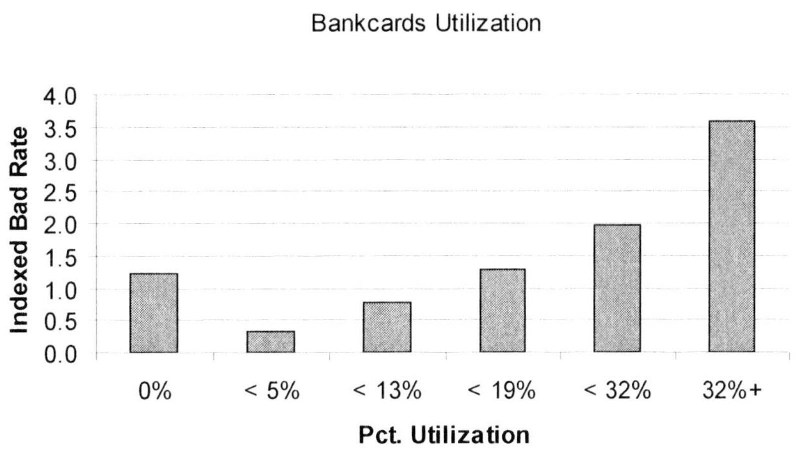

ing. Consider Chart 10. Attribute A is a strong risk predictor on Segment 1, but it is fairly flat on Segment 2. Segment 2, however, represents over 80% population. As a result, this attribute does not show predictive power on the population as a whole. We need a separate scorecard for Segment 1 because it's risk behavior is different than the rest of the population, and it is small enough to "disappear" in a global model.

There are some generally accepted segmentation schemes, but in general, the segmentation process remains empirical. In designing a segmentation scheme, we need to strike a balance between selecting distinct behavior differences and maintaining sample sizes large enough to support a separate model. Statistical techniques like clustering and decision trees can shed some light on partitioning possibilities, but business domain knowledge and past experience are better guides here than any theory could provide.

Unbalanced Data Challenge: Modeling a Rare Event

Risk modeling involves highly unbalanced datasets. This is a well known data mining challenge. In the presence of a rare class, even the best models yield tremendous amount of false positives. Consider the following (hypothetical) scenario.

A classifier threshold is set at the top 5% of scores. The model identifies 60% of bads in that top 5% of the population (i.e., the true positive rate is 60%). That is a terrific bad recognition power. But if the bad rate in the population is 2%, then only 24% of those classified as bad are true bad.

TP/(TP+FP) = (0.6*P)/(0.05*M) = (0.6***0.02*M**)/ 0.05*M = 0.24

Where M is the total population size and P is the number of total bads. (i.e., P = 0.02*M)

If the population bad rate is 1% (P = 0.01*M), then only 12% of those classified as bad are true bad.

TP/(TP+FP) = (0.6*P)/(0.05*M) = (0.6***0.01*M**)/ 0.05M = 0.12

The challenges of modeling rare events are not unique to credit scoring and had been well documented in the data mining literature. Standard tools—in particular the maximum likelihood algorithms common in commercial software pack-

Chart 10.

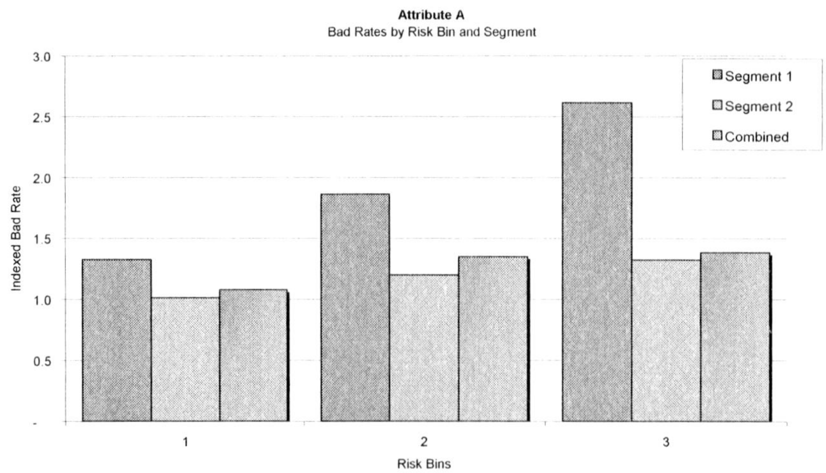

ages—do not deal well with rare events, because the majority class has much higher impact than the minority class. Several ideas on dealing with imbalanced data in model development have been proposed and documented (Weiss, 2004). Most notable solutions are:

- Over-sampling the bads
- Under-sampling the goods (Drummond & Holte, 2003)
- Two-phase modeling

All of these ideas have merits, but also drawbacks. Over-sampling the bads can improve impact of the minority class, but it is also prone to overfitting. Under-sampling the goods, removes data from the training set and may remove some information in the process. Both methods require additional post-processing if probability is the desired output. Two-phase modeling, with second phase training on a preselected, more balanced sample has only been proven successful if additional sources of data are available.

Least absolute difference (LAD) algorithms differ from the least squares (OLS) algorithms in that the sum of the absolute, not squared, deviations is minimized. LAD models promise improvements in overcoming the majority class domination. No significant results with these methods, however, have been reported in credit scoring.

Modeling Challenges: Combining Two Targets in One Score

There are two primary components of credit card losses: bankruptcy and contractual charge-offs. Characteristics of customers in each of these cases are somewhat similar, yet differ enough to warrant a separate model for each case. For the final result, both, bankruptcy and contractual charge-offs need to be combined to form one prediction of expected losses.

Modeling Challenge #1: Minimizing Charge-off Instances

Removing the most risky prospects prior to mailing minimizes marketing costs and improve approval rates for responders. To estimate risk level of each prospect, the mail file is scored with a custom charge-off risk score.

We need a model predicting probability of any charge-off: bankruptcy or contractual. The training and validation data come from an earlier marketing campaign with 24 month performance history. The target class, charge-off (CO) is further divided into two sub-classes: bankruptcies (BK) and contractual charge-offs (CCO).

The hypothetical example used for this model maintains ratio of 30% bankruptcies to 70% contractual charge-offs. Without loss of generality, actual charge-off rates have been replaced by indexed rates, representing a ratio of bad rate to the population average in each bad category. To protect proprietary data, attributes in this sections will be refered to as *Attribute A*, *B*, *C*, and so forth.

Exploratory data analysis shows that the two bad categories have several predictive attributes in common. To verify that *Attribute A* rank orders both bad categories, we split the continuous values of *Attribute A* into three risk bins. Bankruptcy and contractual charge-off rates in each bin decline in a similar proportion. Chart 11 shows this trend.

Some of the other attributes, however, behave differently for the two bad categories. Chart 12 shows *Attribute B*, which rank-orders both risk classes well, but differences between the corresponding bad rates are quite substantial.

Chart 13 shows Attribute C which rank-orders well the bankruptcy risk, but remains almost flat for the contractual charge-offs.

Based on this preliminary analysis we suspect that separate modeling effort for BK and CCO would yield better results than targeting all charge-offs as one category. To validate this observation, three models are compared.

Chart 11.

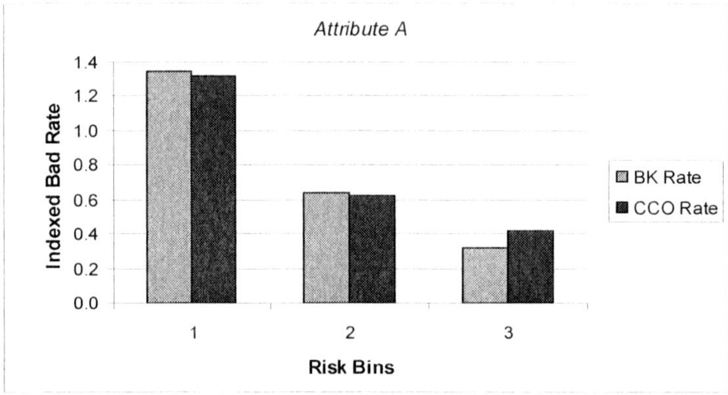

Chart 12.

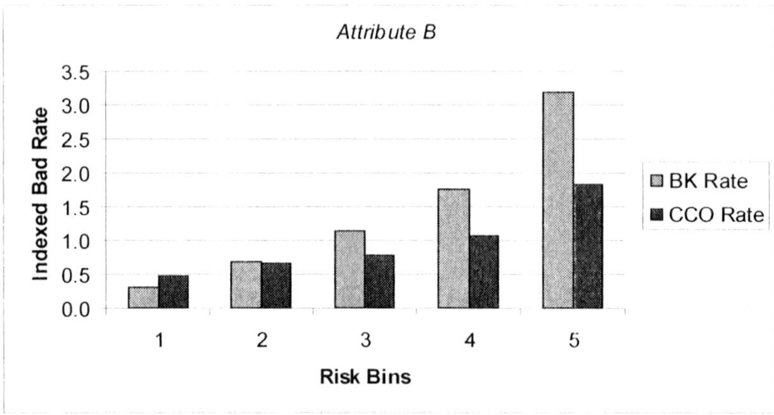

Chart 13.

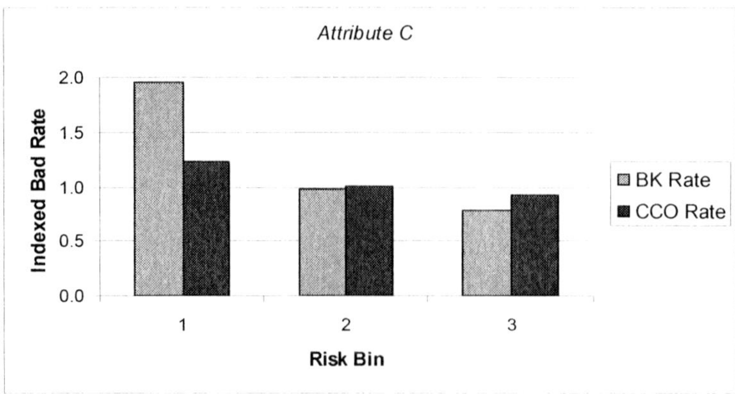

Model 1. Binary logistic regression: Two classes are considered: CO=1 (charge-off of either kind) and CO=0 (no charge-off). The goal is to obtain the estimate of probability of the account charging off within the pre-determined time window. This is a standard model, which will serve as a benchmark.

Model 2. Multinomial logistic regression: Three classes considered: BK, CCO, and GOOD. The multinomial logistic regression outputs probability of the first two classes.

Model 3. Nested logistic regressions: This model involves a two step process.

- **Step1:** Two classes considered: BK=1 or BK=0.

  Let q_i = P(BK=1) for each individual i in the sample. Log odds ratio $z_i = \log (q_i/(1-q_i))$ is estimated by the logistic regression.

  $$z_i = \alpha_i + \gamma_i * \mathbf{X}$$

  where α_i, γ_i is the vector of parameter estimates for individual i and **X** is vector of predictors in the bankruptcy equation.

- **Step 2:** Two classes are considered: CO=1 (charge-off of any kind) and CO=0.

  Logistic regression predicts probability p_i= P(CO=1).
  The bankruptcy odds estimate z_i from Step1 is an additional predictor in the model.

  $$p_i = 1/(1 + \exp(-\alpha_i' - \beta^0_i * z_i - \beta_i * \mathbf{Y}))$$

  where α_i', β^0_i, β_i is the vector of parameter estimates for individual i, and **Y** - vector of selected predictors in the charge-off equation.

We have seen in the exploratory phase that the two targets are highly correlated and several attributes are predictive of both targets. There are two major potential pitfalls associated with using a score from the bankruptcy model as an input in the charge-off model. Both are indirectly related to multicollinearity, but each requires a different stopgap measure.

a. If some of the same attributes are selected into both models, we may be overestimating their influence. Historical evidence indicates that models with collinear attributes deteriorate over time and need to be recalibrated.

b. The second stage model may attempt to diminish the influence of a variable selected in the first stage. It may try to introduce that variable in the second stage with the opposite coefficient. While this improves the predictive power of the model, it makes it impossible to interpret the coefficients. To prevent this, the modeling process often requires several iterations of each stage.

For the purpose of this study, we assume that the desired cut is the riskiest 10% of the mail file. We look for a classifier with the best performance in the top decile. Chart 14 shows the gains chart, calculated on the hold out test sample for the three models. Model 1, as expected, is dominated by the other two. Model 2 dominates from decile 2 onwards. Model 3 has the highest lift in the top decile.

While Models 2 and 3 performance is close, Model 3 maximizes the objective, by performing best in the top decile. By eliminating 10% of the mail file Model 3 eliminates 30% of charge-offs while Model 2 eliminates 28% of charge-offs. A 2% (200 basis points) improvement in a large credit card portfolio can translate into millions of dollars saved in future charge-offs.

Modeling Challenge #2: Predicting Expected Dollar Losses

A risk model predicts probability of charge-off instances. Meanwhile, the actual business objective is to minimize dollar losses from charge-offs.

A simple approach to predicting dollar losses could be predicting dollar-losses directly, through a continuous outcome model, such as multivariable regression. But this is not a practical approach. The charge-off observation window is long; 18-24 months. It would be difficult to build a balance model over such long time horizon. Balances are strongly dependent on the product type and on usage pattern of a cardholder. Products evolve over time to reflect marketplace changes. Subsequently, balance models need to be nimble, flexible and evolve with each new product.

Chart 14.

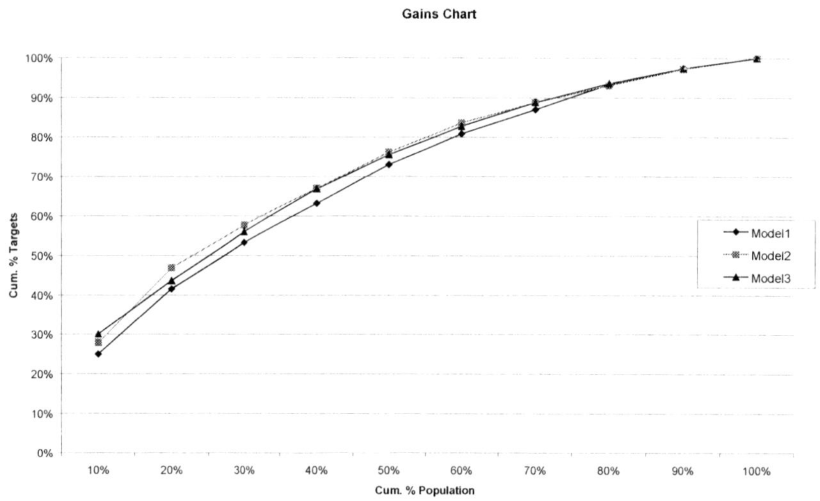

Chart 15.

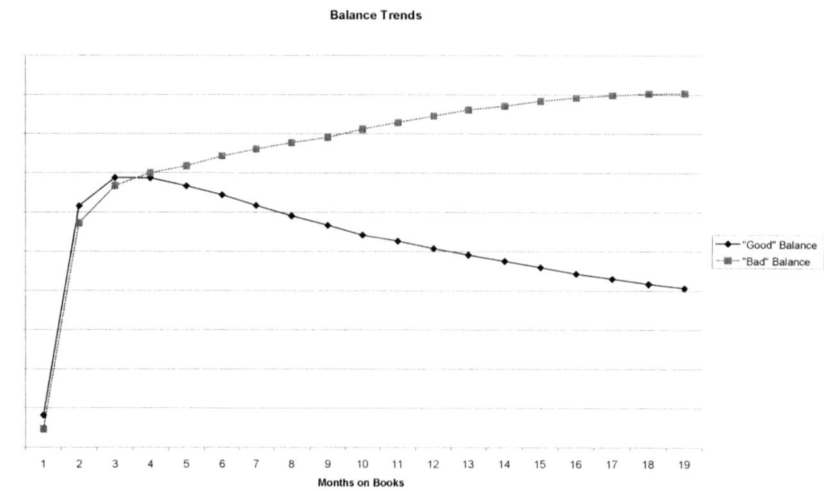

Good and Bad Balance Prediction: Chart 15 shows a diverging trend of good and bad balances over time. Bad balances are balances on accounts that charged-off within 19 months. Good balances come from the remaining population.

As mentioned earlier, building the balance model directly on the charge-off accounts is not practical, due to small sample sizes and aged data. Instead, we used the charge-off data to trend of the average bad balance over time.

Early balance accumulation is similar in both classes, but after a few months they begin to diverge. After reaching the peak in the third month, the average good balance gradually drops off. Some customers pay off their balances, become inactive, or attrite. The average bad balance, however, continues to grow. We take advantage

Chart 16.

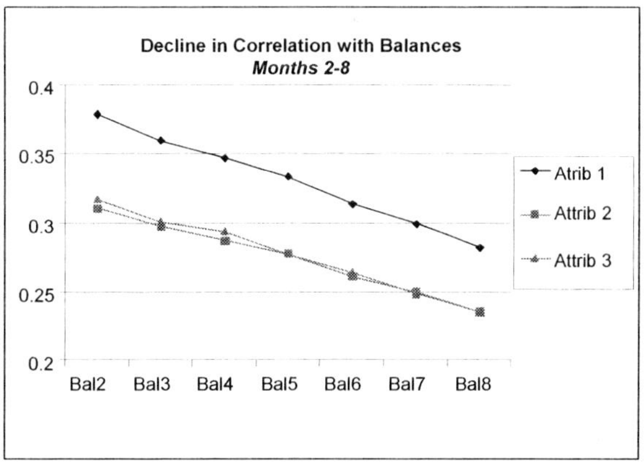

Chart 17.

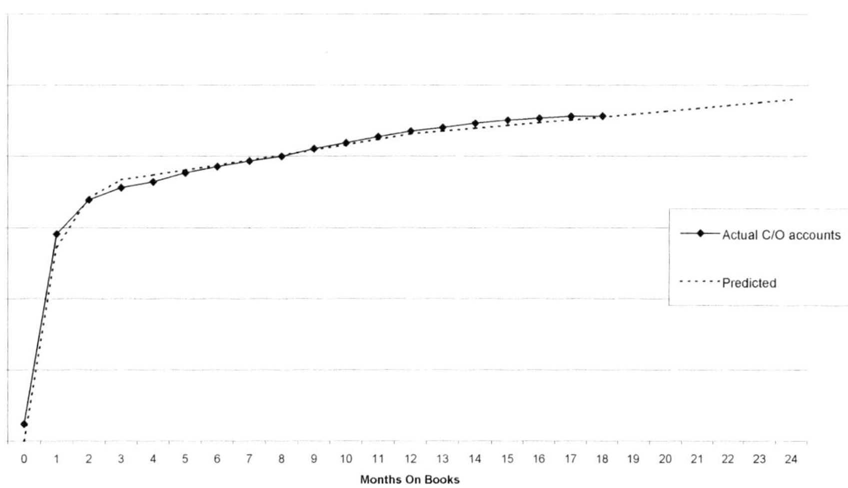

of this early similarity and predict early balance accumulation, using the entire dataset. We then extrapolate the good and bad balance prediction by utilizing the observed trends.

Selecting early account history as a target has an advantage of freshness of the data. A brief examination of the available predictors indicates that their predictive power diminishes as the time horizon moves further away from the time of the mailing (i.e., time when the data was obtained). Chart 16 shows the diminishing correlation with balances over time of three attributes.

The modeling scheme consists of a sequence of steps. First we predict the expected early balance. This model is built on the entire vintage. Then we use observed trends to extrapolate balance prediction for the charged-off accounts. This is done separately for good and bad populations.

Chart 17 shows the result the bad balance prediction. Regression was used to predict balances in month 2 and month 3 (peak). A growth factor f1 = 1.0183 was applied to extrapolate the results for months 5-12. Another growth factor f2 = 1.0098 was applied to extrapolate for months 13-24.

The final output is a combined prediction of expected dollar losses. It combines outputs of three different models: charge-off instances prediction, balance prediction, and balance trending. The models, by necessity, come from different datasets and different time horizons. This is far from optimal from a theoretical standpoint. It is impossible, for example, to estimate prediction errors or confidence intervals.

Empirical evidence must fill the void where theoretical solutions are missing or impractical. This is where the due diligence in on-going predictions validation on out of time datasets becomes a necessity. Equally necessary are periodic tracking of predicted distributions and monitoring population parameters to make sure the models remain stable over time.

Modeling Challenge #3: Selection Bias

In the previous example, balances of customers who charged off as well as those who did not could be observed directly. This is not always possible.

Consider a model predicting the size of a balance transfer request made by a credit card applicant at the time of application. Balance transfer incentives are used in credit card marketing to encourage potential new customers to transfer their existing balances from other card issuers, while applying for a new card.

Balance transfer request will be a two stage model. First, a binary model predicts response to a mail offer. Then, a continuous model predicts size of a balance transfer request (0 if the applicant does not request a transfer.)

Only balance transfer requests from responders can be observed. This can bias the second stage model. This sample is self-selected. It is reasonable to assume that people with large balances to transfer are more likely to respond, particularly if the offer carries attractive balance transfer terms. Thus the balance prediction model built on responders only is likely to be biased towards higher transfer amounts. To make matters worse, responders are a small fraction of the prospect population. If a biased model is subsequently applied to score a new prospect population, it may overestimate balance transfer requests for those with low probability of responding.

This issue was addressed by James J.Heckman (1979). In the presence of a selection bias, a correction term is calculated in the first stage and introduced in the second stage, as an additional regressor.

Let x_i represent the target of the response model.

$x_i = 1$ if individual i responds
$x_i = 0$ otherwise

The second stage is a regression model where y_i represents balance prediction of individual i. We want to estimate y_i with:

$$y_i (\mathbf{X} \mid x_i = 1) = \alpha_i' + \beta_i' \mathbf{X} + \varepsilon_i$$

where $\mathbf{X}$ is a vector of predictors and α_i', β_i' is the vector of parameter estimates in the balance prediction equation built on records of the responders and ε_i is a random error.

If the model selection is biased then $E(\varepsilon_i) \neq 0$. Subsequently:

$E(y_i(\mathbf{X})) = E(y_i(\mathbf{X} \mid x_i = 1)) = \alpha' + \beta_i' \mathbf{X} + E(\varepsilon_i)$ is a biased estimator of y_i.

Heckman first proposed methodology aiming to correct this bias in case of a positive bias (overestimating). His results were further refined by Greene (1981), who discussed cases of bias in either direction.

In order to calculate the correction term, the inverse Mills ratio $\lambda(z_i)$ is estimated from Stage1 and entered in Stage2 as an additional regressor:

$$\lambda_i = \lambda(z_i) = \mathrm{pdf}(z_i) / \mathrm{cdf}(z_i)$$

where z_i is the odds ratio estimate from Stage1, $\mathrm{pdf}(z_i) = (1/\sqrt{(2\pi)})^* \exp(-(z_i^2/2))$ is the standard normal probability density function, and $\mathrm{cdf}(z_i)$ is the standard normal cumulative density function.

$y_i(\mathbf{X}, \lambda_i \mid x_i = 1)) = \alpha' + \beta_i' \mathbf{X} + \beta^0_i * \lambda_i + \varepsilon'_i$ where $E(\varepsilon'_i) = 0$ and

$E(y_i(\mathbf{X})) = E(y_i(\mathbf{X} \mid x_i = 1)) = \alpha' + \beta_i' \mathbf{X} + \beta^0_i * \lambda_i$ is an unbiased estimator of y_i.

Details of the framework of bias correction, as well as error estimate can be found in (Greene, 2000).

Among the pioneers introducing the two stage modeling framework, were the winners of the KDD 1998 Cup. The winning team—GainSmarts—has implemented the Heckman's model in a direct marketing setting, soliciting donations for a non-profit veteran's organization (KDD Nuggets, 1998). The dataset consisted of past contributors. Attributes included their (yes/no) responses to a fundraising campaign, and the amount donated by those who responded. The first step of the winning model was a logistic regression predicting response probability, built on all prospects. The second stage was a linear regression model built on the responder dataset, estimating the donation amount. The final output was the expected donation amount calculated as the product of the probability of responding and the estimated donation amount. Net gain was calculated by subtracting mailing costs from the estimated amount. The benchmark, a hypothetical, optimal net gain was calculated as $14,712 by assuming that only the actual donors were mailed. The GainSmarts team came within a 1% error of the benchmark achieving the net gain of $14,844.

This model was introduced as a direct marketing solution, but lessons learned are just as applicable to two stage modeling in credit scoring models described previously.

More On Selection Bias: Our Decisions Change the Future Outcome

Taking the Heckman's reasoning on selection bias one step further, one can argue that all credit risk models built on actual performance are subject to selection bias. We build models on censored data of prospects whose credit was approved, yet we use it to score all applicants.

A collection of techniques called reject inference has been developed in the credit industry to deal with selection bias and performance of risk models on the un-observed population. Some advocate iterative model development process to make sure that the model would perform on the rejected population as well as on the accepted one. There are several ways to infer behavior of the rejects, from assuming they are all bad, through extrapolation of the observed trend and so forth. But each of these methods makes assumptions about risk distributions on the unobserved. Without observing the unobserved, we cannot verify that those assumptions are true. Ultimately the only way to know that models will behave the same way for the whole population is to sample from the unobserved population. In credit risk this would imply letting higher than optimal losses through the door. It is sometimes acceptable to create a clean sample this way. Particularly if aiming at a brand new population group or expecting very low loss rate based on domain knowledge. But in general, this is not a very realistic business model.

Banasik et al. (2005) introduce a binary probit model to deal with cases of bias selection. They compare empirical results for models built on selected vs. unselected population. The novelty of this study is not just in theoretical framework for biased cases, but also in following up with an actual model performance comparison. The general conclusion reached, is that the potential for improvement is marginal and depends on actual variables in the model as well as selected cutoff points.

There are other sources of bias affecting "cleanness" of the modeling population. Chief among them company evolving risk policy. First source of bias are the binary criteria mentioned earlier. They provide a safety net and are important components of loss management, but they tend to evolve over time. As a new model is implemented, population selection criteria change, impacting future vintages.

With so many sources of bias, there is no realistic hope for a "clean" development sample. The only way to know that a model will continue to perform the way it was intended, is—once again—due diligence in regular monitoring and periodic validation on new vintages.

CONCLUSION

Data mining has matured tremendously in the past decade. Techniques that once were cutting edge experiments, are now common. Commercial tools are widely available for practitioners, so no one needs to re-invent the wheel. Most importantly, businesses have recognized the need for data mining applications and have build supportive infrastructure.

Data miners can quickly and thoroughly explore mountains of data and translate their findings into business intelligence. Analytic solutions are rapidly implemented on IT platforms. This gives companies a competitive edge and motivates them to seek out potential further improvements. As our sophistication grows, so does our appetite. This attitude has taken solid roots in this dynamic field. With this growth, we have only begun to scale the complexity challenge.

REFERENCES

Banasik, J., Crook, J., & Thomas, L. (2005). *Sample selection bias in credit scoring.* Retrieved October 24, 2006, from http://fic.wharton.upenn.edu/fic/crook.pdf

Burns, P., & Ody, C. (2004, November 19). *Forum on validation of consumer credit risk models.* Federal Reserve Bank of Philadelphia. Retrieved October 24, 2006, from http://fic.wharton.upenn.edu/fic/11-19-05%20Conf%20Summary.pdf

Crook, J., Edelman, B., & Thomas, L. (2002). *Credit scoring and its applications.* SIAM Monographs on Mathematical Modeling and Computations.

Duda, R., Hart, P., & Stork, D. (2001). *Pattern classification.* Wiley & Sons.

Drummond, C., & Holte, R.(2002) Explicitly representing expected cost: An alternative to ROC representation. *Knowledge Discovery and Data Mining,* 198-207.

Drummond, C., & Holte, R. (2004). What ROC curves can't do (and cost curves can). *ROC Analysis in Artificial Intelligence (ROCAI),* 19-26.

Drummond, C., & Holte, R. (2003). C4.5, class imbalance, and cost sensitivity: Why under-sampling beats over-sampling. In *Proceedings of the International Conference on Machine Learning, Workshop on Learning from Imbalanced Datasets II.*

Fayyad, U. M., Piatetsky-Shapiro G., & Smyth, P. (1996). From data mining to knowledge discovery. *Advances in Knowledge Discovery and Data Mining.* AAAI/MIT Press.

Furletti, M. (2003). *Measuring credit card industry chargeoffs: A review of sources and methods.* Paper presented at the Federal Reserve Bank Meeting, Payment Cards Center Discussion, Philadelphia. Retrieved October 24, 2006, from http://www.philadelphiafed.org/pcc/discussion/MeasuringChargeoffs_092003.pdf

Greene, W. (1981, May). Sample selection bias as a specification error. *Econometrica, 49*(3), 795-798.

Greene, W. (2000). *Econometric analysis.* Upper Saddle River, NJ: Prentice Hall.

Heckman, J. (1979, January). Sample selection bias as a specification error. *Econometrica, 4*(1) 153-161.

KDD Nuggets. (1998). *Urban science wins the KDD-98 Cup: A second straight victory for GainSmarts.* Retrieved October 24, 2006, from http://www.kdnuggets.com/meetings/kdd98/gain-kddcup98-release.html

Olecka, A. (2002, July). Evaluating classifiers' performance in a constrained environment. In *Proceedings of the Eighth ACM SIGKDD International Conference on Knowledge Discovery and Data Mining,* Edmonton, Canada (pp. 605-612).

Oliver, R. M., & Wells, E. (2001). Efficient frontier cut-off policies in credit portfolios. *Journal of Operational Research Society, 53.*

Provost, F., & Fawcett, T. (2001). Robust classification for imprecise environment. *Machine Learning, 42*(3).

U.S. Department of Treasury. (2005, October). *Thrift industry charge-off rates by asset types.* Retrieved October 24, 2006, from http://www.ots.treas.gov/docs/4/48957.pdf

Weiss, G. M. (2004). Mining with rarity: A unifying framework. *SIGKDD Explorations, 6*(1).

Section VI
Data Mining and Ontology Engineering

Chapter IX
Semantics Enhancing Knowledge Discovery and Ontology Engineering Using Mining Techniques:
A Crossover Review

Elena Irina Neaga
Loughborough University Leicestershire, UK

ABSTRACT

This chapter deals with a roadmap on the bidirectional interaction and support between knowledge discovery (KD) processes and ontology engineering (ONTO) mainly directed to provide refined models using common methodologies. This approach provides a holistic literature review required for the further definition of a comprehensive framework and an associated meta-methodology (KD4ONTO4DM) based on the existing theories, paradigms, and practices regarding knowledge discovery and ontology engineering as well as closely related areas such as knowledge engineering, machine/ontology learning, standardization issues and architectural models. The suggested framework may adhere to the ISO-reference model for open distributed processing and OMG-model-driven architecture, and associated dedicated software architectures should be defined.

INTRODUCTION AND MOTIVATION

Generally, the role of ontologies in knowledge engineering has been deeply investigated since early 1990 such as the research reported by van Heijst (1995) in his thesis mainly dealing with the modalities of defining explicit ontologies and using them in order to facilitate the knowledge engineering processes. However, these earlier approaches have been achieved in the context of

Copyright © 2007, IGI Global, distributing in print or electronic forms without written permission of IGI Global is prohibited.

building knowledge based systems and enhancing the agents' knowledge base. These approaches are not contradictory to the current emergence of Semantic Web technologies using as a core concept the *ONTOLOGY* as "*an explicit specification of a conceptualization*" (Gruber, 1994, p. 200). Recently, ontologies have provided the development of common frameworks for dissimilar systems supporting disparate applications related to engineering, business and medicine. Generally, these applications have a high-level common foundation based on generic concepts and theories. Moreover, generic knowledge and ontology models capture the common aspects of different domains.

Currently, the problems related to *ontology engineering* workbenches, methodologies and tools are quite similar of those that knowledge engineers have approached in order to define knowledge bases. Besides the machine learning is a common artificial intelligence technique used in ontology development as well as in knowledge intensive systems including data mining. Although the ontology and knowledge bases can be independently defined, used, processed and maintained there is not a strict separation between them (Maedche, 2002), and the approach enclosed in this chapter emphasizes the similarities and the differences.

There are not many crossover approaches regarding both knowledge discovery process and ontology engineering, but Gottgtroy, Kasabov, and MacDonell (2003, 2004) have explored the bidirectional interaction and support between the related processes. This interaction is graphically represented in Figure 1.

Figure 1. KD4ONTO4KD

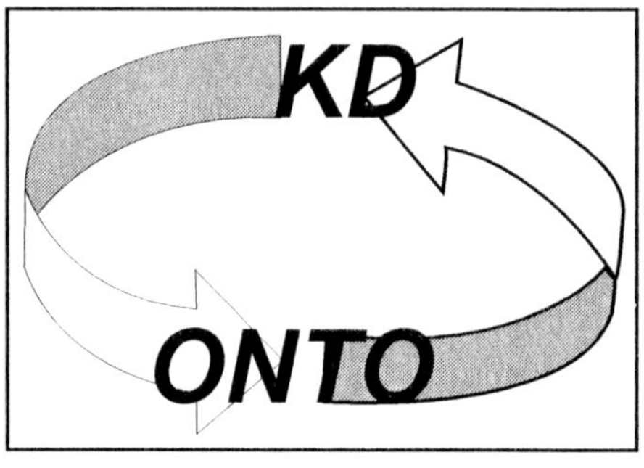

The knowledge discovery process includes several phases, such as data preparation, cleaning and transformation, and each of these phases or steps in the life-cycle might benefit from an *ontology-driven approach* which underpins the semantics in order to enhance the knowledge discovery processes. Applying intelligent data analysis, visualization, and mining techniques to discover and identify meaningful relationships, missing and clustering concepts may contribute to refine ontology models and related processes (Gottgtroy et al., 2003, 2004). On the other hand, as well as Maedche (2002) and Staab (2000, 2001) have introduced a novel approach of applying knowledge discovery to multiple data sources to support the development and maintenance of ontologies and techniques for ontology learning mainly from text.

Nowadays, a very important aspect is the explosive growth of information available on the World Wide Web which makes very difficult to deal with information overload and relevance. These issues can be approached using Web personalization based on Web usage mining which applies mining algorithms such as association rules, sequential patterns and clustering in the context of Web mining. De Moor (2005) suggested an approach based on context dependent ontologies by using so-called pragmatic patterns which are defined as meta- patterns including the ontology models and the context description. It then becomes possible to better deal with information overload and relevance as well as partial, contradicting, evolving ontologies and meaning negotiation.

An ontological approach of data mining systems may also provide the interoperability functionalities of knowledge discovery distributed systems. Furthermore given the present lack of a generally accepted framework for knowledge discovery processing and ontology engineering, *the quest for a unified framework is a major research priority.*

The objectives of this chapter are described in the next section. The main part of this chapter deals with a roadmap which analysing the present status of the related approaches, methodologies and their interaction as well as current and further research issues, requirements and practices in order that knowledge discovery processes and ontology engineering to strongly support each other. The basic concepts, paradigms and models are briefly presented, and an overview of ontology learning issues is also included. Existing methodologies and relevant applications are also presented. The section dedicated towards a semantics enhancing framework and related meta-methodology includes an outline of associated architectural approaches.

Objectives

The main objective of this chapter is related to comprehensively answering the research question: *How can knowledge discovery and ontology engineering support each other?*

The related research questions of this chapter can be formulated as follows:

- How can explicit generic and domain-dependent ontologies ease the knowledge discovery process?
- How can data/text/Web mining contribute to ontology development?

Additional aims are as follows:

1. Providing a holistic approach and a roadmap focused on:
    - Domain-dependent ontology supporting knowledge discovery processes in several stages such as domain understanding, data preprocessing, guiding/supervising the mining process, and model refinement by adding meaning to the results
    - Knowledge discovery refining an ontology model by semantic discovery directed to reveal or leverage new and existing concepts and finding semantic associations in large datasets
2. Outlining the current state-of-the-art of applications considering both knowledge discovery and ontology engineering especially in manufacturing and biomedicine areas
3. Identification and brief presentation of the existing relevant research projects carried out especially in Europe under Framework 5/6
4. Analysis of the gaps in the existing approaches and suggesting potential solutions for bridging them: One of the main gaps is related to knowledge discovery from legacy data, semantic support systems and the harmonization towards integrating heterogeneous data sources which should be supported by ontology. The metadata concept is also addressed.
5. Enhancing existing methodologies such as cross industry standard process for data mining (Crisp – Dm); sample, explore, modify, model, assess (Semma) and so forth with a semantic layer based on common thesauri, vocabulary, taxonomies and ontologies. An extended version of well recognized CommonKads (Schreiber et al., 1999) might be used for the definition of a meta-methodology for knowledge intensive activities including acquisition, discovery as well as ontology engineering.
6. Refining the existing methodologies for ontology extraction, building and semantic discovery such as Methontology, by adding the knowledge intensive activities including acquisition, representation and discovery.
7. Suggesting the key elements of a framework and an associated meta-methodology for

whole life-cycle of a bidirectional interaction between ontology engineering and knowledge discovery.

A ROADMAP OF BIDIRECTIONAL INTERACTION BETWEEN ONTOLOGY ENGINEERING AND KNOWLEDGE DISCOVERY

An Overview of Related Data and Knowledge Models vs. Ontologies

The *data model*s include the conceptual representations embedded in schema definitions, relational and inductive models which may also contain strategic/operational information related to a data warehouse organizational model. A comprehensive and generic model incorporating the description of associated data models may be defined as metadata. The entity relationship (ER) data model and later the semantic data models use higher level and generic metadata definition.

Generally, a data model represents an integrated structure of the data elements usually related to a particular application/system which uses a specific modeling approach for data. Therefore, the conceptualisation, and the vocabulary of a data model are not intended a priori to be shared between applications/systems. Furthermore, due to heterogeneity of the data within the distributed database systems some problems might arise (Kim & Seo, 1991) which can be classified into following three categories (Visser, Stuckenschmidt, Schlieder, Wache & Timm, 2002):

- Syntax (e.g., data format heterogeneity)
- Structure (e.g., homonyms, synonyms, or different attributes in database tables)
- Semantic (e.g., intended meaning of terms in a special context or application)

Besides within some data modeling approaches, the semantics of models often constitute an informal agreement between the developers and the users of the data model and, in many cases, the data model is updated as particular new functional requirements without any significant update in the metadata repository (Spyns, Meersman & Jarrar, 2002).

Data mining defined as "*the non-trivial process of identifying valid, novel, potentially useful and ultimately understandable patterns in data*" (Piatetski-Shapiro & Frawley, 1991) is directed to provide new knowledge and information models based on the intelligent exploration and analysis of large amounts of data stored in databases or/and data warehouses.

*Knowledge model*s range from a mere recalling of facts, to action and expertise, and thus, to a potential and an ability (Schreiber et al., 1999, 2000; Spiegler, 2003). It should be possible to carry the delineation a step further and propose that knowledge is the production of new facts, or even the production of new knowledge, a recursive or reflexive process that is, in fact, an infinite cycle. A generic knowledge model may be defined as a partial combination of at least two models:

1. The conventional transformation of data into information, knowledge and further experiences/wisdom/actions defined mainly by Spiegler (2003)
2. The reverse hierarchy of knowledge preceding information and data defined by Tuomi (1999, 2000)

The following two types of knowledge are widely accepted (Polanyi, 1966):

1. **Tacit knowledge:** Implicit, mental models, and experiences of people
2. **Explicit knowledge:** Formal models, rules, and procedures

Bridging the gap between information technology and knowledge, the main objective of data mining is the identification of valid, novel and useful patterns, and associations in existing data. The acquired knowledge models obtained through data mining capture the history embedded in large datasets usually stored in databases.

The inductive databases (IDBS) contain not only data, but also patterns. Patterns can be either local patterns, such as frequent itemsets, which are descriptive, or global/generic models represented as decision trees, which are predictive. In an IDB, inductive queries can be used to generate (mine), manipulate, and apply patterns. Therefore an IDB framework may be defined as an applied theory for data mining, because it employs declarative queries instead of ad-hoc procedural constructs. Declarative queries are often formulated using constraints and inductive querying is closely related to constraint-based data mining. An IDB framework is also appealing for data mining applications, as it supports the process of knowledge discovery in databases (KDD): the results of one (inductive) query can be used as input for another and nontrivial multistep KDD scenarios can be supported, rather than just single data mining operations.

Ontology concept and associated models still generate some controversies in Artificial Intelligence including knowledge discovery approaches. The ontology concept has a long history in philosophy, in which it refers to the subject of existence. It is also often a misunderstanding with epistemology, which is about knowledge and knowing. In the context of knowledge intensive systems, ontology represents a description (like a formal specification of a program) of the concepts and their relationships related to a domain and/or context. This definition is consistent with the usage of ontology as set-of-concept-definitions, but it may be more generic. Unlike data and domain-dependent knowledge models, the fundamental asset of ontologies is their relative independence of particular applications, that is an ontology consists of relatively generic knowledge that can be reused and shared by different types of applications/tasks (Gottgtroy et al., 2003).

On the other hand, ontology, knowledge and data model have similarities especially in terms of scope and task. They are also context dependent knowledge representation paradigm. Therefore there is not a strict delimitation between generic and specific knowledge in the process of building ontology. Moreover, both modeling techniques are knowledge acquisition intensive tasks and, the resulted models include a partial consideration of the conceptualization issues. In spite of the above differences Gottgtroy et al. (2003) have described and considered the similarities and moreover the fact that data models has incorporated a lot of useful hide knowledge about the domain in its data schemas which may ease the process of building ontologies from data and improve/refine the process of knowledge discovery in databases.

Related Background Theories and The Conceptual Framework

Ontologies have become a key element of several researches related to knowledge issues such as acquisition, representation and reusing as well as semantic based systems. However, the role of ontologies in knowledge discovery and data mining represents a new challenging open issue.

Generally, knowledge discovery and data mining techniques are applied in a centralized manner, requiring a central collection/deposit of data which needs to be extracted and integrated from distributed sites. These processes are directed to obtain a data warehouse which is based on data mart that is a data subset related to selected subjects (Adriaans & Zantinge, 1996). Data warehouse is defined as the extraction and integration of data from multiple sources and legacy systems in an effective and efficient manner. It includes architectures, algorithms, tools as well as organizational and management issues for integrating data/information and adequately storing this information into an integrated data environment.

There is a need to move from such centralized environments to frameworks which are transparent and provide a common understanding of data having also associated meaning, thus opening up the possibility of using semantics to identify and integrate the data in a seamless manner. Visser et al. (2002) have suggested an ontology based information integration directed to solve data heterogenity problems related to syntax, structure and semantics.

The projects enhanced Knowledge Warehouse (eKW), and enhanced Information Retrieval and Filtering for Analytical Systems (enIRaF) currently carried out within the Department of Management Information Systems at Poznan University of Economics, Poland aim to (http://www.kie.ae.poznan.pl/research/projects.html):

- Organize unstructured data in the data warehouse through knowledge warehouse modeling using domain/business ontologies and Semantic Web services
- Deal with an innovative approach which leverages information filtering, knowledge representation, data warehouse, and Semantic Web technologies in order to enable a much higher degree of automation and flexibility in performing operations pertaining to the searching and extracting information
- Create domain-dependent (dedicated) ontology to support knowledge warehouse and information retrieval and filtering especially for business intelligence applications

Therefore the ability to provide a better understanding and common representations of data within a data warehouse, using ontology will be directed to obtain more significant results within the knowledge discovery in databases. Incorporating the semantics into knowledge discovery provides some improvements for a better understanding, interpretation and derivation of new meaningful data and information, which up to now has not been possible. A such conceptual framework is depicted in the Figure 2, and the related architecture including on-line analytical processing (OLAP) is shown in Figure 3. The database administrator human tasks might be complemented by a knowledge discovery administrator who should be responsible for the whole knowledge discovery processes applied into a methodological manner within an organization/enterprise (Gupta, Bhatnagar, & Wasan, 2005).

Maedche and Staab (2000) have defined ontologies as metadata schemas, providing a controlled vocabulary of concepts, each with explicitly

Figure 2. Data mining through a data warehouse based on ontologies

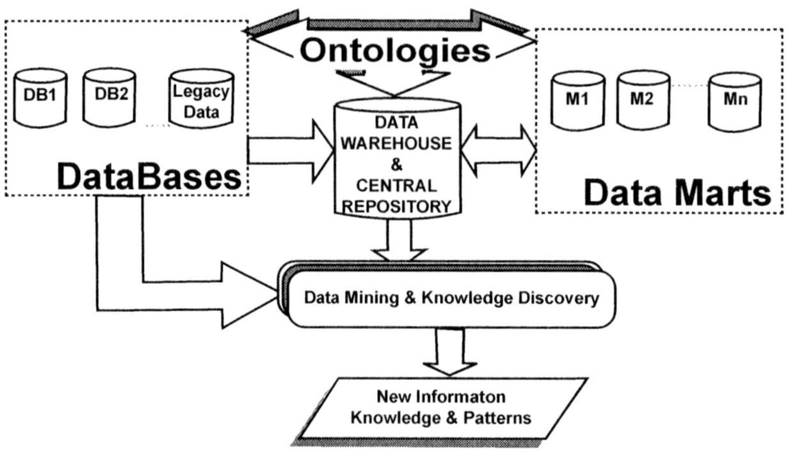

defined and machine-processable semantics. By defining shared and common domain theories, ontologies support people and machines to communicate concisely providing semantics exchange, and not just syntax.

Generally, it is possible to identify the following three generations of approaches related to the ontology theory and practice (Staab & Studer, 2004):

1. Defined and applied in the framework of developing knowledge based systems and knowledge modeling, ontologies are mainly related to domains, methods and tasks. These approaches include CommonKADS, Toronto Virtual Enterprise (Tove) and the earlier version of Protégé.
2. In the context of Semantic Web technology, it has been adopted an ontology-based approach for dealing with heterogeneous data, and in particular, for managing systems interoperability. Ontologies provide the conceptual underpinning which is required to define and communicate the semantics of metadata stored and/or processed. Several efforts have been directed to formalize the Web by powerful ontology and Semantic Web languages such as Rdf, Rdf(s), Owl, Daml+Oil and so forth, and these can be studied through the examination of relevant projects including On-To-Knowledge; Sdk _ cluster of three European initiatives: Sekt (Semantically Enabled Knowledge Technologies), Dip (Data, Information and Process Integration with Semantic Web Services) and Knowledge Web; Deri (Digital Enterprise Research Institute – Making Semantic Web real); Ontoprise® (a semantic technologies provider); Triple20 (a Rdf/Rdf(S)/Owl visualization and editing tool under development at the University of Amsterdam, Human Computer Studies Laboratory); OntoWeb (ontology-based information exchange for knowledge management and electronic commerce); Rewerse (Reasoning on the Web with Rules and Semantics) and so forth Therefore the success of *Semantic Web* by introducing flexible, dynamic and shared web applications and data in several areas strongly depends on quickly and cheaply

Figure 3. Architecture for data warehouse, mining, and OLAP

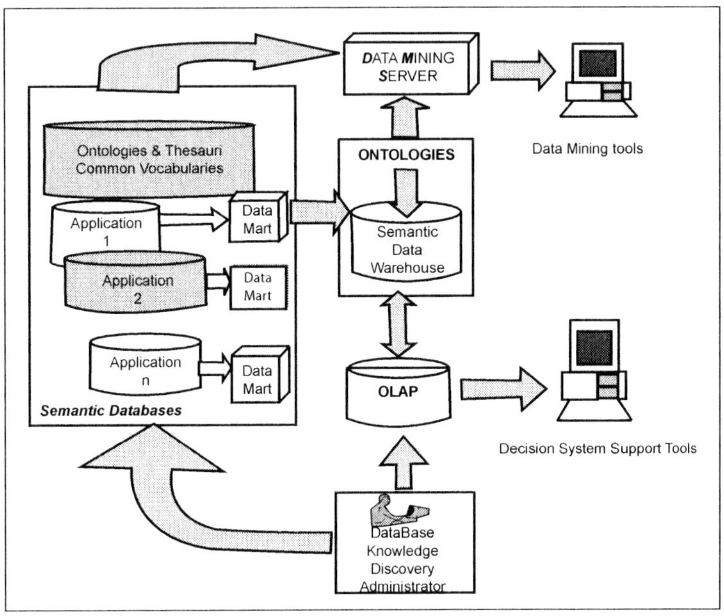

constructing especially domain-specific ontologies (Maedche, 2002).

3. Ontology learning and discovery aim at developing methods and tools that decrease the efforts for engineering and management of ontologies (Maedche, 2002) and they include techniques for extracting, building an ontology from scratch, enriching or adapting an existing ontology in a semi-automatic manner using previously defined sources and thesauri. There are also a few systems for *semantic discovery* which provide support for semi-automatic extraction of relevant concepts and relations between them from (Web) documents and existing ontologies. Ontology/semantic discovery has the roots in Web and text mining which may be a preliminary stage in the process of building an ontology.

The role and contributions of knowledge discovery (KD) towards the *Semantic Web* (SW) systems are briefly presented below (Grobelnik & Mladenić, 2005):

a. SW systems involve and manipulate deep structured knowledge which is composed into ontologies. Since KD techniques are mainly about discovering structure in the data, this can serve as one of the key mechanisms for structuring knowledge. Ontology learning which is usually performed in automatic or semi-automatic mode has the main aim to extract the structure from unstructured data sources into an ontological/knowledge structure being further used in knowledge management approaches.
b. Automatic KD approaches are not always the most appropriate, since often it is too hard or too costly to integrate the available background knowledge about the domain into fully automatic KD workbenches. For such cases there are KD approaches such as "active learning" and "semi-supervised learning" which make use of small pieces of human knowledge for better guidance towards an ideal model (e.g., ontology). The effect is that it should be possible to reduce the amount of human effort by an order of magnitude while preserving the quality of results.
c. SW applications are typically associated with more or less structured data such as text documents and corresponding metadata. An important property of such data is that it is relatively easy manageable by humans (e.g., people are good in reading and understanding texts). In the future it may be expected to deal with the applications in the areas where the data are not so "human friendly" (e.g., multimedia, signals, graphs/networks). In such situations there will be significant emphasis on automatic or semi-automatic methods offered by KD technologies which are not limited to a specific data representation.
d. Language technologies (including lexical, syntactical and semantic levels of natural language processing), are benefiting from KD area because modeling a natural language includes number of problems where models created by automatic learning procedures from rare and costly examples enable to capture the soft nature of a language.
e. Data and corresponding semantic structures change in time. Therefore, it is necessary to adapt ontologies that are modeling the data accordingly using dynamic ontologies. For most of such scenarios an extensive human involvement in building dynamic models from the data is not a feasible solution, since it gets too costly, too inaccurate and too slow. The sub-area of KD called

"stream mining" deals with these kinds of problems and the idea is to be able to deal with the stream of incoming data fast enough to be up to date with the corresponding models (ontologies) evolving in time. Besides this kind of scenarios might not be critical for today's application but may become very important in the future.

f. Scalability is one of the central issues in KD, especially in the sub-areas such as data mining applications which deal with real-life datasets of the terra-byte sizes. SW is ultimately concerned with real-life data embedded in the Web which have exponential growth—currently about 10 billions of indexed Web pages by major search engines. Due to this aspect, the approaches where human interventions are necessary might not be applicable. KD with its focus to scalability will certainly be able to provide some solutions to these open research questions.

According to (Guarino & Poli, 1998) and (Studer, Benjamins & Fensel, 1998) it is possible to define the following types of ontologies:

- **Top-level (generic) ontologies:** These ontologies describe generic concepts or common-sense knowledge such as space, time, matter, object, event, action, and so forth which are independent of a particular domain and specific problem.
- **Domain ontologies:** These describe the terminology and vocabulary related to a generic domain such as manufacturing, medicine, physics, and so forth
- **Task ontologies:** Task ontologies describe the vocabulary related to a generic task or activity such as bank transaction, machine fault/human diagnosis, and so forth.
- **Application ontologies:** These describe concepts depending both of a particular domain and a particular task. They are often a specialization of both domain and task ontologies and correspond to the roles played by domain entities when they perform certain activities.
- **Representational ontologies:** These ontologies do not commit to any particular domain. These ontologies provide representational entities without stating what should be represented. A well-known representational ontology is the *frame ontology* (Gruber, 1993) which defines concepts such as frames, slots and slot constraints allowing to represent knowledge using an object-oriented or frame-based technique.

The modalities of applying the above types of ontologies in order to enhance the knowledge discovery processing methodologies could be formalized as described in the next section.

A Survey of Existing Methodologies

Facilitating Knowledge Discovery and Data Mining

The cross industry standard process for data mining (*CRISP-DM*) model and methodology are widely used for describing and implementing the steps of the KDD process especially in the business domain (Chapman et al., 1999, 2000). However the methodology might be extended for other application areas and the suggested model using ontologies is presented in the Figure 4. The ontologies have enriched every phase of this methodology as follows:

The role of ontologies in *(Business, Manufacturing and Medicine) Domain Understanding* is important in knowledge discovery life-cycle, and it needs a deep analysis towards relevant applications.

Domain ontologies are dynamic/evolving entities for exploring the area of applying discovery techniques prior to committing to a particular task. Semiformal ontologies can help a new user to become familiar with most important concepts and relationships. Next, formal ontologies allow the identification of conflicting assumptions that might not be obvious while a first domain inspection is performed.

Therefore, in this phase it should be also required and possible to apply a top level ontology such as the manufacturing enterprise ontology defined as a taxonomy for supporting project team e-collaboration within an extended enterprise (Lin, 2004). This ontology is shown in Figure 5.

For improving *Data Understanding*, elements of a domain ontology have to be semi-automatically mapped on elements of the data scheme and vice versa. This will typically lead to selecting a relevant part of an ontology (or, multiple ontologies). In this phase both the domain and application ontologies are used. The benefits of this effort might be as follows:

- Identification of missing attributes that should be added to the dataset
- Identification of redundant attributes (e.g., measuring the same quantity in different units) that could be deleted from the dataset

The *Data Preparation* phase is already connected with the subsequent modeling phase. Concrete use of domain ontology thus partially depends on the selected mining tool(s). An ontology may also typically help by identifying multiple groupings for attributes and/or values according to semantic criteria and it may be directed to solve the syntax and semantic conflicts.

In the *Modeling* phase, ontologies might support the design of particular mining sessions and define their attributes. In particular, for large datasets, it might be worthwhile to introduce some ontological bias, for example to skip the quanti-

Figure 4. CRISP-DM enriched with ontology (Based on Chapman et al., 1999, 2000)

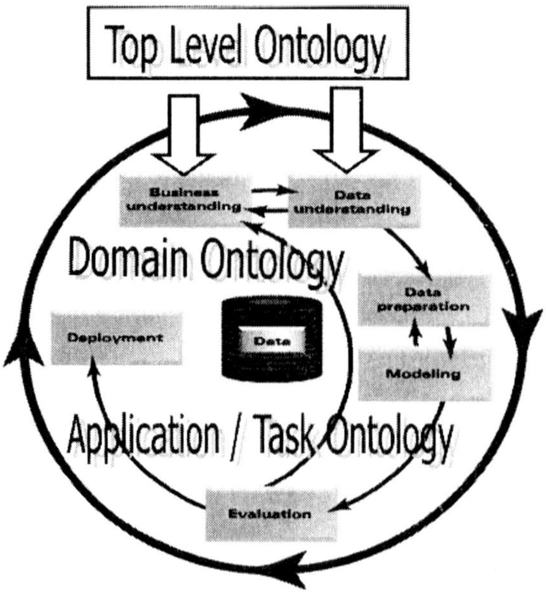

Figure 5. Top level ontology for extended enterprise (Based on Lin, 2004)

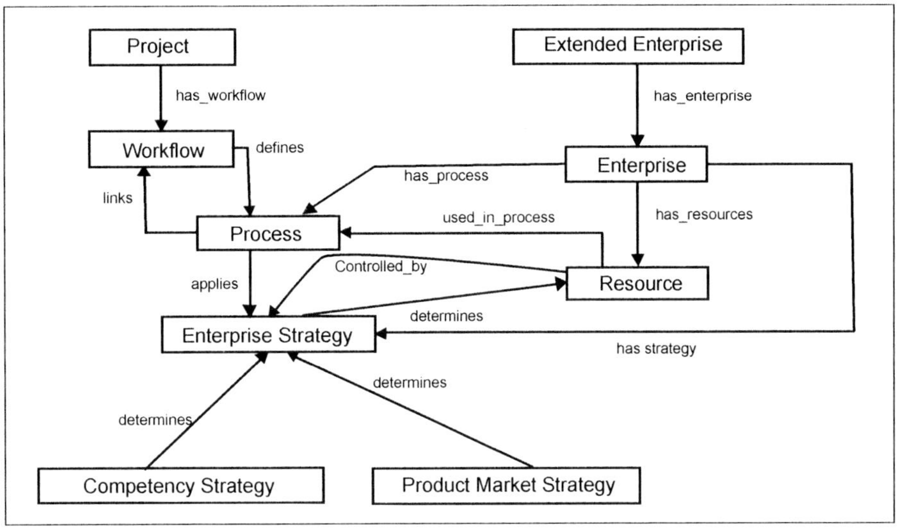

Figure 6. Manufacturing system engineering ontology (Source: Lin, 2004)

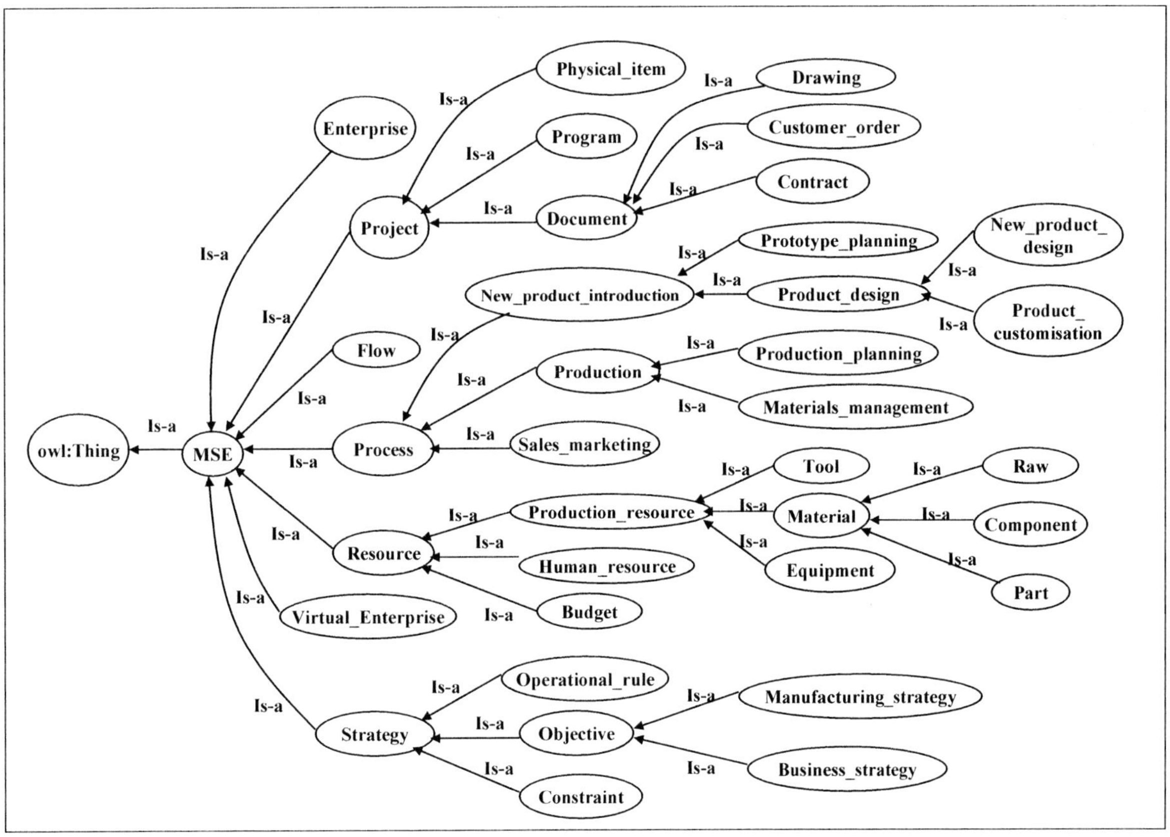

tative examination of hypotheses that would not make sense from the ontological point of view, or, on the other hand, of too obvious ones. The modeling phase usually applies application and task ontologies.

In the *Evaluation* phase, the discovered model(s) have the character of structured knowledge built around the concepts (previously mapped on data attributes), and can thus be interpreted in terms of ontology and associated background knowledge.

In the *Deployment* phase, extracted knowledge is sent back to the application environment/system. An application model using ontological means and the integration of new knowledge can again be mediated by an application/domain ontology. Furthermore, if the mining results are to be distributed across multiple organizations/sites (using a Semantic Web infrastructure) mapping to a shared ontology is required.

Figure 6 shows the OWL representation of a manufacturing system engineering (MSE) model which might be employed as a domain/application ontological model for improving CRISP-DM phases.

*S*elect, explore, modify, model, assess (*SEMMA*) methodology elaborated by SAS Institute Inc. may also take in consideration the ontology within its phases:

- **Sample** the data by extracting a portion of a large dataset containing enough significant information, but having optimal dimension to be manipulated quickly using semantic enhanced data extraction, information filtering and retrieval.
- **Explore** the data by searching for unanticipated trends and anomalies in order to understanding ideas and the trends of the dataset using top level and domain ontologies.
- **Modify** the data by creating, selecting and transforming the variables to focus the model selection process.
- **Model** the data by allowing the software to search automatically for a combination of data that reliably predicts a desired outcome.
- **Assess** the data by evaluating the usefulness and reliability of the findings from the data mining process.

In order to bridge the gap between data mining theory, practice and the application in manufacturing industry, Neaga (2003) proposed a domain-dependent methodology which also may benefit by the advantages of using an approach based of ontology and semantic support systems based on the following considerations:

- It is almost impossible to interpret the results of mining a large database without any domain specification for the applied algorithms. Therefore during the evaluation phase it is recommend to apply the domain/application ontology.
- If data mining is considered to be domain-dependent, the modeling should follow the information as well as knowledge modeling and representation of the application domain.

This methodology is shown in Figure 7, and it has been concluded that knowledge discovery processing should include (Neaga, 2003):

1. Understanding the application domain which involves formation of a whole picture of what exists in the domain, and gathering the relevant facts about the domain as well as rules applying to domain specific data
2. Project definition and an initial objective of data mining exploration
3. Exploring the problem space
4. Exploring the solution space
5. Analysis of the critical factors which may affect the adoption of data warehouse and data mining

6. Preliminary data modeling (auditing) and experimental design
7. Specifying the implementation methods or algorithms
8. Mining the data which includes preparing, surveying and modeling the data
9. Creating mining models
10. Evaluation and validation of the results

This methodology has been proposed to be applied for real-world applications in manufacturing industry and related business issues as described in (Neaga, 2003).

Additionally, the search for patterns and interesting information mainly within texts and Web documents based on ontology may help to solve the following set of specific problems:

- **Unfamiliar vocabulary** such as the technical terminology of some domain (health, legal) may be unfamiliar to users, and an ontology may help by providing a rich network of terms.
- **Faulty/inconsistent meta-tagging:** When the search engine uses meta-tags of documents, the user may not be familiar with the tagging vocabulary, which is typically a controlled vocabulary. Documents may not be consistently tagged.
- **Retrieval of short documents:** (e.g., newswire, items in listings or directories) which might not include a word/term that a user would be looking for, and query expansion is necessary. Furthermore, a document might be so specific as not to include generic terms that the user would be looking for (often the case for technical texts).
- **Ranking documents** by order of generality and by topic

Enabling Ontology Engineering

Nowadays there are several efforts towards methodological approaches of ontology building, maintenance and (re)using and the most well known ontology engineering methodologies are:

METHONTOLOGY which was been developed by a group at Universidad Politécnica de Madrid, Spain and its main aim has been to provide a comprehensive methodology for generic ontology building and maintenance.

ON-TO-KNOWLEDGE which is an ontology-based environment including methodological aspects has been directed to improve knowledge management issues. This comprehensive environment mainly deals with heterogeneous, distributed

Figure 7. Towards an ontology-driven data mining methodology

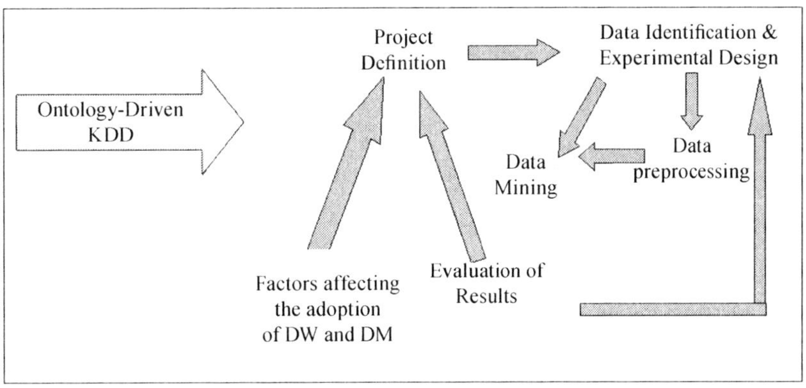

and semi-structured documents typically found in large company intranets and the World Wide Web. It was developed within Information Society Technologies (IST) Program for Research, Technology Development & Demonstration under the 5th Framework Program.

Fernández-López, Gómez-Pérez, and Juristo (1997), Davies, Fensel, and van Harmelen (2003), Gómez-Pérez, Fernández-López, and Corcho (2004) and many other researchers and practitioners have dealt with methodological aspects of ontology building, support tools, and applications.

Methontology supports ontologies building and/or re-engineering mainly at the knowledge level, and has its roots in knowledge engineering especially acquisition, and software development processes defined by IEEE as a standard (Fernández-López et al., 1997; Fernández-López, 1999; Gómez-Pérez et al., 2004). Although this ontology engineering methodology has the foundation in knowledge acquisition and elicitation it does not explicitly consider knowledge discovery for improving the development/building/creation of ontologies. This aspect is suggested in Figure 8. Furthermore, ontology learning represents an alternative for building ontologies and the next section deals with this aspect mainly based on Gottgtroy et al. (2003) and Maedche (2002) and OntoWeb project deliverables (Asunción & David, 2003, 2006). Besides, the knowledge and ontology discovery might refine the ontological computational models. An ontology development environment (Ode) and WebOde were developed in order to provide technological support for Methontology. However, other ontology systems and tool suites can also be used to build ontologies following this methodology such as Protégé-2000, OntoEdit, Kaon and so forth (Staab & Studer, 2004; Sure & Studer, 2002).

Methontology has been initially suggested by the Foundation for Intelligent Physical Agents (Fipa) for building an ontology which enables interoperability across agent based applications. Generally, Methontology guides the whole life-cycle of ontology development through the

Figure 8. Improved Methontology (Based on Fernández-López et al., 1997)

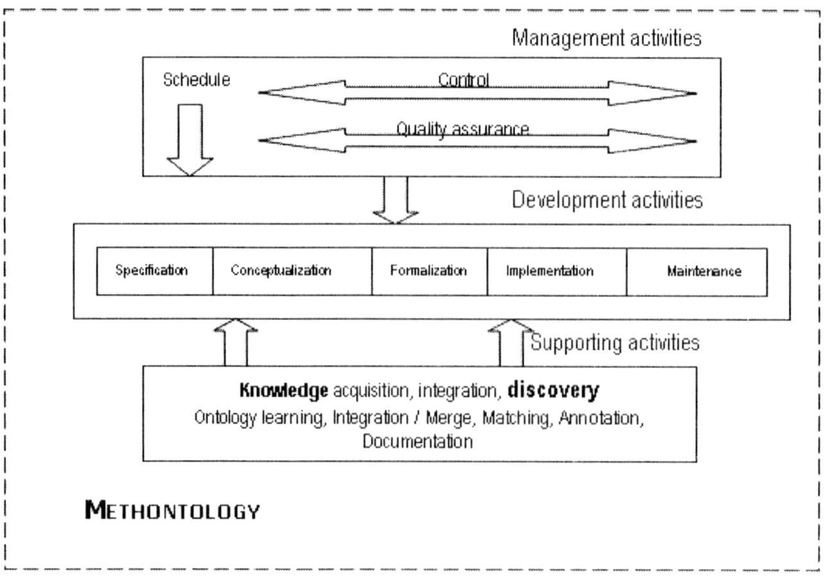

specification, the conceptualization, the formalization, the implementation and the maintenance of the ontology as illustrated in Fgure 8. The main activities are described as follows (de Bruijn, 2003; Fernández-López et al., 1997):

- The **specification** activity states the purposes of ontology, and its potential end-users.
- The **conceptualization** activity organizes and transforms an informally perceived view of a domain into a semi-formal specification using a set of intermediate representations based on tabular and graph notations that can be understood by domain experts and ontology developers. The result of the conceptualization activity is an ontological conceptual model. This activity might use knowledge discovery including text/Web mining in order to gain a deep understanding of a domain based on mining historical data and documents related to a certain domain.
- The **formalization** activity transforms the conceptual model into a formal or semi-computational model. This activity may employ and adapt discovery algorithms such as clustering the concepts, finding associations between concepts and so forth.
- The **implementation** activity develops computational models using ontology languages and systems such as Ontolingua, RDF Schema, OWL and so forth. Tools implement automatically conceptual models in different ontology languages. For example, WebODE imports and exports ontologies from and to the following languages: XML, RDF(s), OIL, DAML+OIL, OWL, PROLOG, and so forth.
- The **maintenance** activity updates and refines the ontology if necessary.

METHONTOLOGY also identifies ontology management procedures such as schedule, control and quality assurance, and support activities such as knowledge acquisition, integration, discovery, evaluation, documentation, and configuration management. Since this methodology attempts to provide a generic methodology for all types of ontologies, the ON-TO-KNOWLEDGE methodology is geared towards the development of application/domain dependent ontologies, more specifically, ontologies for knowledge management applications (de Bruijn, 2003; Sure & Studer, 2002).

Furthermore it has been focused on *acquiring*, *representing*, and *accessing* weakly-structured on-line information sources (Davies et al., 2003) through the following techniques:

- **Acquiring:** Text mining and extraction techniques are applied to reveal semantic information from textual information.
- **Representing:** XML, RDF and OIL are used for describing syntax and semantics of semi-structured information sources.
- **Accessing:** New Semantic Web search systems, and knowledge sharing functionalities.

Based on this survey related to ontology engineering methodologies it is possible to conclude and define the whole ontology development life-cycle supported by a KDD environment as illustrated in Figure 9.

The main stages are described as follows:

- **Ontology creation:** can be done from scratch using a tool such as Protégé for editing and creating class structures and taxonomies (Protégé, 2006). However, this stage may also use the following methods including mining techniques:
  - Text mining can be used to extract terminology from texts, providing a starting point for ontology creation.
  - Often, ontology information is available in legacy forms, such as database schemas, product catalogues, and yellow pages listings. Many of the recently

released ontology editors import database schemas and other legacy formats that is, Cobol copybooks.
    - It is also possible to re-use, in whole or some parts of ontologies that have already been developed. This brings the advantage of being able to leverage detailed work that has already been done by an ontology engineer.
- **Ontology population:** refers to the process of creating instances of the concepts within an ontology and linking them to external sources such as:
    - Ordinary Web pages are a good source of instance information; therefore several tools for populating ontologies are based on annotation of Web pages.
    - Legacy sources of instances are also often available, catalogues, white pages, database tables, and so forth can also be mined while populating an ontology.
    - Population can be done manually or be semi-automated. Semi-automation is highly recommended when a large number of knowledge sources exists.
- **Deployment** which can be performed after an ontology is created and populated. This aspect is explained as follows:
    - The ontology provides a natural index of the instances described in it, and hence can be used as a navigational aid while browsing those instances.
    - More sophisticated methods, such as case-based reasoning, can use the ontology to drive similarity measures for case-based retrieval.
    - DAML+OIL and OWL have capabilities for expressing axioms and constraints on the concepts in the ontology; hence powerful logical reasoning engines can be used to draw conclusions about the instances in an ontology.
    - Semantic integration across all of the various applications is probably the fastest growing area of development for ontology-based systems.
- **Validation, evolution, and maintenance:** Ontologies similar to any other component of a complex system, will need to change if their environment changes. Some changes might be simple responses to errors or omissions in the original ontology; others might be in response to a change in the environment. There are many ways in which an ontology can be validated in order to improve and evolve it; the most effective critiques are based on strict formal semantics of what the class structure means:
    - Extensive logical frameworks that support this sort of reasoning have been developed, and are called description logics.
    - A few advanced tools use automated description logic engines to determine

Figure 9. Ontology development life-cycle

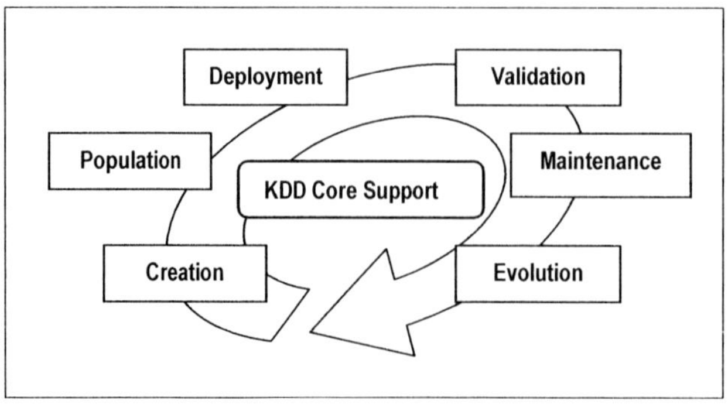

whether an ontology has contradictions, or when a particular concept in an ontology can be classified differently, according to its description.

- These critiques can be used to identify gaps in the knowledge represented in the ontology, or they can be used to automatically modify the ontology, consolidating the information contained within it.

The ontology maintenance may require merging ontologies from diverse sources. The related tools provide:

- Human-centered capabilities for searching through ontologies for similar concepts (usually by name), and mechanisms for merging the concepts
- Support for advanced matching based on common instances or patterns of related concepts

Issues on Ontology Learning

The relevant approaches related to ontology learning are presented in detail within the Deliverables 1.5 of the project OntoWeb (Gottgtroy et al., 2003; Maedache, 2002; Maedche & Staab, 2000, 2001) among others.

As well as Maedche (2002) and Staab (2000, 2001) defined different ontology learning approaches and related methods focused on the following types of inputs: ontology learning from text, dictionary, knowledge base, semi-structured schemata and relational schemata.

Ontology learning methods from texts consist of extracting ontologies by applying natural language analysis techniques to texts. The most well-known approaches are:

Pattern-based extraction is based on the fact that a relation is recognized when a sequence of words in the text matches a defined pattern.

Association rules were initially defined by Agrawal, Imielinski and Swami (1993) related to discover associations between data stored into a database as follows: "Given a set of transactions, where each transaction is a set of literals (called items), an association rule is an expression of the form X implies Y, where X and Y are sets of items. The intuitive meaning of such a rule is that transactions of the database which contain X tend to contain Y" (p. 211). Association rules are used within data mining processing in order to reveal new and hidden information stored on databases if a rough and preliminary objective of the discovery could be defined (Adriaans & Zantinge, 1996). The method applied for ontology learning has been originally described and evaluated in (Maedche & Staab, 2000). This method has been used to discover non–taxonomic relations between concepts, using a concept hierarchy as background knowledge (Maedche & Staab, 2000, 2001).

Conceptual clustering groups concepts according to the semantic distance between each other in order to define hierarchies. The formulae to calculate the semantic distance between two concepts may depend on different factors and must be provided (Faure & Poibeau, 2000).

Ontology pruning has the main objective to build a domain ontology by pruning based on different heterogeneous sources. It has the following steps (Kietz, Maedche & Volz, 2000):

a. A generic core ontology is used as a top level structure for the domain-specific ontology.
b. A dictionary which contains important domain terms described in natural language is used to acquire domain concepts. These concepts are classified into the generic core ontology.
c. Domain-specific and general corpora of texts are used to remove concepts that were not domain specific. Concept removal follows

the heuristic that domain-specific concepts should be more frequent in a domain-specific corpus than in generic texts.

Concept learning consists in incrementally updating a given taxonomy according to the new concepts acquired from real-world texts (Hahn & Schulz, 2000).

Ontology learning from dictionary bases its performance on the use of a machine readable dictionary to extract relevant concepts and relations among them.

Ontology learning from a knowledge base aims to learn an ontology using as source existing knowledge bases.

Ontology learning from semi-structured data is directed to elicit an ontology from sources which have any predefined structure, such as XML schemas.

Ontology learning from relation schemas aims to learn an ontology by extracting relevant concepts and relations from knowledge in databases.

The overall ontology learning process includes the following phases (Maedche & Staab, 2001):

- Merging existing structures or defining mapping rules between these structures allows **importing** and **reusing** existing ontologies.
- Ontology **extraction** models the relevant aspects of the target ontology, with learning support obtained from Web documents.
- The target ontology's rough outline, which results from import, reuse, and extraction, is **pruned** to better mismatch the ontology to its primary purpose.
- Ontology **refinement** benefits from the pruned ontology, but completes the ontology at a fine granularity (in contrast to extraction).
- The target application serves as a measure for validating the resulting ontology.

The above phases and especially the ontology extraction have many similarities with knowledge intensive activities including discovery and by consequence some analogies could be applied. A *discovery approach* constitutes a complementary alternative to this methodology and is based on clustering concepts from text documents or Web pages considering their html structure. This approach starts with an analysis of the structure of texts. Then, a hierarchical clustering is performed to group terms. The basic idea is to consider firstly only the terms having some common characteristics such as title, bold and italic terms, and then the terms occurring in the paragraphs in order to refine and to characterize each cluster. The goal of this step is to finally obtain a concept hierarchy. According to (Aussenac-Gilles, Biébow, Szulman, & Terminae, 2000) it is possible to create a domain model by means of the analysis of a corpus using natural language processing tools and linguistic techniques applied to text.

Text-To-Onto module of Kaon is an ontology learning system that is embedded in Karlsruhe Ontology and Semantic Web infrastructure (http://kaon.semanticweb.org). It is an open-source ontology management and application infrastructure targeted for semantics-driven applications. Besides Kaon Oi-modeler could be applied for using ontologies in order to structure and represent knowledge.

The increased demand for multiple large-scale and complex ontologies arises novel challenges on all tasks related to ontology engineering (i.e., their design, maintenance, merging and integration) and to the operation with ontologies (i.e., the run-time access to ontologies both by human users and by software agents). In all such tasks, understanding and taking into account the implicit knowledge of an ontology is crucial. Nowadays, it is widely accepted that a logical underpinning of ontologies is desirable since it provides a well-defined semantics and allows to rephrase system services of ontology tools in terms of logical reasoning problems. This, in turn, enables one to base such system services on automated reasoning procedures. Such a reasoning support has already proved to be an essential component of state-of-the-art ontology management tools; the range and power of services provided are, however, far from being sufficient.

Therefore the main aim of the some projects such as the European Project focused on *thinking ontologies* (TONES) is to study and develop automated reasoning techniques for engineering and operation with ontologies, and devise methodologies for the deployment of such techniques in advanced tools and applications. This is suggested to be achieved by (1) defining a common semantical framework, based on logic, for ontologies, (2) identifying the key reasoning services needed to support ontology tasks, (3) developing suitable algorithmic techniques for the provision of such reasoning services, (4) investigating and studying the efficient implementation of the techniques, and (5) developing methodologies on how to exploit the reasoning services in tools for ontologies.

Relevant Applications

Hu (2005) has proposed a semantic mining method of digital libraries containing biomedical literature and a dedicated knowledge discovery system called biomedical semantic-based knowledge discovery system (Bio-SbKDS). The mining method for novel connections among the biomedical concepts uses the medical ontologies, MeSH and unified medical language system (UMLS) and it is designed to automatically uncover novel hypotheses and connections/relations among relevant biomedical concepts. Using only the starting concept, and initial semantic relations, the system can automatically generate the semantic types for concepts. Using the semantic types and semantic relations of the biomedical concepts, Bio-SbKDS can identify the relevant concepts collected from Medline in terms of the semantic type and produce the novel hypothesis between these concepts based on the semantic relations. Gottgtroy et al. (2003, 2004) investigated how ontologies and data mining may facilitate biomedical data analysis and present a semantic data mining environment and an initial biomedical ontology case study.

A gene ontology (GO) (http://www.geneontology.org) and UMLS were used in order to define a controlled vocabulary that can be applied to a dedicated genetic knowledge base including characteristics of the organisms. INFOGENE MAP was the defined case study that aims to build a multi-dimensional biomedical ontology (currently composed by six ontologies) able to share knowledge from different experiments undertaken across aligned research communities. INFOGENE MAP was integrated with data mining tools in order to learn and acquire new knowledge from the knowledge discovery process.

This environment is shown in Figure 10, and the associated ontology-driven knowledge discovery process includes ontology preparation, population, instance selection, ontology mining and ontology refining. The experimental design of this framework and the implementation solution are based on PROTÉGÉ-2000, and a system developed at Knowledge Engineering and Discovery Research Institute (KEDRI) of Auckland University of Technology (School of Computer and Information Sciences), New Zealand (www.theneucom.com). NEUCOM is a self-programmable, learning and reasoning system which includes connectionist (Neurocomputing) modules based on the theory of evolving connectionist systems (ECOS) that enables the system to adapt to new inputs and evolve its behavior over time (KEDRI, 2004).

Generally, data mining algorithms such as association rules, K-means, K-medoids as well as some heuristic methods only discover rules in database directly and usually finds the low-level rules which may be huge and hard to understanding. These rules must further use domain knowledge or background knowledge to guide the discovery process in order to produce interesting generic rules. An application of data mining in fault diagnosis (Hou, Gu, Shen, & Yan, 2005) has used an algorithm based on ontology which can discover high-level rules which generalize the low-level rules. This algorithm has the following main phases:

1. Mine for low-level rules as well as recording them and the frequency of them.
2. Generalize the concepts embedded in these rules applying an ontology.
3. Merge concepts if possible.
4. Mine for high-level rules which will have the same coverage as the low-level rules.

The rules discovered by this algorithm based on ontology are more interesting than the general algorithm. Applying it for fault diagnosis in an electric database, multi-level rules are discovered and the high level rules are fewer and clearer.

The state-of-the-art regarding inductive databases (IDBS) reveals the existence of various effective approaches to constraint-based mining (inductive querying) of local patterns, such as frequent item sets and sequences, most of which work in isolation. The European Project *Inductive Queries for Mining Patterns and Models* (IQ) aims to significantly advance the state-of-the-art by developing the theory and practice of inductive querying (constraint-based mining) of global models, as well as approaches to answering complex inductive queries that involve both local patterns and global models. Based on these, showcase applications/IDBs in the area of bioinformatics will be developed, where users will be able to query data about drug activity, gene expression, gene function, and protein sequences, as well as frequent patterns (e.g., subsequences in proteins) and predictive models (e.g., for drug activity or gene function).

These ongoing research and projects demonstrate that knowledge discovery processing and ontology engineering may help each other, but additional interdisciplinary work including the harmonization of data mining standards and systems interoperability is required.

Figure 10. An ontology-driven knowledge discovery framework (Source: Gottgtroy et al., 2003, 2004)

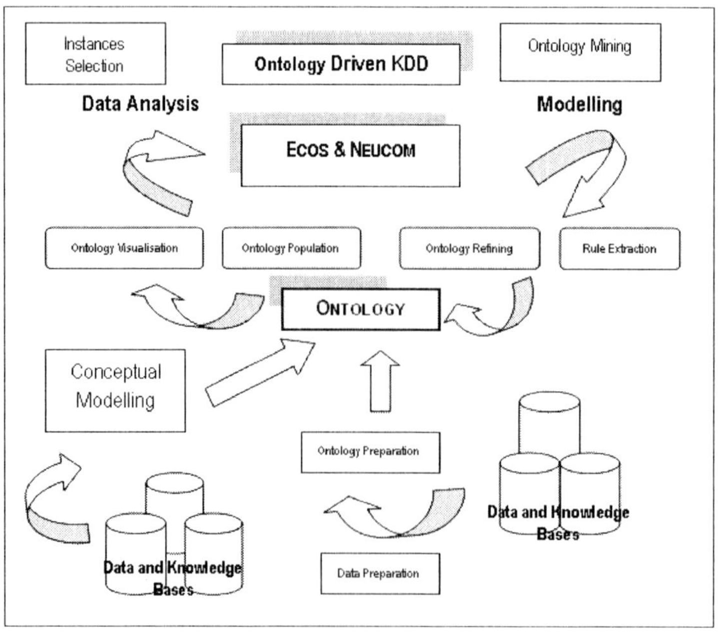

Toward a Semantics Enhancing Framework and a Metamethodology: KD4ONTO4DM

Furthermore despite tremendous potential, knowledge discovery technology and especially for business intelligence applications have not developed and provided solutions as anticipated due to the following main factors (Gupta et al., 2005):

- Current data mining systems/packages require the end-user of the KDD technology to be data mining experts because clear and complete understanding of the KDD process, including the focusing solutions, is essential to successfully steer the KDD process.
- Integrating and processing data from legacy databases still require implementation solutions based on semantic wrappers.
- These systems do not allow inherent sharing of either intermediate results or discovered knowledge among different users from a single KDD process.
- Lack of power to handle continuity in KDD process makes knowledge discovery process a piecemeal approach in environments where databases are continuously evolving.
- Lack of flexibility for (1) dynamically setting mining goals, (2) driving innovation in formulating new business questions and (3) creativity in solving these questions.

Even if knowledge discovery and data mining are quite well established areas of research and practice there is still a need towards a unification of fragmented research and applications which may overcome the existing limitations. The unification process through a bottom up approach should be directed to provide common methods, tools, standards and a meta-methodology which ease the process of applying data mining technology in several areas such as manufacturing, business and medicine. In order to achieve the interoperability between mining systems as well as useful and fined models which trigger into actions a semantic layer based on ontologies is suggested.

On the other hand due to the emergence of Semantic Web technologies, ontology engineering efforts have provided several frameworks and methodologies which require holistic approaches. At present, there are only some attempts towards including knowledge discovery into ontology engineering, and the unification of existing methodologies.

A meta-methodology which captures both knowledge discovery processing and ontology engineering phases could be based such as *CommonKADS* (Schreiber et al., 1999, 2000) or any other high level/abstract methodological software development approach on a so called "*pyramid*" depicted in the Figure 11.

CommonKADS methodology for knowledge engineering and management has been developed by some industry university consortia, and it is nowadays in use worldwide by companies and educational institutions. Within this approach the term knowledge intensive is quite intentionally vague, as it is often difficult to define a strict delimitation between knowledge-rich and knowledge-poor domains. In fact, most complex applications contain components that can be characterized as knowledge intensive processes which may include discovery. Usually, the applications are not classic knowledge-based systems. Beyond information systems applications, practice has demonstrated that several projects in which knowledge plays an important role significantly benefit from the ideas, concepts, techniques, and experiences that derive from this methodology. Therefore, it is possible to extend this approach to knowledge discovery processes and ontology engineering based on the similarities and analogies between knowledge and ontology presented in this chapter as well as the fact that in data mining are used large amounts of data stored in data bases. The fundamental principles of knowledge engineering are defined as follows (Schreiber et al., 1999, 2000):

Figure 11. Methodological pyramid (Based on Schreiber et al., 1999, 2000)

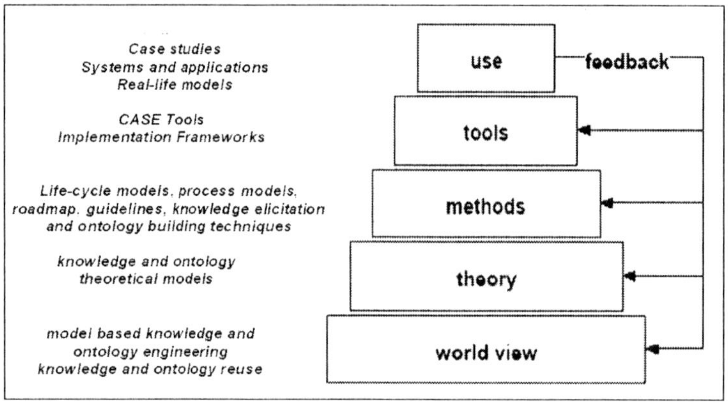

Knowledge engineering is not some kind of "mining from the expert's head" but consists of constructing different aspect models of human knowledge."

"The knowledge-level principle: in knowledge modelling, first concentrate on the conceptual structure of knowledge, and leave the programming details for later."

"Knowledge has a stable internal structure that is analyzable by distinguishing specific knowledge types and roles."

"A knowledge project must be managed by learning from your experiences in a controlled "spiral" way. (pp. 15-17)

These main principles of knowledge engineering might be adapted and/or extended for ontology building, maintenance and reuse as well as *knowledge discovery* processes with the mention that the mining for knowledge used large amounts of data stored in databases. Furthermore, an ontology is the basis for knowledge sharing, communication and reuse and therefore an ontology engineering methodology is interrelated to knowledge intensive activities. The basic idea to develop a library of reusable ontologies in a standard formalism, that each system developer can use have been exploited by knowledge based system development practice and may also be further used for semantic systems development. Almost all ontologies that are nowadays available are concerned with modeling static domain knowledge, as opposed to dynamic reasoning knowledge (e.g., domain models in medicine, power plant, cars, mechanic machines) (Studer et al., 1998). In an advanced representation, an ontology attempts to capture generic valid knowledge, independent of its use, a view closely related to its philosophical definition. However, artificial intelligence researchers quickly gave up to this view, because it turned out that specific use of knowledge influenced its modeling and representation. A weaker, but still strong, concept of ontology is captured within Cyc which aims to represent human common-sense knowledge (Studer et al., 1998). Other researchers and practitioners aim at capturing domain knowledge, independent of the task or method that might use the knowledge.

A framework for knowledge discovery and ontology engineering should adhere to Iso *reference model* for *open distributed processing (Rm-Odp)* (Neaga, 2003). Rm-Odp (ISO/OSI, 1995) provides a conceptual and coordinating environment supporting architectural principles in order to integrate and harmonize the aspects related to the distribution, interoperation and portability of software systems, in such a way that hardware heterogeneity, operating systems, networks, programming languages, databases and management systems are transparent to the user. In this sense, RM-ODP manages complexity through a "separation of concerns," addressing specific problems from different perspectives. It also facilitates the standardization of ODP, able to accommodate current and future standard systems, and maintain consistency among them. RM-ODP includes a brief, clear and explicit specification of concepts and constructs that define semantics, independently of the representation, methodologies, tools and processes used for the development of open distributed systems. RM-ODP offers a vocabulary and a common semantic framework to all the applications' developers and end-users.

The *model-driven architecture* (MDA) elaborated by Object Management Group (OMG) as a high-level abstract model based on unified modeling language (UML) methodology and existing associated profiles should also support a knowledge discovery and ontology engineering framework mainly due to the separation between the platform-independent system model from the implementation solutions. The MDA core includes the meta-object facility (MOF), *common object request broker* architecture (CORBA), XMI/XML and common warehouse metamodel (CWM) as described in Object Management Group (2001).

CONCLUSION AND FURTHER DIRECTION

This chapter presents a holistic literature review related to knowledge discovery processing, ontology engineering methodologies and environments. This approach aims at contributing to a unification of existing methodologies in both areas of knowledge discovery and ontology engineering which may benefit each other from their bidirectional interaction and support. Additional research and experiments are required in order to provide a unified framework and metamethodology which mainly will use the existing knowledge discovery systems as well as semantic tools, applications, and languages.

REFERENCES

Adriaans, P., & Zantinge, D. (1996). *Data mining*. London: Addison-Wesley.

Agrawal, R., Imielinski, T., & Swami, A. (1993). Mining association rules between sets of items in large databases. In P. Buneman & S. Jajodia (Eds.), *Proceedings of the ACM SIGMOD Conference on Management of Data*), Washington, DC (pp. 207-216). ACM Press.

Asunción, G. P., & David, M. A. (2003). *Survey of ontology learning methods and techniques* (OntoWeb Deliverable Report 1.5). Retrieved October, 27, 2006, from http://www.ontoweb.org

Aussenac-Gilles, N., Biébow, B., Szulman, S., & Terminae, S. (2002). Evaluation of ontology engineering environments. In A. Gómez-Pérez & V. Richard Benjamins (Eds.), *Proceedings of the 13th International Conference (EKAW 2002)*, Siguenza, Spain (LNCS). Springer.

Chapman, P., Clinton, J., Kerber, R., Khabaza, T., Reinartz, T., Shearer, C., & Wirth, R. (1999, 2000). *CRISP-DM 1.0 Step-by-step data mining guide*. SPSS Inc.

Davies, J., Fensel, D., & van Harmelen, F. (Eds.). (2003). *Towards the Semantic Web ontology-driven knowledge management*. Australia: John Wiley & Sons Ltd.

de Bruijn, J. (2003). *Using ontologies enabling knowledge sharing and reuse on the Semantic Web* (DERI Tech. Rep.).

de Moor, A. (2005). Patterns for the pragmatic Web (Invited paper). In F. Dau, M.-L. Mugnier, & G. Stumme (Eds.), *Proceedings of the 13th International Conference on Conceptual Structures (ICCS)* (LNAI 3596, pp. 1-18). Heidelberg: Springer.

Faure, D. & Poibeau, T. (2000). First experiments of using semantic knowledge learned by ASIUM for information extraction task using INTEX. In

S. Staab, A. Maedche, C. Nedellec, & P. Wiemer-Hastings (Eds.), *Proceedings of the Workshop on Ontology Learning 14th European Conference on Artificial Intelligence (ECAI'00)*, Amsterdam, The Netherlands. IOS Press.

Fernández-López, M., Gómez-Pérez, A. & Juristo, N. (1997). Methontology: From ontological art towards ontological engineering. In *Proceedings of the Spring Symposium on Ontological Engineering of AAAI*, Stanford University, CA (pp.33-40). AAAI Press.

Fernández-López, M. (1999). Overview of methodologies for building ontologies. In V. R. Benjamins, B. Chandrasekaran, A. Gomez-Perez, N. Guarino, & M. Uschold (Eds.), *Proceedings of the IJCAI-99 Workshop on Ontologies and Problem-Solving Methods*, 4-1-4-13. Retrieved October 27, 2006, from http://sunsite.informatik.rwth-achen.de/Publications/CEUR-WS/Vol-18/

Grobelnik, M., & Mladenić, D. (2005). Automated knowledge discovery in advanced knowledge management. *Journal of Knowledge Management, 9*(5), 132-149.

Gruber, T. (1993). A translation approach to portable ontology specifications. *Knowledge Acquisition, 5*(2), 199-221.

Gruber, T. (1994). Towards principles for the design of ontologies used for knowledge sharing. In N. Guarino & R. Poli (Eds.), *Formal ontology in conceptual analysis and knowledge representation*. Kluwer Academic Publishers.

Gómez-Pérez, A., Fernández-López, M., & Corcho, O. (2004). *Ontological engineering with examples from areas of knowledge management, e-commerce and Semantic Web*. Berlin; New York: Springer-Verlag.

Gottgtroy, P., Kasabov, N., & MacDonell, S. (2003). An ontology engineering approach for knowledge discovery from data in evolving domains. In N. F. F. Ebecken, C. A. Brebbia & A. Zanasi (Eds.), *Proceedings of the Data mining IV*. Southampton; Boston: WIT Press. Retrieved October 27, 2006, from http://www.aut.ac.nz/research/research_institutes/kedri/publications.htm#cpapers

Gottgtroy, P., Kasabov, N. & MacDonell, S. (2004). An ontology driven approach for knowledge discovery in biomedicine. In *Proceedings of the VIII Pacific Rim International Conferences on Artificial Intelligence (PRICAI)* (LNCS). Heidelberg: Springer.

Guarino, N. & Poli, R. (1998). Formal ontologies and information systems. In N. Guarino (Ed.), *Proceedings of FOIS'98* (pp. 3-15). Amsterdam: IOS Press.

Gupta, S. K., Bhatnagar, V., & Wasan, S. K. (2005). Architecture for knowledge discovery and knowledge management. *Knowledge and Information Systems, 7*, 310-336. London: Springer-Verlag Ltd.

Hahn, U., & Schulz, S. (2000). Towards very large terminological knowledge bases: A case study from medicine. In H. J. Hamilton (Ed.), *Proceedings of the 13th Biennial Conference of the Canadian Society for Computational Studies of Intelligence (AI 2000)* (LNCS, pp. 176-186). Springer.

Hou, X., Gu, J., Shen, X., & Yan, W. (2005). Application of data mining in fault diagnosis based on ontology. In *Proceedings of the Third International Conference on Information Technology and Applications (ICITA'05)* (Vol. 1, pp. 260-263). IEEE Computer Society.

Hu, X. (2005). Mining novel connections from large online digital library using biomedical ontologies. *Library Management, 26*(4/5), 261-270.

ISO/OSI, ISO. (1995). *Basic reference model for open systems interconnection (ISO/OSI)*. International Standards Organisation.

KEDRI—Knowledge Engineering and Discovery Research Institute. (2004). Retrieved October 26, 2006, from http://www.aut.ac.nz/research/research_institutes/kedri/, and http://www.theneucom.com

Kietz, J. U., Maedche, A., & Volz, R. A. (2000). Method for semi-automatic ontology acquisition from a corporate intranet. In N. Aussenac-Gilles, B. Biébow & S. Szulman (Eds.), *Proceedings of the EKAW 2000 Workshop on Ontologies and Texts*, Juan-Les-Pins, France (CEUR Workshop Proceedings, 51, 4.1-4.14). Amsterdam. Retrieved October 26, 2006, from http://CEUR-WS.org/Vol-51/

Kim, W., & Seo, J. (1991). Classifying schematic and data heterogeneity in multidatabase systems. *IEEE Computer, 24*(12), 12-18.

Lin, H. K. (2004). *Manufacturing system engineering ontology model for global extended project team*. Unpublished doctoral thesis, Loughborough University, UK.

Maedche, A., & Staab, S. (2000). Discovering conceptual relations from text. In W. Horn (Ed.), *Proceedings of the 14th European Conference on Artificial Intelligence (ECAI'00)*. Amsterdam: IOS Press. Retrieved October 26, 2006, from http://www.aifb.uni-karlsruhe.de/WBS/sst/Research/Publications/handbook-ontology-learning.pdf

Maedche, A., & Staab, S. (2000). Ontology learning for Semantic Web. *IEE Intelligent Systems*, 72-79.

Maedche, A. (2002). *Ontology learning for Semantic Web*. Kluwer Academic Publishers.

Neaga, E. I. (2003). *Framework for distributed knowledge discovery systems embedded in extended enterprise*. Unpublished doctoral thesis, Loughborough University, UK.

Object Management Group (OMG). (2001). *Model-driven architecture (MDA)* (Document No. ormsc/2001-07-01). Architecture Board ORMSC.

Piatetski-Shapiro, G., & Frawley, W. J. (Eds.). (1991). *Knowledge discovery in databases*. AAAI Press/The MIT Press.

Polanyi, M. (1996). *The tacit dimension*. London: Routledge and Kegan Paul.

Protégé. (2006). Retrieved October 26, 2006, from http://www.protege.stanford.edu/

Schreiber, G., Akkermans, H., Anjewierden, A., de Hoog, R., Shadbolt, N., Van de Velde, W., et al. (1999, 2000). *Knowledge engineering and management, The commonKADS methodology*. The MIT Press.

Spiegler, I. (2003). Technology and knowledge: Bridging a "generating" gap. *Information & Management, 40*, 533-539.

Spyns, P., Meersman, R., & Jarrar, M. (2002). Data modelling versus ontology engineering [Special Issue]. *Database Management and Information Systems, 31*.

Staab, S., & Studer, R. (Eds.). (2004). *Handbook on ontologies*. Berlin: Springer-Verlag.

Studer, R., Benjamins, R., & Fensel, D. (1998). Knowledge engineering: Principles and methods. *Data & Knowledge Engineering, 25*, 161-197.

Sure, Y. & Studer, R. (2002). *On-to-knowledge methodology—expanded version* (EU-IST Project IST-1999-10132 Report).

Tuomi, I. (1999, 2000). Data is more than knowledge: Implications of the reversed knowledge hierarchy for knowledge management and organizational memory. *Journal of Management Information Systems, 16*(3), 103-117.

van Heijst, G. (1995). *The role of ontologies in nnowledge engineering.* Unpublished doctoral thesis, University of Amsterdam.

Visser, U., Stuckenschmidt, H., Schlieder, C., Wache, H. & Timm, I. (2002). Terminology integration for the management of distributed information resources [Special Issue]. *Künstliche Intelligenz (KI), Knowledge Management, 16*(1), 31-34.

Chapter X
Knowledge Discovery in Biomedical Data Facilitated by Domain Ontologies

Amandeep S. Sidhu
Curtin University of Technology, Australia

Paul J. Kennedy
University of Technology Sydney, Australia

Simeon Simoff
University of of Western Sydney, Australia

Tharam S. Dillon
Curtin University of Technology, Australia

Elizabeth Chang
Curtin University of Technology, Australia

ABSTRACT

In some real-world areas, it is important to enrich the data with external background knowledge so as to provide context and to facilitate pattern recognition. These areas may be described as data rich but knowledge poor. There are two challenges to incorporate this biological knowledge into the data mining cycle: (1) generating the ontologies; and (2) adapting the data mining algorithms to make use of the ontologies. This chapter presents the state-of-the-art in bringing the background ontology knowledge into the pattern recognition task for biomedical data.

INTRODUCTION

Data mining is traditionally conducted in areas where data abounds. In these areas, the task of the data mining is to identify patterns within the data, which may eventually become knowledge. To this end, the data mining methods used, such as cluster analysis, link analysis and classifica-

Copyright © 2007, IGI Global, distributing in print or electronic forms without written permission of IGI Global is prohibited.

tion and regression, typically aim to reduce the amount of information (or data) to facilitate this pattern recognition. These methods do not tend to contain (or bring to the problem) specific domain specific information. In this way, they may be termed "knowledge-empty." However, in some real-world areas, it is important to enrich the data with external background knowledge so as to provide context and to facilitate pattern recognition. These areas may be described as data rich but knowledge poor. External background information that may be used to enrich data and to add context information, and facilitate data mining is in the form of ontologies, or structured vocabularies. So long as the original data can be linked to terms in the ontology, the ontology may be used to provide the necessary knowledge to explain the results and even generate new knowledge.

In accelerating quest for disease biomarkers, the use of high-throughput technologies, such as DNA microarrays and proteomics experiments, has produced vast datasets identifying thousands of genes whose expression patterns differ in diseased vs. normal samples. Although many of these differences may reach statistical significance, they are not biologically meaningful. For example, reports of mRNA or protein changes of as little as two-fold are not uncommon, and although some changes of this magnitude turn out to be important, most are attributes to disease-independent differences between the samples. Evidence gleaned from other studies linking genes to disease is helpful, but with such large datasets, a manual literature review is often not practical. The power of these emerging technologies—the ability to quickly generate large sets of data—has challenged current means of evaluating and validating these data. Thus, one important example of a data rich but knowledge poor area is biological sequence mining. In this area, there exist massive quantities of data generated by the data acquisition technologies. The bioinformatics solutions addressing these data are a major current challenge. However, domain specific ontologies such as gene ontology (GO Consortium, 2001), MeSH (Nelson & Schopen, 2004) and protein ontology (Sidhu & Dillon, 2005a, 2006a) exist to provide context to this complex real world data.

There are two challenges to incorporate this biological knowledge into the data mining cycle: (1) generating the ontologies; and (2) adapting the data mining algorithms to make use of the ontologies. This chapter presents the state-of-the-art in bringing the background ontology knowledge into the pattern recognition task for biomedical data. These methods are also applicable to other areas where domain ontologies are available, such as text mining and multimedia and complex data mining.

GENERATING OONTOLOGIES: CASE OF PROTEIN ONTOLOGY

This section is devoted to the practical aspects of generating ontologies. It presents the work on building the protein ontology (Sidhu et al., 2006a; Sidhu & Dillon, 2005a, 2006b; Sidhu et al., 2005b) in the section "Protein Ontology (PO)." It then compares the structures of the protein ontology and the well established gene ontology (GO Consortium, 2001) in the section "Comparing PO and GO."

Protein Ontology (PO)

Advances in technology and the growth of life sciences are generating ever increasing amounts of data. High-throughput techniques are regularly used to capture thousands of data points in an experiment. The results of these experiments normally end up in scientific databases and publications. Although there have been concerted efforts to capture more scientific data in specialist databases, it is generally acknowledged that only 20% of biological knowledge and data is available in a structured format. The remaining 80% of biological information is hidden in the unstructured scientific results and texts. Protein ontology (PO) (Sidhu et al., 2006a; Sidhu et al., 2006b; Sidhu et al., 2005a; Sidhu et al., 2005b) provides a common structured vocabulary for this structured and unstructured information and provides researchers a medium to share knowledge in proteomics domain. It consists of concepts, which are data descriptors for proteomics data and the relations among these concepts. Protein ontology has (1) a hierarchical classification of concepts represented as classes, from general to specific; (2) a list of attributes related to each concept, for each class; and (3) a set of relations between classes to link concepts in ontology in more complicated ways then implied by the hierarchy, to promote reuse of concepts in the ontology. Protein ontology provides description for protein domains that can be used to describe proteins in any organism. Protein ontology framework describes: (1) protein sequence and structure information, (2) protein folding process, (3) cellular functions of proteins, (4) molecular bindings internal and external to proteins and (5) constraints affecting the final protein conformation. Protein ontology uses all relevant protein data sources of information. The structure of PO provides the concepts necessary to describe individual proteins, but does not contain individual protein themselves. Files using Web ontology language (OWL) format based on PO acts as instance store for the PO. PO uses data sources include new proteome information resources like PDB, SCOP, and RESID as well as classical sources of information where information is maintained in a knowledge base of scientific text files like OMIM and from various published scientific literature in various journals. PO database is represented using OWL. PO database at the moment contains data instances of following protein families: (1) prion proteins, (2) B.Subtilis, (3) CLIC and (4) PTEN. More protein data instances will be added as PO is more developed. The complete class hierarchy of protein ontology (PO) is shown in Figure 1. More details about PO is available at the Web site: http://www.proteinontology.info/

Semantics in protein data is normally not interpreted by annotating systems, since they are not aware of the specific structural, chemical and cellular interactions of protein complexes. Protein ontology framework provides specific set of rules to cover these application specific semantics. The rules use only the relationships whose semantics are predefined to establish correspondence among terms in PO. The set of relationships with predefined semantics is: {SubClassOf, PartOf, AttributeOf, InstanceOf, and ValueOf}. The PO conceptual modelling encourages the use of strictly typed relations with precisely defined

Figure 1. Class hierarchy of protein ontology

- ProteinOntology
  - AtomicBind
  - Atoms
  - Bind
  - Chains
  - Family
  - ProteinComplex
    - ChemicalBonds
      - CISPeptide
      - DisulphideBond
      - HydrogenBond
      - ResidueLink
      - SaltBridge
    - Constraints
      - GeneticDefects
      - Hydrophobicity
      - ModifiedResidue
    - Entry
      - Description
      - Molecule
      - Reference
    - FunctionalDomains
      - ActiveBindingSites
      - BiologicalFunction
        - PathologicalFunctions
        - PhysiologicalFunctions
      - SourceCell
    - StructuralDomains
      - Helices
        - Helix
          - HelixStructure
      - OtherFolds
        - Turn
          - TurnStructure
      - Sheets
        - Sheet
          - Strands
    - Structure
      - ATOMSequence
      - UnitCell
  - Residues
  - SiteGroup

semantics. Some of these relationships (like SubClassOf, InstanceOf) are somewhat similar to those in RDF schema but the set of relationships that have defined semantics in our conceptual PO model is small so as to maintain simplicity of the system. The following is a description of the set of predefined semantic relationships in our common PO conceptual model.

- **SubClassOf:** The relationship is used to indicate that one concept is a subclass of another concept, for instance: SourceCell SubClassOf FunctionalDomains. That is any instance of SouceCell class is also instance of FunctionalDomains class. All attributes of FunctionalDomains class (_FuncDomain_Family, _FuncDomain_SuperFamily) are also the attributes of SourceCell class. The relationship SubClassOf is transitive.
- **AttrributeOf:** This relationship indicates that a concept is an attribute of another concept, for instance: _FuncDomain_Family AttributeOf Family. This relationship also referred as PropertyOf, has same semantics as in object-relational databases.
- **PartOf:** This relationship indicates that a concept is a part of another concept, for instance: Chain PartOf ATOMSequence indicates that Chain describing various residue sequences in a protein is a part of definition of ATOMSequence for that protein.
- **InstanceOf:** This relationship indicates that an object is an instance of the class, for instance: ATOMSequenceInstance_10 InstanceOf ATOMSequence indicates that ATOMSequenceInstance_10 is an instance of class ATOMSequence.
- **ValueOf:** This relationship is used to indicate the value of an attribute of an object, for instance: "Homo Sapiens" ValueOf OrganismScientific. The second concept, in turn has an edge, OrganismScientific AttributeOf Molecule, from the object it describes.

Comparing PO and GO

Gene ontology (GO Consortium, 2001) defines a structured controlled vocabulary in the domain of biological functionality. GO initially consisted of a few thousand terms describing the genetic workings of three organisms and was constructed for the express purpose of database interoperability; it has since grown to a terminology of nearly 16,000 terms and is becoming a de facto standard for describing functional aspects of biological entities in all types of organisms. Furthermore, in addition to (and because of) its wide use as a terminological source for database-entry annotation, GO has been used in a wide variety of biomedical research, including analyses of experimental data (GO Consortium, 2001) and predictions of experimental results (GO Consortium & Lewis, 2004)). Characteristics of GO that we believe are most responsible for its success: community involvement; clear goals; limited scope; simple, intuitive structure; continuous evolution; active curation; and early use.

It is clear that organisms across the spectrum of life, to varying degrees, possess large numbers of gene products with similar sequences and roles. Knowledge about a given gene product (i.e., a biologically active molecule that is the deciphered end product of the code stored in a gene) can often be determined experimentally or inferred from its similarity to gene products in other organisms. Research into different biological systems uses different organisms that are chosen because they are amenable to advancing these investigations. For example, the rat is a good model for the study of human heart disease, and the fly is a good model to study cellular differentiation. For each of these model systems, there is a database employing curators who collect and store the body of biological knowledge for that organism. This enormous amount of data can potentially add insight to related molecules found in other organisms. A reliable wet-lab biological experiment performed in one organism can be used to deduce attributes of an analogous (or related) gene product in another organism, thereby reducing the need to reproduce experiments in each individual organism (which would be expensive, time-consuming, and, in many organisms, technically impossible). Mining of scientific text and literature is done to generate list of keywords that is used as GO terms. However, querying heterogeneous, independent databases in order to draw these inferences is difficult: The different database projects may use different terms to refer to the same concept and the same terms to refer to different concepts. Furthermore, these terms are typically not formally linked with each other in any way. GO seeks to reveal these underlying biological functionalities by providing a structured controlled vocabulary that can be used to describe gene products, and shared between biological databases. This facilitates querying for gene products that share biologically meaningful attributes, whether from separate databases or within the same database.

Challenges faced while developing GO from unstructured and structured data sources are addressed while developing PO. Protein ontology is a conceptual model that aim to support consistent and unambiguous knowledge sharing and that provide a framework for protein data and knowledge integration. PO links concepts to their interpretation, that is, specifications of their meanings including concept definitions and relationships to other concepts. Apart from semantic relationships defined in "Protein Ontology (PO)," PO also model relationships like sequences. By itself semantic relationships described in "Protein Ontology (PO)" does not impose order among the children of the node. In applications using protein sequences, the ability of expressing the order is paramount. Generally protein sequences are a collection of chains of sequence of residues, and that is the format protein sequences have been represented unit now using various data representations and data mining techniques for bioinformatics. When we are defining sequences for semantic heterogeneity of protein data sources using PO we are not only considering traditional representation of protein sequences but also link protein sequences to protein structure, by linking chains of residue sequences to atoms defining three-dimensional structure. In this section we will describe how we used a special semantic relationship like *Sequence(s)* in protein ontology to describe complex concepts defining structure, structural folds and domains and chemical bonds describing protein complexes. PO defines these

Figure 2. Semantic interoperability framework for PO

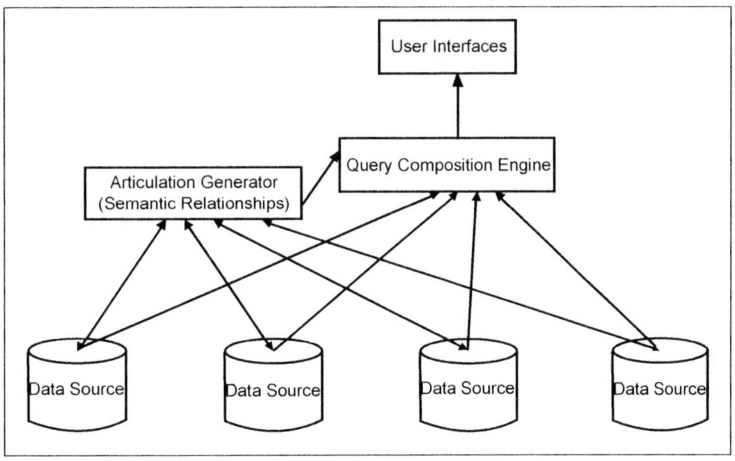

complex concepts as *Sequences* of simpler generic concepts defined in PO. These simple concepts are *Sequences* of object and data type properties defining them. A typical example of *Sequence* is as follows. PO defines a complex concept of *ATOMSequence* describing three dimensional structure of protein complex as a combination of simple concepts of *Chains*, *Residues*, and *Atoms* as: *ATOMSequence Sequence (Chains Sequence (Residues Sequence (Atoms)))*. Simple concepts defining ATOMSequence are defined as: *Chains Sequence (ChainID, ChainName, ChainProperty)*; *Residues Sequence (ResidueID, ResidueName, ResidueProperty)*; and *Atoms Sequence (AtomID, Atom, ATOMResSeqNum, X, Y, Z, Occupancy, TempratureFactor, Element)*. Semantic interoperability framework used in PO is depicted Figure 2.

Therefore, PO reflects the structure and relationships of protein data sources. PO removes the constraints of potential interpretations of terms in various data sources and provides a structured vocabulary that unifies and integrates all data and knowledge sources for proteomics domain (Figure 3). There are seven subclasses of protein ontology (PO), called generic classes that are used to define complex concepts in other PO classes: *Residues*, *Chains*, *Atoms*, *Family*, *AtomicBind*, *Bind*, and *SiteGroup*. Concepts from these generic classes are reused in various other PO classes for definition of class specific concepts. Details and properties of residues in a protein sequence are defined by instances of *Residues* class. Instances of chains of residues are defined in *Chains* class. All the three dimensional structure data of protein atoms is represented as instances of *Atoms* class. Defining *Chains*, *Residues* and *Atoms* as individual classes has the benefit that any special properties or changes affecting a particular chain, residue and atom can be easily added. Protein *Family* class represents protein super family and family details of proteins. Data about binding atoms in chemical bonds like hydrogen bond, residue links, and salt bridges is entered into ontology as an instance of *AtomicBind* Class. Similarly the data about binding residues in chemical bonds like disulphide

Figure 3. Unification of protein data and knowledge

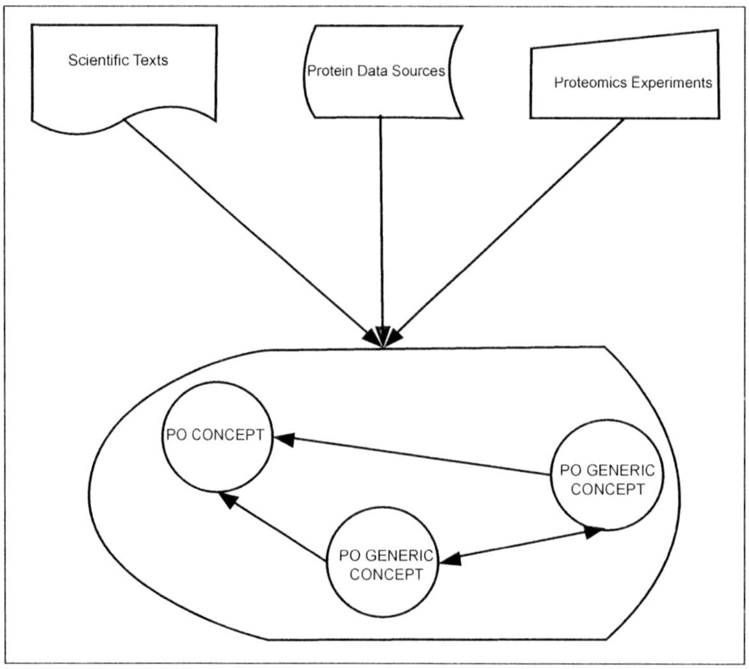

bonds and CIS peptides is entered into ontology as an instance of *Bind* class. All data related to site groups of the active binding sites of proteins is defined as instances of *SiteGroup* class. In PO the notions classification, reasoning, and consistency are applied by defining new concepts or classes from defined generic concepts or classes. The concepts derived from generic concepts are placed precisely into class hierarchy of protein ontology to completely represent information defining a protein complex.

As such PO can be used to support automatic semantic interpretation of data and knowledge sources, thus providing a basis for sophisticated mining of information.

CLUSTERING FACILITATED BY DOMAIN ONTOLOGIES

In this section we demonstrate how to modify clustering algorithms in order to utilise the structure of ontology. In the section "Challenges with Clustering Data Enriched with Ontological Information" we present the differences between clustering data items with associated ontological information compared to clustering data items without this information. In "A Distance Function for Clustering Ontologically Enriched Data," we show how these differences must be met in a clustering algorithm. Finally, "Automatic Cluster Identification and Naming" describes an automatic method of naming and describing the clusters found with the domain ontology.

Challenges with Clustering Data Enriched with Ontological Information

Many algorithms exist for clustering data (Duda, Hart, & Stork, 2001; Theodoridis & Koutroumbas, 1999). However, one of the primary decisions to be made when applying cluster analysis to data, and before choosing a specific algorithm, is the way of measuring distances between data items. Generally this involves defining some distance or similarity measure between data items defined in terms of their attributes.

Just as many clustering algorithms have been defined over a wide variety of data types, so to has a large set of potential similarity and distance functions been devised for comparing data items (Theodoridis & Koutroumbas, 1999). In general, a similarity function measures the degree to which two items are similar to one another. Conversely, a distance function measures how two data items are dissimilar. The choice of distance function for data items is often orthogonal to the particular clustering algorithm used as many clustering algorithms take as input a distance matrix, which contains the results of applying a distance function to each combination of data items. The distance matrix is a square symmetric matrix with each cell *i*, *j* measuring the distance between data items *i* and *j*. The particular distance function used with data items is generally dependent on the type of data being compared. For example, the distance between vectors of real valued data is often defined with the Euclidean distance function, whereas more elaborate functions are required for the sequence data types often found in biomedical datasets.

Thus, the first question we must address when devising a distance function for data enriched with information from ontologies is: what form does the data take? Details will, of course, depend on the particular ontology applied to the data. However, we can make some general comments and apply them in an example of comparing genes based on the associated gene ontology terms. In this example, the "knowledge-poor" or raw data items consist solely of gene names, for example, AA458965 or AA490846, using the GenBank accession codes. These gene names are essentially class labels with no knowledge embedded in them. Hence, there is no useful way to compare them on their own. Ontological information from the gene ontology may be associated with each gene by using the gene ontology database or with the use of a search engine such as SOURCE (Diehn et al., 2003). In our example, the gene ontology associations are shown in Table 1.

Two characteristics regarding the enriched data are apparent. First, there are different numbers of terms from the gene ontology associated with each gene. For the first gene there are four terms whilst the second has six associations. In general, this will be the norm for associations. Second, we do not seem to have accomplished much from the data enrichment. The associated terms can still be regarded as individual class labels for a very large number of classes (more than 16,000). The terms only have meaning in their relationships within the ontology hierarchy.

Thus, algorithms to cluster ontology enriched data items (1) must be able to handle different numbers of terms associated with data items; and (2) must be able to compare terms based on relationships in the ontology.

A Distance Function for Clustering Ontologically Enriched Data

Given the requirements for the clustering of ontologically enriched data developed in the last section, what kind of similarity measure or distance measure is appropriate? Standard measures like Euclidean distance are not applicable because the data contains different numbers of attributes and there is no natural way to define a distance between classes.

One possible approach is suggested by an analogy to comparison of documents in the field of computational linguistics. A common approach in this field is to transform a free form document into a sparse vector of word counts where each position in the vector refers to a different word in the corpus (see, e.g., Chapter 10 of Shawe-Taylor & Cristianini, 2004). This simplified knowledge representation of the text document ignores relationships between words. In the same way that this representation views a document as a vector of word counts, the ontologically enriched data items may be thought of as a vector of occurrences of gene ontology terms. We could devise a long sparse binary vector with each position referring to the presence or absence of an association with each of the thousands of gene ontology terms to the data item. The problem with this knowledge representation is that most of the gene ontology terms apply to only a very few genes in the database. This means that very few similarities could be found between the vectors for different data items. The solution to this difficulty lies in incorporating the relationships within the ontology into the knowledge representation.

Referring back to the example of the two genes in the last section, there is another characteristic of the enriched data that are not, at first, apparent. We can retrieve further enriched data for the genes by tracing back up the gene ontology hierarchy. In the gene ontology, parent terms are more general concepts of child terms. For example, for the gene AA458965 the term GO:0006952 (defense response) can be derived from the term GO:0006955 (immune response) by following the is-a relationship in the ontology. This allows us to retrieve more general terms describing the genes. These more general terms give a sort of

Table 1. Enriched data. First column lists "knowledge-poor" data in the form of GenBank identifiers. Second column lists associated Gene Ontology term identifiers for each gene.

AA458965	GO:0005125, GO:0005615, GO:0006955, GO:0007155
AA490846	GO:0004872, GO:0005515, GO:0007160, GO:0007229, GO:0008305, GO:0016021

Table 2. Enriched data with background associations: First column lists "knowledge-poor" data in the form of GenBank identifiers, rows of second column show gene ontology terms at successive distances from the directly associated terms

AA458965	0: GO:0005125, GO:0005615, GO:0006955, GO:0007155
	1: GO:0005102, GO:0006952, GO:0007154, GO:0050874
	2: GO:0004871, GO:0005488, GO:0007582, GO:0009607, GO:0009987
	3: GO:0050896, 2 x GO:0003674, 2 x GO:0008150
	4: GO:0007582
	5: GO:0008150
AA490846	0: GO:0004872, GO:0005515, GO:0007160, GO:0007229, GO:0008305, GO:0016021
	1: GO:0004871, GO:0005488, GO:0007155, GO:0007166, GO:0043235
	2: 2 x GO:0003674, GO:0007154, GO:0007165, GO:0043234
	3: GO:0007154, GO:0005575, GO:0009987
	4: GO:0009987, GO:0008150
	5: GO:0008150

Note: Some terms are seen multiple times at the same distance or at further distances

background knowledge for the genes. As we trace back terms higher in the hierarchy we successively build up more general background knowledge for the genes. The complete set of associations for the genes in our example is shown in Table 2. It should be clear that the terms associated with the genes differ in importance. Terms that are lower in the hierarchy are more specific to the data items and should be treated as more significant for comparisons between data items. Conversely, terms that are far from the original terms (in terms of distance up the hierarchy) are more general and should play a less significant role in comparison of data items. Furthermore, different child terms may have the same parent term or terms. This means that as we trace back up the ontology hierarchy we may draw in the same term more than once. Consequently, the background knowledge of terms may, and usually will, have duplicated terms.

This observation suggests a method of applying a similar knowledge representation to that used in the field of computational linguistics. Rather than using a binary vector to represent the presence or absence of an association between data item and gene ontology term, we use a real value measure or weighting of the degree of significance of the term to the data item. Terms directly associated with each data item, for example those listed in Table 1, receive a weight value of 1, terms indirectly associated with the data item (i.e., higher in the hierarchy) are given a lower weighting and terms that cannot be reached from terms associated with the data item are assigned 0. This leads to a less sparse vector where comparisons may be made.

A straightforward method of deriving the distance between terms using a weighting scheme like this is to adapt a similarity measure called the Tanimoto measure (Theodoridis & Koutroumbas, 1999). The Tanimoto measure defines a measure of similarity between sets:

$$\frac{n_{X \cap Y}}{n_X + n_Y - n_{X \cap Y}} = \frac{n_{X \cap Y}}{n_{X \cup Y}}$$

where X and Y are the two sets being compared and n_X, n_Y and $n_{X \cap Y}$ are the number of elements in the sets X, Y and $X \cap Y$ respectively.

However, in the current situation, the "sets" being compared are the gene ontology terms for the two genes. As there may be duplicated terms in the lists associated with each data item we adapt the Tanimoto measure to give similarities between bags rather than sets.

Also, as the terms higher in the ontology are less significant in terms of comparison than the more specific terms towards the bottom, we weight the contribution of terms by the distance from the descendent gene ontology term directly associated with the gene. In effect, this results in a "weighted" cardinality of the bag of gene ontology terms. Furthermore, as we are interested in a distance rather than a similarity, we subtract the similarity from 1. The final distance function used, then, is:

$$D_{X,Y} = 1 - \frac{n'_{X \cap Y}}{n'_X + n'_Y - n'_{X \cap Y}} = 1 - \frac{n'_{X \cap Y}}{n'_{X \cup Y}}$$

where X and Y are the bags of terms being compared and n'_X, n'_Y and $n'_{X \cap Y}$ are the weighted cardinalities of the bags X, Y and $X \cap Y$ respectively given by:

$$n'_X = \sum_{i \in X} c^{d_i}$$

where X is the bag of gene ontology terms, d_i is the distance of term of X with index i from its associated descendent in the original set of gene ontology terms for the gene, and c is the weight constant. The weighted cardinality of the other bags is similarly defined.

The more general gene ontology terms provide a context for the understanding of the lower level terms directly associated with genes. The c weight constant allows variation of the importance of the "context" to the comparison. A value of $c = 0$ means that higher level are ignored. A value of 1 considers all terms equally irrespective of their position in the hierarchy and regards the very general terms as overly significant. The c parameter may be viewed as a sort of "constant of gravity" for the clusters. The higher the value of c, the more that distantly related genes are gathered into a cluster. A choice of $c = 0.9$ gives reasonable results.

A similar graph-based approach for determining similarity based on gene ontology relationships to our described above is given in Lee, Hur, and Kim (2004). That approach involves transformation of the gene ontology from a directed acyclic graph into a tree structure and encoding of gene ontology accession codes to map into the tree.

Our similarity function contains several assumptions about ontologies. It treats distances between levels in the ontology as the same. This means that terms that are the same distance away from the terms directly associated to data items have the same effect on the similarity measure. This may not necessarily reflect the knowledge encoded in the ontology. The level of fan-out from a parent to child in the ontology may be an indication of the concentration of knowledge in the ontology. For example, when the fan-out from parent to child is large, this may indicate that the parent concept has been investigated more or is understood better than parents with less fan-out. This and other measures could conceivably be incorporated into the similarity function.

Automatic Cluster Identification and Naming

Once clusters have been identified, the ontology can facilitate inference of cluster descriptions. The descriptions say how data items in the cluster are similar to one another and different to other clusters using the vocabulary of the ontology.

Cluster descriptions are inferred for each cluster using the method shown in the pseudo code in Figure 4. At lines 1 and 2 the algorithm starts with an empty set of definitions and a list of all terms directly associated with the data items in the given cluster. The ontology hierarchy is traversed upwards replacing terms with their parent (more general) terms. Terms are replaced (line 12) only if the parent term is *not* associated with data items in another cluster (or is one of any of the ancestor terms in another cluster). At lines 8 and 14 the algorithm chooses a term to be added to the class description. Line 8 is the case when the top of the hierarchy is reached and line 14 is the case when no parent terms could be found that referred only to the cluster of interest. The output of the algorithm is a list of terms for a cluster that describe in the most general way possible the data items in the cluster (but not so general that it describes another cluster).

Insight into structure within clusters can be gained by examining which data items are associated with terms in the cluster description. It can happen that a subset of the data items in a cluster may have a description that is more concise than the description for all the data items in the cluster. This may be an indication of poor clustering of the data items.

CASE STUDY

This section presents a case study of enriching bio-medical data with the protein ontology. The case study discusses the results of six data mining algorithms on PO data. The protein ontology database is created as an instance store for various protein data using the PO format. PO provides technical and scientific infrastructure to allow evidence based description and analysis of relationships between proteins. PO uses data sources like PDB, SCOP, OMIM and various published scientific literature to gather protein data. PO database is represented using OWL. PO database at the moment contains data instances of following protein families: (1) prion proteins, (2) B.Subtilis, (3) CLIC and (4) PTEN. More protein data instances will be added as PO is more developed. The PO instance store at moment covers various species of proteins from bacterial and plant proteins to human proteins. Such a generic representation using PO shows the strength of PO format representation.

We used some standard hierarchical and tree mining algorithms (Tan & Dillon, in press) on the PO database. We compared MB3-Miner

Figure 4. Pseudo code for cluster identification and naming

```
1   definitions = { }
2   working = terms directly associated with the data items in the cluster
3   while there are terms in working
4       new_working = { }
5       for each term in working
6           parents = parent terms of term
7           if there are no parents
8               add term to definitions
9           else
10              for each parent_term in parents
11                  if parent_term is associated only with this cluster
12                      add parent_term to new_working
13                  else
14                      add term to definitions
15      working = new_working
16  end while
17  definitions is the set of terms describing the cluster.
```

Figure 5. Time performance for prion dataset of PO data

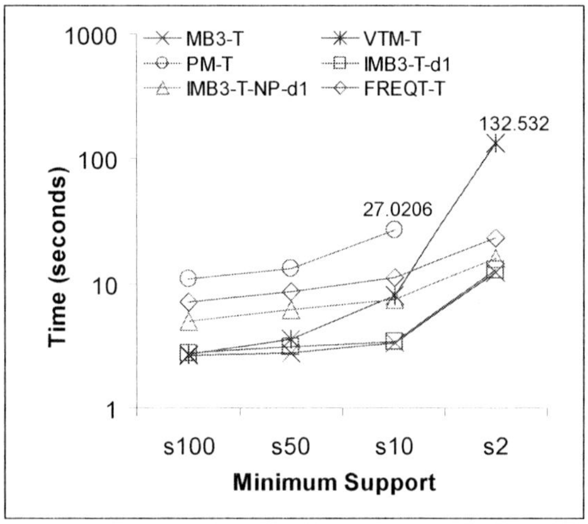

(MB3), X3-Miner (X3), VTreeMiner (VTM) and PatternMatcher (PM) for mining embedded subtrees and IMB3-Miner (IMB3), FREQT (FT) for mining induced subtrees of PO data. In these experiments we are mining prion proteins dataset described using protein ontology framework, represented in OWL. For this dataset we map the OWL tags to integer indexes. The maximum height is 1. In this case all candidate subtrees generated by all algorithms would be induced subtrees. Figure 5 shows the time performance of different algorithms. Our original MB3 has the best time performance for this data.

Figure 6. Number of frequent subtrees for prion dataset of PO data

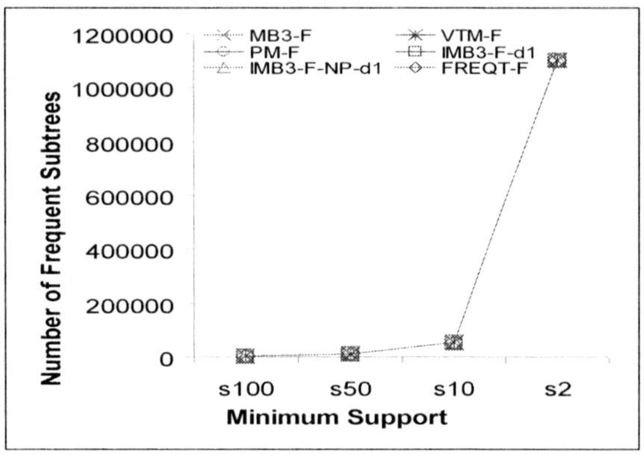

Quite interestingly, with prion dataset of PO the number of frequent candidate subtrees generated is identical for all algorithms (Figure 6). Another observation is that when support is less than 10, PM aborts and VTM performs poorly. The rationale for this could be because the utilized join approach enumerates additional invalid subtrees. Note that original MB3 is faster than IMB3 due to additional checks performed to restrict the level of embedding.

CONCLUSION

We discussed the two challenges to incorporate this biological knowledge into the data mining cycle: generating the ontologies, and adapting the data mining algorithms to make use of the ontologies. We present protein ontology (PO) framework, discuss semantic interoperability relationships between its concepts, and compare its structure with gene ontology (GO). We also demonstrate how to modify clustering algorithms in order to utilize the structure of GO. The results of six data mining algorithms on PO data are discussed, showing the strength of PO in enriching data for effective analysis.

REFERENCES

Diehn, M., Sherlock, G., Binkley, G., Jin, H., Matese, J. C., Hernandez-Boussard, T., et al. (2003). SOURCE: A unified genomic resource of functional annotations, ontologies, and gene expression data. *Nucleic Acids Research, 31*(1), 219-223.

Duda, R. O., Hart, P. E., & Stork, D. G. (2001). *Pattern classification* (2nd ed). New York: John Wiley & Sons.

GO Consortium. (2001). Creating the gene ontology resource: Design and implementation. *Genome Research, 11*, 1425-1433.

GO Consortium & S. E. Lewis. (2004). Gene ontology: Looking backwards and forwards. *Genome Biology, 6*(1), 103.1-103.4.

Lee, S. G., Hur, J. U., & Kim, Y. S. (2004). A graph-theoretic modeling on GO space for biological interpretation of gene clusters. *Bioinformatics, 20*(3), 381-388.

Nelson, S. J., Schopen, M., et al. (2004, September 7-11).The MeSH translation maintenance system: Structure, interface design, and implementation. In M. Fieschi (Ed.), *Proceedings of the 11th World Congress on Medical Informatics*, San Francisco (pp. 67-69).

Shawe-Taylor, J., & Cristianini, N. (2004). *Kernel methods for pattern analysis*. Cambridge: Cambridge University Press.

Sidhu, A. S., & Dillon, T. S. (2006a). Protein ontology: Data integration using protein ontology. In Z. Ma & J. Y. Chen (Eds.), *Database modeling in biology: Practices and challenges*. New York: Springer Science, Inc.

Sidhu, A. S., & Dillon, T. S. (2006b). *Protein ontology project: 2006 Updates*. Invited paper presented at Data Mining and Information Engineering 2006, Prague, Czech Republic. WIT Press.

Sidhu, A. S., & Dillon, T. S. (2005a). Ontological foundation for protein data models. In *Proceedings of the First IFIP WG 2.12 & WG 12.4 International Workshop on Web Semantics (SWWS 2005) in conjunction with On The Move Federated Conferences (OTM 2005)*, Agia Napa, Cyprus (LNCS). Springer-Verlag.

Sidhu, A. S., & Dillon, T. S. (2005a). Protein ontology: Vocabulary for protein data. In *Proceedings of the 3rd IEEE International Conference on Information Technology and Applications (IEEE ICITA 2005)*, Sydney, Australia (pp. 465-469).

Tan, H., & Dillon. T.S. (in press). IMB3-miner: Mining induced/embedded subtrees by constraining the level of embedding. In *Proceedings of PAKDD 2006*.

Theodoridis, S., & Koutroumbas, K. (1999). *Pattern recognition*. San Diego: Academic Press.

Section VII
Traditional Data Mining Algorithms

Chapter XI
Effective Intelligent Data Mining Using Dempster-Shafer Theory

Malcolm J. Beynon
Cardiff University, UK

ABSTRACT

The efficacy of data mining lies in its ability to identify relationships amongst data. This chapter investigates that constraining this efficacy is the quality of the data analysed, including whether the data is imprecise or in the worst case incomplete. Through the description of Dempster-Shafer theory (DST), a general methodology based on uncertain reasoning, it argues that traditional data mining techniques are not structured to handle such imperfect data, instead requiring the external management of missing values, and so forth. One DST based technique is classification and ranking belief simplex (CaRBS), which allows intelligent data mining through the acceptance of missing values in the data analysed, considering them a factor of ignorance, and not requiring their external management. Results presented here, using CaRBS and a number of simplex plots, show the effect of managing and not managing of imperfect data.

INTRODUCTION

The considered generality of the term data mining highlights the wide range of real-world applications that have benefited or could benefit from its attention. It also acknowledges the increasing amount of information (data) available when insights into a problem are the intent. Its remit certainly encompasses the notion of secondary data analysis, as referred to in a definition of data mining given in Hand (1998, p. 112), who state: "*the process of secondary analysis of large databases aimed at finding unsuspected relationships which are of interest or value to the database owners.*"

However, at the start of the 21st century, it could be viewed data mining has matured beyond this, to take in primary data analysis also, where data is

Copyright © 2007, IGI Global, distributing in print or electronic forms without written permission of IGI Global is prohibited.

collected and analysed with a particular question or questions in mind (Hand, 1998). Peacock (1998), highlight the confusion to what is data mining, suggesting it is defined within a narrow scope by some experts, within a broad scope by others, and within a very broad scope by still others. A reason for this confusion is because of the evolution in the range of data mining techniques available to an analyst, many benchmarked using more primary data where results are prior known.

One direction of this evolution is within the environment of uncertain reasoning, which by its definition acknowledges the often imperfection of the considered data. Chen (2001), outlines the rudiments of uncertain reasoning based data mining, highlighting the often reality of the presence of imprecision and incompleteness of the available data to be analysed. Amongst the associated general methodologies considered, including rough set theory (Pawlak, 1982) and fuzzy set theory (Zadeh, 1965), is Dempster-Shafer theory, introduced in Dempster (1967, 1968) and Shafer (1976). DST is often described as a generalisation of the well-known Bayesian theory (Shafer & Srivastava, 1990), noticeably further developed in the form of the transferable belief model (Smets, 1990; Smets & Kennes, 1994). Inherent with DST is its close association with the ability to undertake data mining in the presence of ignorance (Safranek, Gottschlich, & Kak, 1990).

A nascent DST-based technique for object classification and ranking is the classification and ranking belief simplex. Introduced in Beynon (2005a), it encompasses many of the advantages the utilisation of DST can bestow on knowledge discovery and data mining. The advantages highlighted here are central to effective data mining, including; the non-requirement for knowledge on specific data distributions, the ability to work with the presence of missing values without the need for their inhibiting management and the mining of low quality information. CaRBS further offers a visual representation of the contribution of data to the classification of objects using simplex plots, including the concomitant levels of ambiguity and ignorance (Beynon, 2005b).

The main emphasis in this chapter is on the presence of missing values in data and its effect on the subsequent data mining. A need to concern oneself with this issue is that most data mining techniques were not designed for their presence (Schafer & Graham, 2002). The reality is however that there exists a nonchalant attitude to their presence. Exemplified in Barnett (2005), when describing data mining within customer information systems, they comment that, "it is easier to produce accurate reports even when data is missing—through statistical adjustment." It is as though simply managing (replacing) missing values solves the problem, without realising that it brings its own disadvantages, namely a different dataset to that originally available. The CaRBS technique does not require any management of missing values, instead considering them as concomitant ignorance, so allowing data mining on the richness of the original data. This effective utilisation of belief functions (a more general term for DST), offers one direction for the mitigation of the comment in Zaffalon (2002, p. 108), who suggests: "statistical treatment of missing data does not appear to have benefited yet from belief function models."

A "complete" bank rating dataset (with no missing values) is initially analysed using the CaRBS technique. Moreover, a simplified binary classification of the Fitch bank individual rating (FBR) on large U.S. banks is considered, with each bank described by a number of financial variables (FitchRatings, 2003). Similar CaRBS analyses are undertaken when a large proportion of the financial values are denoted missing, with comparable results presented when the missing values are retained and when they are managed through imputation (see Huisman, 2000).

The relative simplicity of the CaRBS technique and visual presentation of findings allows the reader the opportunity to succinctly view a form of DST based data mining. This includes an elucidation of the notions of ambiguity and ignorance in object classification and the negative effects of imposing the management of missing values.

DEMPSTER-SHAFER THEORY, THE CARBS TECHNIQUE, AND MISSING VALUES

The background to this chapter briefly describes the origins and developments of Dempster-Shafer theory, including an example. It is then further exposited through the description of the CaRBS technique for object classification, restricting ourselves to the case of binary classification. Finally, the issues of missing values and their management are briefly presented, the brevity of this description is simply because when using CaRBS there is no reason to manage the missing values.

Dempster-Shafer Theory

Dempster-Shafer theory (DST) is founded on the work of Dempster (1967, 1968) and Shafer (1976), since its introduction the very name causes confusion because it covers several models (Smets, 2002). Hence a more general term often used is belief functions (both used intermittently here). From its introduction, DST has been considered a generalisation (alternative) to the traditional Bayesian theory (Schubert, 1994; Shafer & Srivastava, 1990), with their general mutual existence described in Shafer and Pearl (1990). Alternatively, Shafer (1990) describes belief functions as an alternative language of probability, not as something distinct from it. The relationship between the Bayesian and DST methodologies is further expressed after a discussion on the rudiments of DST is given next.

Formally, DST is based on a finite set of p elements $\Theta = \{o_1, o_2, ..., o_p\}$, called a frame of discernment. A *mass value* is a function m: $2^\Theta \rightarrow [0, 1]$ such that $m(\emptyset) = 0$ ($\emptyset$ - the empty set) and $\sum_{s \in 2^\Theta} m(s) = 1$ (2^Θ - the power set of Θ). Any proper subset s of the frame of discernment Θ, for which $m(s)$ is non-zero, is called a focal element and represents the exact belief in the proposition depicted by s. From a single piece of evidence all assigned mass values sum to unity and there is no belief in the empty set. In the case of the transferable belief model a non-zero mass value can be assigned to the empty set (see Smets & Kennes, 1994).

The set of mass values associated with a single piece of evidence is called a *body of evidence* (BOE), often denoted $m(\cdot)$. The mass value $m(\Theta)$ assigned to the frame of discernment Θ is considered the amount of ignorance within the BOE, since it represents the level of exact belief that cannot be discerned to any proper subsets of Θ. DST also provides a method to combine the BOE from different pieces of evidence, using Dempster's rule of combination. This rule assumes these pieces of evidence are independent, then the function $(m_1 \oplus m_2)$: $2^\Theta \rightarrow [0, 1]$, defined by:

$$(m_1 \oplus m_2)(s) = \begin{cases} 0 & x = \emptyset \\ \dfrac{\sum_{s_1 \cap s_2 = x} m_1(s_1)m_2(s_2)}{1 - \sum_{s_1 \cap s_2 = \emptyset} m_1(s_1)m_2(s_2)} & x \neq \emptyset \end{cases}$$

is a mass value, where s_1 and s_2 are focal elements from the BOEs, $m_1(\cdot)$ and $m_2(\cdot)$, respectively. One point of concern with the combination of evidence is the effect of conflict or inconsistency in the individual pieces of evidence. That is, the notion of conflict (κ) is made up of the sum of the products of mass values from the two pieces of evidence with empty intersection, that is, $\kappa = \sum_{s_1 \cap s_2 = \emptyset} m_1(s_1)m_2(s_2)$. Murphy (2000) discusses the problem of conflict, the larger the value of κ the more conflict in the sources of evidence, and subsequently the less sense there is in their combination. One solution to mitigate conflict is to assign noticeable levels of ignorance to all evidence, pertinently the case when low level measurement are considered (Gerig, Welti, Guttman, Colchester, & Szekely, 2000).

The use of DST does not require concern on prior and conditional probabilities, instead acknowledging certain distributions exist, but which are unknown. The example of the murder of Mr. Jones briefly illustrates this, where the murderer was one of three assassins, Peter, Paul, and Mary, so the frame of discernment Θ = {Peter, Paul, Mary}. There are two witnesses:

- Witness 1, is 80% sure that it was a man, the concomitant body of evidence (BOE), defined $m_1(\cdot)$, includes $m_1(\{\text{Peter, Paul}\}) = 0.8$. Since we know nothing about the remaining mass value it is considered ignorance and allocated to Θ, hence $m_1(\{\text{Peter, Paul, Mary}\}) = 0.2$.
- Witness 2, is 60% confident that Peter was leaving on a jet plane when the murder occurred, so a BOE defined $m_2(\cdot)$ includes, $m_2(\{\text{Paul, Mary}\}) = 0.6$ and $m_2(\{\text{Peter, Paul, Mary}\}) = 0.4$.

The aggregation of these two sources of information (evidence), using Dempster's combination rule, is based on the intersection and multiplication of focal elements and mass values from the BOEs, $m_1(\cdot)$ and $m_2(\cdot)$. Defining this BOE $m_3(\cdot)$, it can be found:

$m_3(\{\text{Paul}\}) = 0.48$, $m_3(\{\text{Peter, Paul}\}) = 0.32$,

$m_3(\{\text{Paul, Mary}\}) = 0.12$ and $m_3(\{\text{Peter, Paul, Mary}\}) = 0.08$.

Amongst this combination of evidence ($m_3(\cdot)$), the mass value assigned to ignorance ($m_3(\{\text{Peter, Paul, Mary}\}) = 0.08$) is less than that present in the original constituent BOEs. Smets (2002) offers a comparison on a variation of this example with how it would be modelled using traditional probability and the transferable belief model.

This brief exposition of DST is noticeable since it shows levels of exact belief (mass values) can be bestowed on subsets of the elements (for example assassins) in some predefined frame of discernment. This in contrast to the, possibly viewed, less general Bayesian approach which would adopt a factorisation of a joint probability distribution into a set of conditional distributions, one for each element in the frame of discernment (Cobb & Shenoy, 2003). It follows, DST captures Bayesian probability models as a special case, whereas DST can only be approximated by a Bayesian approach (see Cobb & Shenoy [2003] and references contained therein). Comber, Law, and Lishman (2004) also state how DST is not a method that considers the evidence element by element as in the Bayesian approach (in particular Bayes' theorem), rather the evidence is considered in light of the elements (hypotheses).

It is worth brief mention that, the Bayesian approach has itself developed to mitigate the incumbency of having to know certain prior distributions, including nonparametric and empirical Bayes procedures (Hjort, 1996; Krutchkoff, 1967; Sarhan, 2003). Heikkinen and Arjas (1998) offer a summary of the non-parametric ideas, including those using a Dirichlet process (or derivative) for specifying a prior, or placing priors on coefficients and other local parameters. The overriding feature being that certain assumptions in some form are present. In the case of DST it is simply that certain distributions do exist but which are unknown.

The CaRBS Technique for Object Classification

The origins of the construction of the nascent CaRBS technique was to enable object classification with a visual interpretation to the results, and allowed for the presence of ignorance because of the use of low level measurements (see Beynon, 2005a). It is concerned with the classification of

Figure 1. Stages within the CaRBS technique for a variable value $v_{j,i}$.

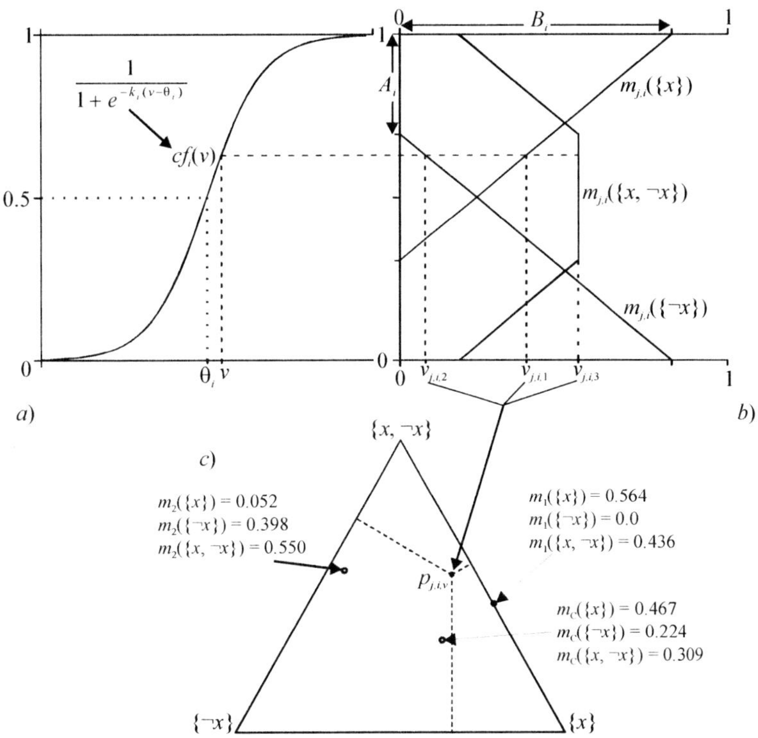

objects, each described by a number of variables. The aim of the CaRBS technique, when undertaking binary classification, is to construct a BOE for each variable value (*variable* BOE), which quantifies that variable's evidential support for the classification of an object to a given hypothesis ($\{x\}$), not the hypothesis ($\{\neg x\}$) and concomitant ignorance ($\{x, \neg x\}$), for an exposition of this process see Figure 1.

In Figure 1, stage *a*) shows the transformation of a variable value $v_{j,i}$ (j^{th} object, i^{th} variable) into a confidence value $cf_i(v_{j,i})$, using a sigmoid function, with control parameters k_i and θ_i. Stage *b*) transforms a $cf_i(v_{j,i})$ into a variable BOE $m_{j,i}(\cdot)$, made up of the three mass values $m_{j,i}(\{x\})$, $m_{j,i}(\{\neg x\})$ and $m_{j,i}(\{x, \neg x\})$, defined by (following Gerig et al., 2000):

$$m_{j,i}(\{x\}) = \frac{B_i}{1-A_i} cf_i(v_{j,i}) - \frac{A_i B_i}{1-A_i},$$

$$m_{j,i}(\{\neg x\}) = \frac{-B_i}{1-A_i} cf_i(v_{j,i}) + B_i,$$

and $m_{j,i}(\{x, \neg x\}) = 1 - m_{j,i}(\{x\}) - m_{j,i}(\{\neg x\})$,

where A_i and B_i are two further control parameters. Importantly, if either $m_{j,i}(\{x\})$ or $m_{j,i}(\{\neg x\})$ are negative they are set to zero before the calculation of the respective $m_{j,i}(\{x, \neg x\})$ mass value. Stage *c*) shows a BOE $m_{j,i}(\cdot)$; $m_{j,i}(\{x\}) = v_{j,i,1}$, $m_{j,i}(\{\neg x\}) = v_{j,i,2}$ and $m_{j,i}(\{x, \neg x\}) = v_{j,i,3}$, can be represented as a simplex coordinate ($p_{j,i,v}$) in a simplex plot (equilateral triangle). That is, a point $p_{j,i,v}$ exists within an equilateral triangle such that the least distance from $p_{j,i,v}$ to each of the sides of the equilateral triangle are in the same proportion (ratio) to the values $v_{j,i,1}$, $v_{j,i,2}$ and $v_{j,i,3}$.

When a series of variables describe each object, a similar number of variable BOEs are constructed. Within DST, Dempster's rule of combination is used to combine the variable BOEs (assuring they are independent). This combination of the variable BOEs, describing an object, produces an *object* BOE associated with its final level of classification to $\{x\}$, $\{\neg x\}$ and $\{x, \neg x\}$. In the case of a binary frame of discernment ($\Theta = \{x, \neg x\}$), since x and $\neg x$ are exhaustive classification outcomes, the combination of two BOEs $m_{j,i}(\cdot)$ and $m_{j,k}(\cdot)$, defined $(m_{j,i} \oplus m_{j,k})(\cdot)$, results in a combined BOE whose mass values are given by the equations in Boxes 1-3.

One concern is on the occasion of very specific information (Gerig et al., 2000; Safranek et al., 1990), they discuss the disadvantage of having this information since it may bias the final classification of objects. This factor implies that the CaRBS technique should consider a problem for which each related variable has a noticeable level of ignorance associated with it and its contribution to the problem (technically this requires at least an upper bound on each of the B_i control parameters, see Figure 1b).

To illustrate the method of combination employed here, two example BOEs, $m_1(\cdot)$ and $m_2(\cdot)$ are considered, with mass values in each BOE given in the vector form $[m_j(\{x\}), m_j(\{\neg x\}), m_j(\{x, \neg x\})]$ as, [0.564, 0.000, 0.436] and [0.052, 0.398, 0.550], respectively. The combination of $m_1(\cdot)$ and $m_2(\cdot)$ is evaluated to be [0.467, 0.224, 0.309], further illustrated in Figure 1*c*, where the simplex coordinates of the BOEs $m_1(\cdot)$ and $m_2(\cdot)$ are shown along with that of the combined BOE $m_C(\cdot)$. This example illustrates the clarity in the interpretation of the interaction between BOEs and their combination that the simplex plot representation allows. In this case, $m_1(\cdot)$ offers more evidential support to the combined BOE $m_C(\cdot)$ than from $m_2(\cdot)$, since the ignorance in $m_2(\cdot)$ is more than that associated with $m_1(\cdot)$. In the limit, a final object BOE will have a lower level of ignorance than that associated with the individual variable BOEs.

The effectiveness of the CaRBS technique is governed by the values assigned to the incumbent control parameters k_i, θ_i, A_i and B_i $i = 1, ..., n$. The necessary configuration is considered as a constrained optimisation problem. Since these parameters are continuous in nature the recently introduced trigonometric differential evolution (TDE) method is utilised (Fan & Lampinen, 2003; Storn & Price, 1997). This evolutionary algorithm, attempts to converge to an optimised configuration through the amendment of a possible configuration with the difference between

Box 1.

$$(m_{j,i} \oplus m_{j,k})(\{x\}) = \frac{m_{j,i}(\{x\})m_{j,k}(\{x\}) + m_{j,k}(\{x\})m_{j,i}(\{x,\neg x\}) + m_{j,i}(\{x\})m_{j,k}(\{x,\neg x\})}{1-(m_{j,i}(\{\neg x\})m_{j,k}(\{x\}) + m_{j,i}(\{x\})m_{j,k}(\{\neg x\}))}$$

Box 2.

$$(m_{j,i} \oplus m_{j,k})(\{\neg x\}) = \frac{m_{j,i}(\{\neg x\})m_{j,k}(\{\neg x\}) + m_{j,k}(\{x,\neg x\})m_{j,i}(\{\neg x\}) + m_{j,k}(\{\neg x\})m_{j,i}(\{x,\neg x\})}{1-(m_{j,i}(\{\neg x\})m_{j,k}(\{x\}) + m_{j,i}(\{x\})m_{j,k}(\{\neg x\}))}$$

Box 3.

$$(m_{j,i} \oplus m_{j,k})(\{x,\neg x\}) = 1-(m_{j,i} \oplus m_{j,k})(\{x\}) - (m_{j,i} \oplus m_{j,k})(\{\neg x\})$$

others. When the classification of a number of objects to some hypothesis and its complement is known, the effectiveness of a configured CaRBS system can be measured by a defined objective function (OB).

From Figure 1c, an object BOE's simplex coordinates' direction (movement) for improved certainty in its final classification is down and to the left (for $\neg x$) or right (for x) vertex. Horizontal movement alters the level of ambiguity in classification, with change specifically in the difference between the respective $m_j(\{x\})$ and $m_j(\{\neg x\})$ mass values in an object BOE. Whereas, vertical downward movement decreases the mass value $m_j(\{x, \neg x\})$, hence a reduction in the level of concomitant ignorance. Within CaRBS, and the use of low level measurements, an objective function should just consider measuring the ambiguity in the classification of the set of objects, and not force the reduction in the inherent ignorance that may be present.

More formally, for objects in the equivalence classes $E(x)$ and $E(\neg x)$, the optimum solution is to maximise the difference values ($m_j(\{x\}) - m_j(\{\neg x\})$) and ($m_j(\{\neg x\}) - m_j(\{x\})$), respectively. The subsequent pair of mean difference values are incorporated into an objective function, defined OB, where optimisation is minimisation with a general lower limit of zero, and is given by (from Beynon, 2005b) can be seen in Box 4.

In the limit, each of the difference values ($m_i(\{x\}) - m_i(\{\neg x\})$) and ($m_i(\{\neg x\}) - m_i(\{x\})$) can attain -1 and 1, then $0 \leq \text{OB} \leq 1$. It is noted, maximising a difference value such as ($m_i(\{x\}) - m_i(\{\neg x\})$) only indirectly affects the associated ignorance, rather than making it a direct issue, a facet related here to the data mining of imperfect data, for which ignorance is an inherent feature.

When the optimisation process has been undertaken, using OB, a final classification (decision) rule is necessary to classify each object to some hypothesis (x) or its complement ($\neg x$). Here, graphical and numerical rules are defined. In Figure 1c, the vertical dashed line down from the $\{x, \neg x\}$ vertex partitions the domain of the simplex plot where the position of an object BOE's simplex coordinate would classify an object to x (right of line) or $\neg x$ (left of line). This graphical rule has a numerical analogy, namely the vertical dashed line partitions where; to the left $m_i(\{x\}) < m_i(\{\neg x\})$ and to the right $m_i(\{x\}) > m_i(\{\neg x\})$.

An indication of the evidential support offered by a variable to the known classification of each object is made with the evaluation of *average variable* BOEs. More formally, again partitioning the objects into the equivalence classes $E(x)$ and $E(\neg x)$, then the average variable BOEs, defined $am_{i,x}(\cdot)$ and $am_{i,\neg x}(\cdot)$, are given by:

$$am_{i,x}(\{x\}) = \sum_{o_j \in E(x)} \frac{m_{j,i}(\{x\})}{|E(x)|},$$

$$am_{i,x}(\{\neg x\}) = \sum_{o_j \in E(x)} \frac{m_{j,i}(\{\neg x\})}{|E(x)|},$$

$$am_{i,x}(\{x, \neg x\}) = \sum_{o_j \in E(x)} \frac{m_{j,i}(\{x, \neg x\})}{|E(x)|}$$

and

$$am_{i,\neg x}(\{x\}) = \sum_{o_j \in E(\neg x)} \frac{m_{j,i}(\{x\})}{|E(\neg x)|},$$

$$am_{i,\neg x}(\{\neg x\}) = \sum_{o_j \in E(\neg x)} \frac{m_{j,i}(\{\neg x\})}{|E(\neg x)|},$$

Box 4.

$$\text{OB} = \frac{1}{4}\left(\frac{1}{|E(x)|}\sum_{o_i \in E(x)} (1 - m_i(\{x\}) + m_i(\{\neg x\})) + \frac{1}{|E(\neg x)|}\sum_{o_i \in E(\neg x)} (1 + m_i(\{x\}) - m_i(\{\neg x\}))\right)$$

$$am_{i,\neg x}(\{x, \neg x\}) = \sum_{o_j \in E(\neg x)} \frac{m_{j,i}(\{x, \neg x\})}{|E(\neg x)|}.$$

As BOEs, the $am_{i,x}(\cdot)$ and $am_{i,\neg x}(\cdot)$ can be represented as simplex coordinates in a simplex plot, so visualising the overall evidential support of each variable to the classification of the objects. Of interest will be the horizontal and vertical distances between the simplex coordinates representing $am_{i,x}(\cdot)$ and $am_{i,\neg x}(\cdot)$, since they exposit the levels of ignorance and ambiguity that may exist in the classification of the objects to x or $\neg x$.

Missing Values

For the last 30+ years (starting with Afifi & Elashoff, 1966; Rubin, 1976), the investigation into the presence and management of missing values in datasets has kept pace with their appropriate analyse. Undoubtedly, the best avoidance of having to analyse incomplete datasets (with missing values present), is through planning and conscientious data collection (De Sarbo, Green, & Carroll, 1986). In the data mining context, this may be impossible when secondary data analysis is undertaken (Hand, 1998).

When utilising the information available in external databases, the lack of knowledge on why a missing value is present may mitigate the ability of the researcher to identify the specific mechanism for its presence and subsequently how to manage its existence (Lakshminarayan, Harp, & Samat, 1999). When the management of the missing values is the issue, the effect of a lack of adequate thought is well expressed by Huang and Zhu (2002, p. 1613): "inappropriate treatment of missing data may cause large errors or false results."

The choices available for their management include the more older non-technical methods, such as case (listwise) deletion and single imputation, against the more modern methods that include maximum likelihood and multiple imputation (Schafer & Graham, 2002). Considering only the non-technical methods, case deletion is a popular approach, whereby individual surveys or cases in a database are discarded if their required information is incomplete. However, this by its very nature incurs the loss of information from discarding partially informative cases (Shen & Lai, 2001).

Imputation is a similarly popular approach to the management of missing values, whereby an incomplete dataset becomes filled-in by the replacement of missing values with surrogates (Huisman, 2000; Olinsky, Chen, & Harlow, 2003). While this appears a relatively simple solution, concomitant dangers have been highlighted, outlined in Dempster and Rubin (1983, p. 8), who state:

The idea of imputation is both seductive and dangerous. It is seductive because it can lull the user into the plausible state of believing that the data are complete after all, and it is dangerous because it lumps together situations where the problem is sufficiently minor that it can be legitimately handled in this way and situations where standard estimators applied to the real and imputed data have substantial biases.

Little (1988) support this danger, suggesting naïve imputations may be worse than doing nothing. Here, the mean imputation approach is employed later in the chapter, whereby a missing value for a given variable is filled in with the mean of all the reported values for that variable. One factor often highlighted is that the distribution characteristics (including variance) of the completed dataset may be underestimated when using mean imputation (Schafer & Graham, 2002).

Within CaRBS, if an attribute value is missing its attribute BOE supports only ignorance, namely $m_{i,j}(\{x, \neg x\}) = 1$ (with $m_{i,j}(\{x\}) = 0$ and $m_{i,j}(\{\neg x\}) = 0$). That is, a missing value is considered an ignorant value and so offers no evidence in the subsequent classification of an object. This means that the missing values can be retained in the analysis rather than having to be imputed or managed in any way, which would change the dataset considered.

FBR DATASET AND CARBS ANALYSES OF COMPLETE AND INCOMPLETE DATA

The main thrust of this chapter briefly describes the FBR dataset considered and then undertakes respective CaRBS analyses on the original complete data, and an incomplete version of the data (when a large proportion of the financial variable values are missing). Comparisons are shown when the missing values are kept in the analysis (treated as ignorant values) and when they are managed (using mean value imputation). The reader is reminded that while classification accuracy is important the ability to accrue insights from only the sparse available data is the underlying motivation for this analysis.

Bank Ratings and Fitch Dataset

One facet associated with the rating agencies, such as Moody's, S&P's and Fitch, is that they shroud their decision-making mechanisms in secrecy. This secrecy has accelerated the attempts to model their rating processes, further it has become a challenge for data mining studies to identify insights into the rating decisions. From the first analyses by Fisher (1959) and Horrigan (1966), techniques utilised include MDA and neural networks amongst others (see Maher & Sen, 1997; Poon, Firth & Fung, 1999 and references contained therein). However, it is interesting that agencies in general have stated that statistical models cannot be used to replicate their ratings (Singleton & Surkan, 1991).

The Fitch Publishing Company issued their first ratings in 1924 (Cantor & Packer, 1995). With respect to the rating of banking institutions, Fitch is considered pre-eminent in its worldwide coverage (Abeysuriya, 2002). Fitch's bank individual rating (FBRs) is investigated here, its introduction was to assess how a bank would be viewed if it were entirely independent and could not rely on external support (FitchRatings, 2003). They state the principal factors to evaluate the banks' FBRs take into account; profitability, balance sheet integrity, franchise, management, operating environment and prospects, as well as other aspects including consistency, size and diversification.

The FBR ratings go from A to E in terms of decreasing strengths of bank individuality (and between sub-levels of graduations). To illustrate, the B definition is given as; a strong bank—there are no major concerns regarding the bank, characteristics may include strong profitability and balance sheet integrity, franchise, management,

Table 1. List of financial variables in FBR dataset

Label	Variable	Category
1. PROV	Loans loss provisions / Net interest revenue	Asset quality (−ve)
2. EQAS	Equity / Total assets	Capital strength (+ve)
3. ROAA	Return on average assets	Profitability (+ve)
4. COST	Cost to income ratio	Expenses management (−ve)
5. LIQ	Liquid assets / Customer & short term funding	Liquidity (+ve)
6. LGAS	Logarithm of total assets	Size (+ve)
7. OWNS	The number of institutional shareholders	Ownership (±ve)
8. SUBS	The number of subsidiaries	Franchise diversification (+ve)

operating environment or prospects. Here the ratings are partitioned into two groups, namely (A, A/B, B) and (B/C, C, C/D, D, D/E, E), in words it discerns between being "at least a strong bank" (denoted FBR-H) and "less than a strong bank" (denoted FBR-L).

The source for the FBR dataset comes from the Bankscope database (Bankscope, 2005), with the data presented in globally standardised templates, which can be compared across banks (Claessons, Demirgüç-Kunt, & Huizinga, 2001). Here, large banks in the U.S. are considered, which have been assigned FBRs. Following Pasiouras, Gaganis, and Zopoundis (2005), eight associated financial variables are utilised here to facilitate the possible discernment of banks between being rated FBR-L and FBR-H, see Table 1.

The financial variables in Table 1, as their categories suggest, cover the main factors that have been previously considered to influence the FBRs assigned (see Pasiouras et al., 2005; Poon & Firth, 2005). The –ve and +ve indicators describe the expected correlation based relationship with achieving a higher FBR (see Pasiouras et al., 2005), in the case of OWNS no direction of association was stated.

Using Bankscope, and the initial desire for a complete dataset with no missing values, there were identified 209 large US banks that have an assigned FBR. Of these banks, 77 and 132, have FBRs assigned the FBR-L and FBR-H classifications, respectively. With respect to CaRBS, the ratings FBR-L and FBR-H are considered the hypothesis x and its complement $\neg x$, respectively. There appears to be a slight imbalance in the numbers of banks assigned FBR-L and FBR-H, the OB used to configure the CaRBS system takes this into account, thus mitigating the often negative influence of such an imbalance (Grzymala-Busse, Stefanowski, & Wilk, 2005).

CaRBS Analysis on the Complete FBR Dataset

The first CaRBS analysis undertaken is on the original complete FBR dataset. The financial variable values of the 209 banks were standardised so they are described with a zero mean and unit standard deviation. This allows the standardisation of the bounds on each control parameter (k_i, θ_i, A_i and B_i), set as; $-2 \leq k_i \leq 2$, $-1 \leq \theta_i \leq 1$, $0 \leq A_i < 1$ and $B_i = 0.4$ (the setting of the B_i values secures the consideration of the financial variables as low level measurements, see Beynon, 2005b). The TDE technique was run five times and the best results adopted, using the run with the least OB value (the TDE operating parameters were amplification control $F = 0.99$, crossover constant $CR = 0.85$, trigonometric mutation probability $M_t = 0.05$ and number of parameter vectors $NP = 100$ (see Fan & Lampinen, 2003). The resultant CaRBS control parameters are reported in Table 2.

The only interpretation given to these control parameters is on the k_i values, the negative and positive values of each k_i signify their correlation based relationship with achieving a higher FBR rating. Reference back to Table 1 shows they are all consistent with what was expected, with the exception of the OWNS financial variable which was not previously assigned such a relationship.

Table 2. Control parameters associated with the eight financial variables

Variables	PROV	EQAS	ROAA	COST	LIQ	LGAS	OWNS	SUBS
k_i	−2.000	2.000	2.000	−2.000	2.000	2.000	−2.000	2.000
θ_i	0.440	−0.006	−0.141	0.624	−0.055	−0.123	0.419	0.209
A_i	0.714	0.967	0.330	0.387	0.393	0.258	0.980	0.258

Using these control parameters, the numerical results for two banks are next presented, namely o_{88} and o_{201}, both known to be classified to FBR-H. The bank o_{88} is first considered, with the construction of the variable BOE $m_{88,3}(\cdot)$ shown, associated with the financial variable ROAA. Starting with the $cf_{88,3}(\cdot)$, using the standardised variable value $v_{88,3} = 0.163$ (from Table 3 presented later) then:

$$cf_{88,3}(0.163) = \frac{1}{1+e^{-2.000(0.163+0.141)}}$$

$$= \frac{1}{1+0.544} = 0.648,$$

using the control parameters in Table 2. This confidence value is used in the expressions making up the mass values in the variable BOE $m_{88,3}(\cdot)$, namely, $m_{88,3}(\{x\})$, $m_{88,3}(\{\neg x\})$ and $m_{88,3}(\{x, \neg x\})$, found to be:

$$m_{88,3}(\{x\}) = \frac{0.4}{1-0.330}0.648 - \frac{0.330 \times 0.4}{1-0.330}$$

$$= 0.387 - 0.197 = 0.190,$$

$$m_{88,3}(\{\neg x\}) = \frac{-0.4}{1-0.330}0.648 + 0.4 = -0.387$$

$$+ 0.4 = 0.013,$$

$$m_{88,3}(\{x, \neg x\}) = 1 - 0.190 - 0.013 = 0.797.$$

For the bank o_{88}, this variable BOE is representative of the variable BOEs $m_{88,i}(\cdot)$, $i = 1, \ldots, 8$, presented in Table 3, along with those for the bank o_{201}. They describe the evidential support from all the financial variables to the bank's FBR classifications (FBR-H in both of these cases).

Amongst the variable BOEs presented in Table 3, for the bank o_{88}, are those associated with contributing only total ignorance, namely, PROV, EQAS and OWNS. This noncontribution is due to these variables not seen to contribute evidence for this bank, and not because they were missing. For both banks, known classified to FBR-H, evidence supporting correct classification requires $m_{j,i}(\{x\}) > m_{j,i}(\{\neg x\})$. These groups of variable BOEs can be combined to construct the object BOEs for the

Table 3. Variable BOEs $m_{?,i}(\cdot)$, $i = 1, \ldots, 8$ for the banks o_{88} and o_{201}

BOEs	PROV	EQAS	ROAA	COST	LIQ	LGAS	OWNS	SUBS
values	10.55	6.400	1.560	56.040	3.550	7.377	1	3
St. values	0.110	−0.889	0.163	−0.245	−0.256	0.033	−0.761	−0.320
$m_{88,?}(\{x\})$	0.000	0.000	0.190	0.302	0.005	0.172	0.000	0.000
$m_{88,?}(\{\neg x\})$	0.000	0.000	0.013	0.000	0.135	0.089	0.000	0.261
$m_{88,?}(\{x, \neg x\})$	1.000	1.000	0.797	0.698	0.859	0.739	1.000	0.739
values	10.01	8.910	1.740	58.22	9.270	8.631	21	1018
St. values	0.079	−0.224	0.373	−0.102	−0.169	2.038	0.973	2.217
$m_{201,?}(\{x\})$	0.000	0.000	0.243	0.276	0.033	0.393	0.000	0.390
$m_{201,?}(\{\neg x\})$	0.000	0.000	0.000	0.000	0.108	0.000	0.000	0.000
$m_{201,?}(\{x, \neg x\})$	1.000	1.000	0.757	0.724	0.859	0.607	1.000	0.610

two banks (defined bank BOEs), producing the two bank BOEs;

$m_{88}(\{x\}) = 0.402$, $m_{88}(\{\neg x\}) = 0.263$, and $m_{88}(\{x, \neg x\}) = 0.335$ for o_{88},

and $m_{201}(\{x\}) = 0.786$, $m_{201}(\{\neg x\}) = 0.024$ and $m_{201}(\{x, \neg x\}) = 0.190$ for o_{201}.

The evidence from the financial variables, towards each bank's FBR classification, can be further presented using the simplex plot method of data representation, see Figure 2.

In Figure 2, each simplex plot concerns a single bank and their FBR classification, based on their financial variables. The simplex plot is a standard domain within which the evidence can be viewed on any bank (shaded region is the domain of the variable BOEs). The base vertices identify where in the domain certainty in the classification of a bank to either FBR-L (left) or FBR-H (right) would be evident. The top vertex is similarly that associated with total ignorance. With levels of ignorance inherent in the evidence from the individual financial variables, their final classification will be someway from these limiting vertices. The variable BOEs ($m_{j,i}(\cdot)$) are labelled accordingly (using financial labels and only those shown which do not contribute total ignorance), the other circles further down the simplex plots represent the resultant bank BOEs ($m_j(\cdot)$).

The banks reported in Figures 2a and 2b (o_{88} and o_{201}) are both classified as being FBR-H, to varying certainty, the correct classifications in each case. One facet of the positions of the variable BOEs, being mostly on the edges of a simplex plot (in both simplex plots), is a direct consequence of the OB used in the optimisation of the evidence. That is, to minimise ambiguity in the final classification results – maximise the difference between the respective $m_j(\{x\})$ and $m_j(\{\neg x\})$ mass values in each bank BOE (so indirectly their variable BOEs). The final FBR classification of each of the 209 banks is next summarily reported, using their bank BOEs representation as simplex coordinates in simplex plots, see Figure 3.

In Figure 3, the simplex plots describe the classification of FBR-L (left) and FBR-H (right) rated banks. As in the simplex plots reported previously, a vertical dashed line partitions where a bank's classification may be correct or incorrect. Considering the 77 FBR-L rated banks, the presentation in Figure 3a shows circles (representing bank BOEs) across much of the lower middle (height) domain of the simplex plot. The different heights of the simplex plots indicate the different levels

Figure 2. Simplex plots of the FBR classification of the banks o_{88} and o_{201}

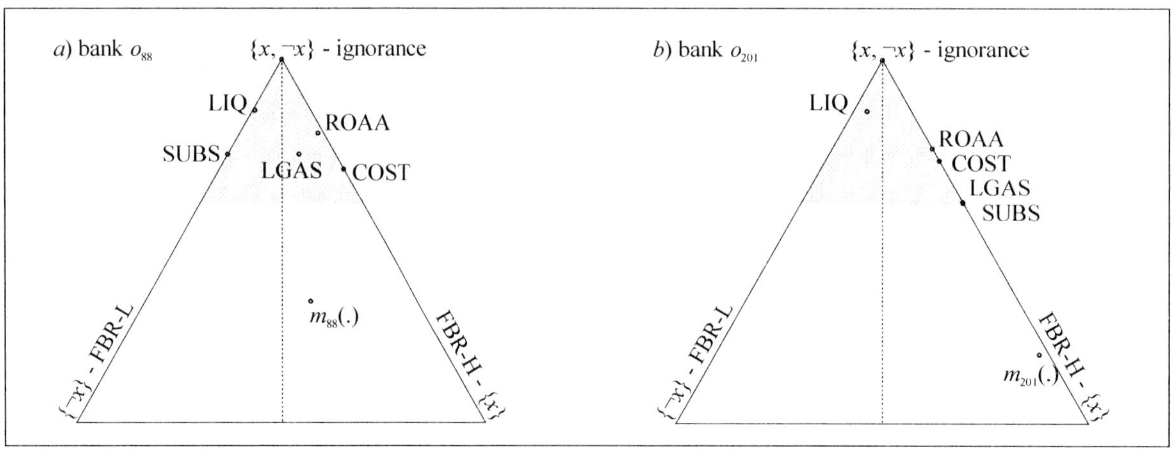

Figure 3. Simplex plots showing the classification of the FBR-L and FBR-H rated banks

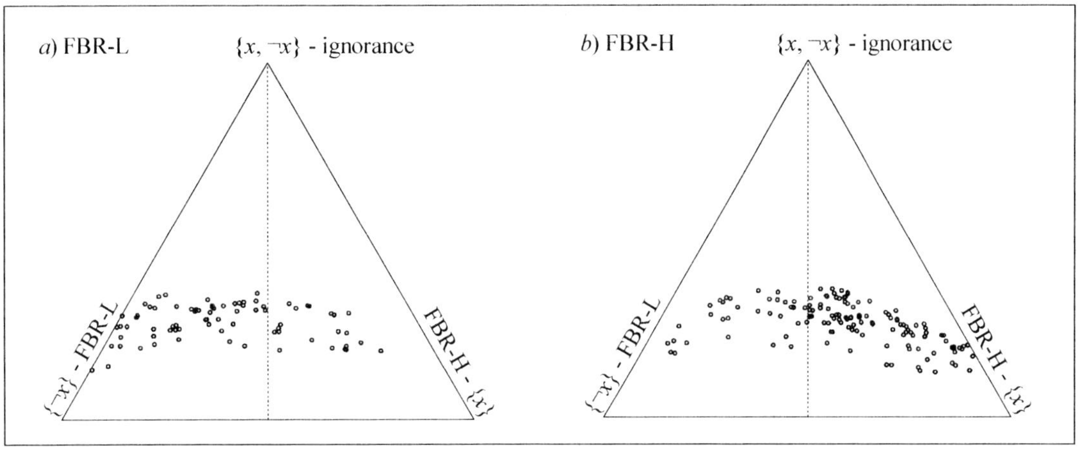

of ignorance associated with the classification of the banks. A similar description can be given for the FBR-H rated banks in Figure 3b.

The dearth of banks represented near the vertical dashed lines may be a consequence of the OB utilised, which minimises ambiguity (hence circles away from dashed line), but does not affect inherent ignorance (hence circles at different heights). In terms of correct classification, 56 out of 77 FBR-L (in 3*a*) and 99 out of 132 FBR-H (in 3*b*) rated banks were correctly classified, giving a total of 155 out of 209 (74.163%) classification accuracy. While benchmarking the accuracy of the results is not the theme of this chapter, using MDA it was found there exists a 66.507% classification accuracy, less than that when using CaRBS (no checks made for normality of group distributions when using MDA).

The CaRBS technique also aids the analyst in the evidential support of each financial variable to discern between FBR-L and FBR-H rated banks. The *average variable* BOEs are calculated separately for those banks differently classified (defined $am_{i,\neg x}(\cdot)$ and $am_{i,x}(\cdot)$). Since they are themselves BOEs, they can be represented as simplex coordinates in a simplex plot, see Figure 4.

In Figure 4, the simplex coordinates labelled '?-L' and '?-H' in the presented sub-domain of the simplex plot (shaded region only shown) denote the positions of the average variable BOEs, $am_{i,\neg x}(\cdot)$ and $am_{i,x}(\cdot)$. The noticeable details include the simplex coordinates associated with the financial variables, ROAA, COST, LGAS and SUBS, which are a distance away from the {*x*, ¬*x*} vertex, so have less overall ignorance associated with the evidence they confer than the others. In the case of the LGAS variable, its large horizontal distance between LGAS-L and LGAS-H further reflects its high ability to discern between the two groups of the differently rated banks.

Figure 4. Simplex coordinates of $am_{i,\neg x}(\cdot)$ '?-L' and $am_{i,x}(\cdot)$ '?-H' average variable BOEs

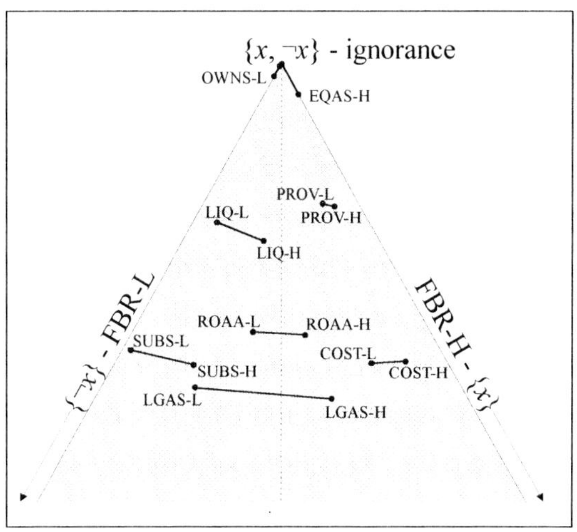

CaRBS Analysis on Incomplete Dataset (With and Without the Management of Missing Values)

This section undertakes similar CaRBS analyses on the FBR dataset, but now when a large proportion of the financial values are denoted as missing. Moreover, 50% of the values are denoted missing, with 8 financial variables and 209 banks this means 836 missing values. The level of incompleteness in this contrived incomplete dataset would be critical since even with their management, through say imputation, the completed dataset would look very different from that originally available (Carriere, 1999). One feature of a CaRBS analysis is that it can operate on an incomplete dataset. It follows, here two analyses are presented, first on the incomplete dataset and then on the "imputed" filled-in dataset (using the mean values of the remaining data values).

When considering the incomplete FBR dataset, where a financial value is missing its associated variable BOE is made up of only total ignorance, namely $m_{j,i}(\{x, \neg x\}) = 1$ (with $m_{j,i}(\{x\}) = 0$ and $m_{j,i}(\{\neg x\}) = 0$). That is, a missing value is considered an ignorant value and so offers no evidence in the subsequent classification of the product. The optimisation process was again undertaken, using TDE on the incomplete dataset, the resultant control parameters are reported in Table 4.

These control parameters are comparable with those in Table 2, the variations are due to the removed financial variable values in this incomplete dataset. To illustrate their utilisation, the bank o_{88} is again considered, with its variable BOEs shown in Table 5.

In Table 5, the dashed lines in some of the financial values of the bank o_{88} show that five of them are now missing (62.5% of its financial evidence missing). On these occasions their variable BOEs are associated with total ignorance. The variable BOEs are again combined to give its bank BOE; $m_{88}(\{x\}) = 0.301$, $m_{88}(\{\neg x\}) = 0.259$ and $m_{88}(\{x, \neg x\}) = 0.440$, for o_{88}, also briefly given here is the bank BOE for o_{201}; $m_{201}(\{x\}) = 0.781$, $m_{201}(\{\neg x\}) = 0.050$ and $m_{201}(\{x, \neg x\}) = 0.169$ (only two missing financial values present for the bank o_{201}, namely EQAS and OWNS). These bank BOEs are next presented using the simplex plot method of data representation, see Figure 5.

Table 4. Control parameters associated with the eight financial variables

Variables	PROV	EQAS	ROAA	COST	LIQ	LGAS	OWNS	SUBS
k_i	−2.000	2.000	2.000	−2.000	2.000	2.000	−2.000	0.227
θ_i	1.000	0.824	−0.400	0.988	0.216	−0.174	−0.202	0.177
A_i	0.879	0.835	0.366	0.673	0.285	0.266	0.284	0.264

Table 5. Variable BOEs $m_{88,i}(\cdot)$, $i = 1, \ldots, 8$ for bank o_{88}

BOEs	PROV	EQAS	ROAA	COST	LIQ	LGAS	OWNS	SUBS
values	-	6.40	1.56	-	-	7.377	-	-
St. values	-	−0.854	0.190	-	-	0.074	-	-
$m_{88,?}(\{x\})$	0.000	0.000	0.252	0.000	0.000	0.194	0.000	0.000
$m_{88,?}(\{\neg x\})$	0.000	0.319	0.000	0.000	0.000	0.061	0.000	0.000
$m_{88,?}(\{x, \neg x\})$	1.000	0.681	0.748	1.000	1.000	0.745	1.000	1.000

Figure 5. Simplex plots of the FBR classification of the banks o_{88} and o_{201}

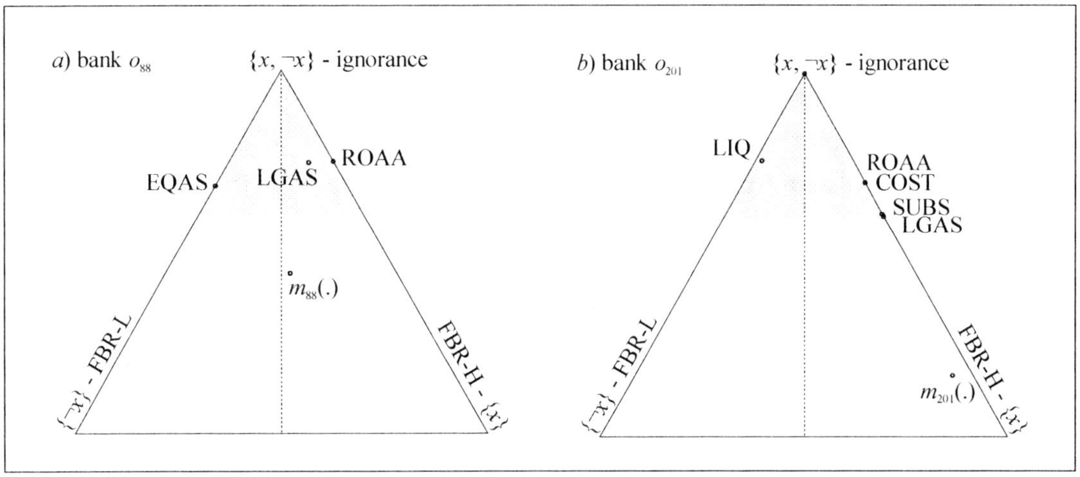

The results in Figure 5*a*, compared with those in Figure 2*a*, for the bank o_{88} show a movement of its bank BOE $m_{88}(\cdot)$ further up the simplex plot and more towards the vertical dashed line. This signifies an increase in associated ignorance and ambiguity for the FBR classification of this bank, mostly a consequence of the missing values in this case. Moreover, there is now no strong evidential support from the COST variable and the incorrect evidence is no longer from LIQ and SUBS but from EQAS. Its position to the right of the vertical dashed line means it is still correctly classified to FBR-H. For the bank o_{201}, the results in Figure 5*b* show little change to those when no missing values were present (see Figure 2b), since the missing values from EQAS and OWNS offered no evidence previously. The results concerning all the banks are shown in Figure 6.

Some of the simplex coordinates of the bank BOEs in Figure 6 are spread further up the respective simplex plots than in Figure 4. This clearly shows the effects of varying the numbers

Figure 6. Simplex plots showing the classification of the FBR-L and FBR-H rated banks

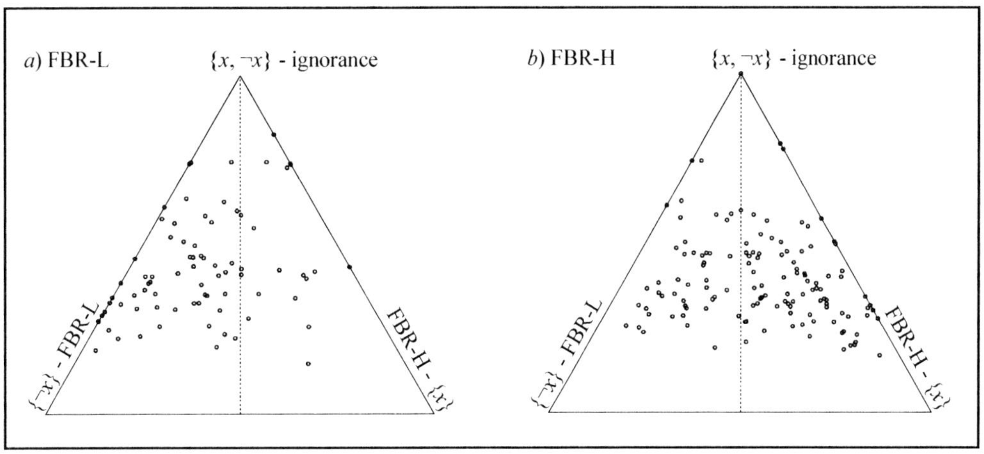

of missing financial values describing each bank. The considerable variations in the heights of the circles in the simplex plots is due to the utilisation of the incomplete dataset and that banks are now described by incomplete sets of financial variables. The variation in the number of missing values illustrates why there are still circles near the base and near the $\{x, \neg x\}$ vertex. In terms of correct classification, 58 out of 77 FBR-L (in 6*a*) and 87 out of 132 FBR-H (6*b*) rated banks were correctly classified, given a total 148 out of 209 (69.378%) classification accuracy (less than when there were no missing values in the dataset).

This section continues with a similar CaRBS analysis to those presented previously, but this time the missing values present in the incomplete FBR dataset are managed using mean imputation (using mean values of those values remaining). Only the simplex plot representations of the evidential support of the financial values to the banks o_{88} and o_{201} are given, see Figure 7.

Figure 7. Simplex plots of the FBR classification of the banks o_{88} and o_{201}

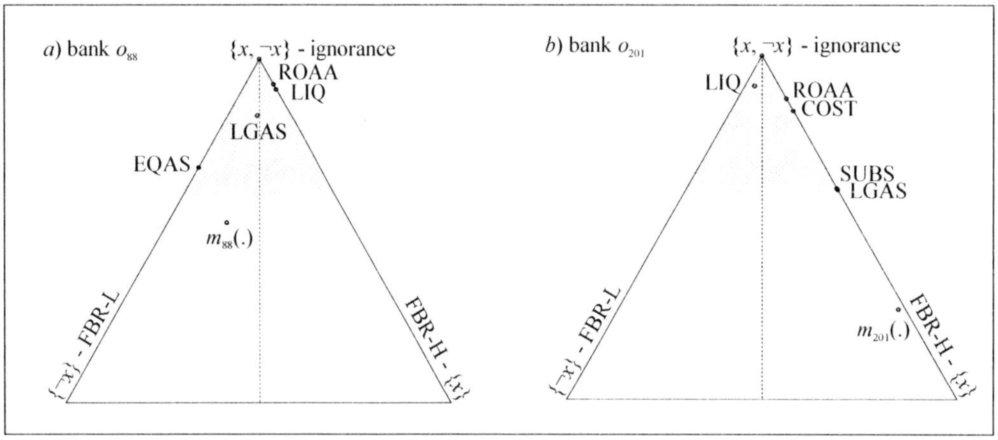

Figure 8. Simplex plots showing the classification of the FBR-L and FBR-H rated banks

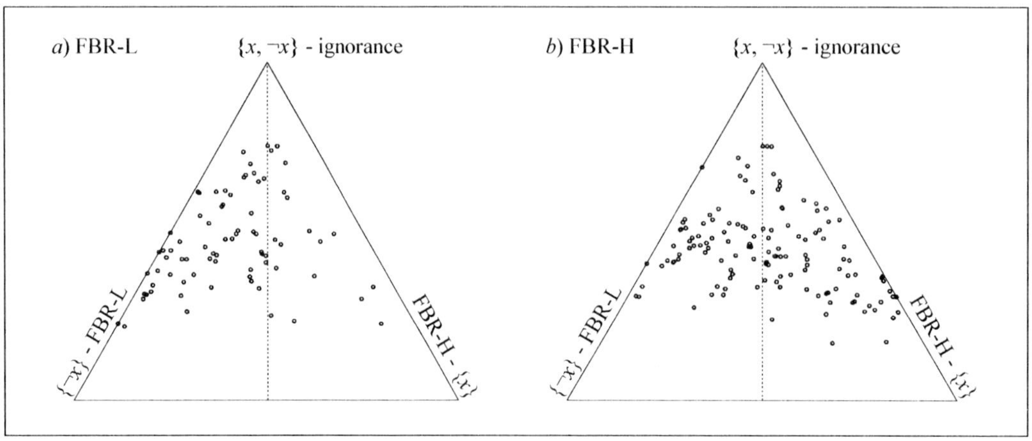

From the details concerning the bank o_{88} in Figure 7*a*, it is now incorrectly classified (to the left of the vertical dashed line). Briefly, this is because of the reduced influence of the ROAA and LIQ variables. The results for the o_{201} bank are similar to those from its previous analyses (see Figures 3 and 5). For all 209 banks, the simplex coordinate based representation of their final bank BOEs are given in Figure 8.

The results in Figure 8 show similar movement up the simplex plots of all the simplex coordinates representing the bank BOEs. One reason for this is that the missing values have been imputed using mean values of those values remaining, but since these are near the centre of the distribution of the variable values, more ignorance will be associated with them (see Figure 1b). It follows, the control parameters are dampened in offering more certain evidence by having to work with these large numbers of mean values present in the filled-in dataset. In terms of correct classification, 59 out of 77 FBR-L (in Figure 8a) and 74 out of 132 FBR-H (Figure 8b) rated banks were correctly classified, given a total of 133 out of 209 (63.636%) classification accuracy. Noticeably, this overall classification accuracy is below that found from the MDA analysis on the original dataset.

The two CaRBS analyses in this section have dealt with the presence of missing values differently, following the results in Figure 4, the evidential contribution of each financial variable in these cases are reported in Figure 9.

The average variable BOEs, $am_{i,x}(\cdot)$ and $am_{i,\neg x}(\cdot)$, shown in Figure 9a are evaluated only on the variable BOEs associated with those financial variables that were not missing, since those missing do not affect the optimisation process at all. It follows, the results in Figure 9a are comparable with those in Figure 4, where it can be seen that there are levels of similarity in the positions shown for all the financial variables. The case is not true for the results in Figure 9b since the optimisation process utilised the imputed missing values, so they need to be included in the average variable BOEs constructed. Most noticeable is that the simplex coordinates are further up the sub-domain of the simplex plot presented.

FUTURE TRENDS

Data mining has to keep pace with the realities of the role it is asked to perform, including the ability to adequately cope with the ever increas-

Figure 9. Simplex coordinates of $am_{i,\neg x}(\cdot)$ '?-L' and $am_{i,x}(\cdot)$ '?-H' average variable BOEs

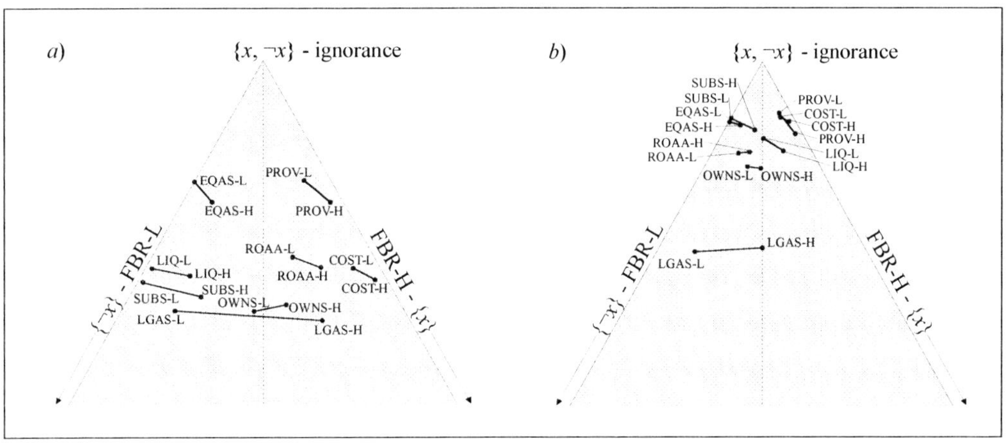

ing size of the datasets they need to analyse. The generality of its definition highlights the ongoing evolution that data mining is experiencing, with an extensive range of techniques available to be employed. Future trends need to encompass the qualities these techniques offer, as well as acknowledge the complexities inherent with the analysed datasets. Nowhere is this more evident than when there is the presence of missing values in a considered dataset. There should be movement away from externally transforming an incomplete dataset, purely to accommodate the utilisation of a more traditional data mining technique, which very often, is not able to internally operate with their presence.

Leading this movement away from such inhibiting management is the utilisation of uncertain reasoning methodologies, including Dempster-Shafer theory (DST). Available data mining techniques, such as classification and ranking belief simplex (CaRBS), demonstrate that accommodating missing values is possible within a technique without having to utilise external management mechanisms. A characteristic of this direction, using CaRBS, is the expressions of ambiguity and ignorance associated with the classification of objects. Moreover, the optimisation of the classification of objects understandably attempts to minimise ambiguity, but does not attempt to directly limit the inherent ignorance that may exist.

CONCLUSION

The technical conclusions from this chapter are twofold. Firstly, the findings inform/remind an analyst that issues such as the presence of missing values and low quality information should not be ignored and data mining techniques need to fully respect their unjustly viewed inhibiting presence. Secondly, uncertain reasoning methodologies such as Dempster-Shafer theory and its developments offer a novel base for current and future data mining techniques, including CaRBS, that will not need to concern themselves with particular complexities—hence offering more realistic analysis and results.

The emphasis on the effects of the presence of missing values in a dataset, also considered here, identifies a cause for concern for all individuals interested in data mining. Now in the 21st century it is ambivalent of analysts to consider the presence of missing values as inhibitory, consequently their management should be carefully considered. This issue is particularly pertinent in data mining, since it is regularly undertaken on large external datasets, which means the presence of missing values may be more probable. Against these issues the appropriateness of uncertain reasoning based techniques looks positive. However, the increased popularity of such techniques is possibly out of the hands of the theorists, instead it requires the applied analysts to be broad minded and have confidence in employing the more nascent approaches.

REFERENCES

Abeysuriya, R. (2002, January). Utility of bank ratings. *ISBL Bankers Journal*, 1-3.

Afifi, A. A., & Elashoff, R. (1966). Missing observations in multivariate statistics. Part 1: Review of the literature. *Journal of the American Statistical Association*, *61*, 595-604.

Bankscope. (2005). Retrieved October 30, 2006, from http://www.bankscope.bvdep.com

Barnett, B. (2005). Data mining and warehousing: The bigger CIS picture. *Public Utilities Fortnightly*, *143*(5), 62-63.

Beynon, M. J. (2005a). A novel technique of object ranking and classification under ignorance: An application to the corporate failure risk problem.

European Journal of Operational Research, 167(2), 493-517.

Beynon, M. J. (2005b). A novel approach to the credit rating problem: Object classification under ignorance. *International Journal of Intelligent Systems in Accounting, Finance and Management, 13*, 113-130.

Cantor, R., & Packer, F. (1995). The credit rating industry. *Journal of Fixed Income, 5*, 10-34.

Carriere, K. C. (1999). Methods for repeated measures data analysis with missing values. *Journal of Statistical Planning and Inference, 77*, 221-236.

Chen, Z. (2001). *Data mining and uncertain reasoning: An integrated approach*. New York: John Wiley.

Claessens, S., Demirgüç-Kunt, A., & Huizinga, H. (2001). How does foreign entry affect domestic banking markets? *Journal of Banking & Finance, 25*(5), 891-911.

Cobb, B. R., & Shenoy, P. P. (2003). A comparison of Bayesian and belief function reasoning. *Information Systems Frontiers, 5*(4), 345-358.

Comber, A. J., Law, A. N. R., & Lishman, J. R. (2004). A comparison of Bayes', Dempster-Shafer and endorsement theories for managing knowledge uncertainty in the context of land cover monitoring. *Computers, Environment and Urban Systems, 28*, 311-327.

Dempster, A. P. (1967). Upper and lower probabilities induced by a multiple valued mapping. *Ann. Math. Statistics, 38*, 325-339.

Dempster, A. P. (1968). A generalization of Bayesian inference (with discussion). *Journal of Royal Statistical Society Series B, 30*, 205-247.

Dempster, A. P., & Rubin, D. B. (1983). Overview. In W. G. Madow, I. Olkin & D. B. Rubin (Eds.), *Incomplete data in sample surveys, Vol. II: Theory and bibliographies* (pp. 3-10). New York: Academic Press.

DeSarbo, W. S., Green, P. E., & Carroll, J. D. (1986). Missing data in product-concept testing. *Decision Sciences, 17*, 163-185.

Fan, H.-Y., & Lampinen, J. (2003). A trigonometric mutation operation to differential evolution. *Journal of Global Optimization, 27*, 105-129.

Fisher, L. (1959). Determinants of risk premiums on corporate bond. *The Journal of Political Economy, 67*, 217-237.

FitchRatings. (2003). Launch of Fitch's bank support rating methodology. Retrieved October 30, 2006, from http://www.fitchrating.com

Gerig, G., Welti, D., Guttman, C. R. G., Colchester, A. C. F., & Szekely, G. (2000). Exploring the discrimination power of the time domain for segmentation and characterisation of active lesions in serial MR data. *Medical Image Analysis, 4*, 3142.

Grzymala-Busse, J., Stefanowski, J., & Wilk, S. (2005). A comparison of two approaches to data mining from imbalanced data. *Journal of Intelligent Manufacturing, 16*(6), 565-573.

Hand, D. J. (1998). Data mining: Statistics and more? *The American Statistician, 52*(2), 112-118.

Heikkinen, J., & Arjas, E. (1998). Non-parametric Bayesian estimation of a spatial intensity. *Scandinavian Journal of Statistics, 25*, 435-450.

Hjort, N. L. (1996). Bayesian approaches to non- and semi-parametric density estimation. In M. Bernado, J. O. Berger, A. P. Dawid, & A. F. M. Smith (Eds.), *Bayesian statistics 5* (pp. 223-253). Oxford: Oxford University Press.

Horrigan, J. O. (1966). The determination of long-term credit standing with financial ratios. *Journal of Accounting Research, 4*, 44-62.

Huang, X., & Zhu, Q. (2002). A pseudo-nearest-neighbour approach for missing data on Gaussian random datasets. *Pattern Recognition Letters*, *23*, 1613-1622.

Huisman, M. (2000). Imputation of missing item responses: Some simple techniques. *Quality & Quantity*, *34*, 331-351.

Krutchkoff, R. G. (1967). A supplementary sample non-parametric empirical Bayes approach to some statistical decision problems. *Biometrika*, *54*(3/4), 451-458.

Lakshminarayan, K., Harp, S. A., & Samad, T. (1999). Imputation of missing data in industrial databases. *Applied Intelligence*, *11*, 259-275.

Little, R. J. A. (1988). Missing-data adjustments in large surveys. *Journal of Business & Economic Statistics*, *6*, 287-296.

Maher, J. J., & Sen, T. K. (1997). Predicting bond ratings using neural networks: A comparison with logistic regression. *Intelligent Systems in Accounting, Finance and Management*, *6*, 59-72.

Murphy, C. K. (2000). Combining belief functions when evidence conflicts. *Decision Support Systems*, *29*, 1-9.

Olinsky, A., Chen, S., & Harlow, L. (2003). The comparative efficacy of imputation methods for missing data in structural equation modelling. *European Journal of Operational Research*, *151*, 53-79.

Pasiouras, F., Gaganis, C., & Zopoundis, C. (2005, December). A multivariate analysis of Fitch's individual bank ratings. In *Proceedings of the 4th Conference of the Hellenic Finance and Accounting Association*, Piraes, Greece.

Pawlak, Z. (1982). Rough sets. *International Journal of Information and Computer Sciences*, *11*(5), 341-356.

Peacock, P. R. (1998). Data mining in marketing: Part 1. *Marketing Management*, *6*(4), 9-18.

Poon, W. P. H., Firth, M., & Fung M. (1999). A multivariate analysis of the determinants of Moody's bank financial strength ratings. *Journal of International Financial Markets Institutions and Money*, *9*, 267-283.

Poon, W. P. H., & Firth, M. (2005). Are unsolicited credit ratings lower? International evidence from bank ratings. *Journal of Business Finance & Accounting*, *32*(9/10), 1741-1771.

Rubin, D. B. (1976). Inference and missing data. *Biometrika*, *78*, 609-619.

Safranek, R. J., Gottschlich, S., & Kak, A. C. (1990). Evidence accumulation using binary frames of discernment for verification vision. *IEEE Transactions on Robotics and Automation*, *6*, 405-417.

Sarhan, A. (2003). Non-parametric empirical Bayes procedure. *Reliability Engineering and System Safety*, *80*, 115-122

Schafer, J. L., & Graham, J. W. (2002). Missing data: Our view of the state of the art. *Psychological Methods*, *7*(2), 147-177.

Schubert, J. (1994). *Cluster-based specification techniques in Dempster-Shafer theory for an evidential intelligence analysis of multiple target tracks*. Department of Numerical Analysis and Computer Science Royal Institute of Technology, S-100 44 Stockholm, Sweden.

Shafer, G. A. (1976). *Mathematical theory of evidence*. Princeton: Princeton University Press.

Shafer, G. (1990). Perspectives in the theory of belief functions. *International Journal of Approximate Reasoning*, *4*, 323-362.

Shafer, G., & Pearl J. (1990). *Readings in uncertain reasoning*. San Mateo, CA: Morgan Kaufman Publishers Inc.

Shafer, G., & Srivastava R. (1990). The Bayesian and belief-function formalisms: A general perspective for auditing. In G. Shafer & J. Pearl (Eds.), *Readings in uncertain reasoning.* San Mateo, CA: Morgan Kaufman Publishers Inc.

Shen, S. M., & Lai, Y. L. (2001). Handling incomplete quality-of-life data. *Social Indicators Research, 55*, 121-166.

Singleton, J. C., & Surkan, J. S. (1991). Modeling the judgement of bond rating agencies: Artificial intelligence applied to finance. *Journal of the Midwest Finance Association, 20*, 72-80.

Smets, P. (1990). The combination of evidence in the transferable belief model. *IEEE Transactions on Pattern Analysis and Machine Intelligence, 12*, 447-458.

Smets, P. (2002). Decision making in a context where uncertainty is represented by belief functions. In R. P. Srivastava & T. J. Mock (Eds.), *Belief function in business decisions* (pp. 17-61). Springer-Verlag.

Smets, P., & Kennes, R. (1994). The transferable belief model. *Artificial Intelligence, 66*, 191-234.

Storn, R., & Price, K. (1997). Differential evolution: A simple and efficient heuristic for global optimization over continuous spaces. *Journal of Global Optimisation, 11*(4), 41-359.

Zadeh, L. A. (1965). Fuzzy sets. *Information and Control, 8*, 338-353.

Zaffalon, M. (2002). Exact credal treatment of missing data. *Journal of Statistical Planning and Inference, 105*, 105-122.

Chapter XII
Outlier Detection Strategy Using the Self-Organizing Map

Fedja Hadzic
DEBII Institute, Curtin University of Technology, Australia

Tharam S. Dillon
DEBII Institute, Curtin University of Technology, Australia

Henry Tan
University of Technology Sydney, Australia

ABSTRACT

Real world datasets are often accompanied with various types of anomalous or exceptional entries which are often referred to as outliers. Detecting outliers and distinguishing noise form true exceptions is important for effective data mining. This chapter presents two methods for outlier detection and analysis using the self-organizing map (SOM), where one is more suitable for categorical and the other for continuous data. They are generally based on filtering out the instances which are not captured by or are contradictory to the obtained concept hierarchy for the domain. We demonstrate how the dimension of the output space plays an important role in the kind of patterns that will be detected as outlying. Furthermore, the concept hierarchy itself provides extra criteria for distinguishing noise from true exceptions. The effectiveness of the proposed outlier detection and analysis strategy is demonstrated through the experiments on publicly available real world datasets.

INTRODUCTION

The fact that real world datasets are often accompanied with various types of anomalous entries, introduces additional challenges to data mining and knowledge discovery. These anomalies need to be detected and dealt with in an appropriate way depending on whether the detected anomaly is caused by noise or is a true exceptional case. An anomalous entry is often referred to as an outlier. The definitions are quite similar throughout the literature and the general intent is captured by the

Copyright © 2007, IGI Global, distributing in print or electronic forms without written permission of IGI Global is prohibited.

definition given by Hawkins (1980): "an outlier is an observation that deviates so much from other observations as to arouse suspicion that it was generated by a different mechanism." Depending on the aim of application the term outlier detection has been commonly substituted by terms such as: anomaly, exception, novelty, deviation or noise detection. Outliers in a dataset correspond to a very small percentage of the data objects. Most data mining algorithms tend to minimize their influence or discard them altogether as being noisy data. However, eliminating outlying objects can result in loss of some important information especially for applications where the intention is to find exceptional or rare events that occur in a particular set of observations. These rare events are mostly of greater interest than the common events in applications such as: fraud detection, network intrusion detection, security threats, credit risk assessment, pharmaceutical research, terrorist attacks, and some financial and marketing applications. In general outlier detection is used in applications where the analysis of uncommon events is important and can provide extensional knowledge for the domain. On the other hand, if the outlying entries are caused by noise it is still important that they are detected and removed from that dataset in order to disallow interference with the learning mechanism. Hence, outlier detection and analysis has become an important task in data mining and knowledge discovery.

The self-organizing map (SOM) (Kohonen, 1990) is an unsupervised neural network that effectively creates spatially organized "internal representations" of the features and abstractions detected in the input space. It is based on the competition among the cells in the map for the best match against a presented input pattern. Existing similarities in the input space are revealed through the ordered or topology preserving mapping of high dimensional input patterns into a lower-dimensional set of output clusters. When used for classification purposes, SOM is commonly integrated with a type of supervised learning in order to assign appropriate class labels to the clusters. After the supervised learning is complete each cluster will have a rule or pattern associated with it, which determines which data objects are covered by that cluster. Due to its simple structure and learning mechanism SOM has been successfully used in various applications and it has proven to be one of the effective clustering techniques (Kohonen, 1990; Sestito & Dillon, 1994).

SOM has been previously used for outlier detection in (Munoz & Muruzabal, 1998), where the trained map is projected using Sammons mapping to find the initial outliers, and thereafter SOMs quantization errors are used for identifying the remaining outliers. Since SOM learns without supervision, abnormalities can be detected without knowing what to expect. This motivated many SOM applications to the problem of intrusion detection on computer networks (Girardin 1999; Heywood & Heywood, 2002; Lichodzijewski, Zincir-Labib, & Vemuri, 2002; Nuansri, Dillon, & Singh, 1997; Rhodes, Mahaffey, & Cannady, 2000; Zanero & Savaresi, 2004). SOM is also an effective tool for data exploration since the formed abstractions can be easily visualized. The work done in Vesanto, Himberg, Siponen, and Simula (1998), aims to improve SOMs visualization capabilities for novelty detection. Another common approach to outlier detection using SOM is to form the initial clusters from normal data objects and then to use a pre-defined distance measure which will indicate the outliers with respect to the clusters set exhibiting normal behavior (Gonzalez & Dasgupta, 2002; Gonzalez & Dasgupta, 2003; Ypma & Duin, 1997).

We propose a different approach to using SOM for outlier detection and analysis. The motivation behind the proposed methods comes from the results obtained in our previous works where SOM was used for classification (Dillon, Sestito, Witten, & Suing, 1993; Hadzic & Dillon, 2005; Sestito & Dillon, 1994) and for detection of frequent patterns from a transactional database

(Hadzic, Dillon, Tan, Feng, & Chang, 2007). When used for classification purposes we observed that some of the resulting clusters could cover only a small subset of data. After applying a type of supervised learning to the produced cluster set, certain clusters may have a very small coverage rate (Dillon et al., 1993; Hadzic & Dillon, 2005; Sestito & Dillon, 1994), indicating that the data objects covered by those clusters are suspected of being outliers.

In (Hadzic & Dillon, 2005) we have adjusted the SOMs learning algorithm so that when used in domains characterized by continuous attributes, rules can be extracted directly from the networks links. A reasoning mechanism was integrated with supervised learning in order to trade off misclassification rate, coverage ratio and the generalization capability. Here the clusters undergo a process of splitting and merging in order to achieve the best classification accuracy using the smallest set of rules (clusters). During this process certain clusters will have a very small coverage ratio but cannot be merged with other similar clusters as the class labels are different amongst the two. The data objects covered by those clusters could in fact be outliers, and further comparison with other similar clusters allows us to more confidently distinguish noise from true exceptional cases. This approach will be referred to as the "reasoning approach."

Another approach to outlier mining using SOM draws from our previous application of SOM for finding frequent patterns in the area of association rule mining (Hadzic et al., 2006) In this case the frequently occurring patterns will influence the organization of the map to the highest degree, and hence after training the resulting clusters correspond to the most frequently occurring patterns. The patterns that are not covered by any clusters have not occurred often enough to have an impact on the self-organization of the map. Such patterns are good candidates for being outliers. For this work the focus will be of course for classification tasks rather than association rule mining. By progressively filtering out the most frequently occurring patterns from the dataset, eventually only the outlying data objects (infrequent patterns) will be left over. These data objects will be validated against the clusters exhibiting the normal behavior within the dataset, in order to distinguish noisy instances from true exceptional cases. This approach will be referred to as the "filtering approach."

The rest of the chapter is organized as follows. In the second section, "Related Works," an overview of some existing approaches to outlier detection is given. The third section, "Outlier Detection Using SOM" describes our filtering and reasoning approaches for outlier detection. Experimental validation and discussion of the proposed techniques is provided in the fourth section, "Experimental Findings," and the fifth section, "Conclusion," concludes the chapter.

RELATED WORKS

Outlier detection problem has its roots grounded in the statistical area where it has been extensively studied to date (Barnett & Lewis, 1994; Hawkins, 1980; Rousseeuw & Leroy, 1987). The common statistical approach to the problem is to model the data points using a statistical distribution and then to determine the outliers as points that deviate from the model. While the method is quite effective, sometimes determining the underlying data distribution poses a problem, especially for high dimensional data. Depth-based approaches (Preparata & Shamons, 1998; Tukey, 1997) avoid the distribution-fitting problem by representing each data point in k-d space. According to a predefined depth definition, each data object is assigned a depth value and small depth values indicate outlying objects. There exist efficient algorithms for smaller k values (Johnson, Kwok, & Ng, 1998; Preparata & Shamons, 1998; Ruts & Rousseeuw, 1996) but the approach does not scale well for increasing k dimensionality.

The notion of a distance-based outlier has been introduced by Knorr and Ng (1998, 2000), where given parameters *d* and *n*, a data object *o* is considered an outlier if no more than n points in the dataset are at a distance *d* or less from *o*. This method is robust to high dimensionality problem, but choosing an appropriate value for parameter *d* can pose a problem as was pointed out in (Ramaswamy, Rastogi, & Shim, 2000). Ramaswamy et al. (2000) extended the notion of distance-based outlier based on the distance of a point from its k_{th} nearest neighbors. Their partition-based algorithm splits the dataset into disjoint subsets and prunes away the points whose distances to their k_{th} nearest neighbors are so small that they cannot possibly make it to the top n outliers. The remaining data points are ranked according to the distance to their k_{th} nearest neighbor, and the points lying at the top of the ranking are considered as outliers.

Clarans (Ng & Han, 1994) and Birch (Zhang, Ramakrishnan, & Livny, 1996) are clustering algorithms which have inbuilt exception-handling mechanisms. Their main objective is to detect clusters present in a dataset, and as such they are more tailored for clustering rather than outlier detection. They consider outliers only in the sense of preventing their interference with clustering. Chakrabarti, Sarawagi, and Dom (1998) define a notion of surprise for market basket analysis. The criteria is based on the number of bits needed to encode an item set sequence using a coding scheme where it takes relatively few bits to encode sequences of items which have steady correlation between items. Thus a sequence with large code length indicates the possibility of surprising correlation. Beside the outlier identification problem, Knorr and Ng (1999) provide "intensional knowledge" for distance-based outliers, which is an explanation as to why the detected outlier is exceptional. This information would help in the evaluation of the identified outliers and the general understanding of data characteristics. The work done in Breunig, Kriegel, Ng, and Sander (2000) assigns to each data object a "local outlier factor," which indicates its deviation degree. The approach is related to density-based clustering and only a restricted neighborhood of each data object is taken into account when determining the outlier factor. There exist many works that, motivated by the curse of dimensionality problem, provide strategies for increasing the efficiency of outlier detection in these situations (Aggarwal & Yu, 2001; Bay & Schwabager, 2003). More recently, Pearson (2005) has provided a more general overview of the detection of different types of anomalies that can occur in data, such as outliers, missing data and misalignments. The focus was on providing an explanation about their cause, implications and consequences, as well as the available methods for dealing with such imperfect data. For an extensional overview and comparison of existing outlier detection methodologies please refer to Hodge and Austin (2004).

As mentioned in introduction, SOM has been previously used for outlier detection but the approaches are somewhat different from that put forward in the present chapter. They rely on distance measures from clusters, or projections from Simmons mappings plus quantization errors. It is not clear if these are able to distinguish between noise and outliers. We interpret outliers as abnormalities in the model representing true clusters with few instances which are distinguished from the main model consisting of clusters with many instances. The novelty of our method is that it is designed to pick out these abnormal clusters.

OUTLIER DETECTION USING SOM

This section describes the strategies used to detect outlying instances using SOM. We start by providing some background knowledge about the SOM algorithm, and proceed to explain in detail the methods used for categorical and continuous data.

General SOM Properties

SOM (Kohonen, 1990) consists of an input layer and an output layer in form of a map (see Figure 1). It is based on the competition among the cells in the map for the best match against a presented input pattern.

Each node in the map has a weight vector associated with it, which are the weights on the links emanating from the input layer to that particular node. When an input pattern is imposed on the network, a node is selected from among all the output nodes as having the best response according to some criterion. This output node is declared the "winner" and is usually the cell having the smallest Euclidean distance between its weight vector and the presented input vector. The winner and its neighboring cells are then updated to match the presented input pattern more closely. Neighborhood size and the magnitude of update shrink as the training proceeds. After the learning phase, cells that respond in similar manner to the presented input patterns are located close to each other, and so clusters can be formed in the map. Existing similarities in the input space are revealed through the ordered or topology preserving mapping of high dimensional input patterns into a lower-dimensional set of output clusters.

When used for classification purposes, SOM is commonly integrated with a type of supervised learning in order to assign appropriate class labels to the clusters. After the learning phase has come to completion, the weights on the links could be analyzed in order to represent the learned knowledge in a symbolic form. One such method is used in "Unsupervised BRAINNE" (Dillon et al., 1993), which extracts a set of symbolic knowledge structures in form of concepts and concept hierarchies from a trained neural network. A similar method is used in the current work. After the supervised learning is complete each cluster will have a rule or pattern associated with it, which determines which data objects are covered by that cluster.

It was mentioned that SOM is good at mapping high dimensional input patterns into a lower-dimensional set of output clusters. As we map higher-dimensional space into a lower-dimensional space, there are only two possibilities. Either the data in lower-dimensional space represents the data from higher-dimensional space in compressed form or the data in the lower-dimensional space is corrupted because there is not enough resolution (map size) to store the data. Putting outlier detection into this context, we will investigate how the mapping of higher dimensional input space onto a lower-dimensional output space can isolate uncommon database behavior.

The notion of *competitive learning* hints that the way knowledge is learnt by SOM is competitive based on certain criteria. Therefore, with a

*Figure 1. SOM consisting of two input nodes and 3 * 3 map*

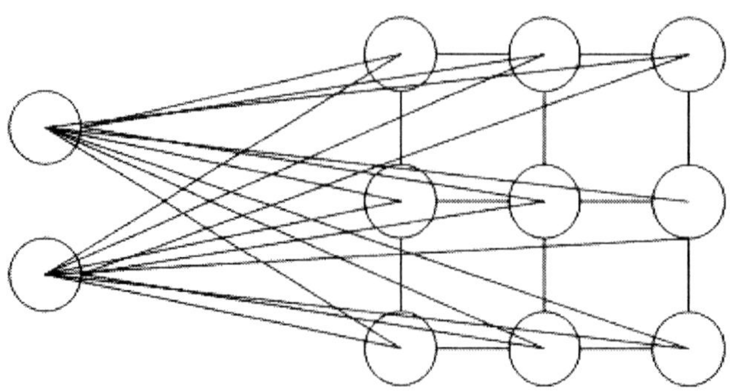

smaller output space the level of competition increases. Patterns exposed more frequently to SOM in the training phase are more likely to be learnt while the ones exposed less frequently are more likely to be disregarded. The frequently occurring patterns will influence the organization of the map to the highest degree, and hence after training the resulting clusters correspond to the most frequently occurring patterns. The patterns that are not covered by any clusters have not occurred often enough to have an impact on the self-organization of the map and are often overruled by the characteristics of frequent patterns. These patterns can be regarded as outliers because their characteristics do not occur often enough in the dataset to allow for the lower-dimensional projection to capture their behavior. The allowed output space for projection will therefore play an important role in the kind of database characteristics that will be learned by SOM. Next we describe the way SOM is used for classification purposes which provides the basis for understanding our outlier detection strategies using SOM.

APPROACH FOR CATEGORICAL DATA

In this section we describe a way SOM can be used for classification purposes when applied to domains characterized with categorical attributes. This provides the basis for understanding our outlier detection strategy using SOM.

Input Transformation

The data used for experiments needed to be adjusted so that it is suitable for SOMs input layer. Each instance from the dataset is represented as a sequence of n bits where n is the number of attributes in the dataset. For a particular instance if an attribute is part of the instance it will have a corresponding value 1; and 0 when the opposite condition occurs.

If a particular attribute has a few categories then an attribute is created for each of the categories. This was the case in the Zoo dataset where the "legs" attribute has been split into six attributes that represent each category of the legs attribute.

Training the SOM

If we let $a(t)$ denote the learning rate between 0 and 1, $x(t)$ the input value at time t, $Nc(t)$ the neighborhood set at time t, m the node and i the link being updated, then the weight update function used in the SOM is (Kohonen, 1990):

$$mi(t+1) = \begin{cases} \{\ mi(t) + a\{t\}[x(t) - mi(t)\ ]\ \} & \text{if } i\ Nc(\text{t}) \\ \{\ mi(t) \qquad\qquad\qquad\qquad \} & \text{if } i\ Nc(t). \end{cases}$$

SOM needs to be trained with a considerable and large number of training data until it settles when it reaches a *terminating condition*. The terminating condition is reached when either, the number of training iterations (epochs) has reached its maximum or the mean square error (*mse*) value has reached its minimum. The *mse* value should be chosen small enough so that the necessary correlations can be learned. On the other hand it should be large enough to avoid the problem of over-fitting which results in a decrease of the generalization capability (Sestito & Dillon, 1994).

Rule Extraction

Once the SOM has been sufficiently trained the pattern(s) that each output node in the map represents need to be determined. This is achieved by analyzing the weight vectors of each node and determining which input is contributory for that node. We have adopted the threshold technique from (Sestito & Dillon, 1994) where an input (i) is considered contributory (1) to an output node (o) if the difference between the weight on the link from i to o and the maximum weight component in the weight vector of o is below a pre-specified threshold. Note also that a threshold is chosen, so that if all the weight components in the weight vector of an output node are below this threshold, than none of the inputs are considered contributory. An input is considered inhibitory (0) if the weight is below a prespecified threshold (T_{inh}), which is commonly chosen to be close to zero. The inputs that are not selected as either of the above are considered as a "don't care" (-1) in the related rule. The output nodes that represent the same patterns are grouped together into a cluster and those clusters now represent the frequent patterns or rules from the database. After the rules have been extracted we should take all rules with no *don't cares* (-1) and some rules with *don't cares* that meet certain decisive factor (Sestito & Dillon, 1994).

From Figure 2 {0,1,0,0,1}, {0,1,1,0,1}, and {0,1,0,1,0} are examples of rules with no don't cares. {1,1,-1,-1,-1}, {1,0,-1,1,-1}, and {-1,-1,-1,1,-1} are rules with don't cares. To determine which don't care rules we should take or discard, we will formulate a means of separating them using a threshold technique. We apply the same principle as threshold technique for extracting rules described in (Sestito & Dillon, 1994) and introduce a *hit count* measure. From Figure 2, the hit count is the value in the bracket, right to the extracted rules. The hit count value of each cell in SOM is normalized against the total epoch. The maximum normalized value, H_{max}, is determined

Figure 2. Extracted rules with and with no "don't cares"

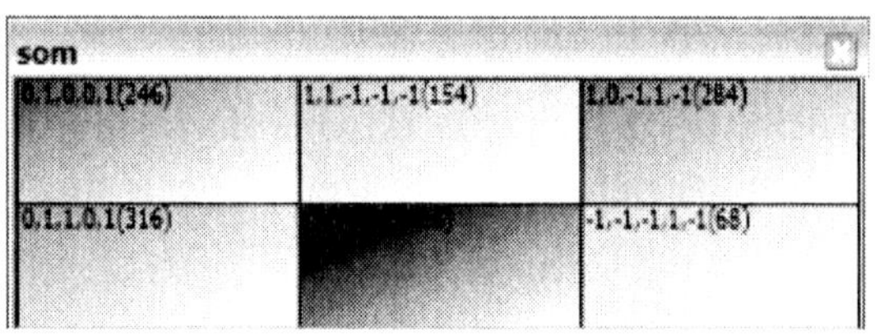

as the fraction of the highest hit count over the number epoch. We take the rules that satisfy:

$$| H_{max} - H_{i} | < T \qquad (1)$$

T is a chosen threshold value with typical value equal to 0.1. Rules that do not satisfy the above equation will be discarded.

Concept Hierarchy Formation

This step is only necessary if the domain at hand can be described by a conceptual hierarchy. The step could be skipped if the rules describing the domain do not have a hierarchical relationship, or such relationships do not improve the generalization capability of the rules. This would be the case if the task was to find unusual patterns from a transactional database. The main interest is in the occurrence of a pattern as opposed to its coverage by the obtained knowledge model, which is of interest in classification tasks.

Once the set of rules is extracted from the trained SOM, a concept hierarchy can be obtained using the method described in (Sestito & Dillon, 1994). The concepts are arranged in a hierarchy where higher-level concepts represent generalizations and lower level concepts represent specializations. The lower-level concepts inherit properties from the higher-level concepts and have additional attribute restrictions. Basically at each step the method works by picking a rule with the smallest number of contributory inputs to form a new concept. The combinations of attributes defining the concept are then replaced by the concept itself in any rules that have that combination. A new set of rules is obtained and new concepts are determined. The whole process is repeated until all the rules are reduced to tautologies, that is, concepts implying themselves (Sestito & Dillon, 1994).

Concept Labeling

Once the conceptual hierarchy is formed a supervised dataset is used in order to label the nodes in the hierarchy. This corresponds to determining the class label that the rule of the node implies. This is achieved by processing the supervised dataset and for each instance triggering those nodes in the hierarchy which most specifically describe that instance. At the end of supervised training each node will have a target vector associated with it which represents the classes that the node was triggered for. Each class will have a weight associated with it, indicating the number of times the concept node was triggered on an instance with that particular class. Ideally each target vector would only have one class, but there could exist a node in the hierarchy that is triggered for multiple classes. This either indicates that the extra instances are suspect of being noisy or that there is large overlap between the classes present in the dataset used for learning. Another possibility is that there was not enough resolution in the output space for the specific characteristics to be learned and hence some nodes in the hierarchy would be too general to distinguish the domain classes.

Map Size and Outlying-ness Relationship

In Hadzic et al. (2006) we have used the above described process for frequent pattern detection problem in the area of association rule mining. The map size determined the number and the frequency of the extracted patterns, and hence the same relationship should exist between the map size and the frequency of data object behavior for it to be considered outlying. The reduction of map size increases the competition between patterns to be projected onto the output space, and hence less frequent patterns will be disregarded. On the other hand, the larger the map the more patterns will be discovered, as there is enough space to project most of the characteristics of the dataset used. As a property of SOM is to compress the input space and present the abstractions in a topology preserving manner, the map size should be chosen with respect to the frequency of database characteristics that the user is after. If the wanted frequency is known then an approximation for map size could be obtained using a heuristic similar to the one used for frequent pattern extraction problem, as described in Hadzic et al. (2006). By filtering out the uncovered instances the outliers would be detected with respect to the wanted frequency.

APPROACH FOR CONTINUOUS DATA

This section demonstrates the isolation of outlying instances during a type of rule optimization process used to trade off misclassification rate (MR), coverage ratio (CR) and generalization power (GP) of the extracted rule set. This step is particularly important in continuous domains where it is often challenging to find the appropriate ranges for the attributes describing a particular rule. The aim is to obtain a rule set which would have low MR and high CR and GP. In order to increase the GP network pruning is a common step which results in simpler rules which in turn are expected to have better GP. The rule optimization process that will be used was previously described in Hadzic and Dillon (2005) where the traditional SOM was adjusted so that symbolic knowledge can be efficiently extracted from continuous domains. In the following sections, we will overview the adjusted SOM and explain the rule optimization technique during which outliers can be isolated.

Continuous SOM (CSOM)

The main difference between the traditional SOM learning algorithm and the continuous

Table 1. CSOM learning mechanism

Normalize input data;
Assign dimension and initialize network;
Set large initial neighborhood and determine decrease factor;
Learning mechanism:
- Initial steps before ranges have been initialized on each link:
- Stimulate the net with given input vector;
- Determine the winner node based upon the smallest Euclidean distance between the input vector and the weighted sum of the inputs to the particular node;
- Update weights for the winning node and its selected neighborhood in following manner:
- Save the initial value as the lower or upper limit of the range based on whether the value of the input vector was greater or smaller than the initial value, respectively, and the new value as the other range limit (the neighborhood may take a value a small distance away from the new value);
- After the ranges on links have been initialized the following procedure will be adopted:
- The winner is determined by a modified Euclidean distance formula.
- The weights of the winner and selected neighborhood are adjusted as:
- If the new input value falls outside of the current range the appropriate lower or upper range is updated to be closer to the new value. The range limit opposite to the updated one is contracted.
- The nodes far away from the winning node are inhibited by applying the opposite of above;

SOM learning algorithm is that the weights on the links between the input and the output layer are in CSOM replaced by a range of values. This difference resulted in an adjustment to the update function and the way neurons compete amongst each other. A brief overview of the CSOM learning mechanism is given in Table 1.

We use the Euclidean distance measure for determining the winner node, which is adjusted once the ranges on the links are initialized. The differences now correspond to the difference from the range limit that the input value is closest to, and if the input value falls within the range the difference is zero.

CSOM Update Function

Since the weights on links are replaced by ranges the updating of network had to be done in a different way. The update function for CSOM is more complex as there are three different possibilities that need to be accounted for. At time t let: m denote the node and i the link being updated, x(t) be the input value at time t, a(t) be the adaptation gain between 0 and 1, Nc(t) be the neighborhood set, INc(t) inhibiting neighborhood set, u(t) be the update factor (the amount that the winner had to change by), *Umi(t)* be the upper range limit for link *i*, *Lmi(t)* be the lower range for link *i*, then the update function can be represented as (Hadzic & Dillon, 2005):

If x(t) > Umi(t)

For winner u(t) = a(t)(x(t) – Umi(t))

Umi(t+1) = { Umi(t) + a(t) [u(t)] } Contract(Lmi(t)) If i Nc(t),

{Umi(t) – a(t) [u(t)] } If i INc(t),

{Umi(t) } If i Nc(t) && i INc(t)

If x(t) < Lmi(t)

For winner u(t) = a(t)(Lmi(t) – x(t))

Lmi(t+1) = { Lmi(t) - a(t) [u(t)] } Contract(Umi(t)) If i Nc(t),

{ Lmi(t) + a(t) [u(t)] } If i INc(t),

{ Lmi(t) } If i Nc(t) && i INc(t)

If Lmi(t) < x(t) < Umi(t)
Update occurs only for i INc(t)
If ((x(t) – Lmi(t)) > (Umi(t) – x(t)))
Umi(t) = { Umi(t) – a(t) [u(t)] }
Else
Lmi(t) = { Lmi(t) + a(t)[u(t)] }

The part of the update function where only inhibiting neighbors are updated is not always required but in our experiments we found that the performance is increased when nodes far away from the winner are inhibited further away from the input. Note that the method "Contract(range)" is used to contract the range in one direction when it is expanded in the opposite direction. Each node in the map keeps record of sorted values that have occurred when that particular node was activated. Until there are not enough values stored, the range of that attribute is contracted using a default factor. Each value has a weight associated with it indicating the confidence of its occurrence. Initially we contract to the point where the first/last value occurred, and at later stages a recursive approach is adopted where we contract past the last value if the weight is below a pre-specified threshold and the difference between the last and the next occurring value is above a certain threshold.

Network Pruning and Rule Extraction

After initial training network pruning is performed for the purpose of removing the links emanating from nodes that are irrelevant for a particular cluster. These links correspond to the attributes whose absence has no effect in predicting the output defined by the cluster. We have used the Symmetrical Tau (Zhou & Dillon, 1991) criterion for measuring the predictive capability of an attribute within a cluster. The necessary information was collected during supervised training where occurring input and target values have been stored for the attributes that define the constraints for a particular cluster. The cluster attributes are then ranked according to the decreasing Symmetrical Tau value and a cut-off point is determined below which all the attributes are considered as irrelevant for that particular cluster. CSOM is then retrained with all the irrelevant links removed and the result is that the newly formed clusters are simpler in terms of attribute constraints. This improved the performance as simpler rules are most likely to have better generalization power. Once the training is completed clusters can be formed from nodes that respond to input space in similar manner. The weight vector of a particular node represents the constraints on attribute ranges for that node. Nodes allocated to a cluster are those nodes whose rules are close enough (in terms of attribute ranges) to other nodes belonging to the same cluster. The initial rule assigned to a cluster will take the highest upper and lower range attribute constraints that occurred amongst its nodes.

Rule Optimization and Outlier Detection

Once the initial rules have been assigned to each cluster the supervised learning starts by feeding the input data with class values on top of the cluster set, activating those clusters with smallest ED to the input instance. When a cluster is activated a link is formed between the cluster and the occurring class value. After sufficient training we could determine which particular class each cluster is implying by inspecting the weights on the links between the clusters and the classes. If a cluster is mainly activated for one particular class than the cluster rule implies that class. When a cluster has weighted links to multiple class values a rule validating approach is adopted in order to split up the rule further until each sub-rule (sub-cluster) predicts only one target value. The supervised learning is continued for a few iterations and eventually each cluster should mainly point to only one class value. This method was motivated by psychological studies of concept formation (Bruner, 1956) and the need for a system capable of validating its knowledge and adapting it to the changes in the domain.

During the validating approach when the winning cluster captured an instance it should not have (i.e., misclassification occurs), a child cluster is created which deviates from the original cluster in those attributes ranges that occurred in the misclassified instance. The attribute constraints in the child cluster will be mutually exclusive from the attribute constraints of the parent so that an instance is either captured by the child or parent cluster, not both. After iteration there could be many children clusters created from a parent cluster. If the children clusters point to other class values with high confidence they become a new cluster (rule), otherwise they are merged back into the parent cluster. During the process the clusters that are not activated are deleted and clusters similar with respect to ED are merged. An example of the structure represented graphically is shown in Figure 3.

In Figure 3, the reasoning mechanism described above would merge the deviatechild1 to C1 and deviatechild1 to C2, deviatechild2 to C3 and deviatechild3 to C3 because they point to the same class value as their parents. The deviatechild2 from C2 and deviatechild1 from C3 become new clusters as they point to different class values than their parents with high weight. The deviatechild2 from C3 points to classValue2 but it is still merged as the small weight on the link to classValue2 could be due to noisy data. However, as the purpose of this work is for outlier detection such child would be separated so that if it cannot be merged with other clusters it is a suspect outlier.

Once the rule optimization process is completed the input file is fed once more on top of the clusters during which each class value of a cluster stores the instance in which it has occurred when that particular cluster was activated. The suspect outliers would be the nodes from the above structure which cannot be merged and whose weights are below a pre-specified threshold (i.e., the nodes were not triggered often). This outlier support threshold should be chosen by user and it reflects the support at which certain database characteristics would be considered as deviating

Figure 3. Example structure after supervised training

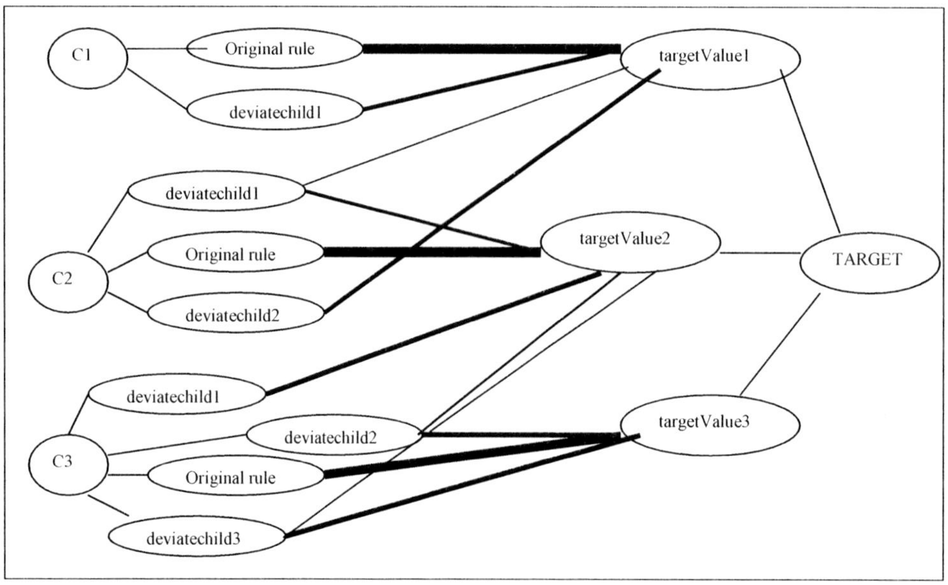

from the norm. Once the instances are stored for each target object we traverse the clusters and print out the instances of target objects whose weight is below the outlier support threshold. These instances are suspect of being outliers and further comparisons with the clusters exhibiting normal behavior would indicate whether those instances are noisy or could in fact be a true exceptional case. The comparisons could be performed using a distance measure such as the ED used in the training phase. The suspect instances are compared with the clusters exhibiting normal behavior for the corresponding class of that instance. Another threshold would be chosen to indicate the distance at which a suspect outlier would be considered as an anomalous entry rather than a true exceptional case.

EXPERIMENTAL FINDINGS

This section describes our experiments performed to test the approaches for categorical and continuous domains. Both approaches were tested using publicly available data from the uci machine learning repository (Blake, Keogh, & Merz, 1998). For testing the filtering approach for categorical domains we have used the "zoo" dataset where the task is to predict the class of an animal based upon various attributes. This dataset naturally contains outlying instances as there are certain animals that deviate from the norm.

For testing the reasoning approach for continuous domains we have used the "iris" dataset which was normalized prior to training using the min-max normalization method. This method preserves all relationships of the data values exactly, and all the constraints detected in normalized form are valid constraints for the domain once they are de-normalized. The Iris dataset consists of four continuous input attributes: sepal-length, sepal-width, petal-length and petal-width. The classification task is to determine the type of the iris flower which can be either iris-setosa, iris-virginica or iris-versicolor. This dataset has some overlapping classes which made it suitable for indicating the problem of distinguishing anomalous entries from true exceptional cases.

Filtering Technique

SOM was trained many times using different sets of learning parameters. A common observation was that when a small output space was used many more instances would be considered as outlying, and the other way around. This is due to the fact that with a small output dimension there is only enough space for the most general database behavior to be projected. On the other hand, extra map resolution allows more space for additional specializations of particular classes to be projected.

By using the method described in the section "General SOM Properties," concept hierarchies for each set of experiments is obtained. During supervised training, if an instance cannot be matched to any of the node rules contained within the hierarchy, it is considered as an outlier. After supervised training the implication of each node in the hierarchy is determined to be the target value that has most frequently occurred in the instances that triggered that particular node. During the supervised training each target value of a node stores the instance in which it has occurred when that particular node was activated. The concept hierarchy is then traversed and whenever a node has a low supported target value which contradicts the implication, the corresponding instances are considered as outliers. To make the following explanation simpler we will refer to a node as an outlier rather than the instance captured by that node. If a node is only rarely triggered it is a suspect outlier. However, if the node itself is a specialization of a more general node that implies the same class, or is a generalization of other more specific nodes that imply the same class, then it is not considered as an outlier. On the other hand, if the node is rarely triggered and it occurs in a separate subtree from other triggered nodes that have implications, it is then regarded as an outlier. Also if two nodes that are rarely triggered exist together in a subtree with no other frequently triggered nodes then they are both considered as outliers, unless the nodes around them all imply the same class. When we refer to a subtree in this case, we refer to all ancestors and descendents of a particular node in the hierarchy. The siblings are not considered, as even if they were implying the same class the rarely triggered node is a suspect outlier since it is separate from the normal behavior for that class. A threshold is chosen at which a node or target value is considered to be rarely occurring. This outlier support threshold should be chosen to reflect the support of a pattern at which it would be considered outlying, and in our experiments this threshold was set to one.

We have inserted 10 noisy instances into the "zoo" dataset which constitutes about 10% of the total dataset. The instances were labeled from o1 to o10, while all the normal instances are labeled by the actual animal name. In this discussion we will consider the results obtained when the map size of 3*2, 6*6 and 8*8 was used. The learning parameters were left the same in all cases, but it should be noted that smaller output space resolution probably does not require as much training time. Furthermore, certain rule extraction thresholds could be adjusted with respect to the map size, but we left all parameters unmodified in our experiments in order to see whether the decrease in the map size was sufficient to detect more outliers. The different set of outlying instances detected by the use of different output dimensions is displayed in Table 2. We split the detected instances into three sets depending on which conditions was used to consider the instance as an outlier. The rarely triggered label does not just refer to rarely triggered nodes but needs to satisfy the extra criteria described in the previous paragraph. We can see the difference in the number of outliers detected by using different output dimensions. With large map sizes the outliers are more often detected from rarely triggered nodes rather than mismatched or unmatched instances. This is because there is enough resolution to extract most of the specialization of various classes, as well as the outlying behaviour. And hence the information is contained in the hierarchy and only through the reasoning applied to the hierarchy, the outliers can be detected. On the other hand a small map size would have many more unmatched outliers as there was only enough resolution for the general behaviour to be learned and hence there are not as many contradictions within the hierarchy. Therefore, the map size could be adjusted according to the type of uncommon behaviour that the user is after

All the artificial outliers were detected by larger map sizes whereas by using the 3*2 map size two artificial outliers were missed. When checked with the concept hierarchy these two outliers were captured by nodes with a low number of attribute constraints, and the classes laying lower in the hierarchy were implying the same class as the outlying instances. The low number of attribute constraints that captured the instance may not capture the characteristics which define the instance as outlying. Only after further specialization, it could be seen that the instance is in fact an outlier. Hence the strategy described above would not consider such instances as outli-

Table 2. The number of different outliers detected by different dimensions

Map Size	3*2	6*6	8*8
Not matched	37	3	2
Mismatched	1	1	0
Rarely triggered	2	18	19

*Table 3. Concept hierarchy and detected outliers for 6*6 SOM*

Map size	Epoch	Neighborhood	Learning rate	Tinh	Detected outliers
6*6	200	5*5	0.3	0.13	
eggs, breathes (1) legs_0 | invertabrate (slug,worm) (2) predator,toothed,backbone,tail |reptile (slowworm) (3) venomous |reptile(pitviper) (1) legs_6 | insect (flea, termite) (2) airborne | (gnat, ladybird) (2) hair | insect (honeybee, housefly, moth wasp) (1) legs_4 | reptile (tortoise) (2) aquatic (3)predator | mammal (platypus) (4)toothed, backbone | amphibian (frog, frog) (5) tail |amphibian (newt) (3) toothed, backbone | amphibian (toad) (4) predator | reptile (tuatara) (1) aquatic, toothed (2) predator | bird (o5) (2) milk, backbone, legs_2, domestic | bird (o4) (1) aquatic, legs_2, backbone, tail, feathers (2) predator | bird (penguin) 3) airborne | bird (gull, skimmer,skua) (2) airborne | bird (duck, swan) (1) feathers,predator,backbone,legs_2,tail | bird (kiwi, rhea) (2) airborne | bird (crow, hawk, vulture) (1) hair,milk,airborne,backbone,legs_5 | insect (o6) (1) feathers,backbone,legs_2,tail | bird (ostrich) (2) airborne | bird (chicken, dove, flamingo, lark, parakeet, pheasant, sparrow, wren) **eggs, legs_0** (1) predator | invertebrate (clam) (2) aquatic | invertebrate (seawasp) (3) toothed, backbone, fins, tail | fish (bass, catfish, chub, dogfish, herring, pike, piranha, stingray, tuna) (1) aquatic, toothed, backbone, fins, tail | fish (carp, haddock, seahorse, sole) **eggs, aquatic, predator** | invertebrate (crab, octopus, starfish) (1) legs_6, | invertebrate (crab, lobster) **feathers, milk, breathes, legs_5, tail** | bird (o8) **predator, breathes, venomous, legs_8, tail** | invertebrate (scorpion) mammal (o9) (root) **milk, predator, toothed, breathes, catsize** (1) backbone (2) aquatic (3) fins, tail | mammal (sealion) (4) legs_0 | mammal (dolphin, porpoise) (5) hair | mammal (seal) (3) hair | mammal (mink) (2) hair | mammal (aardvark, bear, girl) (3) legs_4, tail | mammal (boar, cheetah, leopard, lion, lynx, mongoose, polecat, puma, pussycat, raccoon, wolf) (2) legs_0, tail | mammal (o10) **hair, feathers, airborne, backbone, venomous, legs_4** | mammal (o2) **hair, milk, toothed, backbone, breathes, tail** (1) legs_2 | mammal (squirrel, wallaby) (2) airborne | mammal (fruitbat, vampire) (1) legs_4 | mammal (hare, vole) (2) predator | mammal (mole, opossum) (2) catsize | mammal (antelope, buffalo, deer, elephant, giraffe, oryx) (3) domestic | mammal (calf, goat, pony, reindeer) (2) domestic | mammal (hamster) **hair, milk, airborne, toothed, breathes, legs_4, domestic** | mammal (o3) **hair, milk, toothed, backbone, breathes, legs_2, catsize** | mammal (gorilla) **hair, milk, toothed, backbone, breathes, legs_4, domestic** | mammal (cavy)					**Not matched** seasnake o1 o7 **Mismatched** o9 **Rarely triggered** slowworm tortoise platypus toad tuatara o5 o4 o6 seawasp clam o8 scorpion mink o10 o2 o3 gorilla cavy

Table 4. Inserted outlying instances

sepal-length	sepal-width	petal-length	petal-width	Class
0.75	0.49	0.02	0.15	iris-setosa
0.52	0.9	0.7	0.26	iris-virginica
0.9	0.417	0.595	0.05	iris-versicolor
0.685	0.29	0.02	0.59	iris-setosa

ers. This can commonly occur and we could add extra criterion whereby all the rarely triggered nodes are considered as outliers. This would in fact detect all the outliers, but may detect unnecessary instances if the level of specialization is high within the hierarchy.

The obtained concept hierarchy using the map size of 6*6 is displayed on the left of table 3, where the attributes in bold define the root node of a new sub-tree. The labels of all the instances detected as outliers, is displayed on the right. All the artificial outliers are detected as well as other true exceptions in this knowledge domain. The outlier detection strategy can be verified by the concept hierarchy, and this explains why certain exceptions were not captured. For the rest of the attributes a number is displayed to the left which indicates the level of the concept hierarchy where the attribute occurs. As previously mentioned some nodes could be too general which causes us to miss the specializations which make a particular instance exceptional. If a domain expert was available, we could adopt a more restrictive strategy whereby all the rarely triggered nodes are considered as suspect outliers and the domain expert makes the division between anomalies and true exceptions. However, the described strategy is already efficient in detecting instances which deviate largely from the norm. Since exceptions exist within most of knowledge a domain expert is irreplaceable in these circumstances, and should always provide the final resolution.

Reasoning Technique

The CSOM was trained for 32000 iterations using the following parameters: map size = 8*8; neighborhood = 7*7; learning rate = 0.3; default update factor = 0.02, and node to cluster threshold of 0.02. The default update factor is used when the attribute constraints of the winner node exactly match the input, in order to ensure update in the neighborhood and the inhibiting neighborhood. The node to cluster threshold is the maximum allowed ED between a node and a cluster so that the node is assigned to that cluster. If this value is too small there will be too many clusters formed, and if it is too large there will be too few formed with high misclassification rate. We adopted an approach where the threshold is very small and once clusters are formed, merging between similar clusters and deletion of un-predicting clusters occurs. This produced better results than obtained by trying to find the optimal threshold value. Note that satisfying results could probably be obtained with much less training time, but we decided to use suggestion given in (Kohonen, 1990), iteration number ≈ (map size * 500). We have inserted four outlying instances into the iris dataset (Table 4) which are contradicting to the common set of rules for this domain. Table 5 shows the final cluster set obtained using the method described in the section "Approach for Categorical Data." On the left the clusters are displayed with their corresponding attribute constraints, and on the

Table 5. Cluster set with rules and target vector

C#	Cluster rules	TargetVector
1	0.193994 < sepal_length < 0.19555 0 < sepal_width < 9.36915e-12 0.423993 < petal_length < 0.42601 0.374999 < petal_width < 0.375701	Iris-versicolor – 1
2	0.292 < sepal_width < 0.5 0.15 < petal_width < 0.583	Iris-versicolor – 29 Iris-virginica - 1 Iris-setosa – 1
3	0.333 < sepal_length < 0.361 0.125 < sepal_width < 0.208014 0.475 < petal_length < 0.508 0.416998 < petal_width < 0.5	Iris-versicolor – 4
4	0 < sepal_length < 0.417 0 < petal_length < 0.153	Iris-setosa – 49
5	0.519995 < sepal_length < 0.52 0.899994 < sepal_width < 0.9 0.699994 < petal_length < 0.7 0.259997 < petal_width < 0.26	Iris-virginica – 1
6	0.25 < sepal_width < 0.75 0.708 < petal_width < 1	Iris-virginica – 42 Iris-versicolor – 1
7	0.899309 < sepal_length < 0.9 0.417 < sepal_width < 0.418 0.595 < petal_length < 0.595035 0.05 < petal_width < 0.0503167	Iris-versicolor – 1
8	0.083 < sepal_width < 0.208 0.583 < petal_width < 0.958	Iris-virginica – 5 Iris-versicolor – 2
9	0.417 < sepal_width < 0.583 0.625 < petal_width < 0.708	Iris-virginica – 1 Iris-versicolor – 3
10	0.083 < sepal_width < 0.25 0.15 < petal_width < 0.542	Iris-versicolor – 9 Iris-virginica – 1
11	0.292 < sepal_width < 0.407 0.59 < petal_width < 0.625	Iris-versicolor – 1
12	0.26 < sepal_width < 0.407 0.552 < petal_width < 0.615	Iris-setosa – 1

right of the table the implying target values with the corresponding weight are displayed.

The rule optimization process described in the section "Concept Hierarchy Formation" was applied for 100 iterations. The outlier support threshold was set to two, because during our experimentations we have experienced that in some cases the behavior of two outlying instances could be captured by one cluster. Table 6 shows the instances detected as suspect outliers. By consulting Table 5, it can be seen that these instances were extracted from the clusters that are rarely triggered and/or class objects that have a low support and are contradicting to the normal class implied by their capturing cluster. This high number is due to the existence of overlapping classes in this domain All the inserted anomalous entries were detected and by comparing the attribute values of an instance to the clusters exhibiting normal behavior for the class of the instance,

Table 6. Detected outlying instances

sepal_length	sepal_width	petal_length	petal_width	Class
0.194	0	0.424	0.375	Iris-versicolor
0.556	0.333	0.695	0.583	Iris-virginica
0.75	*0.49*	*0.02*	*0.15*	*Iris-setosa*
0.52	*0.9*	*0.7*	*0.26*	*Iris-virginica*
0.444	0.5	0.644	0.708	Iris-versicolor
0.9	*0.417*	*0.595*	*0.05*	*Iris-versicolor*
0.556	0.208	0.661	0.583	Iris-versicolor
0.528	0.083	0.593	0.583	Iris-versicolor
0.806	0.417	0.814	0.625	Iris-virginica
0.5	0.25	0.78	0.542	Iris-virginica
0.472	0.292	0.695	0.625	Iris-versicolor
0.685	*0.29*	*0.02*	*0.59*	*Iris-setosa*

anomalies could be distinguished from true exceptions. For example in cluster 10 the suspect outlier instance was: 0.5,0.25,0.78,0.542,Iris-virginica. By comparing it to cluster 6 that exhibits normal behavior for the "iris-virginica" class, we can see that the difference in attribute constraints is not large enough for the instance to be regarded as an anomalous entry. The same holds for the instance wrongly captured by cluster 6 (i.e., iris-versicolor). It is a small distance away from its true cluster 2. These examples are true exceptional cases as they are close enough to the common rules but were miscomputed due to the existence of class overlap in the iris dataset. On the other hand instances that are a large distance away from their true clusters can be regarded as anomalous with high confidence. When an instance is captured by a wrong cluster it has more chance of being a true exceptional case as opposed to when it is separate from the existing clusters, especially in the domains with overlapping classes. Furthermore, given the suspect outlying instances a domain expert would have minimal trouble distinguishing anomalies from true exceptions.

CONCLUSION

This work has demonstrated some different ways that the SOM can effectively be used for outlier detection and analysis. The proposed approach detects outliers elegantly by forming abstractions of common behavior and thereby easily isolating uncommon behavior. Furthermore, the dimension of the output space plays a role in the type of database behavior that will be learnt. One could use different dimensions depending on what kind of unusual patterns are desired. The criteria for selecting an entry as an outlier will be more automatic as the proposed techniques converge to the conclusion of which data objects are outliers, rather than relying on some statistical-based heuristics that could be biased in certain ways. Furthermore by detecting outliers in the proposed manner there is a better indication of whether the detected outlier is caused by noise or is in fact a true exceptional case. Making this distinction allows us to clean the datasets from noisy instances and thereby increase the quality of data which is important for effective data mining and knowledge discovery.

REFERENCES

Aggarwal, C. C., & Yu., P. S. (2001, May 21-24). Outlier detection for high dimensional data. In *Proceedings of the 2001ACM SIGMOD International Conference on Management of Data*, Santa Barbara, CA.

Barnett, V., & Lewis, T. (1994). *Outliers in statistical data* (3rd ed.). Chichester, UK: John Wiley & Sons.

Bay, S. D., & Schwabacher, M. (2003, August 24-27). Mining distance-based outliers in near linear time with randomization and a simple pruning rule. In *Proceedings of SIGKDD'03*, Washington, DC.

Blake, C., Keogh, E., & Merz, C. J. (1998). UCI repository of machine learning databases. Irvine, CA: University of California, Department of Information and Computer Science. Retrieved October 30, 2006, from http://www.ics.uci.edu/~mlearn/MLRepository.html

Breunig, M. M., Kriegel, H. P., Ng, R. T., & Sander, J. (2000). LOF: Identifying density-based local outliers. In *Proceedings of ACM SIGMOD International Conference on Management of Data*, Dallas, TX.

Bruner, J. S., Goodnow, J. J., & Austin, G. A. (1956). *A study of thinking*. New York: John Wiley & Sons.

Chakrabarti, S., Sarawagi, S., & Dom, B. (1998). Mining surprising patterns using temporal description length. In *Proceedings of the 24th VLDB Conference*, New York (pp. 606-617).

Dillon, T. S., Sestito, S., Witten, M., & Suing, M. (1993, September). Automated knowledge acquisition using unsupervised learning. In *Proceedings of the Second IEEE Workshop on Emerging Technology and Factory Automation (EFTA93)*, Cairns (pp. 119-28).

Girardin, L. (1999). An eye on network intruder-administrator shootouts. In *Proceedings of the Workshop on Intrusion Detection and Network Monitoring*, Berkeley, CA (pp. 19-28) . USENIX Association.

Gonzalez, F. A., & Dasgupta, D. (2002). Neuro-immune and self-organizing map approaches to anomaly detection: A comparison. In *Proceedings of the 1st International Conference on Artificial Immune Systems* (pp. 203-211).

Gonzalez, F. A., & Dasgupta, D. (2003). Anomaly detection using real-valued negative selection. *Genetic Programming and Evolvable Machines, 4*, 383-403.

Hadzic, F., & Dillon, T. S. (2005, August 10-12). CSOM: self organizing map for continuous data. In *Proceedings of the 3rd International IEEE Conference on Industrial Informatics (INDIN'05)*, Perth, Australia.

Hadzic, F., Dillon, T. S., Tan, H., Feng, L., & Chang, E. (2006). *Mining frequent patterns using self-organizing map* (The annual advanced topics in data warehousing and mining series). Hershey, PA: Idea Group.

Hawkins, D. (1980). *Identification of outliers*. London: Chapman & Hall.

Hodge, V. J., & Austin, J. (2004). A survey of outlier detection methodologies. *Artificial Intelligence Review, 22*, 85-126.

Johnson, T., Kwok, I., & Ng, R. (1998). Fast computation of 2-dimensional depth contours. In *Proceedings of KDD* (pp. 224-228).

Knorr, E. M., & Ng, R. T. (1998, September). Algorithms for mining distance-based outliers in large data sets. In *Proceedings of VLDB Conference*.

Knorr, E. M., & Ng, R. T. (1999). Finding intensional knowledge of distance-based outliers. In *Proceedings of the 25th VLDB Conference*.

Knorr, E. M., Ng, R. T., & Tucakov, V. (2000). Distance-based outliers: Algorithms and applications. *VLDB Journal*, *8*(3-4), 237-253.

Kohonen, T. (1990, September). The self-organizing map. In *Proceedings of the IEEE* (pp. 1464-1480).

Labib, K., & Vemuri, R. (2002). *NSOM: A real-time network-based intrusion detection system using self-organizing maps*. (Tech. Rep.). Davis, CA: Department of Applied Science, University of California.

Lichodzijewski, P., Zincir-Heywood, A., & Heywood, M. (2002). Dynamic intrusion detection using self-organizing maps. In *Proceedings of the 14th Annual Canadian Information Technology Security Symposium*.

Munoz, A., & Muruzabal, J. (1998). Self-organizing maps for outlier detection. *Neurocomputing*, *18*, 33-60.

Ng, R., & Han, J. (1994). Efficient and effective clustering methods for spatial data mining. In *VLDB Conference Proceedings*, San Francisco (pp. 144-155).

Nuansri, N., Dillon, T. S., & Singh, S. (1997, January 7-10). An application of neural network and rule-based system for network management: Application level problems. In *Proceedings of the 30th Annual Hawaii International Conference on System Sciences*, Maui, HI (pp. 474-483) .

Pearson, R. K. (2005). *Mining imperfect data: Dealing with contamination and incomplete records*. Philadelphia: SIAM.

Preparata, F., & Shamons, M. (1998). *Computational geometry: An introduction*. Berlin: Springer.

Ramaswamy, S., Rastogi, R., & Shim, K. (2000). Efficient algorithms for mining outliers from large datasets. In *Proceedings of the ACM SIGMOD Conference* (pp 427-438).

Rhodes, B., Mahaffey, J., & Cannady, J. (2000). Multiple self-organizing maps for intrusion detection. In *Proceedings of the NISSC Conference*.

Rousseeuw, P. J., & Leroy, A. M. (1987). *Robust regression and outlier detection*. New York: John Wiley & Sons.

Ruts, I., & Rousseeuw, P. (1996). Computing depth contours of bivariate point clouds. *Computational Statistical Data Analysis, 23*, 153-168.

Sestito, S., & Dillon, T. S. (1994). *Automated knowledge acquisition*. Sydney: Prentice Hall of Australia Pty Ltd.

Tukey, J. (1997). *Exploratory data analysis*. Addison-Wesley.

Vesanto, J., Himberg, J., Siponen, M., & Simula, O. (1998). Enhancing SOM based data visualization. In *Proceedings of the 5th International Conference on Soft Computing and Information/Intelligent Systems: Methodologies for the Conception, Design and Application of Soft Computing* (pp. 64-67), Singapore. World Scientific.

Ypma, A., & Duin, R. P. W. (1997). Novelty detection using self-organizing maps. In Kasabov, N. Kozma, R. Ko, K. O'Shea, R. Coghill & T. Gedeon (Eds.), *Progress in connectionist-based information systems* (pp. 1322-1325). London: Springer.

Zanero, S., & Savaresi, S. (2004). Unsupervised learning techniques for an intrusion detection system. In *Proceedings of the ACM Symposium on Applied Computing (ACM SAC'04).*

Zhang, T., Ramakrishnan, R., & Livny, M. (1996). BIRCH: An efficient data clustering method for very large databases. *ACM SIGMOD Conference Proceedings* (pp 103-114).

Zhou, X., & Dillon, T. S. (1991). A statistical-heuristic feature selection criterion for decision tree induction. *IEEE Transactions on Pattern Analysis and Machine Intelligence*, *13*(8), 834-841.

Chapter XIII
Re-Sampling Based Data Mining Using Rough Set Theory

Benjamin Griffiths
Cardiff University, UK

Malcolm J. Beynon
Cardiff University, UK

ABSTRACT

Predictive accuracy, as an estimation of a classifier's future performance, has been studied for at least seventy years. With the advent of the modern computer era, techniques that may have been previously impractical are now calculable within a reasonable time frame. Within this chapter, three techniques of resampling, namely, leave-one-out, k-fold cross validation and bootstrapping; are investigated as methods of error rate estimation with application to variable precision rough set theory (VPRS). A prototype expert system is utilised to explore the nature of each resampling technique when VPRS is applied to an example dataset. The software produces a series of graphs and descriptive statistics, which are used to illustrate the characteristics of each technique with regards to VPRS, and comparisons are drawn between the results.

INTRODUCTION

The success of data mining is dependent on the appropriateness and practicality of the mathematical analysis techniques employed. Whether it is based on statistical or symbolic machine learning, an analyst is interested primarily in the final results that they can analyse and interpret. Those theorists interested in researching data mining are aware that one-off analyses using different techniques may produce varying results, including that of the often definitive statistic of predic-

Copyright © 2007, IGI Global, distributing in print or electronic forms without written permission of IGI Global is prohibited.

tive accuracy (as for example in classification problems). More pertinently, these results may highlight further incongruousness such as different characteristic attributes in a dataset viewed as important. For the analyst they are then in a quandary, since they desire confidence in the concomitant interpretation.

One option to mitigate the limited confidence that can be inherent with a one-off analysis, with any technique, is through the use of resampling. For the last 70 years, since the early work on error rate estimation (e.g., Larson, 1931), there has consistently been research undertaken on the benefits of resampling based analysis (e.g., Efron, 1982; Braga-Neto & Dougherty, 2005). Whilst research has considered the statistical consequences of such resampling and related analysis (e.g., Shao & Tu, 1995), how nascent techniques, in particular those based on symbolic machine learning, fully utilize such approaches requires elucidation.

Two questions to consider are; whether accustomed parameters used in resampling are generally appropriate to all data mining techniques, and beyond classification accuracy results are resampling approaches appropriate to elucidate insights such as attribute importance. A relevant example of such an overlapping philosophy is with the work of Leo Breiman, who has undertaken extensive research on the issue of resampling (e.g., Breiman, 1996), but also advocates the need to develop new data mining techniques (e.g., Breiman, 2001).

This chapter demonstrates these questions and the role of resampling in data mining, with emphasis on the results from rough set theory (RST). As a nascent symbolic machine learning technique (Pawlak, 1982), its popularity is a direct consequence of its operational processes, which adhere most closely to the notions of knowledge discovery and data mining (Li & Wang, 2004). Characteristics like this contribute to the adage given in Dunstch and Gediga (1997, p. 594), that underlying the RST philosophy is: "*Let the data speak for itself.*"

However, its novel set theoretical structure brings its own concerns when considered within a resampling environment. Consequently, this chapter offers insights into the resampling issues that may affect practical analysis when employing nascent techniques, such as RST.

The specific data mining technique utilised here is *variable precision rough set theory* (VPRS, Beynon, 2001; Ziarko, 1993), one of a number of developments on the original RST. Other developments of RST include; dominance-based rough sets (Greco, Matarazzo, & Słowiński, 2004), fuzzy rough sets, (Greco, Inuiguchi, & Słowiński, 2006) and probabilistic rough sets (Ziarko, 2005). A literal presentation of the diversity of work on RST can be viewed in the annual volumes of the transactions on rough sets (most recent year 2005). The utilisation of VPRS is without loss of generality to developments such as those referenced; its relative simplicity allows the non-proficient reader the opportunity to follow fully the details presented.

The result from a VPRS analysis is a group of "*if .. then ..*" decision rules, which classify objects to decision classes based on their condition attribute values. VPRS also allows for the misclassification of some objects used in the construction of the decision rules, unlike in RST. One relevant issue is the intent within VPRS (and RST in general) for data reduction and feature selection (Jensen & Shen, 2005), with subsets of condition attributes identified that perform the same role as all the condition attributes in a considered dataset (termed β-reducts in VPRS). These β-reducts are identified prior to the construction of its respective group of decision rules, rather than during their construction as in techniques like decision trees, an issue pertinent when resampling is employed (Breiman, 2001).

A number of resampling approaches are considered here, namely; "Leave-one-out" (Weiss & Kulikowski, 1991), *k*-fold cross validation (Braga-Neto & Dougherty, 2004) and bootstrapping (Chennick, 1999). The VPRS results presented utilise specific software, the preliminary work of which was published in Griffiths and Beynon (2005). Its development to allow for resampling includes the requirement for the automation of the selection of a single β-reduct in each resampling run. A small dataset is utilised in the analysis (part of the well-known wine dataset), which allows for the clear presentation of VPRS results. Illustrative of those from this symbolic machine learning technique, the results include; predictive accuracy, quality classification, and importance of condition attributes and β-reducts.

Variable Precision Rough Set Theory and Resampling

The background presented here covers the rudiments of variable precision rough set theory with an example also given, and the principles underlying a number of resampling approaches—describing in each case the construction of the training and test sets of objects in the individual resampling runs. Throughout this chapter, the emphasis is not on the achievement of best classification accuracy, more the elucidation of other measures available with symbolic machine learning techniques when data mining within a resampling environment. Indeed Breiman (2001), highlights that accuracy may not be the dominant results required by an analyst with interpretation often a major requirement.

Variable Precision Rough Set Theory (VPRS)

Central to VPRS (and RST) is the information system (termed here as the dataset), which contains a universe of objects U (o_1, o_2, ...), each characterised by a set condition attributes C (c_1, c_2, ...) and classified to a set of decision attributes D (d_1, d_2, ...). A value denoting the nature of an attribute to an object is called a *descriptor*, from which certain equivalence classes $E(\cdot)$ of objects can be constructed. That is, condition and decision classes which group the objects together, depending on the indiscernibly of their condition and decision descriptor values, respectively. It is noted, the level of granularity of a dataset (uniqueness of descriptor values), dictates the number and size of the concomitant condition and decision classes.

Since the objects in a condition class may not all be in the same decision class, the proportions of the number of objects in a condition class, which exist in the individual decision classes, can be evaluated. Counting the allocation of objects in all the condition classes in this way leads to the notion of set approximations used in VPRS. For a defined proportionality value β, the β-positive region corresponds to the union of the set of condition classes (using a subset of condition attributes P), with conditional probabilities of allocation to a set of objects Z (using a decision class $Z \in E(D)$), which are at least equal to β. More formally:

β-positive region of the set $Z \subseteq U$ and $P \subseteq C$:
$POS_P^{\beta}(Z) = \bigcup_{\Pr(Z \mid X_i) \geq \beta}\{X_i \in E(P)\}$,

where β is defined here to lie between 0.5 and 1 (An, Shan, & Chan, 1996), Ziarko (1993) considers this within the context of a *majority inclusion* relation. That is, those condition classes in a β-positive region $POS_P^{\beta}(Z)$ each have a majority of objects associated with the decision class $Z \in E(D)$ (further developed in the extended VPRS, see Katzberg & Ziarko, 1996). Other set approximations, in the form of β-negative and β-boundary regions are given as follows (from Ziarko, 1993):

β-negative region of the set $Z \subseteq U$ and $P \subseteq C$:
$NEG_P^{\beta}(Z) = \bigcup_{\Pr(Z \mid X_i) \leq 1-\beta}\{X_i \in E(P)\}$,
β-boundary region of the set $Z \subseteq U$ and $P \subseteq C$:
$BND_P^{\beta}(Z) = \bigcup_{1-\beta < \Pr(Z \mid X_i) < \beta}\{X_i \in E(P)\}$,

From the previous expressions, the β-negative region contains the condition classes not associated with a decision class Z and the β-boundary region contains the condition classes that cannot be considered either associated or not associated with Z. The numbers of objects included in the condition classes that are contained in the respective β-positive regions for each of the decision classes, subject to the necessary β value, make up a measure of the *quality of classification*. That is, the quality of classification, denoted $\gamma^{\beta}(P, D)$, is the proportion of those objects in a dataset that are assigned a classification (correctly or incorrectly), defined by:

$$\gamma^{\beta}(P, D) = \frac{\text{card}(\bigcup_{Z \in E(D)} POS_P^{\beta}(Z))}{\text{card}(U)},$$

where $P \subseteq C$. The meaning of this measure differs to that in the original RST, with the number of objects classified including those misclassified. The $\gamma^{\beta}(P, D)$ measure with the β value means that for the objects in a dataset, a VPRS analysis may define them in one of three states; not classified, correctly classified and misclassified. The proportion of the objects in these states depends on the possibly subjective choice of the desired level of quality of classification $\gamma^{\beta}(P, D)$, and the effects of the implicated β value or subdomain.

VPRS further applies these defined measures by seeking subsets of condition attributes (termed *β-reducts*), capable of explaining the associations given by the whole set of condition attributes, subject to the majority inclusion relation (using a β value). Within data mining, the notion of a β-reduct is directly associated with the study of data reduction and feature selection (Jensen & Shen, 2005). Ziarko (1993) states that a β-reduct (R) of the set of conditional attributes C, with respect to a set of decision attributes D, is:

1. A subset R of C that offers the same quality of classification, subject to the β value, as the whole set of condition attributes.
2. No proper subset of R has the same quality of the classification as R, subject to the associated β value.

The original utilisation of VPRS centred on the *apriori* selection of a β value (Ziarko, 1993). More recent developments such as in Mi et al. (2004) and Li and Wang (2004) have aimed to automate aspects of the VPRS, they order the evaluation of the β value first before β-reduct selection, which limits the relevance of the analysis over the whole β domain (compared to that in Beynon, 2001; Giffiths & Beynon, 2005).

A small example dataset is next considered and associated VPRS results briefly described, taken from Beynon (2001), see Table 1. The presented dataset of seven objects has a low granularity, with only 0 and 1 descriptor values describing the six conditions and one decision attribute.

Table 1. Example dataset

Objects	c_1	c_2	c_3	c_4	c_5	c_6	d_1
o_1	1	1	1	1	1	1	0
o_2	1	0	1	0	1	1	0
o_3	0	0	1	1	0	0	0
o_4	1	1	1	0	0	1	1
o_5	1	0	1	0	1	1	1
o_6	0	0	0	1	1	0	1
o_7	1	0	1	0	1	1	1

Using the dataset in Table 1, the associated condition classes are; $X_1 = \{o_1\}$, $X_2 = \{o_2, o_5, o_7\}$, $X_3 = \{o_3\}$, $X_4 = \{o_4\}$ and $X_5 = \{o_6\}$, similarly the decision classes are $Z_0 = \{o_1, o_2, o_3\}$ and $Z_1 = \{o_4, o_5, o_6, o_7\}$. For a specific β value and decision class, the associated set approximations can be found. Considering the decision class $Z_0 = \{o_1, o_2, o_3\}$ then:

with $\beta = 0.55$; $POS_C^{0.55}(Z_0) = \{o_1, o_3\}$, $NEG_C^{0.55}(Z_0) = \{o_2, o_4, o_5, o_6, o_7\}$, $BND_C^{0.55}(Z_0) = \{\ \}$,

and

with $\beta = 0.8$; $POS_C^{0.8}(Z_0) = \{o_1, o_3\}$, $NEG_C^{0.8}(Z_0) = \{o_4, o_6\}$, $BND_C^{0.8}(Z_0) = \{o_2, o_5, o_7\}$.

Similar set approximations can be found with the other decision class Z_1. The calculation of the quality of classification of the whole dataset is, $\gamma^{0.55}(C, D) = 1.000$ when $\beta = 0.55$, and $\gamma^{0.8}(C, D) = 0.571$ when $\beta = 0.8$. Moving away from specific values of β it can be shown, $\gamma^{\beta}(C, D) = 1.000$ for $\beta \in (0.500, 0.667]$, and $\gamma^{\beta}(C, D) = 0.571$ for $\beta \in (0.667, 1.000]$. These examples highlight the asymmetric relationship that exists between a β value and the quality of classification, namely a low or high β value infers relatively high or low quality of classification, respectively. For an analyst, whether a balance between these values is the solution or a more subjective choice is one question that a resampling approach may contribute an appropriate solution to.

A number of β-reducts exist for the dataset presented in Table 1, over different β subdomains. These include, $\{c_3, c_6\}$ for $\beta \in (0.500, 0.600]$, and $\{c_1, c_2, c_5\}$ for $\beta \in (0.667, 1.000]$, which respectively include the β values 0.55 and 0.8 considered previously. With a β-reduct, the associated minimal set of decision rules is then constructed using the method given in An et al. (1996). In summary, for the condition classes associated with a decision class, the descriptors that discern them from the others are identified. These descriptors are called prime implicants and form the basis for the condition parts of the constructed decision rules (with further reduction in the prime implicants also possible). For the two β-reducts considered here, the associated minimal sets of decision rules are as follows (where strength infers the number of objects the rule covers):

For the β-reduct $\{c_3, c_6\}$ then:

If $c_3 = 1$ and $c_6 = 0$ then $d_1 = 0$ with strength 1 and proportion correct 1.000

If $c_6 = 1$ then $d_1 = 1$ with strength 5 and proportion correct 0.600

If $c_3 = 0$ then $d_1 = 1$ with strength 1 and proportion correct 1.000

For the β-reduct $\{c_1, c_2, c_5\}$ then:

If $c_2 = 1$ and $c_5 = 1$ then $d_1 = 0$ with strength 1 and proportion correct 1.000

If $c_1 = 0$ and $c_5 = 0$ then $d_1 = 0$ with strength 1 and proportion correct 1.000

If $c_2 = 1$ and $c_5 = 0$ then $d_1 = 1$ with strength 1 and proportion correct 1.000

If $c_1 = 0$ and $c_5 = 1$ then $d_1 = 1$ with strength 1 and proportion correct 1.000

The presented rules have spaces in their condition parts, which are cases of redundant prime implicants. These two sets of constructed decision rules illustrate the asymmetric relationship between the β value and the concomitant quality of classification. The decision rules of the β-reduct $\{c_3, c_6\}$ classify all seven objects ($\gamma^{\beta}(\{c_3, c_6\}, D) = 1.000$ for $\beta \in (0.500, 0.600]$). However, the middle rule only correctly classifies three out of the five objects it covers, hence the upper bound of 0.600 for the β value that allows $\{c_3, c_6\}$ to be a β-reduct. For the β-reduct $\{c_1, c_2, c_5\}$, only four out of seven objects are classified ($\gamma^{\beta}(\{c_1, c_2, c_5\}, D) = 0.571$ for $\beta \in (0.667, 1.000]$), but the rules correctly classify all the objects they cover, hence the upper bound of 1.000 for the β value in its associated subdomain.

Leave-One-Out

The technique of leave-one-out is attributed to Lachenbruch and Mickey (1968). Within each run, one object is left out of the training set and forms the test set. The constructed classifier (set of decision rules in VPRS) based on the $n - 1$ objects in the training set is then tested on the remaining single object in the test set. There are n runs in this process, hence for every run the classifier is constructed on nearly all the objects, and each object will at some point, during the process, be used as a test object. The error rate is taken as the number of incorrectly classified single test objects over n. Mosteller and Tukey (1968) are accredited with describing the first general statement of what they termed, simple cross validation, which is now commonly known as leave-one-out analysis, they state (p. 111): "*Suppose that we set aside one individual case, optimise for what is left, then test on the set-aside case. Repeating this for every case squeezes the data almost dry.*"

For sample sizes of over 100, leave-one-out is considered an accurate almost completely unbiased estimator of the true error rate (Weiss & Kulikowski, 1991). Historically, this method was considered computationally expensive and was only applicable to smaller datasets.

K-Fold Cross Validation

The *k*-fold cross validation method was proposed by Stone (1974) and is a generalization of the leave-one-out resampling approach. Within this method the sample information system is split into *k* folds (subsets) of equal size, moreover the number of objects in each fold is equal (or as near as can be). For example, 200 objects may be split into 10 ($k = 10$) equally sized folds of 20 objects (objects selected randomly). Nine of these folds (90% of the dataset) would be used to train the classifier; the remaining set would be used to test the classifier. For each run a different fold out of the 10 available folds would be left out for use as a test set.

The advantage of the *k*-fold cross validation is expressed clearly in Weiss and Kulikowski (1991). Moreover, due to the random selection of the folds, different *k*-fold cross validation experiments can lead to different classification error rates. Hence, it is recommended to build the folds such that decision class is properly presented, in the right proportion, in both training and test sets, often termed stratified *k*-fold cross validation (see, e.g., Thomassey & Fiordaliso, 2005), which may improve error estimation (Witten & Frank, 2000). With respect to the value of *k* utilized, a number of studies have used $k = 10, 9, 5$ and 2 (e.g., Zhang et al., 1999). A simplistic formulae to evaluate *k* was presented in Davison and Hinkley (1997), namely $k = \min(n^{1/2}; 10)$, where n is the number of objects in the dataset (see also Wisnowski, Simpson, Montgomery, & Runger, 2003).

The *k*-fold cross validation approach requires less runs than the leave-one-out approach and is subsequently less computationally expensive. Considering today's computational power it may be difficult to justify using *k*-fold cross validation, at least the 10-fold variation. However, if one was to consider the size of some of the modern day datasets then cross-validation is still a relevant and practical resampling approach. Indeed, something like 40-fold cross validation may offer an appropriate compromise. It should also be pointed out though, that given a succinctly large dataset, a simple train-and-test technique is a perfectly acceptable method for estimating the true error rate. Braga-Neto and Dougherty (2005) demonstrate a development called *r*-repeated *k*-fold cross validation, whereby a *r* number of cross validations are undertaken using different partitions of the data into folds.

Bootstrapping

The bootstrap resampling approach was introduced in Efron (1979, 1982), and has received much attention and scrutiny over the last 30 years (Chennick, 1999). It draws a random sample of n, from a dataset of size n, using sampling with replacement. This constitutes the training set, objects that do not appear within the training set constitute the test set. For example, given a sample of 200 objects, sampling with replacement n times will yield a training set of 200 objects (some objects may be duplicated more than once). On average the proportion of the objects appearing in the original dataset and the training set is 0.632 (0.368 are therefore duplicates of them), hence the average proportion of the testing set is 0.368 (Weiss & Kulikowski, 1991). These proportions are central to one of the methods for estimating the true error rate.

There are a number of valid methods for estimating the error rate within the bootstrap approach (Chennick, 1999). Two of the acknowledged methods that yield strong results are the e0 and 0.632B bootstrap estimators (see Braga-Neto & Dougherty, 2005; Furlanello, Merler, Chemini, & Rizzoli, 1998; Merler & Furlanello, 1997). The e0 measure is the average of the test set error rates, it is a low variance measure that is biased pessimistically (since the classifier is trained on average on only about two thirds of the available data), but produces strong results when the error rate estimate is large. The 0.632B estimator is a linear combination equation, $(0.368 \times app) + (0.632 \times e0)$, where "app" is the apparent error rate. The 0.632B has low variance but is biased optimistically; its strongest results are produced when the true error rate is low. Initial research considered between 25 and 200 runs as necessary within bootstrapping to obtain a good estimate of the true error rate (Efron, 1983; Wisnowski et al., 2003).

Although leave-one-out is a virtually unbiased estimator for datasets with a 100 or more objects, given a small dataset the value for the error rate estimation has high variance. Conversely, given a small sample, the bootstrap estimator, leads to a more biased estimator, but with lower variance. Hence the bootstrap approach is often considered superior to leave-one-out (but not in all examples). A variant similar in principle to the stratified k-fold cross validation is the balanced bootstrap (Chennick, 1999), whereby each sample is made to appear exactly the same number of times as there are runs in the computation.

VPRS WITH RESAMPLING AND ANALYSIS OF WINE DATASET

The main thrust of this chapter reports a series of analyses using VPRS, the results found are from the utilisation of the three different resampling approaches described previously. The well-known wine dataset is analysed, available at http://www.ics.uci.edu/~mlearn/MLRepository.html. The VPRS software utilised here (Griffiths & Beynon, 2005), is developed from its original ability to only perform one-off analyses, with single training and test sets of objects generated, to enable the defined resampling. Before the presentation of results, a theoretical understanding of how VPRS adopts the necessary automated structure that allows resampling based analysis is described (see Beynon, Clatworthy, & Jones, 2004). As such this is a demonstration of how a nascent symbolic machine learning technique evolves within a resampling environment for data mining.

VPRS with Resampling

In each resampling run, the following stages of a VPRS analysis need to be performed (automated); identification and selection of an acceptable β-reduct, construction of a minimum set of decision rules, and classification and prediction of training and test sets of objects. Also defined here, is the β_{min} value, which is the lowest of the (largest) proportion values of β that allowed the set of condition classes to be in the β-positive regions constructed, with respect to the level of the quality of classification considered. That is, a β value above this upper bound would imply at least one of the contained condition classes would not be given a classification. To illustrate, for the β-reduct $\{c_3, c_6\}$ associated with the information system in Table 1, its $\beta_{min} = 0.6$.

The main concern in this automating process is the selection of a single β-reduct in each resampling run from the many β-reducts that may be identified. Following Beynon et. al. (2004), a criteria list is employed (not unique), with the following ordered properties inherent with the selected β-reduct:

1. **The highest quality of classification possible:** Infers the selected β-reduct(s) will assign a classification to the largest possible number of objects in the training set part of a dataset. A consequence being the rules constructed may miss-classify a number of objects. It is then more probable that the β subdomains associated with the selected β-reduct(s) are at the lower end of its general domain of (0.5, 1], subsequently the respective β_{min} values may be less than 1.
2. **The highest β_{min} value from those associated with the β-reduct(s) selected in (1):** Infers the selected β-reduct(s) will have the highest proportional level of majority inclusion general to all the contained condition classes with their decision classes, of the relevant β-positive regions.
3. **Least number of condition attributes in the β-reduct(s) selected in (2):** Infers a selected β-reduct will have the least complex decision rule set. This follows the science tenet of Occam's Razor (Domingos, 1999), whereby if a choice is available, then the simpler model should be chosen. Here, a β-reduct with less condition attributes would be chosen over one with more condition attributes to exact a simpler model. Since this criterion follows criteria *i*) and *ii*), information quality such as the number of objects classified is not affected.
4. **The largest subdomain of β associated with the β-reduct(s) from those selected in (3):** Infers a selected β-reduct will have been chosen from the largest choice of β value (largest subdomain). This criterion replicates a level of stochastic subjectivity, namely a random choice of a β value would more probably mean this selected β-reduct would be chosen.

Once only a single β-reduct is identified, there is no need to go through the remaining selection criteria (initial studies have shown the criterion *iv* is often not required since a single β-reduct is identified before it is reached). In the case of more than one β-reduct identified after criterion *iv*, a single β-reduct is then randomly selected from this group.

The automated method of deciding which rule predicts the decision for an object in a test set is from Słowiński (1992). Moreover, a measure of the distance (*dist*) between each constructed decision rule and an object is computed for those condition attributes that determine each rule. An object x is described by the condition attribute descriptor values $c_1(x)$, $c_2(x)$, ..., $c_m(x)$, with $m \leq$ card(C). The distance of object x from rule y is measured by:

$$dist = \frac{1}{m}\left\{\sum_{l=1}^{m}\left[k_l\left(\frac{|c_l(x) - c_l(y)|}{v_{l\max} - v_{l\min}}\right)^p\right]\right\}^{\frac{1}{p}}$$

where; p is a natural number selected by an analyst; $v_{l\max}$, $v_{l\min}$ are the maximal and minimal descriptor values of c_l, respectively; k_l is the importance coefficient of condition attribute c_l; m is the number of condition attributes in a decision rule. It follows, the value of p determines the importance of the nearest rule. A small value of p allows a major difference with respect to a single condition attribute to be compensated by a number of minor differences with regard to other condition attributes, whereas a high value of p will overvalue the larger differences and ignore minor ones. In this case the values $p = 2$ (implying least squares fit), and $k_l = 1$ for all l (equal importance amongst the condition attributes).

Leave-One-Out Analysis

As the first occasion of the analysis of the wine dataset in this chapter, it is briefly described and an *apriori* level of continuous value discretisation (CVD) also reported. Here, the first eight continuous condition attributes (chemical constituents); c_1 (Alcohol), c_2 (Malic acid), c_3 (Ash), c_4 (Alcalinity of ash), c_5 (Magnesium), c_6 (Total phenols), c_7 (Flavanoids), c_8 (Nonflavanoid phenols), are used to classify 178 different objects (Italian wines) to three different decision classes (cultivars) labelled $d = 0$ (59), 1 (71) and 2 (48). The values in brackets identify the numbers of wines separately classified to the three decision classes. The data mining question here is whether the wines from the three different cultivators can be discerned using the eight chemical constituents considered. Moreover, with VPRS, can decision rules be identified that classify future wines, also how many and which chemical constituents should form the condition parts of the necessary decision rules.

The considered dataset includes an imbalance between the objects contained in the decision classes, here this is not affected, but can be formulated into a balanced dataset (see, e.g., Grzymala-Busse, Stefanowski, & Wilk, 2005). Returning to the dilemma described by Occam's Razor, the possible desire to work with a relatively small number of "more general" rules may mean the need to reduce the granularity of a dataset, through CVD. The subject of CVD is a research topic in itself (see Beynon, 2004). The software utilised has inbuilt CVD capabilities, a discretisation of the eight continuous condition attributes is reported in Figure 1.

In Figure 1, each condition attribute is partitioned into two intervals (identified by the relatively crude unsupervised equal-width method). Briefly, the snapshot shows for each condition attribute the three values that define the two intervals which categorize them, the dataset created would look similar to that presented in Table 1 (using 0 and 1 labels). For the first condition attribute, Alcohol (c_1), the two intervals are (0, 12.93] (for 0) and (12.93, 14.83] (for 1), future values above 14.83 would also be included in the neighboring interval. Also shown towards the bottom left corner of the snapshot is a pull down window that lists the available CVD methods (in this case choosing equal width for the Nonflavanoid phenols (c_8) condition attribute). This CVD transformed dataset is used in all the resampling undertaken

Figure 1. Snapshot of CVD of eight condition attributes

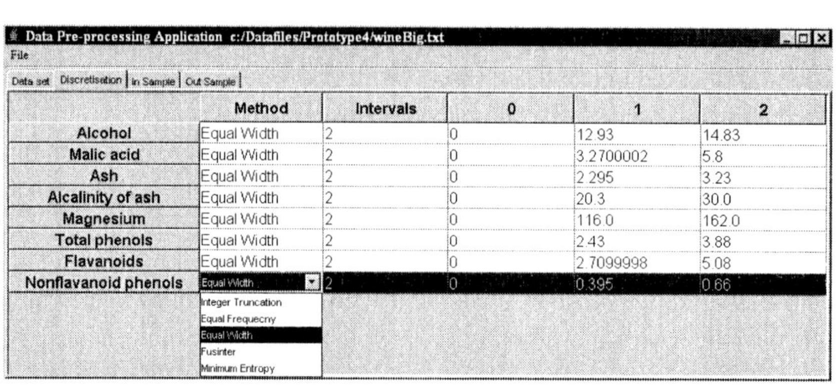

in this section of the chapter (it is noted this is a very low granularity dataset suggesting the future miss-classification of objects may be prevalent).

A leave-one-out approach with VPRS on the wine dataset means there are 178 individual resampling runs to be made, in each run one object is removed and used as the test set. A series of results that encompasses the rudiments of the benefits from a leave-one-out based resampling approach is first described, see Figure 2.

The table of results given in Figure 2, includes the descriptive statistics from the 178 individual runs, including; minimum, maximum, mean, median, mode, standard deviation and skewness. These statistics cover the VPRS based measures of; prediction accuracy, quality of classification, correct classification, number of condition attributes, and the number of decision rules in the identified β-reducts (see the description of VPRS measures in the background section).

The *predictive accuracy* results in this case indicate a mean of around 68.539% of the test set objects correctly classified (relatively low value since crude CVD employed). The quality of classification and correct classification measures are particularly associated with VPRS, since it is not necessarily so that all objects in the training set are assigned a classification. Using the mean values reported in the table in Figure 2, with 177 objects making up a training set, 171 (96.559%) of them are classified, of these 131 (76.423%) and 40 (23.577%) are correctly and incorrectly classified, respectively. Moving away from classification accuracy, these results were based on the information content of around four of the eight condition attributes, with on average nine decision rules employed in each resampling run.

The table presented is positioned above a choice of more in-depth expositions of some of these and other measures, in this case it is a histogram describing the number of condition attributes in the selected β-reducts in the resampling runs. The shape of the histogram is dominated by the 139 occasions out of the 178 runs that 4

Figure 2. Descriptive statistics and histogram from leave-one-out analysis

Resampling Analysis c:/Datafiles/Prototype4/wineBig.txt

Overall Summary | Summary Stats

	Minimium	Maximum	Mean	Median	Mode	Standard Deviation	Skewness
Prediction Accuracy	0.0	100.0	68.53933	100.0	100.0	46.43590633656608	-2.0325221890991414
Quality of Classification	93.22034	98.870056	96.55948	96.61017	96.61	0.6540595919617803	-0.1431252373270784
Correct Classification	63.276836	89.26553	76.34095	76.83616	76.83	4.203035618242402	-0.1959516752036951
Number Of Condition Attributes	3.0	8.0	4.1685395	4.0	4.0	1.062496054783752	0.7730465330895178
Number of Decision Rules	3.0	42.0	9.157304	8.0	8.0	7.581614183474893	0.8260486741846507

Frequency of Beta Reduct Size | Frequency Of Condition Attribute | Frequency of Identified Reduct

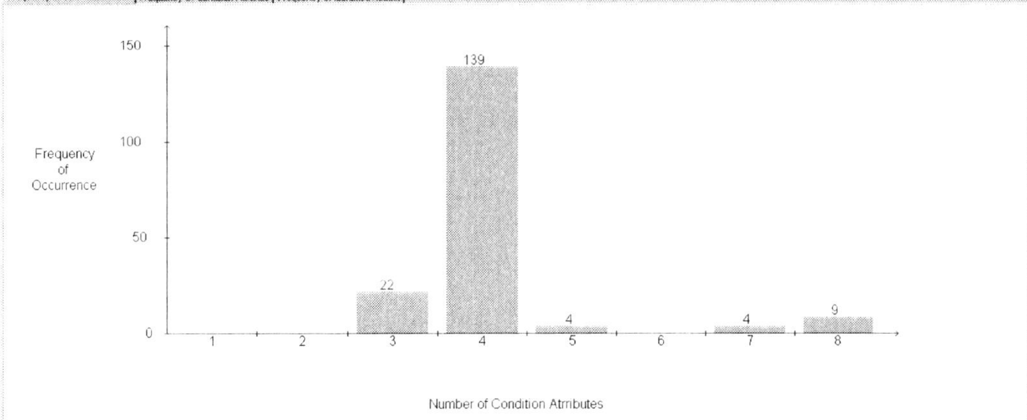

condition attributes made up the finally selected β-reduct each time. This domination is mostly due to the limited differences in the considered training sets throughout the runs (a feature of the leave-one-out resampling approach). However, the occasions when a different number of condition attributes make up a β-reduct indicate that the stability of the size of the β-reduct selected is not assured even when the training sets differ only by one object.

Two further histograms of the details from the leave-one-out resampling approach are presented. Moreover, the measures of the frequency of occurrence of the different condition attributes in the selected β-reducts (top) and frequency of occurrence of specific β-reducts (bottom), see Figure 3.

The top histogram in Figure 3 reflects the influence of the individual condition attributes to discern the Italian wines between the three cultivators. It shows the condition attributes, c_1, c_2, c_4 and c_7, are noticeably most present in the selected β-reducts. The bottom snapshot shows the top ten most frequently selected β-reducts (in decreasing order of frequency), in this case the β-reduct $\{c_1, c_2, c_4, c_7\}$ is most often selected. One interesting finding in the bottom histogram is the third placed β-reduct $\{c_1, c_2, c_3, c_4, c_5, c_6, c_7, c_8\}$, which is the whole set of condition attributes, showing that on nine occasions there were no

Figure 3. Histograms of frequency of occurrence of condition attributes and β-reduct selection in leave-one-out analysis

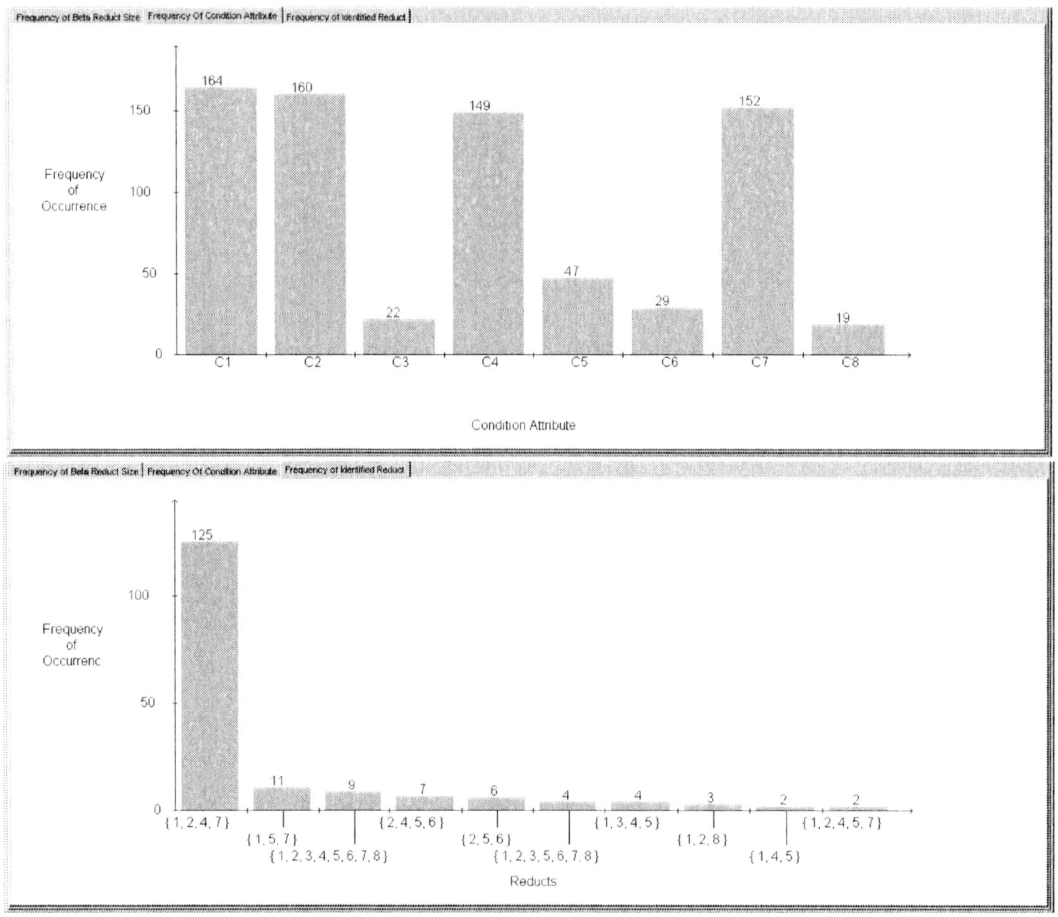

alternative β-reducts associated with the dataset (possibly due to its low granularity).

The snapshots presented in Figures 2 and 3 are closely dependent on each other, here supporting the size and content of a single β-reduct that should be considered "offers the most insights into the wine classification problem" (following the ordered criteria given previously), including the interpretation of the associated constructed set of decision rules (see later).

k-fold Cross Validation Analysis

The second resampling approach, *k*-fold cross validation, is linked to leave-one-out in terms of the convergence of the former to the latter (Shao, 1993). Hence the results presented here should be read with this in mind, and comparisons made where appropriate, with those from the leave-one-out analysis. The resampling literature heavily supports the use of 10-fold cross validation (Davison & Hinkley, 1997), meaning 10 runs are undertaken, unlike the 178 with the leave-one-out approach. The same snapshots that appeared for the elucidation of the leave-one-out approach are considered here, starting with the table of descriptive statistics and histogram of the number of condition attributes in the selected β-reducts, see Figure 4.

The classification accuracy based statistics presented in the table in Figure 4 do not look particularly different from those describing the leave-one-out analysis (see Figure 2). However, the histogram shows the number of condition attributes in the final selected β-reducts range from one to eight (only ten runs made). This suggests a relatively large number of different β-reducts may be selected (in only ten runs). If classification accuracy is the only issue for the data mining taking place then there is no problem, but the fact that different β-reducts are most probably being identified means little insight may be achieved from the data mining undertaken. This concern is further investigated by looking at the frequency of occurrence of the individual condition attributes and selected β-reducts, see Figure 5.

The results presented in Figure 5 further mitigate the ability to achieve insights into the

Figure 4. Descriptive statistics and histogram from 10-fold cross validation analysis

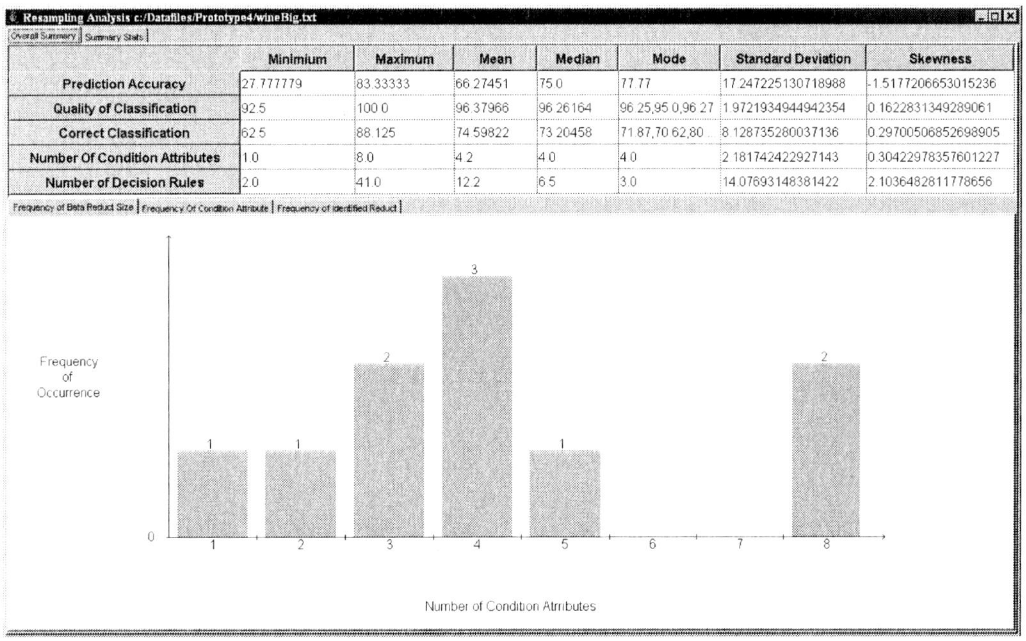

	Minimium	Maximum	Mean	Median	Mode	Standard Deviation	Skewness
Prediction Accuracy	27.777779	83.33333	66.27451	75.0	77.77	17.247225130718988	-1.5177206653015236
Quality of Classification	92.5	100.0	96.37966	96.26164	96.25,95.0,96.27	1.9721934944942354	0.1622831349289061
Correct Classification	62.5	88.125	74.59822	73.20458	71.87,70.62,80...	8.128735280037136	0.29700506852698905
Number Of Condition Attributes	1.0	8.0	4.2	4.0	4.0	2.181742422927143	0.30422978357601227
Number of Decision Rules	2.0	41.0	12.2	6.5	3.0	14.07693148381422	2.1036482811778656

classification of the condition attributes in this wine classification problem. Indeed, in the bottom histogram nine different β-reducts were selected from the ten runs undertaken. Of note is that the prominent β-reduct $\{c_1, c_2, c_4, c_7\}$ identified in the leave-one-out analysis was never selected in this 10-fold cross validation (the β-reduct $\{c_1, c_2, c_4, c_7, c_8\}$ was selected). The findings here highlight that due to the many stages of a VPRS analysis, even when automated, there is the scope for wide variations in the results that may be found. One solution to this ambiguity is to undertake the *r*-repeated *k*-fold cross validation (Braga-Neto & Dougherty, 2005).

One supposed advantage of 10-fold cross validation is the less computational expense needed to acquire the necessary results than say leave-one-out. When time is not an issue then cross-validation with a larger number of folds could be more pertinent, due also here to the lack of conclusive findings from a 10-fold cross validation approach. In this case a 40-fold cross validation based analysis is briefly described, utilising 40 resampling runs, see Figure 6.

The top histogram in Figure 6 shows a number of condition attributes regularly occurring in the selected β-reducts, with only c_3, c_6 and c_8 not appearing in around at least half of the β-reducts

Figure 5. Histograms of frequency of occurrence of condition attributes and β-reduct selection in 10-fold cross validation

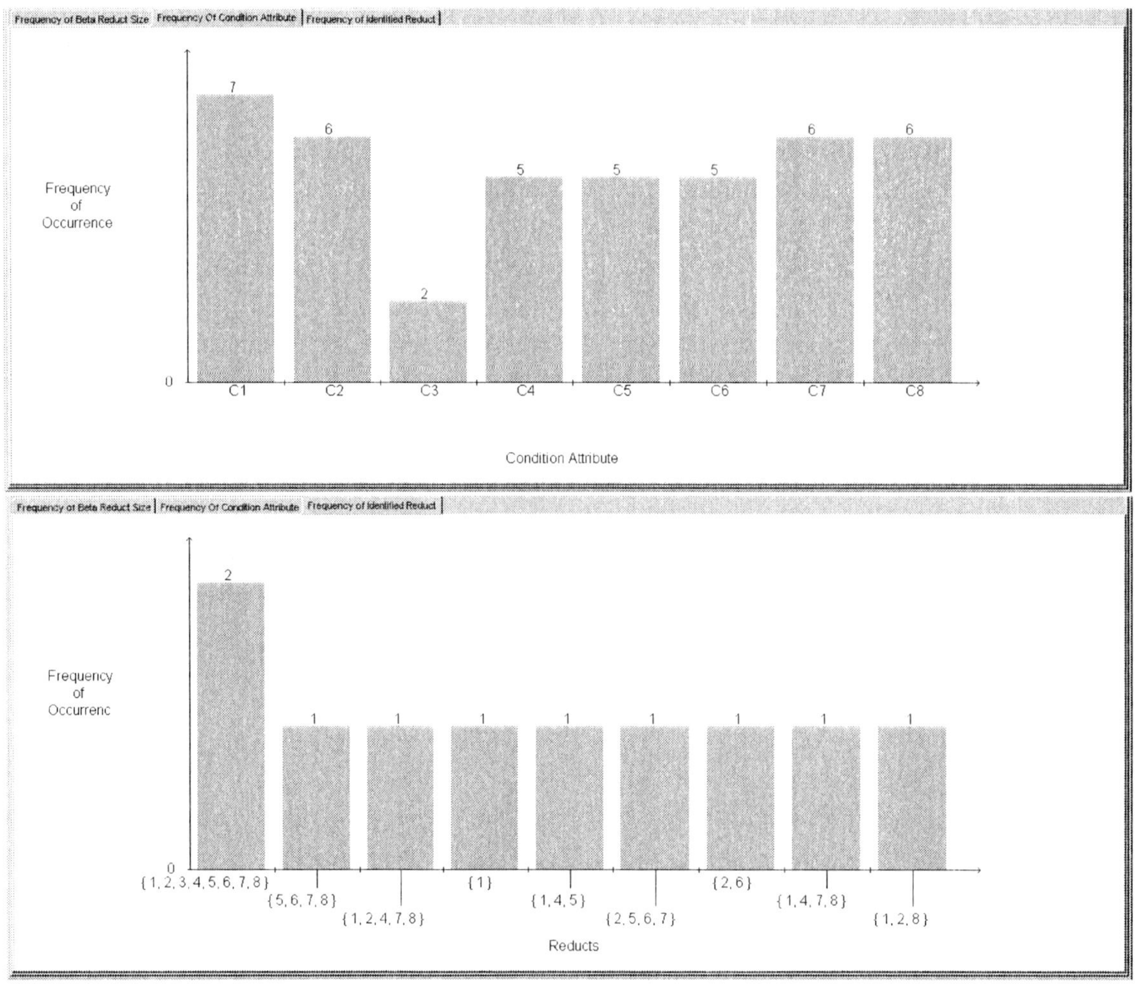

selected. The evidence in the bottom histogram shows the β-reduct $\{c_1, c_2, c_4, c_7\}$ is selected more times than any other. These results look more similar to those from the leave-one-out analysis than the 10-fold cross validation, not surprising since by having 40 folds there are more objects in the individual training sets analysed.

However, is similarity what the analyst should be concerned with. That is, in the case of the 10-fold cross validation in each run there were around 160 and 18 objects in the training and test sets, respectively, not greatly different from the situation in the 40-fold case. An analyst needs to be aware of the instability of results, especially with respect to those offering insights into the importance of certain condition attributes (this is before interpretation of the decision rules constructed would be made).

Bootstrapping Analysis

The third resampling approach, namely bootstrapping, requires the construction of training sets which are of the same size as the original training set. The objects in the training set are drawn using sampling with replacement. One parameter associated with bootstrapping is the number of runs to undertake, whilst any number between 25

Figure 6. Descriptive statistics and histogram from 40-fold cross validation analysis

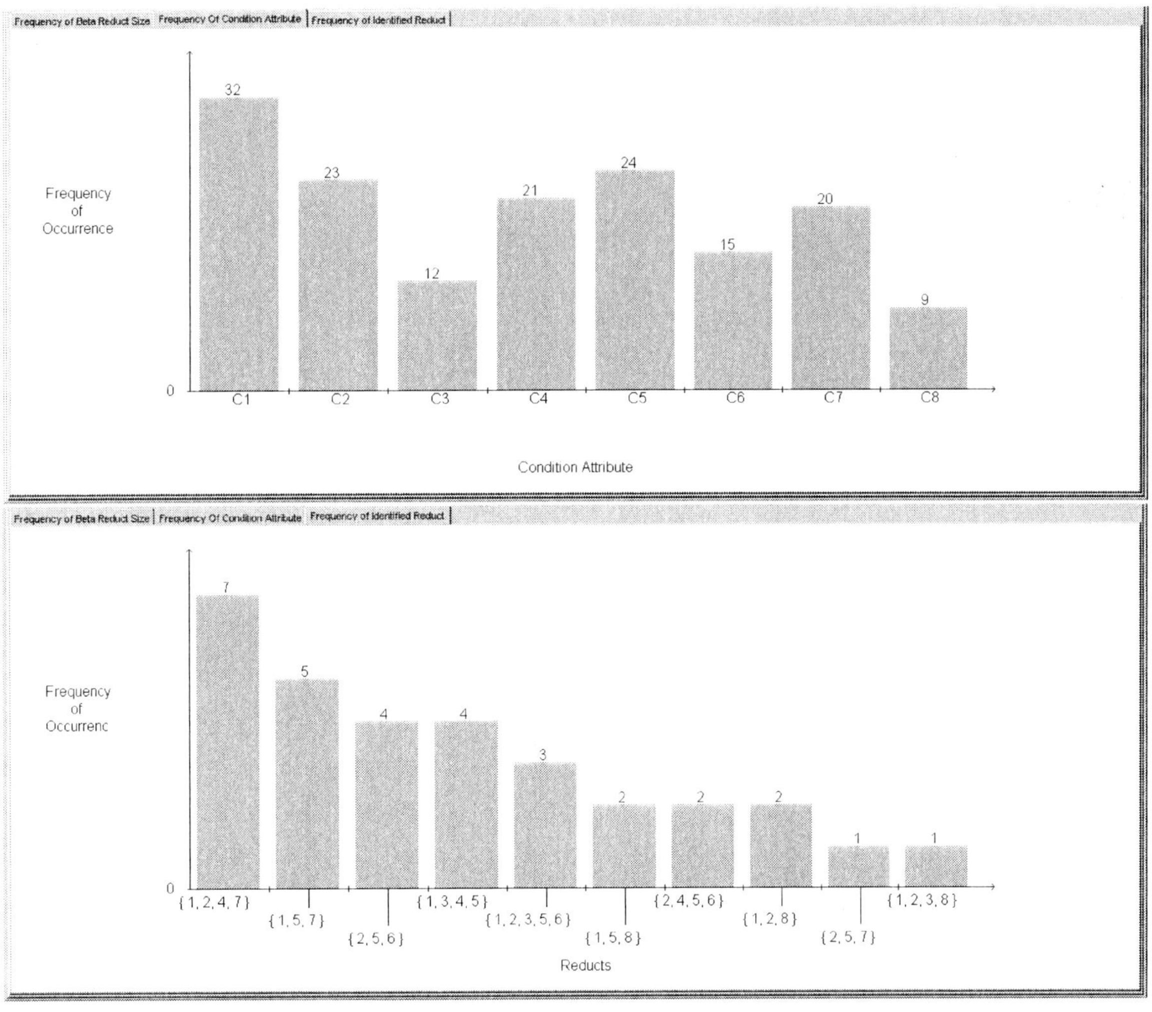

and 200 is recommended (Erfon, 1983), here 800 runs are undertaken. For consistency, the same snapshots of the resampling based results as for the other resampling approaches are presented, see Figure 7.

The descriptive statistics results presented in the table in Figure 7, are again consistent with those in the previous resampling undertaken. The histogram presented offers results that may not have been expected. That is, with 800 runs undertaken this is far more than any undertaken in the previous resampling reported, so it would be hoped that a level of convergence has occurred. This, may be true for the classification accuracy results, but clearly there is no stability in the number of condition attributes in a selected β-reduct. How the bootstrapping runs identify the important condition attributes and β-reducts is reported in Figure 8.

The histograms presented in Figure 8 offer further doubt that stable results have been found. In the case of the importance of the condition attributes, with the exception of the c_1 condition attribute there is little difference in the frequency of occurrence of the others. The elucidation of the selected β-reducts is also concerning, with the β-reduct $\{c_1\}$ clearly most often selected. The concern here is because decision rules based only on the c_1 condition attribute, which is described only by the 0 and 1 descriptor values, means at least one of the decision classes of wine would not be assigned by the associated decision rules.

The question then is, why when using VPRS with bootstrapping are the results on the condition attribute importance and selected β-reducts measures not conclusive? The answer may lie in the constructed condition classes. That is, with bootstrapping the same objects may appear more than once in the training set, hence there will be a smaller number of larger sized condition classes constructed. This would necessitate a smaller number of condition attributes necessary

Figure 7. Descriptive statistics and one histogram from bootstrapping with 800 runs

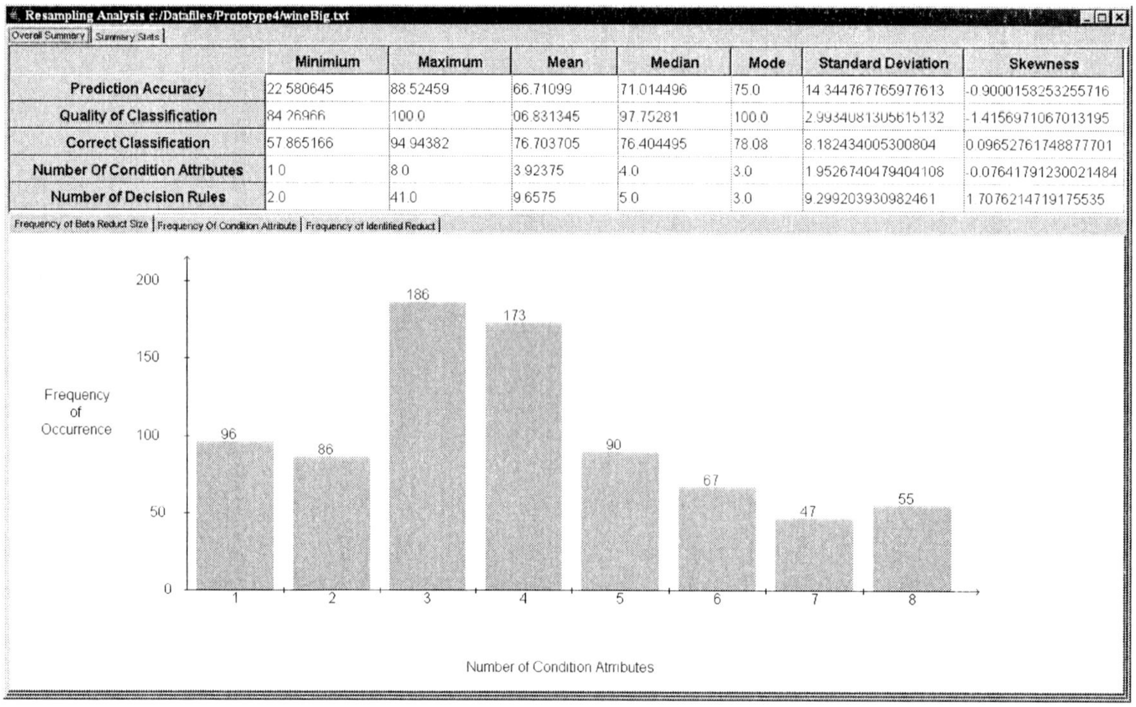

	Minimium	Maximum	Mean	Median	Mode	Standard Deviation	Skewness
Prediction Accuracy	22.580645	88.52459	66.71099	71.014496	75.0	14.344767765977613	-0.9000158253255716
Quality of Classification	84.26966	100.0	06.831345	97.75281	100.0	2.9934081305615132	-1.4156971067013195
Correct Classification	57.865166	94.94382	76.703705	76.404495	78.08	8.182434005300804	0.09652761748877701
Number Of Condition Attributes	1.0	8.0	3.92375	4.0	3.0	1.9526740479404108	-0.07641791230021484
Number of Decision Rules	2.0	41.0	9.6575	5.0	3.0	9.299203930982461	1.7076214719175535

to discern the condition classes associated with different decision classes, so resulting in smaller β-reducts. The results here suggest very small numbers of condition attributes were necessary, resulting in this case in a number of occasions when only the β-reduct $\{c_1\}$ was selected (the next larger β-reducts ranked follow a converse argument).

Further, with bootstrapping resampling is it fair to rank order the β-reducts in a similar way to that with the other resampling approaches. That is, the statistical results suggest an average and median of four condition attributes make up a β-reduct, hence showing a ranking of those β-reducts with four condition attributes may be more pertinent. In Figure 8, the one β-reduct with four condition attribute identified is $\{c_1, c_2, c_3, c_6\}$, similar in two condition attributes to the heavily supported $\{c_1, c_2, c_4, c_7\}$ β-reduct from the other resampling analyses. A similar elucidation can be given on the importance of condition attributes - only looking at selected β-reducts with four condition attributes. This suggested approach limits the number of bootstrapping runs which contribute evidence, hence with VPRS and possibly other symbolic learning techniques there

Figure 8. Two histograms from bootstrapping with 800 runs

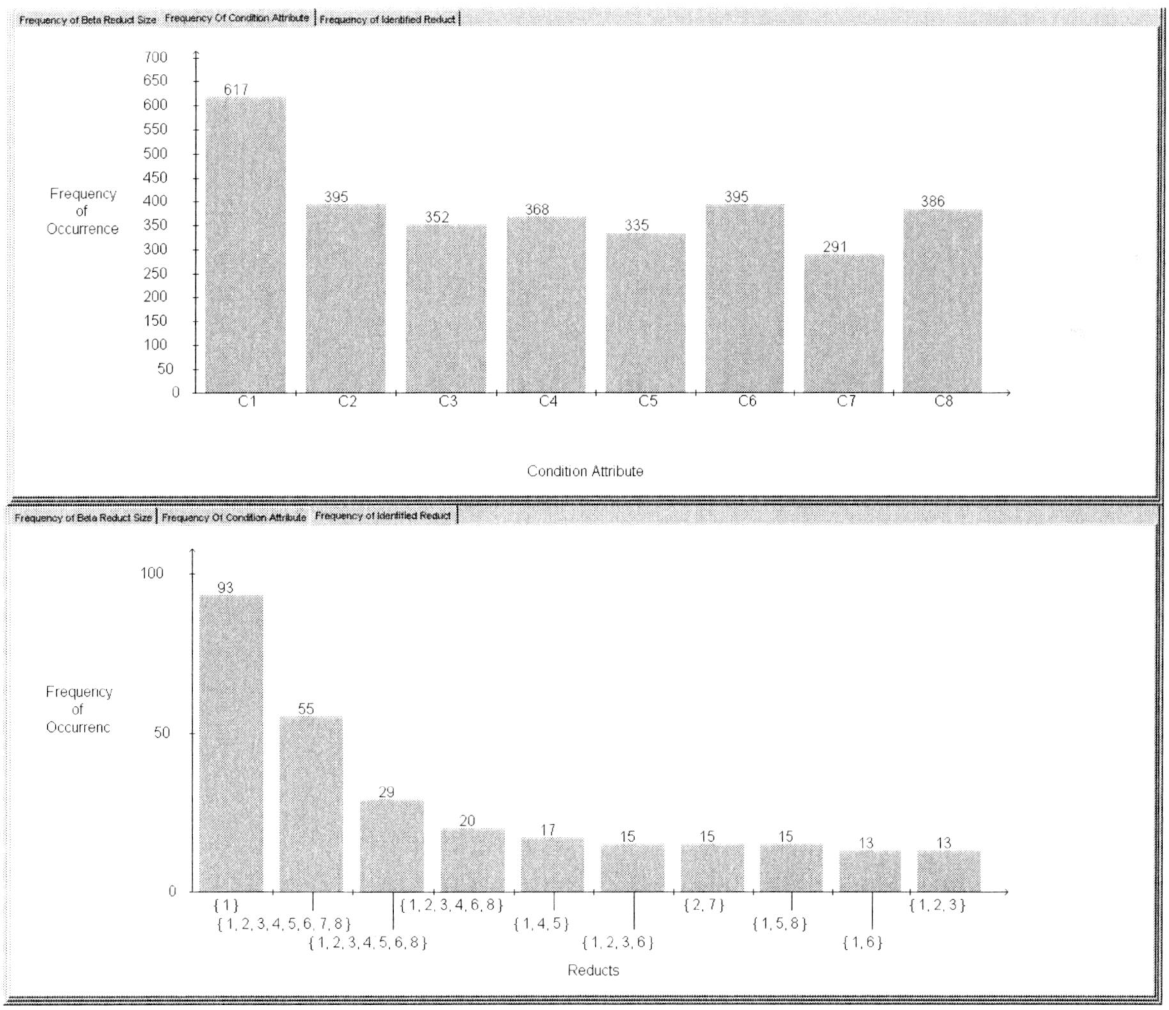

Figure 9. β-reducts identified from the full dataset

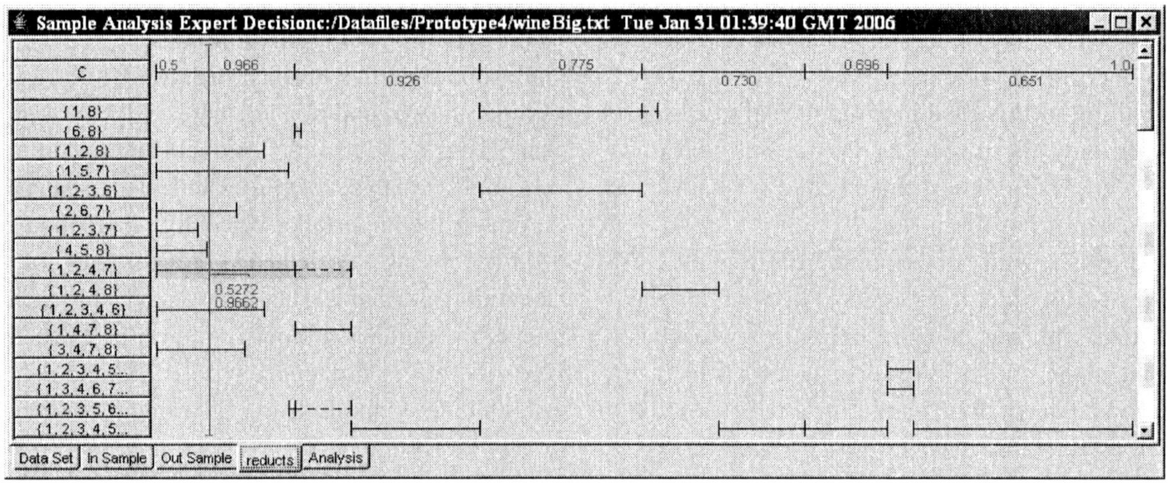

is the need to perform noticeably large numbers of runs, compared to the numbers mentioned in the related literature.

Presentation of Decision Rules

This subsection demonstrates the types of decision rules found using the VPRS software, based on the resampling results presented previously. Moreover, concentrating on the leave-one-out and *k*-fold cross validation resampling analyses, a β-reduct made up of four condition attributes and specific condition attributes c_1, c_2, c_4 and c_7 are viewed as particularly influential, indeed the actual β-reduct $\{c_1, c_2, c_4, c_7\}$ was most often selected. With these constraints, the full dataset of 178 wines was used as the training set and a VPRS analysis undertaken, see Figure 9.

In Figure 9, a snapshot of the VPRS software shows a window that contains all the β-reducts associated with this training set (full dataset). Moreover, each row of the graph-like diagram represents a subset of the condition attributes and the *solid lined subdomain* of the general β domain of (0.5, 1] shown, identifies where it would be considered as a β-reduct. In this case there were a total of 17 β-reducts, the spread of these domains highlight the intractable issue of β-reduct selection.

The shaded band over the β sub-domain (0.500, 0.571] for the β-reduct $\{c_1, c_2, c_4, c_7\}$, shows it is chosen by an analyst to be used for the data mining of the dataset. With respect to data mining this window offers it in its truest form, namely any of these solid-lines sub-domains could be chosen and a subsequent group of decision rules constructed from the associated β-reduct. Indeed these solid-lines sub-domains appear like veins in a seam worthy to be mined in a mountain of available information, the very essence of what data mining is Linoff (1998). The associated rules for the β-reduct $\{c_1, c_2, c_4, c_7\}$ are shown in Figure 10.

A total of eight minimal decision rules make up the rule set presented in Figure 10, of these two, two and four classify objects to the decision classes denoted by 0, 1 and 2, respectively. In the case of the third rule, it classifies 69 objects (has highest strength) to the decision class 1, with 55 of these correctly classified. Utilising the CVD results in Figure 1, this would allow the third rule to be written as:

Figure 10. Decision rules associated with β-reduct $\{c_1, c_2, c_4, c_7\}$

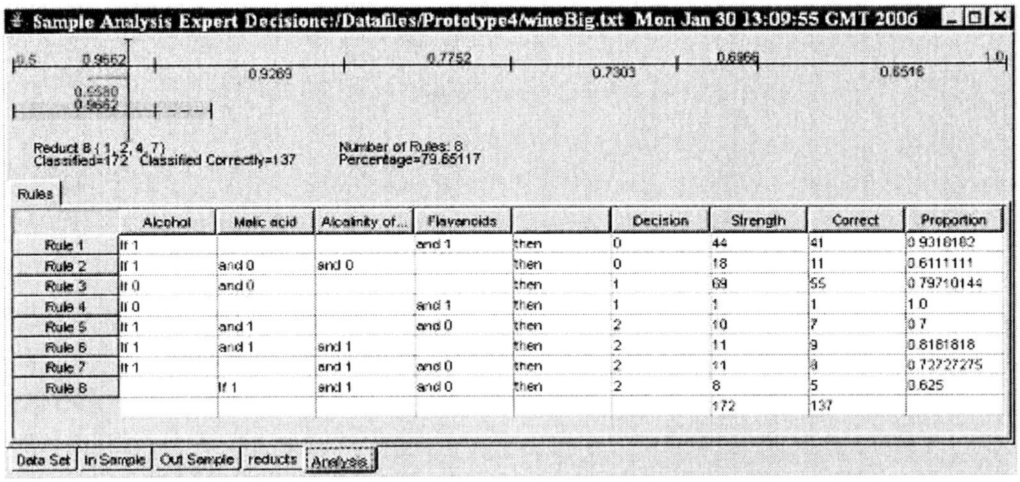

If Alcohol greater than 12.93 and Malic Acid less than or equal to 3.27 then the wine is associated with cultivator 1, based on 69 wines and probability of correct classification is 79.710%.

This latter finding highlights the insightfulness that VPRS and other symbolic machine learning techniques can bring to any data mining undertaken.

FUTURE TRENDS

It is fair to say that the diversity of the theoretical field of data mining means future trends are difficult to be specific on. The practical realisation is that different techniques have their own range of traits, which may advantage and/or disadvantage them with respect to expectations by an analyst. Whichever technique, how they benefit from being implicit in a resampling approach needs to be understood.

The example of the VPRS technique for data mining described in this chapter, illustrates the unique realities of cultivating a resampling based analysis with a nascent symbolic machine learning technique. For an analyst interested in insightful results using techniques like VPRS, the future trend must incorporate more importance to findings away from simply classification accuracy and include measures such as attribute importance.

The latter part of this chapter started using the term stability, and this holds one direction also, namely how resampling approaches can measure the stability of the more data reduction related results that may exist (identification of β-reducts in VPRS). Perhaps the analysts who ultimately use the plethora of data mining techniques that exist and continue to be developed should direct future trends since insights are what they desire. Ultimately, this means that theorists need to listen more to what the analysts want.

CONCLUSION

Error rate estimation and resampling, due to their importance, are justifiably considered in their own research studies. However, how they benefit the wide range of data mining techniques is little understood by analysts. The results presented here show that the chosen resampling approaches, leave-one-out, *k*-fold cross-validation and bootstrapping, can elucidate similar and different data mining based results, when using a symbolic learning technique, namely variable precision rough set theory (VPRS).

Once the analysis moves away from concerning itself with classification accuracy, the level and type of resampling may have dramatic effects on the more insightful findings such as the importance of the considered condition attributes and so forth. In the case of VPRS it may mean different β-reducts identified and subsequently different sets of decision rules. Further, VPRS (RST in general) attempts to identify the redundant attributes in a dataset, resampling strengthens this redundancy investigation considerably, but it needs to be controlled and understood so stable findings are taken further.

The specific results identify discrepancies between the important attributes found using leave-one-out and *k*-fold cross-validation against those from the bootstrapping approach. The difference in these approaches is that bootstrapping operates with replacement when constructing the training sets (unlike non-replacement with the others). The subsequent datasets, with multiplicity of objects, seem to dramatically affect the selection of a single β-reduct in each resampling run, using the predefined criteria. Importantly though, there are still encouraging trends between the sets of results.

There appears to be a level of convergence between leave-one-out and 40-fold cross validation, raising the question of what is the most appropriate value for *k* in *k*-fold cross-validation within a VPRS environment? Further more, although bootstrapping on first appearance does not support the findings of 40-fold or leave-one-out, it is pertinent to realise that the most selected β-reducts with bootstrap resampling contained three or four attributes which correlates with the findings of the other resampling methods. Clearly a much deeper investigation will be needed to understand the full effects of resampling within a VPRS environment. These initial findings have highlighted the short falls in the software, but elucidate the necessary areas that should be taken into consideration in future studies.

REFERENCES

An, A., Shan, N., Chan, C., Cercone N., & Ziarko, W. (1996). Discovering rules for water demand prediction: An enhanced rough-set approach. *Engineering Applied Artificial Intelligent, 9*, 645-653.

Beynon, M. (2001). Reducts within the variable precision rough set model: A further investigation. *European Journal of Operational Research, 134*, 592-605.

Beynon, M. J. (2004). Stability of continuous value discretisation: An application within rough set theory. *International Journal of Approximate Reasoning, 35*, 29-53.

Beynon, M. J., Clatworthy, M. A., & Jones, M. J. (2004). A prediction of profitability using accounting narratives: A variable precision rough set approach. *International Journal of Intelligent Systems in Accounting, Finance & Management, 12*, 227-242.

Braga-Neto, U., & Dougherty, E. (2004). Is cross-validation valid for small-sample microarray classification? *Bioinformatics, 20*(3), 374-380.

Braga-Neto, U., & Dougherty, E. (2005). Exact performance of error estimators for discrete classifiers. *Pattern Recognition, 38*, 1799-1814.

Breiman, L. (1996). Bagging predictors. *Machine Learning, 24*, 123-140.

Breiman, L. (2001). Statistical modeling: The two cultures. *Statistical Science, 16*(3), 199-231.

Chennick, M. (1999). *Bootstrap methods: A practitioner's guide*. New York: Wiley & Sons.

Davison, A. C., & Hinkley, D. V. (1997). Bootstrap methods and their application. Cambridge, UK: Cambridge University Press.

Domingos, P. (1999). The role of Occam's Razor in knowledge discovery. *Data Mining and Knowledge Discovery, 3*, 409-425.

Duntsch, I., & Gediga, G. (1997). Statistical evaluation of rough set dependency analysis. *International Journal of Human-Computer Studies, 46*, 589-604.

Efron, B. (1979). Bootstrap methods: Another look at the jackknife. *Annals of Statistics, 7*, 1-26.

Efron, B. (1982). *The jackknife, the bootstrap and other re-sampling plans*. Philadelphia: SIAM.

Efron, B. (1983). Estimating the error of a prediction rule: Improvement on cross-validation. *Journal of American Statistical Association, 78*, 316-331.

Furlanello, C., Merler, S., Chemini, C., & Rizzoli, A. (1998). An application of the bootstrap 632+ rule to ecological data. In M. Marinaro & R. Tagliaferri (Eds.), *Neural Nets WIRN-97*. MIT Press.

Greco, S., Matarazzo, B., & Słowiński, R. (2004). Axiomatic characterization of a general utility function and its particular cases in terms of conjoint measurement and rough-set decision rules. *European Journal of Operational Research, 158*(2), 271-292.

Greco, S., Inuiguchi, M., & Słowiński, R. (2006). Fuzzy rough sets and multiple-premise gradual decision rules. *International Journal of Approximate Reasoning, 41*(2), 179-211.

Griffiths, B. & Beynon, M. J. (2005). Expositing stages of VPRS analysis in an expert system: Application with bank credit ratings. *Expert Systems with Applications, 29*(4), 879-888.

Grzymala-Busse, J., Stefanowski, J., & Wilk, S. (2005). A comparison of two approaches to data mining from imbalanced data.. *Journal of Intelligent Manufacturing, 16*(6), 565-573.

Jensen, R., & Shen, Q. (2005). Fuzzy-rough data reduction with ant colony optimization. *Fuzzy Sets and Systems, 149*, 5-20.

Katzberg, J. D., & Ziarko, W. (1996). Variable precision of rough sets. *Fundamenta Informaticae, 27*, 155-168.

Lachenbruch, P., & Mickey, M. (1968). Estimation of error rates in discriminant analysis. *Technometrics, 10*, 1-11.

Larson, S. C. (1931). The shrinkage of the coefficient of multiple correlation. *Journal of Educational Psychology, 22*, 45-55.

Li, R., & Wang, Z.-O. (2004). Mining classification rules using rough sets and neural networks. *European Journal of Operational Research, 157*, 439-448.

Linoff, G. (1998, January). Which way to the mine? *Systems Management*, 42-44.

Merler, S., & Furlanello, C. (1997). Selection of tree-based classifiers with the bootstrap 632+ rule. *Biometrical Journal, 39*(2), 1-14.

Mi, J.-S., Wu, W.-Z., & Zhang, W.-X. (2004). Approaches to knowledge reduction based on variable precision rough set model. *Information Sciences, 159*, 255-272.

Mosteller, F., & Tukey, J. W. (1968). *Data analysis, including statistics. Handbook of Social Psychology*. MA: Addison-Wesley.

Pawlak, Z. (1982). Rough sets. *International Journal of Information and Computer Sciences, 11*(5), 341-356.

Shao, J. (1993). Linear model selection by cross validation. *Journal of the American Statistical Association, 89*, 550-559.

Shao, J., & Tu, D. (1995). *The jackknife and booststrap*. New York: Springer-Verlag.

Słowiński, R. (1992). *Intelligent decision support: Handbook of applications and advances in rough set theory.* Dordrecht: Kluwer Academic Publishers.

Stone, M. (1974). Cross-validation choice and assessment of statistical predictions. *Journal of the Royal Statistical Society B*, *36*(2), 111-147.

Thomassey, S., & Fiordaliso, A. (in press). A hybrid sales forecasting system based on clustering and decision trees. *Decision Support Systems.*

Peters, J. F., & Skowron, A. (Eds.). (2005). *Transactions on rough sets II* (LNCS 3135). Berlin: Springer-Verlag.

Weiss, M. S., & Kulikowski, A. C. (1991). *Computer systems that learn: Classification and prediction methods from statistics, neural nets, machine learning, and expert systems.* San Francisco: Morgan Kaufmann.

Wisnowski, J. W., Simpson, J. R., Montgomery, D. C. & Runger, G. C. (2003). Resampling methods for variable selection in robust regression. *Computational Statistics & Data Analysis*, *43*, 341-355.

Witten, I. H., & Frank, E. (2000). *Data mining.* San Diego: Academic Press.

Zhang, G., Hu, M. Y., Patuwo, B. E. & Indro, D. C. (1999). Artificial neural networks in bankruptcy prediction: General framework and cross-validation analysis. *European Journal of Operational Research*, *116*(1), 16-32.

Ziarko, W. (1993). Variable precision rough set model. *Journal of Computer and System Sciences*, *46*, 39-59.

Ziarko, W. (2005). Probabilistic rough sets. In *Proceedings of Rough Sets, Fuzzy Sets, Data Mining, and Granular Computing: 10th International Conference RSFDGrC2005* (LNCS 3641, pp. 283-293).

About the Authors

Xingquan Zhu is an assistant professor in the Department of Computer Science and Engineering at Florida Atlantic University, Boca Raton, Florida (USA). He received his PhD in computer science (2001) from Fudan University, Shanghai (China). He was a postdoctoral associate in the Department of Computer Science, Purdue University, West Lafayette, Indiana (USA) (February 2001 to October 2002). He was a research assistant professor in the Department of Computer Science, University of Vermont, Burlington, Vermont (USA) (October 2002 to July 2006). His research interests include data mining, machine learning, data quality, multimedia systems, and information retrieval.

Ian Davidson is currently an assistant professor of computer science at the State University of New York (SUNY) at Albany (USA). Prior to this appointment he worked in Silicon Valley most recently for SGI's MineSet datamining group. He publishes and serves on the program committees of most AI and data mining conferences. He has a PhD from Monash University under the supervision of C.S. Wallace.

* * *

Jose Ma. J. Alvir is a statistician at Pfizer, Inc. (USA) where he supports outcomes research. He received his PhD from Columbia University after graduating magna cum laude with a sociology degree from the University of the Philippines. Jose is an accomplished musician, having played roles such as Jesus Christ in *Jesus Christ Superstar* and Kurt von Trapp in *The Sound of Music*. He is an alumnus of the elite world-acclaimed Philippine Madrigal Singers and currently sings with groups in NYC. A track runner in college, he has run five sub-3 hour marathons. He is married to his wife, Gloria, and has a daughter, Marie-Therese.

Copyright © 2007, IGI Global, distributing in print or electronic forms without written permission of IGI Global is prohibited.

Malcolm J. Beynon received his BS and PhD in pure mathematics and computational mathematics from Cardiff University, Cardiff (UK) (1989 and 1993, respectively). He is currently a reader at Cardiff Business School, Cardiff University, having also worked in the computing and mathematics departments of the same university. His current research areas surround uncertain reasoning, including theoretical development and application based studies. He is the author of over 80 journal articles, book chapters and conference papers. Dr. Beynon is a member of the Multi-Criteria Decision Making and Operations Research Societies, and is on the editorial boards of a number of journals.

Tilmann Bruckhaus is director of analytics at Numetrics Management Systems (USA) where he uses machine learning technology to predict cost, time-to-market and productivity of complex technology projects. Before joining Numetrics he was chief architect of data mining and analytics at Sun Microsystems where he oversaw the conception, implementation and delivery of predictive analytics capabilities for a billion-dollar, telemetry-based business. Tilmann received the Sun Software Innovation Award for these contributions. He also received a research fellowship from the IBM Centre for Advanced Studies and modeled the productivity of software development projects at IBM Canada. Tilmann earned a PhD, summa cum laude, from McGill University for this research. He holds patents in object-oriented programming, multimedia, and machine learning.

Javier Cabrera is director of the Biostatistics Institute at Rutgers University (USA). He earned his PhD at Princeton University (1983) and has been with Rutgers University (since 1984). He was a professor for two years at the National University of Singapore and at the Hong Kong University of Science and Technology. He is a Henry Rutgers fellow and a Fulbright fellow and he works in the areas of biostatistics, data mining, and statistical computing. His research has been funded by NSF and by Singapore's STB. He has published over 50 research articles and two books in statistics and biostatistics.

Frank Caridi is head of clinical trials statistics and outcomes research statistics for Pfizer Global Research and Development in New York (USA). He received his MS (1972) and PhD (1980) in mathematical statistics from Rutgers University. He has over 30 years of experience in the application of statistics in the health care industry. For the last 24 years he has worked at Pfizer, Inc. on the design and analysis of numerous clinical trials and statistical preparation of regulatory submissions. More recently he has turned his attention to integrating statistical application into health outcomes research at Pfizer.

Elizabeth Chang is currently director of the Frontier Technology for Extended Enterprise Centre (Centre for Extended Enterprise and Business Intelligence) at Curtin Business School, Curtin University of Technology, Perth (Australia). She is the vice-chair of the Work Group on Web Semantics (WG 2.12/12.4) in Technical Committee for Software: Theory and Practice (TC2) for International Federation for Information Processing (IFIP). Professor Chang has published over 200 scientific conference and journal papers including two co-authored books. The themes of these papers are in the areas of ontology, software engineering, object/component-based methodologies, e-commerce, trust management and security, Web services, user interface and Web engineering, as well as logistics informatics.

Tharam S. Dillon is the dean of the Faculty of Information Technology at the University of Technology, Sydney (UTS) (Australia). His research interests include data mining, Internet computing, e-commerce, hybrid neurosymbolic systems, neural nets, software engineering, database systems and computer networks. He has also worked with industry and commerce in developing systems in telecommunications, health care systems, e-commerce, logistics, power systems and banking and finance. He is editor-in-chief of the *International Journal of Computer Systems Science and Engineering* and the *International Journal of Engineering Intelligent Systems*, as well as co-editor of the *Journal of Electric Power and Energy Systems*. He is the advisory editor of the *IEEE Transactions on Industrial Informatics*. He is on the advisory editorial board of *Applied Intelligence* published by Kluwer in the U.S. and *Computer Communications* published by Elsevier in the UK. He has published more than 400 papers in international and national journals and conferences and has written four books and edited five other books. He is a fellow of the IEEE, fellow of the Institution of Engineers (Australia) and fellow of the Australian Computer Society.

Pinar Duygulu has received her PhD from the Department of Computer Engineering at Middle East Technical University (Turkey). During her PhD studies, she was a visiting scholar at the University of California at Berkeley. After being a postdoctoral researcher at Informedia Project at Carnegie Mellon University, she joined the Department of Computer Engineering at Bilkent University (Turkey). She was a senior researcher in CLSP summer workshop at Johns Hopkins University (summer 2004). Her current research interests include computer vision and multimedia data mining, specifically in object and face recognition on the large scale and semantic analysis of large image and video collections.

Christos Faloutsos is a professor at Carnegie Mellon University (USA). He has received the Presidential Young Investigator Award by the National Science Foundation (1989), seven "best paper" awards and several teaching awards. He has served as a member of the executive committee of SIGKDD; he has published over 140 refereed articles, one monograph, and holds five patents. His research interests include data mining for streams and networks, fractals, indexing for multimedia, and bio-informatics databases and performance.

Benjamin Griffiths graduated with a Joint Honours BS in mathematics and computer science from the University of Wales Cardiff (UK) (2002). He is currently working towards his PhD at Cardiff Business School, where his research interests include data mining within variable precision rough set theory (VPRS), error rate estimation and classifier aggregation. Additional research work includes feature selection for VPRS and the impact of imbalanced datasets within the VPRS resampling environment.

Le Gruenwald is a professor in the School of Computer Science at the University of Oklahoma (USA) and a program director of data management systems at the National Science Foundation. She received her PhD in computer science from Southern Methodist University (1990). She was a software engineer at White River Technologies, a lecturer in the Computer Science and Engineering Department at Southern Methodist University, and a member of technical staff in the Database Management Group at the Advanced Switching Laboratory of NEC (USA). Her major research interests include mobile databases, sensor databases, Web-enabled databases, real-time main memory databases, multimedia databases, data warehouse, and data mining. She is a member of the ACM, SIGMOD, and IEEE Computer Society.

Fedja Hadzic is a member of the eXel research group at the University of Technology Sydney (Australia). He has obtained his BS of computer science at the University of Newcastle, and has completed a BS (Honours) in information technology at the University of Technology Sydney. His current research is mainly focused in the area of data mining and ontology learning. He was a part of the "UTS Unleashed!" robot soccer team (2004). His research work has been published in a number of international conferences. Further research interests include knowledge representation and reasoning, artificial life, life-long learning, automated scientific discovery, robotics and metaphysics.

Paul J. Kennedy is a senior lecturer in the Faculty of IT, University of Technology, Sydney (Australia). He received his PhD in computing science (1999). His research interests are in data mining applied in domains such as bioinformatics, text mining and marketing, particularly using kernel methods with data enriched with ontologies. He leads the e-Bio group in FIT, UTS which interrogates and visualizes complex biomedical datasets with data mining methods. Other projects involve genetic algorithms, particularly involving genotype to phenotype mappings and neural techniques. He regularly consults to industry and is a general chair of the 2006 Australasian Data Mining Conference.

Taghi M. Khoshgoftaar is a professor of the Department of Computer Science and Engineering, Florida Atlantic University (USA) and the director of the graduate programs and research. His research interests are in software engineering, software metrics, software reliability and quality engineering, computational intelligence applications, computer security, computer performance evaluation, data mining, machine learning, statistical modeling, and intelligent data analysis. He has published more than 300 refereed papers in these areas. He is a member of the IEEE, IEEE Computer Society and IEEE Reliability Society. He was the general chair of the IEEE International Conference on Tools with Artificial Intelligence (2005).

Weiguo Liu received his PhD from Boston University (2001) and he is assistant professor in the Department of Geography and Planning of University of Toledo (USA). His research interests range from theory to applications of GIS, remote sensing, and artificial neural networks (ANNs). His current research efforts include integrating spatial data mining (geographical knowledge discovery) and GIS to resolve real-world geographic problems related to environmental health and land-use change (especially urbanization monitoring, simulation and prediction).

Jason H. Moore is the Frank Lane Research Scholar in Computational Genetics and associate professor of genetics and of community and family medicine at Dartmouth Medical School in New Hampshire (USA). He holds adjunct appointments in the Department of Biological Sciences at Dartmouth College, the Department of Computer Science at the University of New Hampshire and the Department of Computer Science at the University of Vermont. He serves as the director of the Dartmouth Computational Genetics Laboratory, the Dartmouth Bioinformatics Shared Resource and the Dartmouth Initiative for Supercomputing Ventures in Education and Research.

Elena Irina Neaga is a researcher within the Informatics Institute at the University of Amsterdam, The Netherlands. She received a PhD (2003) from Loughborough University, Leicestershire (UK) for the research and thesis focused on the definition of a framework facilitating distributed knowledge discovery systems embedded in the extended enterprise. Other appointments include lecturer at the "Gh.

Asachi" Technical University of Iasi, Romania, and postdoctoral researcher at the Research Consortium in Forest Industry (FORAC) from Laval University, Quebec (Canada). She published several papers, and a book regarding knowledge engineering and management, as well as Web technologies. Her research interests and expertise fall in the areas of applied knowledge discovery, ontology engineering, enterprise systems interoperability, standardization aspects, legal issues, and regulatory ontologies for supporting virtual organizations.

Ha Nguyen received his MS in statistics from American University (1982) and his PhD in statistics from Princeton University (1986). After graduation, he worked for one year at the Bureau of the Census in Suitland, Maryland and joined the pharmaceutical industry afterwards. He spent 12 years at Merck Research Labs in Rahway, supporting preclinical work and clinical work in pulmonary. He joined Aventis Global Marketing group (2001) and supported products in diabetic, anti-infective, respiratory areas. He later moved to Pfizer (USA) (2004) where he is currently a clinical trial statistical lead supporting CNS, ophthalmology, oncology, and pain therapeutic areas.

Anna Olecka's educational background includes mathematics from the University of Warsaw (Poland) and operations research from RUTCOR, Rutgers University. While working for several major banks (First USA, Fleet Boston, Barclays), Olecka had an opportunity to apply data mining solutions in credit risk, marketing and collections. Prior to financial institutions, she worked for Business Operations Analysis, an internal consulting organization at AT&T Labs (Bell Labs). It was at AT&T where she developed interest in machine learning and pattern recognition. She was a principal investigator on a project, *Customers Identification Through Call Pattern Matching*, for which AT&T has obtained two U.S. patents.

Jia-Yu Pan received his PhD from Carnegie Mellon University (USA) (2006). His main research interest is in data mining, especially for multimedia data and graphs. His work on multimedia mining has received student paper awards at the PAKDD 2004 and ICDM 2005 conferences. He received a MS from National Taiwan University and a BS from National Chiao Tung University (Taiwan).

Petra Perner is the director of the Institute of Computer Vision and Applied Computer Sciences (IBaI) in Leipzig (Germany). She received her BS in electrical engineering (1981) and her PhD in computer science (1985). She worked at the Technical University of Leipzig (1985 to 1991) where she was the head of the research group "Opto-electronic Inspection and Diagnosis Systems." She was a visiting scientist at the Fraunhofer-Institute of Non-Destructive Testing in Saarbrücken (1991) and then she worked as a visiting scientist at IBM T.J. Watson Research Center in Yorktown Heights, New York (1992). She was the chair of the Technical Committee 17 Machine Learning and Data Mining of the International Association of Pattern Recognition (IAPR) and is currently the chair of the IFIP working group computer vision. She has been the principal investigator of various national and international research projects. She received several research awards for her research work and has been recently awarded with three business awards for her work on bringing intelligent image interpretation methods into business. Her research interest is image analysis and interpretation, machine learning, data mining, image mining and case-based reasoning. Recently, she is working on various medical and biomedical applications and e-commerce applications.

Naeem Seliya is an assistant professor of Computer and Information Science at the University of Michigan-Dearborn (USA). He received his PhD in computer engineering from Florida Atlantic University, Boca Raton, Florida (2005). His research interests include software engineering, data mining and machine learning, application and data security, bioinformatics, and computational intelligence. He is a member of IEEE and ACM.

Amandeep S. Sidhu is a structural bioinformatics researcher at Faculty of IT, University of Technology Sydney (Australia) with expertise in protein informatics. He is currently working on the Protein Ontology Project with Professor Tharam S. Dillon. His research interests include biomedical ontologies, structural bioinformatics, proteomics, XML enabled Web services, and artificial intelligence. His work in these fields resulted in 27 scientific publications.

Simeon Simoff is currently an associate professor in information technology and computing science and head of e-Markets Research Group at the University of Technology, Sydney (Australia). He is also co-director of the Institute of Analytic Professionals of Australia. He is known for the unique blend of interdisciplinary scholarship and innovation, which integrates the areas of data mining, design computing, virtual worlds and digital media, with application in the area of electronic trading environments. His work in these fields has resulted in nine co-authored/edited books and more than 170 research papers, and a number of cross-disciplinary educational programs in information technology and computing. He is co-editor of the CRPIT series "Conferences of Research and Practice in Information Technology." He has initiated and co-chaired several international conference series in the area of data mining, including The Australasian Data Mining series AusDM, and the ACM SIGKDD Multimedia Data Mining and Visual Data Mining series.

Henry Tan is a PhD student working under supervision of Professor Tharam S. Dillon, graduated from La Trobe University (2002) with a BS of computer system engineering (honours) and nominated as the most outstanding honours student in computer science. He is the holder of the ACS Student Award (2003). His current research is mainly focused in the area of XML association mining. Other research interests include neural networks, AI, game and software development. His research work has been published in a number of international conferences. He is currently on leave working for Microsoft, Redmond (USA) as a software design engineer.

Hyung-Jeong Yang is a lecturer at School of Electronics and Computer Engineering, Chonnam National University (South Korea). She worked as a postdoctoral researcher at Carnegie Mellon University for two years partially funded by Korea Science and Engineering Foundation. She has received her PhD, MS, and BS from Chonbuk National University (South Korea). Her current research interests include e-design for collaborative product development, multimedia data mining, biometrics, and e-learning.

Jianting Zhang received a BS (1993) and MS (1996) in geography from Nanjing University (China) and MS (2001) and PhD (2004) in computer science from the University of Oklahoma (USA). He is currently doing his postdoctoral studies at the Long Term Ecological Research (LTER) office at the

University of New Mexico (USA) and works as a research scientist in NSF large ITR Scientific Environment for Ecological Knowledge (SEEK) project. His is interested in multiple disciplinary researches on data management and data analysis, such as spatial databases, GIS applications, scientific workflows, and data mining of geospatial and biological data.

Index

Copyright © 2007, IGI Global, distributing in print or electronic forms without written permission of IGI Global is prohibited.